Championing Child Care

POWER, CONFLICT, AND DEMOCRACY:
AMERICAN POLITICS INTO THE TWENTY-FIRST CENTURY

ROBERT Y. SHAPIRO, EDITOR

POWER, CONFLICT, AND DEMOCRACY:
AMERICAN POLITICS INTO THE TWENTY-FIRST CENTURY

ROBERT Y. SHAPIRO, EDITOR

This series focuses on how the will of the people and the public interest are promoted, encouraged, or thwarted. It aims to question not only the direction American politics will take as it enters the twenty-first century but also the direction American politics has already taken.

The series addresses the role of interest groups and social and political movements; openness in American politics; important developments in institutions such as the executive, legislative, and judicial branches at all levels of government as well as the bureaucracies thus created; the changing behavior of politicians and political parties; the role of public opinion; and the functioning of mass media. Because problems drive politics, the series also examines important policy issues in both domestic and foreign affairs.

The series welcomes all theoretical perspectives, methodologies, and types of evidence that answer important questions about trends in American politics.

Championing Child Care

Sally S. Cohen

COLUMBIA UNIVERSITY PRESS   NEW YORK

COLUMBIA UNIVERSITY PRESS
Publishers Since 1893
New York   Chichester, West Sussex
Copyright © 2001 Columbia University Press
All rights reserved

Library of Congress Cataloging-in-Publication Data

Cohen, Sally Solomon.
  Championing child care / Sally S. Cohen.
    p. cm. — (Power, conflict, and democracy)
  Includes index.
  ISBN 0-231-11236-X (cloth : alk. paper) — ISBN 0-231-11237-8
    (pbk. : alk. paper)
    1. Child care—Government policy—United States. 2. Child care—
  Political aspects—United States. 3. Child care services—Government policy—
  United States. 4. Child care services—Law and legislation—United States.
  I. Title. II. Series.
  HQ778.63 .C62 2001
  362.71′2—dc21

                                                      2001028627

Dedicated to the memory of my father,
Louis Arnold Solomon, a great champion

Contents

Foreword

During my tenure in the Senate I have been privileged to witness the extraordinary political forces that have shaped the development of federal child care policy over the past two decades. Today, when issues as diverse as tobacco control and environmental regulation routinely employ child-friendly rhetoric, it is difficult to imagine that in 1983, when Senator Arlen Specter and I established the first Senate Children's Caucus, children's needs were more typically an afterthought in federal policy. At that time, while limited federal involvement in education and health care had reached a general degree of acceptance, the idea of a federal role in child care had not recovered from serious defeats in the 1970s. In subsequent years, from the position of chairman and then ranking member of the Senate Subcommittee on Children and Families, I have seen support for a federal role in child care advance dramatically with legislation such as the historic Child Care and Development Block Grant Act of 1990 and have watched progress stall from indifference and partisan squabbling. In recent years I have become cautiously optimistic that child care has finally achieved a position on the federal agenda where it can no longer be easily dismissed.

Although enduring concerns remain in the minds of many that federal support for child care encourages parents to abrogate their responsibilities for child rearing, most now acknowledge that in many American families the parents must work. That economic reality coupled with the societal judgment embodied in welfare reform that welfare recipients, even those with very young children, should be in the workplace has helped to focus national attention on the critical role of affordable child care in promoting self-sufficiency. The growing recognition of employers that employees with stable and affordable child care arrangements are more reliable workers has also had a role in positioning child care as a critical ingredient in maintaining a productive workforce.

Most recently the debate over the federal role in child care has been shaped by developments in unlikely sectors–medical research and law enforcement. Compelling research demonstrating that the early years of life present finite opportunities for children to learn and thrive has triggered unprecedented interest in the quality of child care. Although debates still rage over what constitutes "quality care," this research has contributed to the movement away from the view of child care as strictly "baby-sitting" and toward the expectation that child care should facilitate healthy child development.

Law enforcement statistics highlighting the rise in crimes committed by adolescents in the hours immediately after school have helped to spark bipartisan concern about the lack of available care for school-age children. Bolstered by the involvement of police chiefs and mayors, policymakers have begun to embrace the idea that structured, productive after-school activities can both keep communities safer and create opportunities for educational enrichment. Advocates for programs for school-age children have also capitalized on the fact that nonparental care for older children tends to generate less concern than the same care for younger children.

Sally Cohen's book artfully constructs the complex constellation of political factors that has determined the outcome of child care deliberations since 1970. As Cohen points out, no single individual or political party has been successful in advancing child care policy alone. Substantive progress has been made only when policymakers have come together from both sides of the aisle to support child care initiatives. She also aptly demonstrates how the ongoing ambivalence of policymakers across the political spectrum about nonparental child care, particularly for very young children, has colored the debates of the past thirty years.

As Cohen illustrates, presidential interest has played an important role in advancing policy. However, while presidential leadership is critical, it is not by itself sufficient for successful enactment of child care legislation. In addition, she highlights the powerful role that grassroots and organized interests on the national level have played in sustaining the issue and capitalizing on political opportunities. Cohen's *Championing Child Care* is a valuable addition to this national discussion. Cohen demonstrates why increasing participation of women in the labor force is only a partial explanation for our child care policies. Her in-depth and thorough analysis illuminates the political factors that have shaped federal child care policies since 1970, an important story that needs to be told. Taking a historical view of child care gives us a better understanding of effective policies and why some policies, like federal child care standards, have repeatedly failed. Cohen demonstrates the strong link between child care legislation and societal interests and concerns, including evolving attitudes toward women and the increasing media and academic attention to research on early brain development.

Cohen's book offers an inside glimpse into the powerful forces that have contributed to our national child care agenda. This book is a critical tool for anyone interested in child care—federal and state legislators, executive branch officials, advocacy groups, child care and early education professionals, and students of public policy. Individuals of all political persuasions with a stake in social policies for children should read this book to learn more about this fascinating chapter in American family policy. I commend Cohen for making this valuable contribution to our understanding of the politics and policies that have shaped child care in America.

Senator Christopher Dodd

Acknowledgments

As with any project that spans several years and bridges different stages of one's professional life, in writing this book I owe thanks to many individuals. I am particularly grateful for the guidance and insight provided by faculty at Columbia University when as a doctoral student I embarked upon the study of child care politics and policy. In particular, Lawrence Brown, Richard Pious, Richard Nelson, Sheila Kamerman, and John Colombotos were a vibrant team of dissertation advisers whose perspectives helped create the vision for this book years later. Robert Shapiro's advice and review of various chapters were invaluable.

At Yale University I was fortunate to work with colleagues at the School of Nursing who encouraged me to write the book. Donna Diers has always been a special source of inspiration, graciously reviewed several drafts of early chapters, and helped me pull together seemingly disparate themes. Judith Krauss reviewed drafts of later chapters and shared responsibilities that enabled me to devote time to writing the book. I thank Margaret Grey for helping to make available funding for research assistance. Catherine Gilliss facilitated the grant of a sabbatical from the university, which enabled me to complete the manuscript. Ted Marmor at the Yale School of Management helped sharpen my thinking and writing. Lynn Sennett gave wise editorial advice. I also thank Linda Juszczak, Dorothy Needham, Stephanie Webb, Emily Sadinsky, Kathleen Ennis, and Vanessa Morgan for their research assistance. Kevin Morrissey and the late Barry Bluestein were catalysts for converting the project into book form.

Background research for this book led me to several libraries and archives. At Yale University, Sandra Peterson facilitated the retrieval of numerous government documents, and Jocelyn Tipton guided searches of public opinion data. Scott Parham helped with research at the Nixon Project in the early 1990s. Dallas Lindgren guided archival research at the Minnesota Historical Society. The Yale Center for the Humanities provided a small grant to subsidize research at the Minnesota Historical Society.

I appreciate the scores of individuals who generously gave their time to be interviewed, explained the nuances of child care politics, and reviewed manuscript excerpts. As a condition of their consenting to be interviewed, I cannot identify them by name. Nonetheless, a few can be singled out for their outstanding contributions. First and foremost, Helen Blank at the Children's Defense Fund tirelessly commented on the entire manuscript and numerous rewrites. Her institutional memory, political sensitivity, concern for objective and accurate writing, and generous giving of her time helped shape this book in uncountable ways. Joan Lombardi also reviewed several chapters. Her insights and good cheer were much appreciated. Staff to legislators from both parties in the House and Senate offered important information. Ruby Takanishi and Margaret Blood were instrumental in broadening my analyses and networks.

Excerpts from this book were presented as papers at the American Political Science Association's annual meetings in 1998 and 1999. Gary Mucciaroni, Christopher Klyza, and Michael Hagen offered useful feedback that was incorporated into the final manuscript. At Columbia University Press, John Michel offered wise counsel from the book's inception through completion. His sense of humor was a welcome relief on many occasions. Sabine Seiler copyedited the manuscript. Irene Pavitt, Anne McCoy, and the other members of the editorial and production staff patiently converted the manuscript pages to bound book. I also appreciate the advice of the anonymous reviewer whose careful review illuminated how the book related to other aspects of welfare and family policy.

I am incredibly thankful to Sarah Zaino, whose administrative and editing assistance kept me on course. Her research and organizing talents are invaluable treasures. Finally, I thank my husband, Arnold, and son, Aaron, for the many hours of family time that they had to forgo as I wrote the book. Arnold's belief in the importance of the book and Aaron's acceptance of my prolonged absences enabled me to keep on going. Indeed, writing the book while working and raising a preschool child showed me firsthand the importance of quality child care.

Abbreviations

AAUW	American Association of University Women
ABC	Act for Better Child Care
ACCESS	Affordable Child Care for Early Success and Security Act
ACF	Administration for Children and Families
ACLU	American Civil Liberties Union
ACYF	Administration for Children, Youth, and Families
AEI	American Enterprise Institute
AFDC	Aid to Families with Dependent Children
AFSCME	American Federation of State, County, and Municipal Employees
AFT	American Federation of Teachers
AJC	American Jewish Congress
AJLI	Association of Junior Leagues, International
APHSA	American Public Human Services Association (formerly APWA)
APWA	American Public Welfare Association (changed to APHSA in 1998)
CACFP	Child and Adult Care and Food Program
CAMPUS	Child Care Access Means Parents in School Act
CBO	Congressional Budget Office
CCAC	Child Care Action Campaign
CCDBG	Child Care and Development Block Grant
CDF	Children's Defense Fund
CDGM	Child Development Group of Mississippi
CIDCARE	Creating Improved Delivery of Child Care: Affordable, Reliable, and Educational

CLASP	Center for Law and Social Policy
CWA	Concerned Women for America
CWLA	Child Welfare League of America
DCTC	Dependent Care Tax Credit
DLC	Democratic Leadership Council
DOL	Department of Labor
DPC	Domestic Policy Council
EITC	Earned Income Tax Credit
EOA	Economic Opportunity Act
ERA	Equal Rights Amendment
FAP	Family Assistance Plan
FERA	Federal Emergency Relief Administration
FIDCR	Federal Interagency Day Care Requirements
FRC	Family Research Council
FSA	Family Support Act
FWA	Federal Works Administration
FWI	Families and Work Institute
GAO	General Accounting Office
HEW	Department of Health, Education, and Welfare
HHS	Department of Health and Human Services
ILGWU	International Ladies Garment Workers Union
JOBS	Job Opportunities and Basic Skills Training Program
LWV	League of Women Voters
NACCRRA	National Association of Child Care Resource and Referral Agencies
NACDE	National Association for Child Development and Education
NACO	National Association of Counties
NAEYC	National Association for the Education of Young Children
NBCDI	National Black Child Development Institute
NCCA	National Child Care Association
NCJW	National Council of Jewish Women
NCSL	National Conference of State Legislatures
NEA	National Education Association
NGA	National Governors Association
NICHD	National Institute of Child Health and Human Development
NIOST	National Institute on Out-of-School Time
NOW	National Organization for Women
NWLC	National Women's Law Center

OBRA	Omnibus Budget Reconciliation Act of 1981
OCD	Office of Child Development
OEO	Office of Economic Opportunity
OMB	Office of Management and Budget
PBJI	Program for Better Jobs and Income
PRWORA	Personal Responsibility and Work Opportunity Reconciliation Act
SEIU	Service Employees' International Union
SSBG	Social Services Block Grant
SSI	Stenholm-Shaw One
SSII	Stenholm-Shaw Two
TANF	Temporary Assistance for Needy Families
TCC	Transitional Child Care
TEACH	Teacher Education and Compensation Helps
21st CCLC	21st Century Community Learning Centers
UAW	United Auto Workers
USCC	U.S. Catholic Conference
WIC	Special Supplemental Nutrition Program for Women, Infants, and Children
WIN	Work Incentive Program
WPA	Works Progress Administration
WRAP	Washington Research Action Project

Championing Child Care

1 Introduction

Millions of parents start each day with a flurry of activity that includes placing their children safely in someone else's hands for the rest of the day. Regardless of whether parents entrust their children to relatives, friends, or child care providers, working parents are constantly confronted with the difficulties of arranging for child care while they work. They must locate caregivers who can ensure their children's safety and promote their development. And they must be able to afford the fees, which poses further challenges, especially for low-income working families. Most Americans agree that decisions regarding child care are best left to parents. However, for many families, securing good quality child care is not easily accomplished without the help of family, friends, employers, government entities, and the clout of child care public policies.

The basic premise of this book is that changes in political institutions shaped the politics and outcomes of child care public policies, defined here as federal laws and regulations. Political institutions include Congress and the executive branch. Moreover, changes in organized interests—defined here as national and state organizations representing women, children, labor unions, welfare, education, child care, and other interests—interacted with such institutions to influence child care policy outcomes. Appreciation of how organized interests (also referred to as interest groups) evolved over time further enhances understanding of American child care policies. *Championing Child Care* offers an alternative to the oft-repeated claim that the increased participation of women in the labor force explains the rising interest in child care and subsequent legislative developments. Another important assumption underlying this book is that understanding the politics of previous child care policymaking episodes helps make subsequent strategies more successful.

This book answers the following questions: How were the politics of child care legislation affected by structural changes among political institutions? Which aspects of the relationships among political institutions most influenced the process and outcome of child care deliberations? What patterns over the past thirty years can be discerned to inform future deliberations about child care policy?

In the United States, for various reasons, child care historically has not been a major government priority. This is in contrast to some other industrialized nations, in particular the Scandinavian countries and France, that offer substantial government support for child care.[1] Canada and the United Kingdom have "moderate" government involvement in child care, more closely resembling the mix of public- and private-sector child care initiatives in the United States.[2] Differences among countries are partially attributable to cultural values. Laissez-faire individualism, which characterizes American culture and political norms, emphasizes free markets and the private sector, not government subsidies. In the United States policymakers first rely on markets to cover child care needs. However, because forces of supply and demand do not always meet the child care needs of many families, government involvement becomes increasingly important. Determining the nature of that involvement generates debate.

Many Americans have a hard time delegating the rearing of children to others. Publicly sponsored child care often connotes images of parents, especially mothers, relinquishing their responsibilities and abandoning their children to institutional facilities. Actually, as the book explains, publicly sponsored child care gives parents the flexibility to use a wide range of providers, including members of their extended families. A January 1998 poll by Louis Harris and Associates revealed Americans' continuing ambivalence toward child care as a government responsibility. When asked "Who do you think should be primarily responsible for ensuring that families have access to child care," 60 percent responded that individuals should be responsible, 23 percent preferred business or employers, and 15 percent indicated the government.[3]

Public opinion polls also suggest a persisting unease with mothers of young children working. In the 1998 General Social Survey conducted by the

National Opinion Research Center, 41 percent of respondents agreed that "a preschool child is likely to suffer if his or her mother works." Each time this question was asked since 1985 men were more likely than women, by 10 to 15 percentage points, to think that way.[4] Given the large and growing number of working mothers, these data reflect a gap between the policy preferences of many Americans and the realities that many families face.[5]

Starting in the late 1980s a new interest in child care emerged that led to the enactment of landmark child care legislation in 1990. This ended nearly two decades of political stalemate. In the mid-1990s work requirements under welfare reform and interest in programs for preschool and school-age children prompted further attention to child care. Discussion of the politics surrounding these different events and outcomes forms the essence of this book.

Why Study Child Care Politics?

By the mid-1990s more than 32 million children aged fourteen and under had mothers in the workforce and required some type of child care arrangement, including after-school care.[6] Mothers who did not work may also have placed their children in child care, especially preschool programs. From 1970 to 1997 the total number of children between the ages of three and five enrolled in preprimary programs increased from 4.1 to 7.9 million, representing an increase from 37.5 to 64.9 percent of all children in that age group.[7] With 1.5 million children receiving federal child care assistance and another 13 million being eligible but not receiving support,[8] the politics behind the federal government's role in this growing sector of American social and economic life warrant explanation.

Child care policymaking encompassed many issues on the political agenda, ranging from tax and budget policies to welfare reform and separation of church and state. It evoked questions about the role of women, the well-being of children, and the balance between federal and state responsibilities. Furthermore, unraveling the story of child care legislation over the past thirty years points to the legacies of past events in current policies. With the federal government spending over $17 billion on child care and related programs in fiscal year (FY) 2001, it is important to understand the dynamics behind these various initiatives (table 1.1).

Studying the politics of child care legislation also points to advantages and disadvantages of specific strategies, such as direct subsidies or tax credits.

TABLE 1.1 Federal Spending on Child Care and Related Programs,
FY 2001

Program	Amount (billion $)
CCDBG (discretionary portion)	2.0
CCDBG (entitlement portion)	2.6
Child and Adult Care Food	1.7[a]
Dependent Care Tax Credit	2.2[b]
Dependent Care Assistance	0.4[b]
Social Services Block Grant	0.3
Head Start	6.2
21st Century Community Learning Centers	0.8
Other	1.0
Total	**$17.2**

[a]Estimated, Department of Agriculture.
[b]Estimated, Joint Committee on Taxation.

Source: Melinda Gish and Karen Spar, Child Care Issues in the 106th Congress (Washington,
D.C.: Congressional Research Service, 18 February 2000); author's estimates.

The book's thirty-year span allows for analyses of the puzzles and patterns
that characterized the politics of child care legislation during that period. A
three-decade overview enables policymakers, scholars, and the public at
large to appreciate the strides that have been made in child care policymaking and to debunk common myths. Exploring the politics over time also
illustrates how "things are seldom what they seem." That is, assumptions
regarding which party is better for child care and which presidents most
advanced child care policymaking may be proved wrong after a closer examination of the politics.

A major premise of this book is that federal child care policies matter.
With devolution placing an increasingly large emphasis on state policies,
many scholars have lost sight of the importance of federal child care legislation. In fact, the large growth of state child care spending of the 1990s is

largely due to the funds that states received from the federal child care block grant. In addition, federal policies are important in establishing how far states *may* go and what they *must* do to receive federal child care funds. Federal child care policies also set a precedent for coordination among various state and local programs, such as Head Start, public health, education, and social services, all of which are connected to child care and the well-being of millions of families with children.

This book depicts the different problems child care policies addressed and the various ways policymakers defined child care politically. It shows that shifting institutional structures affected who had access to decision makers and who controlled the agenda, and that none of these factors alone determined final child care policy outcomes. This book also illustrates the time and effort needed to convert a social condition (i.e., increasing numbers of children needing regular nonparental care) into a policy problem (child care bills). In the process, unpredictable political forces created opportunities for and impediments to arriving at policy solutions. One example of the unexpected was the support child care legislation received from Republican legislators, even some conservatives. Such nuances emerge once one understands the major themes and details of child care policymaking as presented in this book.

Why Championing?

Why call this book *Championing Child Care?* Why not just entitle it "The Politics of Child Care Legislation," which is the book's primary focus? Including the word "championing" in the title and referring to "champions" throughout the text brings to life the struggles to advance child care legislation. In telling the story of child care legislation, this book explains how certain individuals on both sides of the aisle have been champions. Their endurance, commitment, and perspectives have been invaluable to the advancement of child care policies.

At each critical episode of child care legislation one can identify champions of child care policymaking who were willing to invest time, resources, money, and ideas to improve child care policies. Some of these individuals were presidents or other well-known figures. Other champions were federal bureaucrats, state advocates, or concerned individuals who were less well known and acted politically to improve the quality of child care. In all cases, it was championing—negotiating, advocating, articulating, and persisting—that made their efforts valiant and important.

Championing of child care is not limited to those at one end of the political or ideological spectrum. In its fullest sense the championing of child care includes liberals, conservatives, and moderates alike. Thus, this book is about the web of child care policymaking, the turbulence it produced, and the different approaches, including tax policies and calls for a return to traditional family values, that child care prompted when it landed on the public or legislative agenda.

Why 1970 to 1999?

The years 1970 to 2000 are a particularly rich time for studying the politics of child care legislation. They are characterized by marked demographic changes, expansion of the child care industry, and significant shifts in the structural and procedural aspects of American political institutions. The thirty years this book covers include three major child care policymaking episodes. The first was in the late 1960s and early 1970s, made infamous by President Nixon's 1971 veto of legislation featuring a national child care program. The second major episode started in the late 1980s and ended with the enactment of landmark child care legislation in 1990. The third major event was the 1996 welfare act, with its provisions that changed the contours of federal child care policy. Events in the intervening years and after 1996 are also discussed.

Between 1970 and 2000 the legislative and executive branches of the federal government underwent significant changes. Among them were shifts in partisan control of Congress with the 1980 Republican victory in the Senate, its return to Democratic dominance in 1986, and the GOP takeover of both the House and the Senate in 1994. National elections in 1976, 1980, and 1992 switched party control of the White House. The executive branch experienced a centralization of power within the Office of Management and Budget (OMB) and a changing relationship among OMB and other executive agencies involved with child care.

The last three years of the twentieth century were also marked by tremendous social and economic transformation, which created new interest in child care.[9] In 1998 the *New York Times* magazine ran a "Special Issue on the Joy and Guilt of Modern Motherhood." In discussing conflicts between work and home, Andrew Cherlin emphasized the dramatic expansion of child care usage since the 1970s.[10] Between 1965 and 1994, the number of preschool children with employed mothers increased from 3.8 to 10.3 million.[11] In 1995, 14.4 million children under five years of age, comprising 75 percent of all children that age, had some type of regular child care arrangement. Many of these children were in more than one setting per week. Forty-nine percent of children under five years of age were cared for by nonrelatives, including nearly 6 million children who were placed in organized child care facilities (table 1.2).[12] Another 24.7 million children between the ages of five and fourteen had parents employed or in school in 1995.[13] From another perspective, James L. Hymes Jr. chronicled the many changes in early childhood education between 1971 and 1990.[14] The advocacy groups involved with child care grew in number over the same period, while other aspects of their organizing endured.

The demographic change most frequently associated with child care policies was the surge of women in the paid labor force since World War II, in particular since the late 1960s (figure 1.1 and table 1.3). Most significantly, employment rates for women with children under the age of six soared from 25.3 percent in 1965 to 62.3 percent in 1996. The rate also more than doubled for women with children under the age of three, for whom participation rates in the labor force increased from 21.4 to 59 percent over the same time period. By 1996 employment rates for women with children aged six years or older were well above 70 percent. Although most women worked full time, many were employed part time.[15] During the 1970s, 1980s, and 1990s those seeking stronger government investments in child care often cited the increasing number of working mothers to justify their cause. But as this book demonstrates, child care legislation was about much more than growing numbers of working women. If the number of working women alone determined child care policy outcomes, we would have arrived at different solutions many years ago.

One of the most dramatic changes in family life since 1970 was the more than doubling in the number of children raised by only one parent, rising from 8 million to almost 20 million in 1996.[16] Most of these single parents are women who typically have fewer relatives to assist with child care. They often are in low-paying jobs or are the sole breadwinners for

TABLE 1.2 Primary Child Care Arrangements Used for Preschoolers (children under age 5) by Families with Employed Mothers: Selected Years, 1965–1995

Type of arrangement	February 1965	Fall 1977[4]	Winter 1985	Fall 1990	Fall 1995
Number of children (in thousands)	3,794	4,370	8,168	9,629	10,047
Percent	100[1]	100	100	100	100
By father	10.3	14.4	15.7	16.5	16.6
By grandparent	(NA)	(NA)	15.9	14.3	15.9
By other relative	36.0[2]	30.9[2]	8.2	8.8	5.5
By nonrelative in child's home	18.5	7.0	5.9	5.0	4.9
By nonrelative in provider's home	19.6	22.4	22.3	20.1	23.5[5]
Organized child care facilities	8.2	13.0	23.1	27.5	25.1
Day/group care center	(NA)	(NA)	14.0	20.6	21.6
Nursery school/preschool	(NA)	(NA)	9.1	6.9	5.9
Head Start	(NA)	(NA)	(NA)	(NA)	1.5
Mother cares for child at work[3]	6.7	11.4	8.1	6.4	5.4
Other arrangements	0.7	1.0	0.8	1.3	2.9

NA Not available
[1]Percentages reported only for children with mothers working full-time
[2]Data include grandparents
[3]Includes mothers working for pay at home or away from home
[4]Data only for the two youngest children under 5 years of age
[5]Includes 15.7 percent in family day care and 7.8 percent in care by other nonrelatives.

Sources: Bureau of the Census, "Primary Care Arrangements Used for Preschoolers by Families with Employed Mothers: Selected Years, 1977 to 1994," Internet release date, 14 January 1998, available at: http://www.census.gov/population/socdemo/child/p70-62/tableA.txt, accessed 17 December 2000; Bureau of the Census, Trends in Child Care: Arrangements of Working Mothers, Current Population Reports, P23-117 (Washington, D.C.: Government Printing Office, 1982), 6, 43; Kristin Smith, Who's Minding the Kids? Child Care Arrangements: Fall 1995, Current Population Reports, P70-70 (Washington, D.C.: Bureau of the Census, 2000), 11.

FIGURE 1 Labor Force Participation Rates of Women by Youngest Child

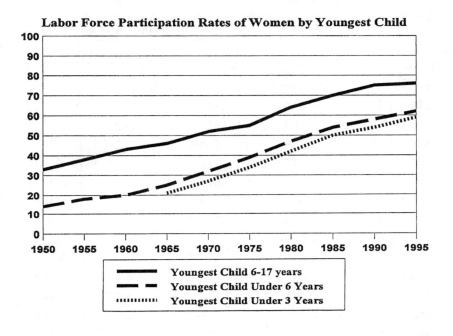

Labor Force Participation Rates of Women by Youngest Child

Legend:
— Youngest Child 6-17 years
– – Youngest Child Under 6 Years
⋯⋯ Youngest Child Under 3 Years

Source: U.S. House, Committee on Ways and Means, *1998 Green Book*, 105th Cong., 2d sess., 19 May 1998, 661.

their household. Since the 1970s single mothers have had lower labor force participation rates than their married counterparts, but the 1996 welfare reform could change this.

Many leading economists have shown that despite upward mobility for many Americans, the income gap persists.[17] During the 1980s families and incomes at the lower end of the income distribution "lost ground" while those at the top gained. At the same time, high- and low-income families made more strides than those in the middle.[18] These trends raise questions regarding who should benefit from state and national child care policies.

TABLE 1.3 Labor Force Participation Rates of Women
by Age of Youngest Child, Selected Years, 1950–1996

| | | | All children under age 18 | |
| | | | Under age 6 | |
	Total	Age 6–17	Total	Under 3
March 1950	21.6	32.8	13.6	NA
March 1960	30.4	42.5	20.2	NA
March 1970	42.4	51.6	32.2	27.3
March 1975	47.3	54.8	38.8	34.1
March 1980	56.6	64.3	46.8	41.9
March 1985	62.1	69.9	53.5	49.5
March 1986	62.8	70.4	54.4	50.8
March 1987	64.7	72.0	56.7	52.9
March 1988	65.0	73.3	56.1	52.5
March 1989	65.7	74.2	56.7	52.4
March 1990	66.7	74.7	58.2	53.6
March 1991	66.6	74.4	58.4	54.5
March 1992	67.2	75.9	58.0	54.5
March 1993	66.9	75.4	57.9	53.9
March 1994	68.4	76.0	60.3	57.1
March 1995	69.7	76.4	62.3	58.7
March 1996	70.2	77.2	62.3	59.0

Source: U.S. House, Committee on Ways and Means, 1998 Green Book, 105th Cong., 2d sess.,
19 May 1998, 661.

Federal child care policies have targeted poor and low-income families who
spend a proportionately higher share of their income on child care. But
many middle-class families also face challenges of arranging suitable care
for their children.

Finally, in 1998, despite the nation's economic largesse, 18.7 percent
of all children under eighteen lived in families with incomes below the

federal poverty level. (In 1998 the official poverty threshold for a family of four was $16,660.) The 13.3 million children in poverty in 1998 comprise a 3 million increase in the overall number of children who were poor since 1979. Poverty rates among children below age six are higher than those for older children.[19] In 1997, 22 percent of all children under age six lived in families with incomes below the federal poverty level, and another 20 percent were in families with incomes below 185 percent of the poverty threshold. These data reflect an overall drop in the child poverty rate from its high in 1993, but rates are still above those reported in the early 1970s.[20] Children in poverty are at risk for many physical, social, cognitive, and emotional problems.[21] Early childhood programs offer many benefits, especially for disadvantaged children,[22] and are important in reversing possible deleterious effects of poverty.

In response to these social and economic trends the child care industry grew dramatically over the past three decades. Between 1977 and 1990 the total number of center-based child care programs tripled from 18,307 to 55,960, with enrollment quadrupling from 897,000 to 3.8 million children.[23] In 1999 states reported 102,458 regulated child care centers, nearly a 16 percent increase from 1991.[24] Family child care providers, most of whom were unregulated, also grew in number although at a slower rate than center-based care. In 1999, 290,667 regulated family child care providers were reported in the United States; most were small family child care homes.[25]

One of the most significant changes for early education programs over the past three decades was the growth of state and local involvement in prekindergarten programs. These programs, which often entailed collaboration among Head Start, public education, and community child care providers, changed the contours of child care policymaking.

Finally, over the past thirty years, new knowledge emerged about the impact of child care on child development. Political debates in the late 1960s and early 1970s had featured arguments about the harmful effects of child care on children. In the ensuing years empirical data showed that good quality child care was not harmful to children and was perhaps beneficial. Research on early brain development had a significant impact on many aspects of early childhood policymaking, too. This book integrates these political, social, economic, and empirical developments in deciphering the politics of American child care policymaking between 1970 and 2000.

Context of the Book

Organizing Framework

The author used several frameworks to explain policy change. The book is not meant to confirm any of these theories. Rather they help explain the series of events pertaining to child care legislation over time. Frank R. Baumgartner and Bryan D. Jones's model of punctuated equilibrium is of particular relevance.[26] They explain that structural shifts within political institutions and changing definitions of the policy problem create periods of "relative stability" followed by periods of "rapid change."[27] The latter leave in place new structures to guide subsequent child care policymaking efforts. *Championing Child Care* uses Baumgartner and Jones's framework in identifying key junctures at which major child care bills were introduced and debated (1971, 1990, and 1996), describing the politics surrounding each of these events, and then identifying the new political structures and the negotiations among individuals associated with them that evolved in the intervening years.

According to Baumgartner and Jones, issue definition is "the driving force" for determining the stability and instability of political systems because it has the potential to mobilize people and groups who were "previously disinterested." *Championing Child Care* shows how issue definition was fundamental to the politics of child care legislation. Issue definition is essential for engaging new constituencies and framing the terms of the debate. In addition to issue definition, structural changes among political institutions, often as a result of changes in partisan control, may also result in new issues emerging on the agenda or old ones being redefined. Thus, issue definition combined with institutional control "make[s] possible the alternation between stability and rapid change that characterizes political systems."[28]

Scholarship by Paul Sabatier and Hank Jenkins-Smith on advocacy coalitions provides another framework for explaining child care politics.[29] Advocacy coalitions are composed of "people from a variety of positions (elected and agency officials, interest group leaders, researchers) who share a particular belief system—i.e., a set of basic values, causal assumptions, and problem perceptions—and who show a non-trivial degree of coordinated activity over time."[30] Under the advocacy coalition framework, policy change requires a time frame of ten years or more, which makes it particularly useful for this study. Opposing coalitions reach a consensus through "policy-oriented learning," which "refers to relatively enduring alterations of thought or behavioral intentions that result from experience and are concerned with the attainment (or revision) of policy objectives."[31] By understanding the variables affecting their belief system and responding to exogenous events, individuals adjust their position.[32]

Between 1970 and 2000 one major advocacy coalition lobbied for child care legislation. It included some organizations, legislators, and individuals with long-standing, consistent involvement with child care legislative debates. Other participants were marginally involved, and some were more engaged at certain times than others. All members of the coalition accepted the importance of a strong role for the federal government in child care policymaking.

Groups and individuals in the opposing coalition included individuals, legislators, and organizations with a different set of beliefs about the government's role in the child care arena—one that emphasized parental choice, states' rights, and minimal government intervention. They did not form a formal coalition and were not as cohesively organized as their liberal counterparts. By the 1990s, partly as a result of policy learning, the views of both sides had converged but only to a very limited extent. Philosophical differences between each camp contributed to ongoing divisiveness in child care policymaking.

Other minor advocacy coalitions also were part of child care policymaking, sometimes in inchoate forms. In particular, the politics of enacting the 1990 child care legislation heightened ongoing conflicts among organizations over separation of church and state. Although this is not presently a key issue for child care (having been resolved, to some extent, in the 1990 legislation), it produced distinct coalitions among organizations participating in child care policymaking in the late 1980s.

In sum, by focusing on issue definition, political institutions, and advocacy coalitions and by taking a perspective that allows for analysis over time, the story of child care politics comes to life. These structures offer vistas through which a host of political and socioeconomic forces can be examined.

What Makes This Book Different

This book fills significant gaps in the policy sciences and child care literature.[33] It differs from the many publications on child care policies, which are cited throughout the book, in that its focus is on the politics, not the policy analyses. Its goal is not to tout a particular policy option, such as a universal system, but rather to show the importance of political negotiations in understanding contemporary child care policies.

Other authors wrote historical perspectives on child care and related policies, but typically without the political analysis of this book.[34] Most recently, Sonya Michel offered a detailed history of child care policies since the late 1800s, explaining why the United States failed to establish a universal system of child care.[35] Her work is based on the premises that child care is an undervalued public policy and that universal child care is a desirable goal.

Gilbert Steiner's books on children's and family policies analyzed of some of the same issues covered in this book. However, his discussions of children and family policy, including but not limited to child care, ended in the late 1970s.[36] Marion Frances Berry's *The Politics of Parenthood* covered some of the same terrain as *Championing Child Care* but did not go beyond 1990.[37] Berry examined the politics of child care and parenthood in the workplace, government, and elsewhere, depicting the prevalence of the "mother-care" tradition and its effect on women's social, political, and economic status since the early 1900s. In contrast, this book examines the politics of child care in one domain, policymaking at the federal level since 1970, and shows how the themes that Berry presented were among the many factors that influenced American child care policies. Other scholars covered the politics of child care legislation between 1970 and 1990[38] but not with the breadth of this project.

Sheila B. Kamerman and Alfred J. Kahn's 1987 book on child care is a classic for understanding public and private sector child care policies through the late 1980s.[39] In subsequent comparative analyses of child care and other family policies they demonstrated how the United States differs from, and often lags behind, other industrialized nations.[40] Their recent and most ambitious project offers a multifaceted view of family policies from 1960 to the mid-1990s in the United States, Canada, Great Britain, and New Zealand. Family policy experts from these four countries analyzed the relationship between family change and family policy, including broad political, social, and economic developments.[41] Kamerman and Kahn found that none of these four countries had explicit comprehensive national child care policies.[42] *Championing Child Care* elaborates on many of the political themes for American child care policymaking that Kamerman and Kahn noted in a comparative context.

Edward Zigler's abundant contributions to the literature on child development and early childhood policymaking are invaluable for anyone examining these issues.[43] William T. Gormley Jr.'s scholarship, especially his book, *Everybody's Children*, provides insightful analyses on state regulation of child care following the implementation of the 1990 child care provisions.[44] *Championing Child Care* also adds to the literature of case studies in social policy formation.[45] Although each case study has a particular focus, taken together this literature enriches our understanding of the public policy process. Theodore R. Marmor's analysis of Medicare policymaking includes the same period as this book (1970s to 2000) and reaches similar conclusions regarding structural factors that affect policymaking.[46]

Finally, this book is part of a renewed focus on institutions that many contemporary political scientists and historians have favored. This return to institutionalism is not limited to political science; fields such as economics, law history, and sociology have also experienced a renewed interest in the topic.[47]

New institutionalism is different from the so-called old institutionalism that prevailed until the mid-twentieth century in that the political scientists interested in "old institutionalism" viewed Congress, the presidency, the bureaucracy of the executive branch, and organized interests as static, emphasizing their rules, norms, and cultures. The old institutionalism focused on the central role of the law in governance and the formal features of the Constitution, such as the presidency and Congress. Scholars also studied the major institutional aspects of political systems, such as whether they were parliamentary, presidential, or federal versus unitary, and offered normative analyses of what comprised good government.[48]

Starting in the 1950s political scientists developed behavioral models of political action that sought to identify what motivated individuals (i.e., voters or public officials) to take certain actions. As a result, economic theories of choice and rationality came to the forefront of political science. According to such theories, political actors were deemed to be "rational utility maximizers." For example, legislators would vote in ways to maximize their chance of being reelected.[49] Rational choice and behavioral theories tend to reduce collective behavior to individual actions.[50]

For the past two decades, political scientists working under the rubric of the new institutionalism have pursued many different avenues of study. One approach incorporates rational choice, political behavior, bargaining, and politics with the parameters of institutional structures, rules, and procedures.

It examines how such structures and procedures shape the context in which political actors function.[51] Such approaches are relevant to the politics of child care legislation in that rules of lawmaking and the structure of Congress shaped the politics of child care policymaking in many ways. Moreover, changes in congressional structures and rules in the mid-1970s and the mid-1990s influenced both the process and the outcome of the politics of child care legislation in subsequent years.

Another line of inquiry, historical institutionalism, explains how the choices made when an institution or policy is formed (or not formed) create enduring legacies for subsequent policies. Historical institutionalists frequently refer to the concept of path dependency, "in which preceding steps in a particular direction induce further movement in the same direction," creating a type of inertia of policymaking.[52] The notion of path dependency is relevant to American child care policymaking in that a reluctance to provide government assistance to families with working mothers and young children as early as the beginning of the twentieth century established a precedent that was hard to break. President Nixon's veto of the 1971 child care bill further contributed to legislators' unwillingness to endorse a federal child care program. The monumental breaking of that inertia in 1990 with the enactment of the first freestanding federal child care program established a pattern of child care policymaking (block grants to states with certain parameters) that proved difficult to disturb when child care landed on the legislative agenda in subsequent years.

Other institutionalists point to the constitutional structure and institutional fragmentation of American government as explanations for what they consider lags in government involvement in social policies. For example, according to Sven Steinmo, the underdevelopment of the American welfare state can be explained by several institutional aspects of American government. In particular, Steinmo points to the American federalist system, which divides authority between a central government and the states, separation of powers between a legislative and an executive branch of government, fragmentation within Congress, and the large influence of interest groups as factors that impede the creation of a more active government role in the social policy arena.[53] The story of child care policymaking over the past three decades illustrates how many of these institutional constraints shaped the contours of the debates and the policy outcomes. Finally, institutionalism offers an alternative to American exceptionalism as an explanation for the uneven involvement of government in many social policy arenas. As

Steinmo and Jon Watts remarked, "In the end, culturalists offer quite static explanations. What we need is a better understanding of the relationship between what people think about government and what government does (or does not) do."[54]

Of relevance to the politics of child care legislation, new institutionalism claims that political institutions influence how interests organize, how much access and power they are likely to have, and what positions they might take. For child care, the ability of certain groups and ideas to prevail at specific junctures was related to who had access to decision making. Often this depended on which party controlled Congress or the White House. Other factors, such as the balance between legislative and executive branches of government, also were important.

Political institutions shape the rules and other aspects of the strategic environment, giving priority to certain groups and ideas over others.[55] As Baumgartner and Jones observed, the "structural bias inherent in any set of political institutions" helps explain how certain groups or individuals have an advantage in mobilization and, consequently, in achieving certain policy outcomes.[56] In the chapters that follow, historical institutionalism allowed the author to trace how changes evolved over time; political institutions provided the lenses for understanding how decisions were made.

Research Questions

This book answered several key research questions. First, why did child care legislation take the course it did at each of the critical junctures (1971, 1990, and 1996) and in the intervening years? How did the players interact to enable lawmakers to arrive at these three different solutions? Second, based on the premise that something other than demographic factors determined child care policies, how did institutional structures interact to influence child care policy outcomes? Finally, what do the politics of child care legislation over the past thirty years suggest for the future?

While conducting research for this book, three additional questions emerged that are answered in the final chapter. First, once child care bills were introduced in Congress, why was it so difficult for legislators to pass legislation that a president willingly signed? Second, why were some of the most significant changes in child care policymaking enacted under a Republican president (1990) and a GOP Congress when Democrats were typically the promoters of government investment in child care? What do the answers to these questions reveal about American public policymaking? Finally, how did organized interests influence child care policies? In particular, if child care was an important policy concern, largely because of the influx of women into the workforce, why were women's groups not in the forefront of child care advocacy?

These are questions that emphasize the "how" and "why" of child care politics.[57] Answering them also requires knowing "who" was involved and "what" the major issues and sequence of events were. Government documents and archival evidence were useful in answering such questions but only insofar as they revealed aspects of the story that were publicly recorded. Other case study methodologies, especially interviews with individuals who participated in the politics of child care legislation, enabled the author to delve beneath the surface and obtain information that was not otherwise available.

This book's multiple case studies provided opportunities to compare and contrast three major periods in child care policymaking—1971, 1990, and 1996. This required that the same questions be asked for each case and that there be sufficient similarities and differences among cases to allow analysis. All three cases pertained to national child care legislation involving Congress, the executive branch, and organized interests. Over time, some of the individual players and structural aspects of the institutions changed. Thus, these three cases contained enough similarities and differences to allow a meaningful analysis.

The author conducted interviews with 114 individuals involved with child care policymaking since the early 1970s.[58] This included past or present members of Congress, congressional staff, executive branch officials, interest group representatives from state or national organizations, state officials, and policy analysts from academic or private research entities. Slightly over half of the interviews were conducted in the early 1990s as part of a previous research project. The rest were conducted between 1996 and 1999. Approximately half the interviews were conducted in person and the rest by phone. Some individuals were interviewed more than once to obtain perspectives at different times. To ensure accuracy and avoid the risk of "being co-opted by respondents,"[59] the author made every attempt possible to ask the same question of many individuals, to have key informants review the text, and to obtain feedback from unbiased and well-informed experts.

All interviews were conducted with the understanding that the interviewees' names and organizations would not be revealed in subsequent analyses unless the author was explicitly granted permission to do so. In such cases, respondents were given the opportunity to review and revise the text that included their citations. The author often asked respondents to review excerpts from the text, even if they were cited anonymously, to ensure that the material was accurate. Quotations in the text without attribution are taken from such interviews, and these sources remain anonymous to protect respondents' identities.[60] Throughout the text, in order to protect the interviewees' identities, interviewees are quoted verbatim without notes identifying the source. When interviewees granted permission to be explicitly cited, their names and the dates of the interviews are revealed in the endnotes.

Interviews were not tape-recorded. Instead, the author took handwritten notes that were later typed so as to preserve as much as possible the respondent's exact words and the interchange between author and respondent. The decision not to tape-record was based on the assumption that people would talk more freely without the tape recorder, a premise many interviewees reiterated. Moreover, interviews were intended to provide insight and clarify certain issues, not to obtain verbatim transcriptions for subsequent analysis of language or content. The advantages of this method in terms of the respondents' candor and spontaneity outweighed the disadvantages of losing their precise wording.[61]

Overview of the Book

The book takes a chronological approach to child care policymaking. Chapter 2 describes the politics of the 1971 bill establishing a universal and comprehensive child care program, which President Nixon vetoed. The chapter includes the themes that helped place child care on the legislative agenda, differences between how leaders in the House and Senate handled the legislation, alignment of organized interests, and divisiveness within the executive branch that led to President Nixon's veto. Readers will be intrigued with how some of the key players in these early years went on to obtain high positions within government, party politics, and social policymaking.

Chapter 3 covers the years between 1972 and the late 1980s, describing the ongoing efforts of certain members of Congress to keep child care legislation alive, despite fierce opposition from conservatives, including an anonymous smear campaign. This chapter describes the contentious politics over the establishment of federal child care requirements and the enactment of major child care legislation under the Family Support Act of 1988 (FSA).

Chapter 4 illuminates the politics of the most critical juncture in the history of American child care policymaking. It closely follows the path of child care legislation from the late 1980s through enactment in 1990 as a package that included expansion of the earned income tax credit and the creation of two new federal child care programs. The 1990 bill demonstrated the importance of both tax credits and programmatic initiatives as venues for child care policies. This chapter presents the politics among organized interests across the ideological continuum, including but not limited to the major child care coalition, led by the Children's Defense Fund (CDF) and its outspoken president, Marian Wright Edelman. The chapter ends with explanations for the different political outcomes in 1971 (presidential veto) and 1990 (enactment).

Chapter 5 reviews the politics of implementing the child care provisions of the 1990 law. In many ways, regulatory battles mirrored the politics of enactment. The chapter also looks at the impact of President Clinton's election on child care policymaking.

Chapter 6 examines child care as part of welfare reform, starting with the Republican takeover of Congress in 1994 and the ensuing structural and procedural shifts in Congress. It follows the sequence of events that led to the enactment of welfare reform in 1996, concentrating on how child care was part of those deliberations and how new congressional structures and procedures influenced the legislative outcomes. Differences between this round of child care legislation and the two previous ones are discussed throughout the chapter.

Chapter 7 depicts how child care legislation became part of other issues, including crime prevention, school readiness, tax policy revisions, and the negotiations between states' attorneys general and the major tobacco companies. In contrast to the 1970s, by the late 1990s most lawmakers, regardless of party affiliation, agreed that the federal government had a role to play in child care policymaking. However, debates continued over federal funding levels, the types of tax reforms that would best meet the needs of families with children, and the type of families that should benefit from various child care policies.

Chapter 8 describes the nuances of child care policymaking at the state level and how federal legislation affected and interacted with states' decisions pertaining to child care and early education. A book on federal child care policymaking would be incomplete without some discussion of how states implemented such policies and linked them with Head Start, child care, and other early education programs.

The final chapter discusses patterns of child care policymaking over the last thirty years of the twentieth century. It focuses on the structural aspects of American political institutions that both facilitated and impeded the formation of child care policies. The chapter explains why child care policies have come so far since 1970 and identifies opportunities for future advancement. These insights make it possible to look ahead with cautious optimism to the path child care legislation will take in the century ahead.

2   Politics of Child Care Legislation, 1971

The child care debates of the late 1960s and early 1970s broke new ground. For the first time, lawmakers considered a national child care program separate from a wartime initiative or welfare policy. Nonetheless, each time child care had landed on the congressional agenda, whether during the Depression or the postwar years, it had generated heated discussions about working mothers and the government's role in caring for children. By 1971 legislators and interest groups who worked on a comprehensive child care bill were confident it would become law. After all, both chambers of Congress endorsed the measure; it met the goals of various organizations, and the president had made a commitment to helping children in the early years of life. Thus, President Richard M. Nixon's veto sent a strong message of defeat to child care advocates.[1] A close look at the politics reveals that Nixon cannot be blamed alone for the downfall of child care legislation in 1971.

Prelude to Child Care Legislation of 1971

Foreshadowing of Later Years

At the beginning of the twentieth century, day nurseries and other initiatives provided care for children of impoverished working women.[2] In 1933 President Franklin Roosevelt established emergency nursery schools under the Federal Emergency Relief Administration (FERA) and the Works Progress Administration (WPA). These nursery schools were designed to protect the health and welfare of poor preschool children in rough economic times. As the first federally funded child care programs, they established a precedent of targeting poor children.[3] These nurseries also were intended to create jobs for unemployed professionals on relief rolls. Thus, about 90 percent of the staff were teachers, social workers, or nurses who easily became skilled in caring for young children.[4] By 1943 more than 300,000 children were attending emergency nursery schools on a regular basis.[5]

Emergency nursery schools engendered controversy regarding the appropriateness of the government's involvement in child rearing. Many federal officials and social work professionals preferred that religious and other voluntary organizations provide child care for impoverished families. They contended that the federal government should not usurp mothers' rightful roles. One proponent of government-subsidized child care centers, Susan B. Anthony II (niece of the well-known suffragette), referred to her opponents as the "at home as usual" champions.[6] The same term could describe those opposed to federal child care programs for decades to follow.

Labor shortages during World War II generated a growing demand for workers, including women, and eliminated the need for federally sponsored work programs. As women were called to work in defense industries, the demand for child care grew.[7] In 1942 President Roosevelt agreed to use funds from the Community Facilities Act of 1941 (referred to as the Lanham Act) to help states pay for child care centers.[8] By 1943 WPA nurseries funded by the Lanham Act were placed under the Federal Works Administration (FWA). In the transition from the WPA to the FWA many child care programs were closed because they did not meet the Lanham Act criteria of being in an area affected by the war.[9]

The use of Lanham funds for child care did not come about easily. Many government officials and private welfare leaders were reluctant to invest in child care, preferring instead that mothers assume primary responsibility for rearing their children. Congressman Fritz Lanham (D-Tex.) was among those who opposed the use of funds from legislation bearing his name for the subsidization of child care.[10] He was joined by others who felt that women should be "driven, if necessary, back to their homes, where they belong, to look after these children."[11] Those opposed to federal child care funding were less concerned with the well-being of children and more worried about the proper role of women. Even government officials were divided over federal funding of child care programs. Some thought that group child care facilities would harm children's relationships with their mothers and create an undesirable decline in parental contact with children[12]—another theme that would resonate through the debates for years.

Implementation of Lanham Act funding for child care presented challenges, largely because responsibility for administering Lanham Act funding for child care rested with more than one federal agency, often working together with state welfare and education agencies. Moreover, only a handful of states invested in child care programs, seeing it as a responsibility of the federal, not the state, government. In addition, local officials responsible for applying for and administering federal child care assistance often stalled and stymied the flow of federal child care funds.[13]

In spite of the reluctance on the part of some federal officials to support child care programs, in February 1944 the FWA reported that more than 2,240 centers received Lanham Act funds for nearly 66,000 children. Eventually, depending on the source, 105,000 to 129,000 children received child care assistance under the Lanham Act. Some accounts place the number considerably higher. The exact amount is hard to know because Children's Bureau officials often inflated the figures to emphasize the importance of the program, and some children were counted more than once.[14] Nonetheless, the millions of federal and state dollars spent on child care under this law still fell short. Based on estimates from the Women's Bureau, Lanham funds only reached 10 percent of the 1 million children in need.[15]

Lanham Act funding for child care ended as the war drew to a close. Only California and New York continued to allocate funds for Lanham child care programs; New York finally ended its funding in 1948. Over the next three decades, California revised its Lanham child care programs and combined them with the state's extensive child care system. Congress continued to authorize Lanham child care funds for the District of Columbia until 1953.[16]

In sum, the influx of women into the workforce during the war presented opportunities for redefining the role of women and establishing a federal commitment to child care. The end of the war brought about a desire to return to the prior status quo. In the case of child care, this meant keeping mothers at home and child care as a private matter, free of government involvement. Contrary to what many policymakers expected, women did not relinquish their jobs after the war. Instead, the percentage of working mothers rose steadily from 18 percent in 1946 to 42 percent in 1970.[17] Despite these trends, attempts to establish cohesive policies for children and families in the postwar era were often derailed by the controversies child care legislation engendered.

Linking Child Care and Welfare

From the mid-1940s to the early 1960s, child care did not receive much attention, other than at conferences that federal agencies or private organizations sponsored.[18] One such event was the 1960 National Conference on the Day Care of Children sponsored by the U.S. Women's Bureau and the U.S. Children's Bureau. Conference attendees made twenty-five recommendations, including obtaining child care funds from local, state, and federal sources.[19] One of the conference organizers was Elinor Guggenheimer, who remained pivotal to the politics of child care for another thirty-five years.

In the early 1960s President Kennedy proposed expanding child care to welfare recipients to encourage self-sufficiency.[20] A 1962 welfare law (P.L. 87-543) earmarked appropriations for child care. To receive these allocations, states were required to match federal funds, provide child care when it was "in the best interest of the child and the mother," and have state laws with criteria for establishing such need.[21] Many states did not implement welfare child care programs. In 1967 enactment of the Work Incentive Program (WIN) authorized the federal government to pay 75 percent of the costs of child care for children of WIN trainees.

The WIN child care provisions and subsequent welfare discussion emphasized "employment-oriented day care," defined as care required for recipients of welfare assistance as they looked for employment. Child care advocates complained that this type of care was custodial and comprised nothing more than extended baby-sitting. Joseph Reed, executive director of the Child Welfare League of America (CWLA), referred to this as the "ghettoiz[ing] of day care centers for children from welfare families."[22] The same arguments were echoed during ensuing debates regarding welfare reform in the 1980s and 1990s.

Child Care Lands on the Legislative Agenda

Child care legislation in the late 1960s followed the footsteps of Great Society programs intended to eliminate poverty or at least to ameliorate its effects. The notorious 1971 child care bill envisioned a universal and comprehensive child care program, with parents paying according to income. The politics of child care legislation in the early 1970s generated controversies over the appropriateness of a universal federal child care program and its implementation at the local level. To appreciate why, it is useful to understand the bill's origin and how it landed on the legislative agenda.

Head Start and the Importance of the First Five Years

Child care legislation was based largely on the popularity of Head Start as an antipoverty measure for children. Authorized in 1965 under the Office of Economic Opportunity (OEO), Head Start served as a model for many child care legislative proposals. Representative John Brademas (D-Ind.), who introduced child care legislation in the House, noted during his committee's extensive hearings on child care, "If we hadn't had Project Head Start, I dare say we wouldn't be having these hearings this morning, and nobody would give a tinker's damn about preschool program's anyway."[23]

The introduction of child care legislation and the popularity of Head Start can both be traced to rising interest in children, whether through desegregation of public schools or enactment of Medicaid, the Elementary and Secondary Education Act (P.L. 89-110), or other initiatives. The importance of child care as a children's issue was illustrated when the 400 delegates to the 1970 White House Conference on Children ranked comprehensive family-oriented child development programs as their most important concern.[24]

Child care legislation and the popularity of Head Start stemmed from a new emphasis on a child's environment during the first five years of life. If children had stimulating and nurturing environments, the thinking went, then they would become well-adapted adults. Renowned academicians such as Bruno Bettelheim, Urie Bronfenbrenner, Bettye Caldwell, and Edward Zigler often testified before Congress on the importance of early childhood intervention.[25] Most child development specialists explained the importance of the interaction between environmental and genetic factors in shaping a child's development. However, as one of Head Start's leading architects noted, in the translation of academic research to the political arena complex relationships became simplified. Discussions of early childhood legislation during the 1960s could be characterized as "environmentalism run amok."[26]

Child Care Holds Promise for Education, Labor, and Women's Interests

Advocates of child care legislation often pointed to the rising number of women in the workforce to justify their bills. In 1970, 32.2 percent of married women with children under the age of six were in the labor force compared with 13.6 percent in 1950. Women with children between the ages of six and seventeen were employed at a rate of 32.8 percent in 1950, reaching 51.6 percent in 1970 (see table 1.3).[27] The Children's Bureau estimated that more than 17 million children under eighteen had working mothers in 1965. About 4.5 million children were under six, another 6.4 million were six to eleven years of age, and 6.4 million were between twelve and seventeen years old. Across income levels, economic necessity prompted most women to work. Most children with working mothers (46 percent) were cared for at home by someone other than their mothers; 28 percent were cared for by their working mothers, who worked only while their children were at school or took care of them while working; and 18 percent were cared for away from home, including 2 percent in group- or center-based care.[28] In later years, these proportions shifted as the number of children in nonparental and, especially, center-based care grew enormously (see table 1.2).

Apart from helping families with working mothers, some legislators viewed child care as a component of education policy. The enactment of two landmark education laws in 1965—the Elementary and Secondary Education Act and the Higher Education Act (P.L. 89-329)—led some policymakers, most notably members and staff of the House Select Subcommittee on Education, to view child care as the next logical component of federal education policymaking.

Controversy arose over which entities in the public or private sector should administer child care programs, whether federally funded or not. Education organizations, such as the National Education Association (NEA), which is both a public education advocacy group and a union for many public school teachers, argued that public schools should "be expanded to absorb the responsibility for care of children at the preschool level, as well as develop programs to care for older children who need day care services outside of regular school hours."[29] Welfare and social service professionals wanted to place responsibility for child care with welfare departments or community and social service agencies whose staff were already administering child care programs under welfare. Antagonism between these two camps characterized the politics of child care in the late 1960s and the decades that followed.

Labor organizations were strong supporters of child care in the late 1960s. They successfully lobbied for 1969 federal legislation (P.L. 91-86) amending the Taft-Hartley Act by permitting labor unions and employers to establish trust funds to provide child care centers for children of employees. This provision opened the door for expanded child care benefits for labor union members and emphasized the importance of child care as a labor concern. Union leaders testified before Congress that initiatives sponsored by employers and unions were insufficient to meet the needs of their members.[30] The membership of some unions, such as the International Ladies Garment Workers Union (ILGWU) and the Amalgamated Clothing Workers, was close to 80 percent female.[31] Many of these women earned low wages and faced difficulties in arranging for affordable child care.

In the late 1960s women became increasingly politically active, due largely to the women's movement. The National Organization for Women (NOW), formed in 1966, identified child care as a one of its earliest policy priorities. In advocating for child care as a universally available benefit, NOW called for "child care facilities established by federal law on the same basis as parks, libraries, and public schools . . . as a community resource to be used by all citizens from all income levels."[32] The National Council of Jewish Women (NCJW) gained notoriety for its 1972 study, *Windows on Day Care*.[33] Written by Mary Keyserling, former director of the U.S. Women's Bureau, it was one of the first comprehensive reports on child care facilities. The study portrayed many unsafe and inadequate child care situations. Legislators and lobbyists used the report's findings to substantiate the need for greater federal child care assistance even into the 1980s. In 1971 twelve women were elected to the House of Representatives, several of whom introduced and lobbied for child care legislation. Among them were Representatives Bella Abzug (D-N.Y.), Shirley Chisholm (D-N.Y.), and Patsy Mink (D-Hawaii).

Yet, despite leadership displayed by women in Congress, NOW's formal positions, NCJW's study, and the support of other women's organizations (such as the League of Women Voters [LWV], American Association of University Women [AAUW], and Association of Junior Leagues, International [AJLI]), most feminists in the late 1960s and early 1970s were not involved with child care legislation. This was mainly because they were fighting for other issues such as abortion and the Equal Rights Amendment

(ERA). By the mid-1970s, the ERA took precedence over every other item on the women's agenda.[34] Another explanation for the inconsistent involvement of feminist organizations with child care advocacy was the concern that "identification of child care with the women's movement would reinforce the traditional societal perception of woman as homemaker and caregiver." When feminists addressed child care as a policy issue, they tended to focus on the needs of middle-class women and overlooked the problems low-income mothers encountered when working.[35]

Edelman as the Lead Child Care Advocate

The leader of advocacy for federal child care legislation since the late 1960s was Marian Wright Edelman. Her interest in child care began with her involvement with civil rights and as a board member of the Child Development Group of Mississippi (CDGM) in the early 1960s.[36] The organizers of CDGM were civil rights activists who envisioned social change through empowerment of local communities. They planned and implemented programs in child development in the South as a way of encouraging "maximum feasible participation" of participants. The Economic Opportunity Act (EOA), which funded many of these community initiatives under the OEO, required such participation as a way of encouraging programs to be responsive to local needs and to empower constituents. Linkages between civil rights and social programs during the 1960s were forged through community organizing and political advocacy for social policies.[37]

CDGM was one of many community-based programs that merged civil rights and social concerns. It was an alliance among local ministries, national civil rights groups (such as the Student Nonviolent Coordinating Committee), and Northern liberal volunteers. After the enactment of Head Start in 1965, CDGM received $1.4 million as one of the first summer Head Start programs. That year CDGM enrolled more than 5,000 preschool children in eighty-four community centers across Mississippi. Another of CDGM's goals was to sidestep state bureaucracies that were slow to enact and implement civil rights laws.[38]

Conflict between CDGM's leaders and federal officials hampered its progress. Senator John Stennis (D-Miss.), a "bedrock" segregationist, used his position as senior member of the Senate Appropriations Committee to call for an investigation into how CDGM managed its funds. Although CDGM's "rudimentary recordkeeping" procedures made it vulnerable to such audits, it was not clear that its practices warranted the OEO decision to withdraw federal funds.[39] Although Congress renewed CDGM's funding in 1966, lapses in funding and negative national publicity disrupted what was already a highly contentious initiative.

CDGM illustrated the political turbulence associated with child development programs in the late 1960s, especially when combined with community activism. It drew attention to child development and the care of children as national issues. The experience Edelman and her colleagues had with the reluctance of Mississippi and other southern states to implement civil rights reforms made them extremely skeptical of any federal child care legislation that put state authorities in control. As Edelman explained at a 1971 congressional hearing on child care:

> I have no confidence whatsoever that this . . . or any administration would say to the Governor of Mississippi or the Governor of California: "We're sorry, but we will not fund your child development programs because your plan does not place proper emphasis on the poor or because you are not providing adequately for Black or Chicano children or because there is not enough community participation."[40]

Edelman's launching pad for her political activities after CDGM was the Washington Research Action Project (WRAP), which she started in 1968. She also led the Ad Hoc Coalition for Child Development, consisting of approximately twenty labor, civil rights, education, welfare, and women's organizations. These groups were united through their interest in a comprehensive federal child care program and their preference to keep power at the local level as much as possible. The Day Care and Child Development Council of America, a national child care advocacy group, lobbied for child care legislation but did not take a leadership role. Nor had its directors forged strong linkages with labor, civil rights, and other interests. It was a member of the coalition of organizations for a federal child care program in the early 1970s but folded shortly thereafter.

Moving Child Care Through Congress

By the late 1960s the forces just described spurred interest in federal child care legislation. Between February 1968 and May 1971 Congress held hearings on child development and child care bills lasting more than thirty days. Although the sponsors of child care legislation in both chambers and their staffs worked well together, each house handled the issue differently. The main sponsor of child care legislation in the House was Representative Brademas. Walter Mondale (D-Minn.) took the lead in the Senate. They worked together to obtain bipartisan support for their bill. By the fall of 1971, members of Congress had reached agreement on child care legislation, but enduring consensus and approval from the executive branch proved illusive.

Child Care Legislation Debuts in the House of Representatives

Child care legislation landed on the legislative agenda at the end of the liberal 1960s and at the dawn of an era of rising conservatism in the United States. President Richard M. Nixon was elected in 1968 with nearly the same popular vote (43 percent) as the Democratic candidate, Hubert Humphrey. George Wallace, running on the American Independent Party ticket, received nearly 14 percent of the popular vote. Nixon won the election by capturing a majority of the electoral votes. Although Nixon's election signaled success for the Republicans, he was the first president elected in over one hundred years who failed to "bring in at least one house of the new Congress of his own political persuasion in his initial election to the White House."[41] In Nixon's first term, Democrats retained control of both houses, although in the Senate the margin was closer than in the House.[42] Because no one party controlled both executive and legislative branches of government, policymaking was largely partisan and often contentious. Nixon wanted approval of the Republican Party's major constituencies, including its growing conservative branch. At the same time, he had to work with Democrats in Congress and acknowledge that he lacked a strong popular mandate for governance. He often collided with mainstream Democrats who controlled congressional committees and leadership positions.

Representative Carl Perkins (D-Ky.) chaired the House Committee on Education and Labor. It included the Select Subcommittee on Education, which was the source of most House-sponsored child care legislation during the late 1960s and early 1970s. Perkins, representing a poor, rural district, was elected to Congress in 1948 and appointed chair of the Committee on Education and Labor in 1967. Representative Brademas, chair of the House Select Subcommittee on Education, explained that Perkins's "concern for the well-being of his low-income constituents made him an ardent advocate of federal social programs. . . . He was a strong liberal in his views, and his . . . self-effacing demeanor concealed superb political skill."[43] Ironically, Perkins demonstrated his shrewd political skills in opposing Brademas during the final days of child care deliberations.

In 1967 the fourth-ranking Democrat on the House Select Subcommittee on Education, Representative Mink, introduced one of the first child care bills of the late 1960s: the Preschool Centers Supplementary Education Act (H.R. 10572). The purpose of Mink's bill was to improve the quality of child care in nonprofit centers through a $300 million increase in federal funding to states for educational services and equipment, using a formula based partly on the number of working mothers in each state.[44] As with other female legislators, Mink's concern about child care policy stemmed from her personal experiences. Reflecting on those years she later explained, "I was a young attorney working full-time and needed care for my children, more than just custodial care. I saw what a tremendous problem it was in my community, and realized that if it was a problem for me, then it must be a problem for others."[45] She drafted her bill, gathered twenty-four Democratic sponsors and convinced Representative Dominick V. Daniels (D-N.J.), then chair of the Select Subcommittee on Education, to hold hearings. But that was as far as the bill went.

To appreciate the significance of Mink's child care initiative one must place it in the context of the times. In the late 1960s Congress had dealt with child care primarily through welfare and Head Start, not as a freestanding bill. Moreover, because Mink was not the select committee chair, to get her colleagues, most of whom were men, to pay attention to the issue of child care took some effort. Her bill paved the way for subsequent child care initiatives.

In 1969 Brademas became the chair of the House Select Subcommittee on Education. A former Rhodes scholar with a doctorate in political science, he had "deeply felt views about education and its place on the national agenda."[46] (Brademas was elected to Congress in 1958 and lost to a conservative candidate who ran on Ronald Reagan's coattails in 1980.) Brademas, Mink, and Representative Ogden Reid (R-N.Y.), the ranking minority member of the select subcommittee, drafted the Comprehensive Preschool Education and Child Day-Care Act of 1969 (H.R. 13520). Reid, more liberal than the other Republicans on the Committee on Education and Labor, switched to the Democratic Party in 1973. Brademas, Reid, and Mink acquired broad bipartisan support for their child care bill, including the cosponsorship of the ranking Republican on the Committee on Education and Labor, Representative Albert Quie (R-Minn.). Other GOP committee members, such as Representatives Orval Hansen of Indiana and John R. Dellenback of Oregon, also supported their bill. H.R. 13520 was to provide comprehensive preschool education programs to assist children in reaching their full potential and "to enhance the ability of families to more fully participate in regular educational, employment, training and other social and economic activities."[47] The bill targeted economically disadvantaged children through grants to states. It authorized coverage of children three to five years old for a range of comprehensive child care services.[48]

Congressional staff involved with the initial drafting of the bill were Jack Duncan, staff director for Brademas's subcommittee on education; Martin LaVor, minority senior staff for the Committee on Education and Labor; and Martha Phillips, staff to the House Republican Research Committee. These staffers developed strong and positive working relationships as they worked on child care legislation. As Duncan explained:

> Brademas pulled together a wide coalition of Democrats and Republicans, and we thought we had the White House on board. Brademas was very good at building coalitions, and as we moved through the intellectual community, consulting with university experts, we built a coalition of conservatives and liberals . . . and we thought we had a no-lose situation, just using common sense.[49]

The congressional environments of the late 1960s, when child care legislation was first introduced, and the 1980s, when it reappeared, differed substantially. In the earlier years, there were far fewer staff, so LaVor and Duncan, although of different parties, worked closely together. They were unencumbered by the many layers of congressional staff that existed decades later and would have made such collaboration more difficult. As LaVor explained, "in the late 1960s there were no people other than Duncan, [Sid] Johnson [staff to Mondale], and LaVor. That was it. As hearings were held, then more and more people learned about the issue and became interested."[50]

Both LaVor and Duncan credited Phillips for having educated them about the importance of child care as a policy issue. As with Mink and other women in the political arena at the time, much of her concern about child care was based on firsthand experience in arranging care for her children while she worked. Phillips's collaboration with LaVor and Duncan also illustrated the bipartisan nature of child care legislation when the first bills were drafted and shows the different political environment that existed then. Years later, not being on staff for one of the standing committees responsible for child care, Phillips would probably not have been involved in formulating the committee's proposed bill.

Between November 1969 and March 1970 Brademas's Select Subcommittee on Education held seventeen days of hearings on child care legislation—fourteen in Washington and three in Chicago. Experts on child developmental and others in the fields of early education, social work, and child health responded favorably to the bill. Their main criticism was that eligibility not be limited to children between the ages of three and five but include younger and older children. They were also concerned that eligibility not be limited to economically deprived children or to center-based care.[51] On September 10, 1970, Brademas's subcommittee voted out the bill, but there was not enough support to get the bill beyond the full Committee on Education and Labor. Reportedly, labor and civil rights groups successfully lobbied the full committee to oppose the bill because they claimed it gave states too large a role.[52] Democrats on the full education committee also faced opposition from their Republican counterparts, who by 1970 had their own child care proposal.

Republicans Propose a Child Care Legislative Alternative

In October 1969, for reasons that are unclear, Dellenback switched from being a cosponsor of the 1969 Brademas bill to viewing the Democrats' bills as "ill-considered and inflationary." One could speculate that he and the other Republicans either wanted to claim credit for their own bill or wanted to push for legislation that would appeal more to moderate and conservative Republicans than the Brademas bill did. Child care under Nixon's welfare reform proposal, the Family Assistance Plan (FAP), was not a satisfactory alternative for the Republicans on the Committee on Education and Labor "because it was under consideration by a different committee [Ways and Means] and because it focused on a single group of recipients."[53] Welfare reform was one of Nixon's major priorities in his first term. In 1970 and again in 1971 the House passed welfare legislation based on Nixon's FAP proposal. The bill (H.R. 1) included child care provisions insofar as it was required to enable welfare recipients to engage in work training or be employed. But opposition from liberals on the Senate Finance Committee to aspects of the bill pertaining to a proposed guaranteed income level and other issues killed the FAP in Congress.[54] For Nixon and his advisers, who were determined to get welfare reform through Congress, child care legislation was a distraction and a competing domestic policy initiative. Most White House staff had little use for child care legislation that was not connected to welfare. However, some White House officials and legislators envisioned using the Mondale–Brademas bill as the basis for child care under welfare reform if H.R. 1 were to become law.

Without White House interest and given what Dellenback described as the "special compelling needs" for child care legislation,[55] Republicans drafted an alternative to the Brademas and Mondale bills. Phillips described their approach:

> I worked with Dellenback, Hansen, and Quie. . . . I tried to tell them that finding child care was a problem for the middle class, too . . . that we needed child care for more than just rescuing inner city kids from the drawbacks of poverty, and not to think of child care only as a community empowerment issue, as it was being pushed by many people and groups. . . . This was an idea ahead of its political time, that still hasn't caught on. Eventually, we did our Republican thing, and had the attitude that if the administration came along, fine.[56]

The Republican child care proposal was not as ambitious as Brademas's. As Hansen explained, instead of expanding the federal government's commitment to a new comprehensive endeavor, the goal of H.R. 15776 was "to mobilize federal initiatives . . . in an orderly, carefully coordinated, comprehensive approach."[57] As such, it combined all the federal preschool and child care programs under a single effort administered by the federal Office of Child Development (OCD). It also funded child care for economically disadvantaged children below the age of compulsory school attendance and for children of working mothers, whether or not economically disadvantaged, based on a sliding fee schedule.[58]

As Phillips recalled, the Democrat and Republican bills of 1969 had a lot in common. Most important, they were both looking to strengthen the role of the federal government in the area of child care. Members of Congress from both parties wanted some kind of child care bill, separate from child care under welfare reform.[59]

A Revised Brademas Bill Goes Forward

In 1971 Brademas introduced the Comprehensive Child Development Act of 1971 (H.R. 6748), a revised version of his 1969 bill. The new bill had broad bipartisan sponsorship from other members of the Committee on Education and Labor, including Republicans Quie, Dellenback, Hansen, and Reid. Brademas also benefited from the input of Edward Zigler, professor of child psychiatry at Yale, whom Nixon appointed head of the OCD in April 1970. The premise underlying Brademas's child care bill, as well as Senator Mondale's companion bill, was that child care was a right for all children, regardless of family income. At the same time, both bills placed priority on economically disadvantaged children by providing free care for families with incomes below a certain level and by offering services aimed at improving the development of impoverished children. The legislation provided the framework for a universally available comprehensive child care program that parents could use voluntarily. It also allocated money for child development (child care) programs for federal employees.

One of the major stumbling blocks was the issue of prime sponsorship — determining the level of government that would administer child care programs funded under the bill. Many liberals, in particular organizational members of Edelman's Ad Hoc Coalition for Child Development, wanted prime sponsorship to rest with the smallest government entity possible. This was congruent with their distrust of state authorities and their preference for keeping responsibility as close as possible to the people participating in the program. Others were more moderately inclined and wanted to balance state and local interests. When House subcommittee members voted on child care in 1970, at the suggestion of Representative Quie, they considered allowing the six cities with populations over 1 million (Chicago, Detroit, Houston, Los Angeles, New York, and Philadelphia) to be considered "ministates" for the purposes of this bill. In so doing, these six cities could develop their own child care plans to address the special and complex needs of large urban areas. They could qualify for larger allocations and be eligible for a "greater share of total dollars" than if they were included under a state plan.[60] But the idea of making large cities eligible to be prime sponsors, which was originally conceived as a rational solution to a distribution problem, became an extremely politically charged issue and ultimately contributed to the demise of the bill. Some subcommittee members questioned the 1 million population cutoff point. They argued that other large cities with fewer people faced similar difficulties. As a result, when the House subcommittee members reported the bill in 1970, they made the nineteen cities with populations of 500,000 eligible to be prime sponsors.

Between 1970 and 1971, when the members of the select subcommittee rewrote their bill for the Ninety-second Congress, they were swayed by the coalition of interest groups representing civil rights, labor unions, women, welfare, and education organizations that opposed *any* type of population criteria for prime sponsorship. Therefore, the legislation (H.R. 6748) that Brademas introduced in 1971 had states as prime sponsors and left open the population level at which cities would be eligible for prime sponsorship. As Quie explained, this "totally disregarded the concept that we had envisioned when we originally considered the idea that the large cities of this country have so many unique problems, because of their size, that they should be considered separately."[61] As a compromise, when the subcommittee reported out the bill in September 1971, its members agreed to setting eligibility for prime sponsorship at a population figure of 100,000, making ninety-five cities eligible. As Phillips explained:

> We were melding together the Democratic and Republican bills, when we caved in and were led down a primrose path. A whole bunch of cities were identified as being large enough to be prime sponsors. . . . Eventually, each representative identified the cities in his or her district, and the bottom line for prime sponsorship kept getting lower and lower.[62]

Brademas and Perkins got along on most issues, but the issue of prime sponsorship was an exception. Perkins opposed the criterion of a population of 100,000 for prime sponsorship because it would bypass the very small towns that were part of his district. He then used his power as committee chair to change the bill's content. Although the full committee approved the child care bill on September 23, 1971, by a vote of twenty-eight to three, with one abstention, Perkins prevented the committee's bill from moving to the House floor. Instead, when the House debated child care legislation, he introduced an amendment dropping the eligibility level for prime sponsor-

ship to a population total of 10,000. Then Brademas introduced an amendment, identical to the committee-approved H.R. 6748, which the House
passed by a vote of 186 to 183, with 62 abstentions. Thus, Perkins lost to
Brademas on the prime sponsor issue by a three-point vote. In retaliation,
Perkins did not appoint Brademas to the conference committee. Brademas
described this episode as the only "such encounter" he had with Perkins in
the twenty-two years Brademas had been serving on the committee.[63] With
Perkins on the conference committee, the prime sponsorship level dropped
to 5,000, accommodating small rural communities in accordance with the
preferences of many organized interests.

Although the full House committee passed the child care amendments,
Quie and several of his GOP colleagues voiced their insistence that certain
changes be made before they would support the bill. In particular, they
wanted prime sponsorship granted only to public entities and were concerned about the bill's overall expenditures.[64] Their concerns foreshadowed
what lay ahead.

Child Care and the Senate

Child care legislation took a slightly different course in the Senate. The
Committee on Labor and Public Welfare has traditionally been one of the
most liberal committees, partly because it included some Northern liberal
Republicans who worked well with liberal Democrats. Senator Mondale
introduced the Senate companion to the 1969 Brademas child care bill.
Mondale based his 1969 Head Start and Child Development Act (S. 2060)
on Brademas's bill. Thus, Mondale's child care bill amended the reauthorization of the EOA by creating a new federal child care program based on
Head Start. The main purpose of S. 2060 was to help impoverished children.
As Mondale explained, "This measure . . . would greatly strengthen and expand programs in early childhood development. It would offer preschool
children from poverty areas needed health care, nutritional aid, educational
assistance, and social services. It would attack the conditions of poverty that
can cripple a child's intellect for life."[65]

The Subcommittee on Employment, Manpower, and Poverty, chaired
by Senator Gaylord Nelson (D-Wash.), held hearings on the Mondale bill
in August 1969 and February 1970 but never reported a bill out of committee. This was probably because of controversy in Congress over the reau-

thorization of the OEO program, which included the child care legislation. In the Senate, as in the House, there was interest in revising the child care legislation in response to feedback from interest groups, academics, and other members of the child care policy community.

In April 1971 Mondale introduced a revised child care bill, the Comprehensive Child Development Act (S. 1512). As chair of the newly formed Subcommittee on Children and Youth of the Committee on Public Welfare, he had new influence, although he still had to yield to the power of the full committee chair. Mondale's bill had bipartisan support of twenty-eight senators and Republicans from the full committee. As with Brademas's bill, the premise underlying Mondale's proposal was that all children had a right to child care. Thus, by 1971, both Mondale and Brademas envisioned a universal child care program available to families on a voluntary basis, with priority going to poor children and fees on a sliding scale, depending on family income. Based on the Head Start model, their bills also featured an array of comprehensive services, in areas such as health, nutrition, and psychosocial support.

Under Mondale's S. 1512 any local unit of government or public or nonprofit agency was eligible to be a prime sponsor. Similar to the Brademas bill, Mondale's proposal included advisory councils and local policy councils that were required to have substantial parental input based on Head Start's parental participation requirements. Mondale and his staff director, A. Sidney Johnson, worked closely with Edelman and her partners among organized interests—more so than Brademas and his staff. This was probably because of a natural affinity between the labor and welfare jurisdiction of the committee and the constituents of the coalition. In contrast, Brademas and the House committee staff approached child care primarily in the context of education.

Edelman and Mondale worked closely together on child care. In January 1971, after Mondale assumed the chairmanship of the newly formed Subcommittee on Children and Youth, he asked Edelman for her "assistance in developing a Comprehensive Child Development Act, building upon our experience in Headstart." He wrote:

> In order to develop the best possible bill, I would like to call upon the expertise of persons like yourself. . . . I would welcome your judgments on the essential components of such legislation, and would also like to ask your assistance in bringing together the ideas and opinions of

similar groups who would make useful inputs at this stage in the development of a national program.[66]

Mondale and Edelman shared a concern for the well-being of children. Mondale's appointment as the first chair of the new Subcommittee on Children and Youth, and his speech "Justice for Children," which the *New Yorker* later published, exemplified his commitment to children's policies.[67] Brademas, too, was concerned about children as he approached child care from an education perspective. Any differences between Mondale and Brademas were overshadowed by their fervor for child care legislation and their willingness to collaborate as they moved their legislation through Congress.

In July 1971 the Senate Committee on Labor and Public Welfare voted unanimously to approve the EOA reauthorization, including the Mondale child care amendment. The Senate approved the bill that September by a vote of forty-nine to twelve. A conference committee worked out differences between the House and Senate child care bills, but not without rancor.

Child Care Survives Conference Committee, but with Serious Bruises

In October and November 1971 the conference committee for the Economic Opportunity Amendments of 1971 met to hammer out their differences. With regard to child care (Title V), the conferees agreed to a new comprehensive child development program that would be "available to children whose parents or legal guardians shall request them regardless of economic, social, and family backgrounds."[68] Children from low-income families, especially those enrolled in Head Start projects, were given priority. Prime sponsorship was granted to states and localities with a population of 5,000 or more, giving eligible cities priority over states. Families with incomes below a certain level would receive services at no charge, while other families paid according to a fee schedule based on their income. The funding level was set at $2.5 billion for FY 1973, such sums as necessary for subsequent years, and a planning grant of $100 million for FY 1972.[69]

Between September 1971 (when the House and Senate passed child care legislation as part of their respective OEO reauthorizations) and November of that year (when the conference committee reached an agreement), opposition to child care legislation grew. Some of the opposition came from conservatives who had opposed the child care legislation all along. Conservative columnist James J. Kilpatrick called the bill the "boldest and most far-reaching plan ever for the advanced Sovietization of American youth."[70] Republicans in Congress and the White House, joined by conservative Democrats, opposed the bill because of its potential to "destroy parental authority and indeed the family."[71] Conservative members of Congress, such as Senators William Buckley (R-N.Y.) and Strom Thurmond (R-S.C.), shared these sentiments. According to Buckley, proposals for a federal child care program "threaten[ed] the very foundations of limited government and personal liberty."[72] Representative John Rarick (R-La.), a staunch opponent to child care legislation, described it as a way of "replac[ing] U.S. parents with the Federal Government and the home with a national institution."[73] Most legislators did not share the extremist views of these conservatives. But against a backdrop of Cold War tension (which threatened liberal values) and increasing conservatism among lawmakers and the public at large, the opposition to child care legislation gathered momentum.

One of the most significant aspects of the dwindling support for child care legislation when it was in conference committee was the defection of the some of the bill's original sponsors, in particular Representative Quie. Quie, Dellenback, and other GOP members opposed the conference report primarily because of language concerning the eligibility levels for prime sponsorship, which they thought would make the child care program totally unmanageable. As the conference committee was ending its negotiations, Quie announced unexpectedly, "I won't sign the conference report." LaVor explained in an interview that "none of the arguments raised by James Kilpatrick or other conservatives were ever a factor in Quie's decision." Instead, he realized that "money would be the distraction because there would be fighting for money all the time." With so many small units of government eligible, legislators would get involved in fighting for the towns within their jurisdiction, and in the long run it would be "hurting kids."[74] Addressing his colleagues on the House floor, Quie explained his position:

> I wish I could come before you and urge you to support the conference report, but I cannot. To me this conference report is an administrative monstrosity. It is impossible for it to work out properly. . . . This is not the local control program that many expected but rather control residing in the Federal Government that should go . . . primarily [to] the State.[75]

Even Zigler, who had been an ardent supporter of the bill, opposed it as it came out of conference because of the prime sponsorship changes.[76] Not all Republican conferees opposed the bill. Representative Reid and Senator Jacob Javits (R-N.Y.) sided with Perkins in approving the bill.

Several individuals who worked on the 1971 bill thought that Edelman's insistence on lowering the eligibility level for prime sponsorship, her unwillingness to compromise on the issue, and her influence among liberal legislators made the bill unpalatable even to politicians who had originally supported and helped draft it. One person close to the issue commented that Edelman's reluctance to negotiate was a hindrance to the bill's advancement. Some speculated that if Edelman had been willing to cut a deal, it might have been easier to find common ground and Congress might have enacted a bill. While this might have been true of the early stages of the bill, by November 1971, as the conferees met, opposition to the bill within White House circles and pressure from the governors was probably too strong for the bill's advocates to overcome, even if there had been administrative revisions.

Nation's Governors Exert Influence

Quie and his fellow Republicans were not alone in their reluctance to put small local authorities in control of administering the bill's programs. Many of the nation's governors staunchly opposed the conference bill because it bypassed the states in administering child care programs. Unlike other organized interests, whose strategies consisted of testifying at hearings and writing letters, the governors had the advantage of influence, status, and an inside track to Nixon and members of Congress. As early as June 1971, Charles A. Byrley, director of the National Governors' Conference, wrote to Quie (and most likely to other legislators, too) conveying the governors' concerns about proposed comprehensive child development legislation, which the House Select Education Subcommittee was marking up at the time. In Byrley's words, "[The bill's] bypassing of state government diminishes the opportunities for a State to play a positive role in enabling the utilization of existing . . . resources and systems . . . to complement a child development program." The governors also opposed linking child care legislation to child care under welfare. As Byrley explained, "Of major concern to us also is a provision . . . which would, in effect, fold into this new legislation the day care services now provided through a State and under . . . Title IV of the Social Security Act [welfare]. . . . If day care services provided through a State under this broad authority for social services are folded into this new legislation, we believe that the disadvantages would outweigh the advantages of this provision."[77] In December 1971, when child care legislation was in conference committee, many governors expressed their opposition to child care through letters and telegrams sent to members of the conference committee and to President Nixon. Governor Arch A. Moore Jr. of West Virginia, chairman of the National Governors Conference, sent a telegram to President Nixon on October 19, 1971, saying:

> The child development section of H R 10351 and S 2007 is deeply prejudicial against the on-going child development programs of the states. . . . On behalf of the National Governors Conference, I urge you to encourage the conference committee to delete those sections of the bill that would diminish in any manner the state role in administering these programs. . . . Muc [sic] of the good already accomplished will be negated if the states do not have a major role in coordinating the child development proposals embodied in H R 10351 and S 2007.[78]

Following Moore's lead, several other governors from both parties sent telegrams to Nixon and the conferees urging them to oppose the child care bill.[79] A few, such as Governor Richard B. Ogilvie of Illinois, wrote in support of the bill.[80] Perkins responded to the accusations that states lacked authority by pointing out "specified instances" in which the conference report permitted designation of states as primary sponsors. But the chorus of opposition from the governors was compounded by the disapproval of White House staff who were lining up to write Nixon's veto of the EOA, singling out child care as the primary target.

Nixon and Child Care: A Battle Among the President's Men

Despite rhetoric about the importance of the first five years of life, Nixon was not much interested in child care beyond its connection to welfare reform. His decision to veto the OEO reauthorization bill and to single out the child care amendment was the culmination of power struggles among his staff, which ended with White House conservatives defeating Secretary of Health, Education, and Welfare (HEW) Elliot Richardson.

Nixon's Fading Interest in Early Childhood

A useful starting point for understanding Nixon's child care policies is his "Special Message to Congress on the Nation's Antipoverty Programs," delivered on February 19, 1969. In this speech he addressed the need for a federal commitment to early childhood programs and acknowledged the importance of the first five years of life by saying, "So crucial is the matter of early growth that we must make a national commitment to providing all American children an opportunity for healthful and stimulating development during the first five years of life."[81] Legislators and interest groups advocating the Mondale–Brademas child care legislation frequently cited this speech in arguing that Nixon had a commitment to uphold in the area of early childhood education. In April 1969 Nixon reaffirmed his concern for all American children under the age of five. He also announced the creation of the OCD, under the secretary of HEW, Robert Finch.[82] The OCD staff was to develop standards for federal early childhood programs across the country, ranging from Title IV of the Social Security Act (which included welfare) to Head Start (see chapter 3).[83]

Finch was slow to appoint an OCD director. In August 1969 Checker Finn, assistant to Daniel Patrick Moynihan, Nixon's adviser on urban affairs, explained to Moynihan that the "O.C.D. needs to get moving" because Nixon had "promised day care for 450,000 more children as part of F.A.P., [but] . . . no one [was] thinking about how to deliver it."[84] Finally, in April 1970, Edward Zigler was appointed as the first OCD director.[85] His assignments included the design of child care under Nixon's welfare reform proposal (FAP), revising the federal child care requirements, administering Head Start, and representing the administration, or at least HEW, before Congress on comprehensive child care legislation.

Finn was one of the first within White House circles to sound the alert on the issue of child care and early childhood development. In a memo dated October 2, 1969, he urged Moynihan to consider the "implications of the proposed day-care program for early child development in general and Head Start in particular." He noted that Head Start had "not been very successful," and that it would "probably be a grave mistake" if Head Start were to be "unthinkably adapted for day care . . . lock[ing] it in further as *the* way for the federal government to engage in early childhood activities" (emphasis in original).[86]

Controversy in the late 1960s and early 1970s over Head Start focused on the results of a Westinghouse study,[87] which failed to prove that Head

Start made any significant long-term difference in children's cognitive development. Experts on early childhood development were quick to point out that due to the study's methodological flaws, its findings were inconclusive and that the study even had produced some positive findings.[88] However, their rebuttals had only slight impact on Nixon's domestic policy staff.

Administration Specifications: Round One to Richardson

Finch's replacement as secretary of HEW in 1970, Elliot Richardson, was one of the few Nixon officials who saw the need for a more activist approach to child care. In 1970 Richardson directed the OCD Interagency Task Force to prepare alternative administration strategies for child development legislation. The task force completed its work by February 1971, and Richardson presented the department's preferred strategies to the OMB for clearance. But the "philosophical points of internal contention between HEW and OMB" over day care legislation quickly surfaced.[89] OMB preferred to limit any new federal child care commitment to the provisions of Nixon's welfare reform proposal. One of the strongest opponents to expanding the administration's commitment to child care beyond H.R. 1 was Richard P. Nathan, OMB assistant director, who in September 1971 became HEW's deputy undersecretary for welfare reform planning. In 1968, Nathan chaired one of the presidential transition task forces on public welfare. In addition to questioning whether the nation was ready to "extend public responsibility for education to the preschool years, as envisioned by the Mondale–Brademas proposals," it was understood within presidential and legislative circles that Nathan and OMB officials were reluctant to endorse any program that would "undercut" child care under H.R. 1 or compete with welfare reform.[90]

Under Richardson's leadership, HEW supported child care programs along the lines of the Mondale–Brademas bills but with modifications to meet Nixon's conditions in the areas of cost, prime sponsorship, and income eligibility. Richardson never accepted the OMB position. According to John Iglehart, then a reporter for the *National Journal*, "[Richardson] told OMB he would assume that the Administration's position was the HEW position unless Mr. Nixon personally told him otherwise. The president never did."[91] Richardson claimed his arguments in favor of a more generous child care bill were strengthened by the president's previous commitment to the first five years of life.[92]

Lack of agreement among Nixon's staff over child care produced delays in delivering Nixon's child care package and made it difficult for Mondale and Brademas to negotiate with the executive branch. By the time the White House issued its child care specifications in June 1971, congressional committees were nearly finished with their deliberation of child care legislation. Moreover, White House staff neither promoted its child care package nor secured a legislative sponsor for it.

The Nixon administration's child care specifications were similar to the Republican child care bill of 1970, which Dellenback and others had introduced; both emphasized the consolidation of federal child care programs. Cities with populations of at least 500,000 were eligible as prime sponsors. Free child care was to be available to families of four with annual incomes below $4,320, with others participating on a sliding scale based on income. The White House would not budge beyond a $1.2 billion authorization level, which would include $350 million in new funding for day care under FAP and Head Start. The Mondale–Brademas child care bill, which passed out of conference committee in the fall of 1971, authorized $2.5 billion for FY 1973.[93]

Richardson acted as a broker between congressional committee chairs with whom he had fostered good will, and White House officials, who he assumed would eventually agree to a compromise on the child care bill. But although he worked hard to persuade Nixon to sign the bill, he lost to the "budget cutters" and conservatives inside the White House.[94]

White House Conservatives Make Headway

Not until the fall of 1971, when both chambers were moving swiftly on the OEO reauthorization, did White House staff take a serious interest in child care. Staffers demonstrated their ambivalence by submitting amendments to the House bill (H.R. 6748) only thirty minutes before the full Committee on Education and Labor marked up the bill, which did not give anyone much chance to review the administration's positions or negotiate with members of Nixon's staff.[95]

As part of Nixon's 1969 reorganization of the White House staff, he changed the name of the Bureau of the Budget to OMB and established the Domestic Policy Council (DPC). The division of responsibility between OMB and the DPC fluctuated, eventually evolving into a shared partnership. Especially after the appointment of George Shultz as OMB director in July 1970, it became clear that "OMB's views would be sought after rather than avoided."[96]

Nixon's staff involved with child care legislation included John Ehrlichman, chief assistant for domestic affairs, who worked closely with Harry Robbins "Bob" Haldeman, Nixon's chief of staff and main gatekeeper. Both Ehrlichman and Haldeman played important roles in funneling information to Nixon, who disliked meeting with people one-on-one and relied on his closest aides to handle many aspects of policy decision making. This resulted in a hierarchical White House structure and system, which required staff to work through Ehrlichman and Haldeman in handling domestic issues.[97] These structural aspects of Nixon's staff influenced how people communicated in shaping his child care policies.

On October 6, 1971, Paul H. O'Neill, assistant director of OMB, sent a memo to Kenneth Cole, Ehrlichman's deputy director, on the conference issues of the EOA reauthorization. Child care was one of several issues he identified as major concerns.[98] O'Neill was not alone in voicing his concerns about child care legislation. On October 12, Patrick Buchanan, one of Nixon's special assistants and speech writers, sent Ehrlichman and Cole editorials and articles espousing the conservative position. Buchanan listed reasons for a veto of the child care legislation. First, it was too expensive. Moreover, he argued that it wasn't child care; it was "child development," and "this far-reaching proposal has hardly been debated and discussed at all." Moreover, it would place the federal government "massively and directly into the raising of children." Finally, the bill was inconsistent with Nixon's welfare program, which "is designed to help bring the family together; this thing is an incentive for the family to break apart, for each to pursue separate careers—while the State takes over the children."[99]

On November 2, 1971, as the child care bill was in conference, Cole wrote to Ehrlichman suggesting that he tell Richardson to redirect his message. Specifically, he wanted Richardson to make the distinction between child care for working mothers and the Mondale–Brademas child development centers, which would relieve parents of their responsibilities for training and educating their children.[100]

Richardson was in an awkward position. For months, he had been working with Mondale, Brademas, and GOP members of Congress in an attempt to reach a consensus on child development legislation. Richardson had worked hard at negotiating a bill that would appease both President Nixon and the majority in Congress. Based on Nixon's public statements on the importance of the first five years of life, Richardson had reason to believe that he could craft a compromise that was acceptable to his boss. But without any firm direction from either Nixon or his aides, Richardson was basically on his own. He had been trying to get an appointment with Nixon since late September 1971. Although Nixon had "indicated his willingness to have this meeting," by early November, White House staff had postponed it more than once. On November 6, Richardson told Ehrlichman that he still wanted to meet with Nixon, and a meeting was set for November 15, with the understanding that Ehrlichman would also attend.[101]

Written communications between Richardson and Ehrlichman show that by the time Richardson met with Nixon, it was fairly clear that Nixon would veto the bill. The meeting was more a matter of form than of substance. On November 9 Ehrlichman sent Richardson some background materials on child care, including a ten-page paper that harshly criticized the child care legislation. The author of the paper made a distinction between "day care," which the administration supported under H.R. 1, and "child development," which would be harmful to children because its advocates were preoccupied with a Soviet-style child-rearing techniques that would "supplant" the traditional family.[102]

Within a few days, Richardson responded in detail to the materials Ehrlichman had sent him. Richardson explained how this bill would offer a supplement to family life and give local authorities strong control, consistent with Nixon's New Federalism.[103] Richardson argued that although some of the child developmentalists might favor government intervention, the current bill reflected their concern for "flexibility, community level control, and freedom."[104] Richardson restated his case against a veto, saying, "I cannot understand the objective of a veto, unless it is to end Head Start entirely, since I feel we are achieving what amounts to a limited extension of Head Start. The particular veto justifications are hard to fathom."[105] Richardson's description of the bill as a "limited extension" of Head Start understated the bill's scope and intent, given that the bill would provide child care to all families in need, regardless of income. Richardson was doing his best to placate both sides and to find ways to present the bill as favorably as possible to Nixon.

In another memorandum to Ehrlichman, Richardson went to even greater lengths in arguing against a veto. He explained how the bill was changed in conference committee due to the "commitment" of some key Republican legislators so as to devise "an acceptable bill." According to

Richardson, the conferees accepted the administration's positions on several issues, except for the overall funding levels, which Richardson questioned as grounds for a veto when other critical elements were in place. In his final recommendation, Richardson cautiously opposed a veto:

> It would be premature on my part to make a firm recommendation that the President sign this measure, as we are not aware of all the final details of the bill to be reported by the Conference Committee. However . . . it is my belief that a presidential veto would be a major error. The credibility of the President's commitment to the first five years of life is certainly at stake, as is the integrity of our relationship with those Members of Congress who have done so much to bring about the result we have repeatedly claimed we wanted.[106]

To prepare Nixon for his meeting with Richardson, Ehrlichman briefly summarized a few of Richardson's reasons for supporting the conference bill. He indicated the level of importance it held for Richardson by mentioning that there was a "remote chance the Secretary might threaten to resign over this."[107] Scant archival documentation of the meeting implied that Nixon remained unconvinced of Richardson's recommendations. According to Ehrlichman, Richardson gave a detailed explanation of the child care issue, including the "exceedingly embarrassing position" a veto would place him in, given the testimony cleared by OMB and presented before congressional committees supporting aspects of the bill. Richardson also made a push for Nixon's signing the bill if limits were placed on the funding level. Nixon "made no comment beyond the Secretary's effectiveness being noted [sic]."[108] It is understandable why Richardson did not make much headway with Nixon. Even before he walked into the Oval Office, conservatives in the White House had the upper hand in voicing their opposition to the child care bill.

On November 17, with the OEO reauthorization bill moving out of conference and Richardson having made his unsuccessful attempt to get Nixon to endorse it, Buchanan wrote to Haldeman, Ehrlichman, and Cole explaining why he would be well suited to write a stinging veto message that targeted child development and legal services legislation:

> Understand that the final appeals for "Child Development" are being made before an altogether unsympathetic court, and that the execution is likely to take place as currently scheduled. If so, as I have versed

myself fairly well in the matter . . . I would like to have a crack at drafting the veto. The "lobbies" for the bills . . . are going to howl whether the veto is indulgent or not—so the veto message . . . ought to be designed to appeal to the majority of the country, and to energize some of those who care most strongly and who are vocally opposed.[109]

By December 9, Buchanan submitted a draft to Haldeman, "as requested."[110] Buchanan was not the only one drafting the message. Special assistant Ray Price and one of his speech writers, John K. Andrews Jr., also gave it a try. Buchanan was then assigned to revise Andrews's draft. This revised draft became the veto message. Choosing Buchanan to write the veto message had certain implications. As William Safire, another speech writer for Nixon observed, "When Nixon wanted to take a shot at somebody, he turned to [Patrick] Buchanan . . . when he wanted a vision of the nation's future, he turned to [Raymond] Price."[111]

Buchanan made another claim for a harshly worded message and the political implications of the veto in his memorandum to Haldeman accompanying the final draft. He wrote, "Since we are certain to get our lumps from the opposition even with a Milquetoast veto, we ought to reap the rewards of an unequivocal one. . . . This is one measure where we *can* get some mileage with the Conservatives; and maybe help abort a few things."[112] This was hardly the first time that Buchanan pushed the conservative view within White House circles. For example, on January 6, 1971, he had sent the president a seven-page memo entitled "Trouble on the Right." His list of the conservatives' "on-going and new grievances against the President and the Administration" included concerns that Nixon was "adopting a liberal Democratic domestic program." Buchanan also expressed fear that losing the conservatives' support could jeopardize Nixon's bid for reelection in 1972.[113] These concerns probably figured into the political calculations pertaining to the veto.

The final veto, although less harsh than Buchanan's original draft, was a combination of the Andrews and Buchanan versions. It deleted Buchanan's language about the psychiatric damage that child care would inflict on children. But it kept Andrews's descriptions of Nixon's activities on behalf of disadvantaged children through expansions of the food stamp, Medicaid, and maternal and child health programs.[114] White House staff probably wanted to balance criticism of the child care bill with a portrayal of Nixon as caring for the welfare of poor children.

On December 10, 1971, Nixon delivered his veto message. Referring to the child care provisions as "the most deeply flawed provision of this legislation," he stated that it pointed "far beyond what this administration envisioned when it made a 'national commitment to providing all American children an opportunity for a healthful and stimulating development during the first five years of life.'"[115] He also said that the intent of Title V, although laudable, was "overshadowed by the fiscal irresponsibility, administrative unworkability and family-weakening implications of the system it envisions." Moreover, "our response to [the challenge to do more for America's children] must be . . . to cement the family in its rightful position as the keystone of our civilization."[116] Devoting more than half the veto message to child care, Nixon offered nine specific reasons for vetoing the child care provisions. Among them were that the need for this type of child development program had not been demonstrated and that to some degree its provisions duplicated efforts in H.R. 1. He objected to the bill's "altering the family relationship" and to its $2 billion price tag, which he estimated would easily grow to $20 billion. He also claimed that "states would be relegated to an insignificant role." The most frequently quoted excerpt from the veto message was his contention that "for the Federal Government to plunge headlong financially into supporting child development would commit the vast moral authority of the National Government to the side of communal approaches to child rearing over against [sic] the family-centered approach."[117] Citing only the last sentence minimizes other aspects of the bill that were problematic for Nixon, White House staff, and members of Congress from both parties.

Immediately after Nixon signed the veto, Steve Kurzman (HEW assistant secretary for legislation), Frank Carlucci (OMB assistant director), and Ron Ziegler (the president's press secretary) held a press conference. Ziegler emphasized that the veto was not an "abandonment" of the president's commitment to the first five years of life or a rejection of day care altogether. Instead, the president was against "an ill-conceived, unwieldy, unworkable, and exorbitantly expensive program." In a nod to the governors and others who were concerned about the bill's administrative structures, Ziegler also emphasized that the president opposed the bill's "bypassing of state governments" in the administration of such a "massive program."[118] Reading between the lines, Nixon and his men were acknowledging the opposition to the Mondale–Brademas bill not just from conservatives, but also from many Republican and Democratic governors, who opposed placing administrative authority for the child care programs at the local level.

The exact reason for the veto is unknown. Richardson and Brademas thought it was a way of appeasing conservatives who were worried about Nixon's overtures to China. Some Republicans speculated that Nixon vetoed the bill to dampen competition from a conservative Republican, Representative John Ashbrook of Ohio, who was considering running against Nixon in the 1972 primaries.[119] Archival evidence points to the political benefits the veto was intended to reap in conservative circles and suggests the governors' influence.

On December 10, the Senate voted against the veto by fifty-one to thirty-six, with twelve abstentions. The vote was fifteen short of the two-thirds majority required by the Constitution for a veto override. This marked the demise of legislation on child development and child care for years to come.

By 1971 women were entering the work force in increasing numbers, underscoring the need for federal child care legislation. However, changing demographics alone cannot bring about social change. Many legislators and organizations felt threatened by a federal universal child care program. The program was a lightning rod for a host of controversies. Lack of presidential support for a sweeping change in the nation's child care system, regardless of how the politics of the administration shaped that decision, was another strike against the bill. Divisiveness within liberal circles over the prime sponsorship issue weakened support for the child care provisions.

Nixon's inability to carry out his pledge to help young children was exacerbated by power struggles within the executive branch. Richardson's inability to influence Nixon on child care was not an isolated case but part of the exclusion of departmental staff in presidential decision making, which became characteristic of Nixon's tenure.[120] It also reflected the strong ascendancy of conservative ideology within the Nixon White House and the growing influence of OMB on the president's decision making. Nineteen years later, when child care reappeared on the congressional agenda, presidential domestic policymaking was concentrated within OMB. Officials from the Department of Health and Human Services (HHS) were hardly involved in the legislative bargaining. By the mid-1990s, a new structure within HHS devoted to child care expanded department officials' influence on child care policymaking.

The overlap between child care and welfare policies also created controversies over how to mesh welfare-related child care with a broad federal child care program. Lack of empirical data on the relationship between child care and child development made it difficult to counter accusations about the detrimental effects of child care. Almost twenty years later, some of these factors changed, while others persisted. In the interim, social, economic, and political shifts reconfigured the context in which policies about child care were made.

3 From Political Stalemate to Welfare Entitlement, 1972–1988

Throughout the 1970s advocates of a federal child care program failed to recapture the momentum of previous efforts. While legislation for such an initiative languished, proposed federal interagency child care requirements (FIDCR) generated a controversy that lasted for over a decade. At the same time, the 1970s and 1980s witnessed enormous changes in the social and economic fabric of American life. In the child care arena new organizations formed that had an impact on subsequent legislative efforts. In political circles organized interests with a conservative propensity grew in size and influence and helped elect many right-wing candidates to office. The 1980 presidential election of Ronald Reagan forced those seeking an expanded federal role in child care to fight against retrenchment of government support for child care. By the end of Reagan's second term, welfare reform legislation enacted in 1988 included the first federal child care guarantee.

The Demise of Child Care Legislation

Following Richard Nixon's 1971 veto of the OEO reauthorization, Senator Walter Mondale and Representative John Brademas introduced revised child care bills. Despite their efforts, congressional support for child care legislation never reached the fervor of 1971. Instead, conservative opposition to federal child care bills became increasingly vocal and organized interests sparred over the details of proposed child care bills. Even a unified Democratic government, with Jimmy Carter in the White House and Democrats in control of Congress, failed to enact legislation creating a new federal child care program.

Brademas and Mondale Fight to Recapture Interest in Child Care Legislation

In 1972 Mondale introduced the Comprehensive Head Start, Child Development, and Family Services Act of 1972 (S. 3617), which the Senate easily passed on June 20, by a vote of seventy-three to twelve. Compared with the 1971 vetoed child care provisions, Mondale's 1972 bill granted states more authority, had simpler administrative mechanisms, set the eligibility level for prime sponsorship at a population figure of 25,000 instead of 5,000, and had less funding. Although the Senate passed Mondale's bill by a safe margin, some senators sang the familiar refrain about the "family-weakening implications" of these child care provisions. They opposed what they considered the federal government's interference in family life and discouragement of mothers from staying home to care for their children.[1]

In February 1972 the House Committee on Education and Labor passed legislation (H.R. 12530) reauthorizing the EOA. Unlike Mondale's bill, Brademas's legislation lacked a separate title for child development but included child care provisions under Head Start. Representative Albert Quie and other Republicans on the committee opposed the child care provisions because they felt the committee "did not attempt to meet the concerns expressed by the President." They accused "the majority on the Committee [of] misleading the public in the entire area of child development by suggesting that the increase in Headstart dollars and the changing of a few provisions will address the child development questions."[2] Demonstrating growing ambivalence toward a federal child care initiative, the House voted 234 to 127 in favor of Quie's motion to send the bill back to the committee, where it languished.[3] Without a bill approved by the House, child care legislation stood little chance of enactment. In September 1972 Nixon signed legislation (P.L. 92-424) reauthorizing the EOA through 1974; the bill lacked any new child care provisions.

In 1973 Mondale held hearings, "The American Family: Trends and Pressures."[4] He deliberately focused on families, as opposed to child care, to deflect conservatives' criticism that earlier child care legislation undermined the importance of families. Mondale's staff director, A. Sidney John-son, explained this strategy in a letter to Marian Wright Edelman:

> The point will be to bring to the attention of Americans that there are a number of forces already at work in this country that are pulling families apart . . . and that it is not day care programs that rip them apart, but rather other kinds of pressures. . . . Among other things we hope to show that child development legislation is designed to sup-port families that are already under attack, rather than to destroy them as our opponents contended with some success around the time of the veto.[5]

In December 1973 Johnson suggested that Mondale introduce child care legislation as a "vehicle for identifying goals, keeping [the] issue alive, and holding hearings." They could decide later if they wanted to push for en-actment. Probably anticipating flack from conservatives, Johnson suggested that the next bill "drop all references to services 'as a matter of right' [or] universal coverage."[6]

In July 1974 Mondale and Brademas introduced the Child and Family Services Act (S. 3754/H.R. 15882). Compared with earlier child care legis-lation, its authorization levels were lower, it was a separate bill unattached to the EOA reauthorization, and it lacked any type of population requirement for prime sponsorship—thus avoiding the issue that had evoked so much debate in previous years. Mondale and Brademas conducted joint hearings on their bill in August,[7] but by the end of 1974 neither had succeeded in moving his bill out of committee. Some of the difficulties they faced were attributable to the nation's preoccupation with the Watergate scandal and upcoming midterm elections. But even without those distractions, child care legislation would have languished. In response to conservative criticism, Mon-dale and Brademas shifted the framing of child care legislation from a uni-versal right, which would especially benefit poor children, to a way of main-taining family cohesiveness in the face of growing economic and social pressures. But this shift went largely unnoticed as conservatives launched one of the most devastating attacks on federal child care legislation.

On February 7, 1975, Mondale and Brademas reintroduced legislation (S. 626/H.R. 2966) identical to the 1974 child care bills and held joint hearings on it across the country.[8] By the end of 1975 it was clear that Congress would not be passing any child care bills, largely because of an anonymous smear campaign. The organizers of the campaign inundated congressional offices with thousands of letters and distributed an unsigned leaflet entitled "Raising Children—Government's or Parents Rights?"[9] They targeted the offices of Mondale and Brademas in what Mondale labeled "an outrageous and totally dishonest propaganda attack" on the Child and Family Services Act.[10]

The smear campaign was disturbing in several ways. First, it was anonymous; none of the fliers were signed. Furthermore, the information circulated was blatantly untrue. The writers of the flier attacked the Mondale–Brademas bill as a "soviet-style system of communal child rearing" and claimed that, if passed, it "would take the responsibility of the parents to raise their children and give it to the Government." Martin LaVor, staff to Republicans on the House Subcommittee on Select Education, explained that the brochure cited legislators out of context. He noted that although legislators had legitimate reasons to be concerned about pending child care legislation because of questions it raised about the delivery system and because of its funding, "in all of the thousands of letters that have come into the Congress, none have addressed these issues, and not one . . . has specifically mentioned the cost of funding this bill if it should become law." Instead, he explained, "these letters are the result of fear, innuendo, and deception."[11] They illustrated the organizers' ignorance of the bill's intent and their outrageous assumption that Mondale and Brademas had Communist sentiments in introducing it.

The smear campaign lasted from late 1975 through the spring of 1976. According to a 1976 *Newsweek* article, Mondale had to hire two additional staffpersons to handle the 2,000 to 6,000 letters he received daily in opposition to his bill. In May 1976 the Senate Committee on Labor and Human Resources requested permission to print an additional 25,000 copies of its background material on the bill to distribute in efforts to set the record straight.[12] As Brademas explained, the intensity of the anonymous campaign "made it very difficult for anyone to get close to this legislation for some time."[13]

Divisiveness Grows Among Interest Groups Advocating a Comprehensive Child Care Bill

In addition to conservative opposition, child care remained an issue surrounded by controversy because of the divisiveness among child care advocates. Organized interests feuded over who should be responsible for administering proposed federally funded child care programs. Several groups favored giving public schools responsibility for child care, arguing that this would foster school readiness among preschoolers and provide a level playing field for all children in a community. The AFL-CIO came out with a position statement endorsing public schools as the sponsors of child care legislation.[14] The NEA took a similar position and proposed that all child care funding "be statutorily assigned to the assistant secretary of education."[15] Not all unions sided with the AFL-CIO and NEA. For example, the American Federation of State, County, and Municipal Employees (AFSCME) "feared that public school prime sponsorship would result in a near monopoly of services by the public schools."[16] This would run counter to maintaining a diverse child care system, responsive to the needs of various types of children, families, and communities. When asked about placing so much responsibility for child care delivery in the hands of public schools, Edelman responded, "I am opposed to giving schools a whole new set of responsibilities when they are so far from meeting the ones they already have."[17]

Another turf issue that characterized child care policymaking in the 1970s and 1980s and, to some extent, also in the 1990s was divisiveness between proprietary and nonprofit child care providers. Members of the nonprofit child care community thought that "profit-making entrepreneurs" had no place in the delivery of child care, Head Start, or other human services programs, especially if they were to be eligible for federal funds.[18] Proprietary providers opposed federal policies that excluded them as eligible grantees. These rifts among organized interests and the providers they represented made it difficult to reach consensus on proposed child care bills. However, they were not as serious an impediment as the conservative opposition.

The Cranston Child Care Fiasco

The 1976 presidential election of Jimmy Carter with Mondale as vice president created a new political environment. Carter received 50 percent of the popular vote. His GOP rival, incumbent Gerald Ford, received 48 percent. Many child care advocates assumed that with Democrats controlling both the White House and Congress and Mondale as vice president, the timing was once again right to push for federal child care programs. But as they later learned, even a unified Democratic government was insufficient for enacting child care legislation.

In the late 1970s Senator Alan Cranston (D-Calif.) was the main sponsor of child care legislation and the chair of the renamed Subcommittee on Child and Human Development of the Committee on Labor and Human Resources. In 1977 and 1978 Cranston held hearings on "future federal legislation involving child care and child development." His efforts were reinforced by Department of Labor (DOL) data released in March 1977 indicating that for the first time a majority of mothers of children under eighteen worked outside the home, two-thirds of them full time. Over 6 million children under the age of six had working mothers.[19] Organizations testifying at the hearings tried to avoid the controversy over who would administer child care programs. For example, the CWLA urged Cranston not to specify in his bill who or what would constitute a prime sponsor. The Day Care and Child Development Council (formerly the National Child Day Care Association) favored a diverse system not dominated by any single agency or approach. Edelman, having established the CDF in 1973, testified on behalf of eighty-seven organizations that had reconvened as the Ad Hoc Coalition on Child Development.[20]

In February 1979 Cranston introduced the Child Care Act of 1979 (S. 4). Shortly thereafter, letters opposing the bill began trickling into congressional offices. Many newspapers published editorials against the bill with rhetoric similar to that of the 1975 anonymous campaign against child care legislation. James Kilpatrick, conservative syndicated columnist, wrote several scathing pieces. In one article, "Launching Another Disaster," he described Cranston's bill as "the same old coon with another ring around his tail."[21]

In March 1979 Susanne Martinez, staff to Cranston, convened a meeting of organizations interested in child care. Some of the groups, especially CDF, "complained that Cranston's bill was not strong enough" and expressed concern about its funding of for-profit child care agencies and public schools. Following the meeting, Martinez spoke with many of the groups' representatives individually, and most said they supported Cranston's measure. However, CDF opposed Cranston's legislation, and as Martinez explained, "without CDF's support, we could not be productive on the bill."[22]

On March 13, 1979, Edelman and Ellen Hoffman, CDF's director of governmental affairs (formerly staff to Mondale on women's issues), wrote to Cranston that although his bill was "certainly a step in the right direction toward developing quality child care legislation, many serious substantive problems remain[ed] from CDF's point of view." Edelman and Hoffman claimed that the bill placed children at risk for custodial care because its funding was too low and its standards and delivery system were inadequate. Their plan was to propose changes to Cranston and seek a House sponsor for their positions.[23]

CDF and Cranston also disagreed over whether proprietary child care providers should participate in a federal program. Cranston didn't oppose granting authority to proprietary providers. As Martinez explained, "He didn't want any one group to hold a monopoly on child care. In part this was based on what he had seen in California . . . where schools had always been involved . . . and, as in many other states, there was a blend of propri-etary with nonprofit child care."[24]

Divisiveness among organized interests took a back seat to HEW oppo-sition. On February 20, 1979, the second day of hearings on S. 4, Arabella Martinez, assistant secretary for Human Development Services, shocked Cranston and his colleagues by announcing that the Carter administration opposed the Cranston bill. In her testimony, she said:

> Serious questions remain, for example, as to what constitutes the best way to achieve quality child care, and what the federal role and re-sponsibility should be. . . . [The] increase in the number of working women does not necessarily imply that those women want or need center-based or formal, governmentally supported care. . . . We do not believe that another categorical program for child care is warranted at this time.[25]

HEW opposition combined with the divisiveness among the interest groups and the formidable conservative opposition to federal involvement in child care led Cranston to cancel the third day of hearings and pull the bill off the books.[26] He called a press conference on March 15 during which he announced his cancellation of hearings scheduled for March 20 and the markup scheduled for March 27. As he put it, "What was needed was not more hearings but more unanimity."[27]

Explaining Carter's Lackluster Interest in Child Care Legislation

For long-time advocates of comprehensive child care legislation, Carter's lack of support for a major child care bill was puzzling. However, from another angle, it was reasonable given the political and economic considerations of a moderate Democratic president facing an increasingly conservative Congress. Moreover, Carter was preoccupied with other social issues, such as welfare reform and low-income energy assistance, so child care was not a priority for him.[28]

President Carter's opposition to child care legislation came most likely from OMB. Peggy Pizzo, who in 1979 was a special assistant to the commissioner for the Administration for Children, Youth and Families (ACYF) and then in 1980 became an assistant director for Carter's domestic policy staff, explained that "there was an OMB directive, either verbally or in writing . . . that the administration position would be in opposition to the bill."[29] Suzanne H. Woolsey, OMB associate director for human and community affairs, strongly opposed an expansion of the federal government's commitment to child care activities. In a 1977 article on child care and the federal government published in *Daedalus*, Woolsey argued:

> The data seem to show that there is far more interest in informal care in the home or the extended family than anyone would gather from the public debate. . . . Instead, policy makers are importuned by ideological and interest group pied pipers, promising to rid us of various forms of pestilence: oppression of women, a thoroughly unworkable welfare system, emotional disturbance, and school failure.[30]

Woolsey had a valid point about the diversity of child care arrangements parents used. Census Bureau data for 1977 reported that 13 percent of employed mothers with children under five used organized child care facilities, 29 percent relied on care from nonrelatives, and approximately 35 percent relied on relatives.[31] But these data fail to indicate the need for child care in family or organized child care settings. Furthermore, as the number of working parents who relied on child care rose, the quality of the care their children received was questionable. Pizzo noted that most OMB staff probably agreed with Woolsey because of their interest in holding down federal spending.[32] However, the explanation for Arabella Martinez's opposition to S. 4 does not lie with Woolsey alone. As is often the case, chance and serendipity also were at play.

The day before Cranston's child care hearing, Washington, D.C., was hit with a terrible snowstorm, forcing many federal offices to close. This left no time for the typical exchange of information that usually occurred in the preparation of testimony, and consequently communication over the hearing among HEW, OMB, and Cranston's staff was minimal. Whether because of the weather or poor planning, Arabella Martinez failed to offer what might have been a more carefully worded explanation of the reasons for the Carter administration's opposition to the Cranston bill.

Even if OMB had instructed Martinez and her staff at HEW to oppose the bill, she could have responded in other ways. For example, she could have supported the bill's provisions for resource and referral programs and training and at least have shown some willingness to work with child care constituencies. According to Pizzo,

> Had the HEW players been a little more creative in how they balanced their response, they could have come up with some provisions that would have helped parents in how they made choices for their children's care. Even if you walked through the eye of the needle with Suzanne Woolsey, you still could have opposed the bill but found ways to help parents in finding quality care.[33]

Cranston made the same point during the hearings, saying, "I would find HEW's position more credible if your agency acknowledged the need for a systematic and coordinated approach such as provided in S. 4, but said that the Federal Government did not want to pay the price at this point."[34] In fairness to Arabella Martinez, it must be noted that she was at a disadvantage because there were few top-level HEW officials who appreciated the complexities of child care and its meaning to the interest groups involved. As Pizzo explained:

> I don't think most of the Carter subcabinet staff, with the exception of Dick Warden [assistant secretary for legislation] and Peter Libassi [general counsel] understood how deeply the Washington advocacy groups felt about child care. . . . But Warden and Libassi could not take on the issue of child care legislation on their own. It needed to be handled by the appropriate assistant secretary, in this case, Martinez.[35]

In 1979 HEW was not nearly as involved with child care legislation as it had been in 1971, mostly because in the later years HEW lacked a strong high-level advocate for child care legislation who negotiated with Congress and the White House, as Elliot Richardson had done in the early 1970s. Even had HEW had such leadership, OMB probably would have prevailed because of its rising influence over domestic policymaking. Its policies were more congruent with those of the growing conservatism of the late 1970s than with those of the more liberal-oriented HEW, and OMB's staff was mindful of Carter's fiscal conservatism and intent to reduce the federal bureaucracy. Thus, OMB played a pivotal role in child care policymaking in 1979, just as it had done eight years earlier and would do again ten years later.

Although not altogether opposed to the federal government taking a role in solving social problems, Carter was hesitant to involve the federal government fiscally and administratively in every domestic arena.[36] According to Stuart Eizenstat, Carter's domestic policy staff director, Carter was more conservative than many of the other presidential candidates, but he still was a Democrat with a strong concern for the social problems facing the country. "And yet at the same time . . . he recognized that the resources weren't there to do everything he or the groups wanted."[37] The result was an ongoing tension between Carter and the many liberal Democratic constituencies.[38] Finally, the last two years of Carter's presidency (1978 and 1979) were what Eizenstat defined as the "austerity phase," characterized by inflation, rampant unemployment, and the need to control the federal budget deficit.[39] Thus, new spending for child care programs in 1979 was not fiscally feasible. Moreover, there was little evidence that child care was a priority for the public at large.

Federal Interagency Day Care Requirements

Ambivalence toward comprehensive child care legislation was complicated by another major issue: Federal Interagency Day Care Requirements (FIDCR).[40] Conflicts surrounding the establishment of federal child care standards preoccupied government officials and interest groups involved with child care for decades. Some claimed it was the major child care issue on the policy agenda after Nixon's veto.

The issue must be traced back to the late 1960s, when Congress mandated interagency day care regulations as part of the Economic Opportunity Amendments of 1968 (P.L. 90-222). Secretary of HEW Wilbur Cohen selected Jule Sugarman, associate director of the Children's Bureau and former director of Head Start, to chair the interagency panel charged with writing the FIDCR. Under Sugarman's guidance, the panel developed FIDCR that were comprehensive in outlook yet vague, except for child–

staff ratios, the issue that raised the most controversy. These FIDCR were included in the 1971 child care bill Congress passed, and they came to symbolize the minimum standards that organizations advocating the bill would accept. Edward Zigler, when appointed director of the OCD in 1969, found the FIDCR too ambiguous to be enforceable. With HEW Secretary Richardson's consent he revised them, assuming that they would apply to child care under Nixon's proposed new welfare plan once enacted. Zigler issued the revised FIDCR in 1972.[41]

Nixon's 1971 veto of legislation with a proposed federal child care program made groups such as the CWLA and WRAP skeptical of any efforts on behalf of the Nixon administration in the area of child care policy. Even though the 1972 FIDCR were more rigorous than the 1968 version, these groups still preferred the earlier requirements. "To the advocates of comprehensive day care, loyalty to the 1968 FIDCR had become the test of commitment to the proper care of children."[42] Ultimately, the 1968 FIDCR prevailed because of OMB's opposition to the 1972 version; its staff was concerned about the costs that enforcement of the FIDCR would impose on providers and the federal government.[43] Conservative legislators and proprietary child care providers also opposed them, claiming that the costs of administering them would force many centers to close.

The FIDCR lay dormant until late 1974 when President Gerald Ford signed legislation (P.L. 93-647) creating Title XX of the Social Security Act, which granted funds to states for social services such as child care. The law required states to adhere to a modified version of the 1968 FIDCR as a condition of receiving federal child care payments under Title XX and Title IV (welfare) of the Social Security Act. Because of the ongoing confusion and controversy surrounding FIDCR, Congress also directed HEW to complete a report on the appropriateness of federal child care requirements.[44] In drafting regulations for child care under Title XX, HEW used Zigler's 1972 child–staff ratios, leading to a bitter battle among organized interests and HEW officials. But by the mid-1970s, the nonprofit child care community was pushing for the 1972 requirements because they were the most stringent version. Led by CWLA and AFL-CIO, these groups threatened to sue HEW if it did not enforce the 1972 requirements. The proprietary child care providers continued to oppose the rules.

This controversy pushed the FIDCR into the legislative arena. The main opponent to the FIDCR was Senator Russell Long (D-La.), chair of the Senate Finance Committee, who opposed the FIDCR mainly because of costs they would impose on providers. Senator Mondale, the lead advocate of the FIDCR, favored enforcement because of their importance to the well-being of children. OMB, not wanting the federal government to be involved in federal child care regulations, preferred that states be responsible, which would also reduce federal expenditures. HEW, while not totally opposed to this argument, wanted to postpone promulgating federal child care requirements until completion of its study on the appropriateness of federal child care regulations. All of this disagreement created years of heated debates among legislators, executive branch officials, and organized interests, resulting in a stalemate and delays in implementing any federal child care regulations. Between 1975 and 1977 President Ford signed several bills that postponed enforcement of the most controversial aspect of the FIDCR—child–staff ratios—until 1978.[45] This delayed the decision until completion of the pending appropriateness study and well into a new presidential administration. When finally released in 1978, the long-awaited study did not call for increases in staff–child ratios, nor did another major national child care report.[46] This was contrary to the consensus among child care professionals who considered high staff–child ratios essential for fostering child development. It also left HEW in a bind as to how to handle the ratios in proposed federal child care regulations.

In June 1979 HEW Secretary Joseph Califano proposed revised federal child care regulations that outlined three options for staff–child ratios from which Califano would choose a final figure.[47] HEW needed to find a middle ground that would simultaneously protect children in child care settings and satisfy those within the Carter administration, especially OMB, who were keen on reducing the federal government's regulatory role. CDF, the National Association for the Education of Young Children (NAEYC), and more than thirty other national, state, and local groups, along with certain individuals, such as Zigler and Mary Keyserling (who had written the NCJW child care study), approved of the proposed regulations and expressed their preference for the most stringent staff–child ratios.[48] They considered the proposed regulations as "the most minimal requirements for a floor of safety for children in federally funded care . . . not recommended practices or goals for superior quality care."[49] The CWLA led a third group of organizations that opposed the proposed rule as too lax, but this group did not have a very large or influential following.[50] As in the past, proprietary providers, joined by conservatives, opposed the proposed rule altogether. HEW held ten regional meetings, a national forum, and one hundred state and national meetings between June 15 and September 21, 1979, to solicit public comments.[51]

At the height of this controversy, in 1979, approximately 18,300 licensed child care centers served about 900,000 children, 70 percent of whom were preschoolers. About 8,000 centers enrolled children who received federal child care assistance.[52] The FIDCR would apply to center-based as well as family child care that fell under Titles IV (welfare) and XX of the Social Security Act and other major federal programs, such as the Elementary and Secondary Education Act.

In March 1980, under the leadership of Carter's second HEW secretary, Patricia Harris, HEW drafted a final set of federal interagency child care standards.[53] The change in command at HEW gave those in favor of relaxed FIDCR time to make headway within HEW. Pizzo got hold of the proposed standards one week before they were to be published. Realizing how weak they were, she immediately prepared an analysis showing how they would "endanger children as well as put Carter in a bad position" because even the proposed FIDCR under Nixon would have done a better job at protecting children in child care. She and Harley Frankel (former head of the Head Start and the child care division within the ACYF) met with Eizenstat privately at his home one evening to express their concern.

After hearing Pizzo's analysis, Eizenstat immediately called Secretary Harris and told her to postpone issuing the requirements. Eizenstat had been a supporter of the FIDCR and sided with CDF and others in their attempts to get them promulgated. Harris assumed that her staff's proposed requirements would meet Carter's preference for a minimal federal regulatory role. Eizenstat's response was that economic deregulation was not the same as protecting young children. He agreed with Pizzo and others who argued that higher-quality child care would result in long-term cost-savings for the education and health systems and thus be worth the investment of public funds.[54] Eizenstat tried to convince Carter to go along with the stricter FIDCR, but apparently Carter had a "governor's perspective," and cost was a major concern. "He just felt real strongly that the federal government shouldn't be involved here."[55]

Shortly after Eizenstat delivered his instructions to Harris, HEW issued final FIDCR that were tighter than the version Harris had originally endorsed. The most controversial component, child–staff ratios for three- to five-year-olds, was changed somewhat, making them acceptable to a majority of the groups involved in the discussions. By the fall of 1980, with HEW poised to implement the FIDCR after nearly twelve years of protracted debates, the proprietary day care providers launched a successful letter-writing campaign to members of Congress opposing the FIDCR and pointing to the costs they claimed the high staffing ratios would impose on child care providers. They easily convinced Senator Long to insert a provision in the FY 1981 budget reconciliation bill (S. 2885) suspending implementation of the new child care standards for one year. Long claimed that the postponement would save $20 million and provide more time to review the standards. In saying that the FIDCR would be too costly, he claimed to have the support of the next "Republican standard bearer," Ronald Reagan. Long explained his reasoning on the Senate floor:

> Having discussed this sort of thing with [Reagan], my impression of his view is that this cost of day care centers is getting very much out of line by insisting on all sorts of educational components and various other things that run up the cost to where it is unreasonable and unpractical. . . . To try to provide these types of standards is going to require a lot of day care centers to shut down and it is going to increase the costs and it seems to me that it is an area that can be deferred for a while.[56]

Senator Cranston proposed an amendment on the Senate floor that would have retained the FIDCR. He questioned "the appropriateness" of including language pertaining to the FIDCR in reconciliation legislation, explained that most child care centers serving Title IV children were already in compliance with the staffing ratios, and noted that suspending the FIDCR would not save the federal government $20 million, as its opponents claimed. But Cranston's amendment lost by a vote of seventeen to seventy-two.[57] With House acceptance of the Senate's provisions, the 1980 reconciliation bill silenced the FIDCR debate. In the following year Congress enacted reconciliation legislation (P.L. 97-35) that made many sweeping social policy changes, including eliminating the FIDCR altogether and replacing Title XX's categorical programs with the Social Services Block Grant (SSBG).[58]

In sum, thirteen years after HEW issued the original FIDCR, with much legislative and bureaucratic haggling in between, federal child care standards fell from the agenda, at least for the time being. Their demise demonstrated the unwillingness of Congress to endorse policies that required child care providers across the country to adhere to minimum federal standards. As a result, it was left to the states to determine the quality of care for millions of children in child care settings; this meant that many children were in unsafe environments and received child care of questionable quality. Once again, as in 1971, child care policies were characterized by a stalemate.

The Early 1980s: Retrenchment and Regrouping

Ronald Reagan's 1980 presidential election and the Republican gains in Congress that year ushered in a new era of domestic policymaking characterized by growing conservatism. Reagan captured almost 51 percent of the popular vote, compared with Carter's 41 percent, and Independent candidate John Anderson's nearly 7 percent. Republicans captured control of the Senate by a margin of 53 to 46 (and 1 Independent). Senator Orrin G. Hatch (R-Utah) became the chair of the Committee on Labor and Human Resources. At this point, Hatch considered child care a state responsibility and had little interest in any type of federal child care program. Senator Jeremiah Denton (R-Ala.) replaced Cranston as chair of the renamed Subcommittee on Aging, Family, and Human Services; in 1983 it became the Subcommittee on Family and Human Services. In 1985 it was renamed the Subcommittee on Children, Family, Drugs, and Alcoholism and chaired by Senator Paula Hawkins (R-Fla.). As a result of the 1980 elections, House Democrats lost 33 seats but retained a strong margin (243 to 192) over Republicans. Thus, a split in party control of Congress and a conservative GOP president created new challenges for those seeking federal support for child care.

Reflecting the fiscal and political conservative mood of the times, one of Reagan's first bills, the Omnibus Budget Reconciliation Act of 1981 (OBRA) (P.L. 97-35), decreased Title XX funding for child care and other social services. Specifically, among its many changes in social policy, OBRA 1981 combined the programs under Title XX into a SSBG and lowered the entitlement ceiling from $2.9 to $2.4 billion. Congress also reduced expenditures for child care under welfare.[59] Much of the pressure to curtail spending for child care and other social programs stemmed from the proliferation of conservative think tanks and organizations in the 1970s. Liberal think tanks and organizations also increased in number. However, among think tanks focusing on national issues, those with a conservative bent outnumbered those with a liberal preference by nearly two to one between 1976 and 1995.[60] Many of these well-endowed conservative think tanks entered the national political arena in opposition to liberal calls for a strong federal presence in social programs, including child care. The Heritage Foundation, founded in 1973, marked a new direction in conservative think tank advocacy with its explicit commitment to overturning liberal policies and its bold advocacy agenda.[61] Heritage and other new conservative think tanks and organized interests strengthened the constituency that mobilized in opposition to proposals for increased spending for child care. Starting in the late 1980s they significantly altered the direction of child care legislative deliberations by introducing bills that garnered enough support to be formidable competition to their liberal opponents.

Several scholars have examined the changes among organized interests in Washington, D.C., over the past few decades. Comparisons across studies are hampered by different definitions and terms. Nonetheless, a common finding is the increase between 1960 and 1980 of interest groups with national representation. In particular, groups representing social welfare, women, and citizens' interests rose in number during those years.[62] Many organizations at both ends of the ideological spectrum flourished, or at least remained viable, because of patronage from foundations, wealthy individuals, business firms, government, or other entities.[63] Thus, when child care reemerged on the legislative agenda in the late 1980s, its politics were characterized by a larger and more well-endowed constellation of organized interests, especially those representing conservative concerns.

Conservatives and the Politics of Ideas

To explain fully the rise of conservatism during the 1970s is beyond the scope of this work.[64] However, some understanding of the increase in conservatism and its accompanying organized interests during the 1970s is important for appreciating the different policy outcomes for child care in 1971 and 1990.

Starting in the early 1970s, conservatives sought to reclaim political control from liberals. Their "weaponry" consisted mostly of "ideas" in addition to data demonstrating what they perceived as the failure of many federal social programs. Recognizing the need to increase support for their ideas, conservatives "accelerated" their "building of an intellectual infrastructure."

They channeled their resources into creating think tanks and research entities that could promote public policies based on conservative principles.[65] Much of the growth of conservative think tanks, such as the Heritage Foundation, was due to the successful engagement of the business community in conservative political activities. One conservative strategy was to heavily subsidize conservative-leaning think tanks that would provide the "theoretical and intellectual justification for alternatives to the Keynesian welfare state."[66]

The Heritage Foundation became the "flagship of the conservative intellectual movement." It was founded in 1973 by Edwin J. Feulner and Paul M. Weyrich, both of whom were aides to conservative members of Congress. In 1971 and 1972 Feulner and Weyrich organized the House Republican Study Committee, which sought to amass and disseminate research supporting conservative policies. Feulner became the committee's director. The "immediate spur to the creation of the Republican Study Committee" was a concern among conservatives, such as Buchanan and Weyrich, that many of their fellow Republicans were too willing to "embrace the [Nixon] administration's social agenda, especially the FAP and the Child Development Act."[67]

Feulner and Weyrich launched the Heritage Foundation with a $250,000 grant from Joseph Coors, the brewery entrepreneur, who was an "ardent propagator of conservative causes."[68] Heritage's earliest campaigns included attacks against national health insurance, welfare programs, and federal support of child care centers.[69] From an annual budget of over $2 million in 1977, the foundation's resources grew to $18 million in 1991. Free competitive enterprise and limited government were two of the principles the Heritage Foundation championed aggressively. As Feulner noted, "Many other think tanks have been overly cautious in deciding just how far they can opine . . . and the result is that their impact has not been nearly as effective as it should be. We set out to change this."[70] By the mid-1980s, many White House officials and lobbyists for conservative organizations viewed Heritage's Robert Rector as a major social policy analyst among conservative interest groups involved with child care.[71] These conservative organizations also played a key role in bringing tax policies to the table as part of child care policymaking. The emergence of conservative organizations offering alternatives to liberal calls for new federal child care programs was an important structural change that influenced subsequent child care policies.

Several other organizations with conservative leanings and an interest in family policy, including child care, were born during the 1970s and 1980s.

For example, the Family Research Council (FRC) was started in 1980 to provide expertise and information on issues, such as parental autonomy and responsibility, and the effects of the tax system on the family. FRC's president in the late 1980s and early 1990s was Gary Bauer, formerly the domestic policy adviser in the Reagan administration. He and policy analyst William Mattox Jr. often testified against any new federal child care program and proposed tax policy revisions to address the needs of families with children.[72] Other conservative organizations formed in the 1970s that became active opponents of a new federal child care program included the Eagle Forum (founded in 1972) and Concerned Women for America (CWA, founded in 1979).

One study reported that between 1992 and 1994, twelve conservative foundations granted $210 million to support conservative policy objectives. Of that amount, 38 percent went to national think tanks and advocacy groups, almost half of which was awarded on an unrestricted basis. This steady support has "anchored" key conservative institutions and given them a strong "offensive capacity" to influence social policy for nearly two decades.[73]

Contrasting New Right and Liberal Views

Conservative organizations flourished in the 1970s and even more so in the 1980s during Reagan's presidency. His 1980 election coaxed the merging of the new right wing and religious constituencies and enhanced the formation of a "coalition of militant Protestants and Catholics united around religious and moral issues." This coalition had formidable political strength, because it "[mobilized] the nation's 75 million right-leaning Christians" even though they did not always agree with one another philosophically.[74]

The growing strength of the religious right gave a boost to people of all religious denominations who wanted religion woven more into daily activities and even into programs and services sponsored by the government, such as education and child care. In addition to evangelicals and fundamentalists, such ideas had appeal to other religious groups, including Orthodox Jews and Mormons. Reagan's support of the religious right gave renewed support to those advocating issues, such as prayer in school and federal funding of religious education, that liberals viewed as a threat to the Constitution's separation of church and state.[75] Many political observers identify the conservatism that grew during the 1970s as the "New Right," distinguishing it from the more traditional or moderate Republicanism that was associated with politicians such as Governor Nelson Rockefeller of New York. Many Northern moderate Republicans had been aligned with Democrats in support of child care legislation.

A distinguishing feature of the New Right's agenda was its attention to moral and social concerns—what became known as family issues. Eventually, these became the dominant themes of conservative political arguments in America.[76] Political commentator E. J. Dionne has described the conservative gains in the area of family policy during the 1970s and early 1980s:

> By linking their movement to "profamily" themes, conservatives gained ground in the short term on two fronts. They furthered their image as "populists" by identifying with "average families" against feminists who were cast as upper-class "elitists." And conservatives softened their image as advocates of rugged individualism by presenting the family as a buffer against the economy's harshness; the family was a "haven in a heartless world."[77]

Conservatives became known for their outspokenness on family policy, even if it embodied a notion of family that was inconsistent with the realities of American life of the 1980s. Liberals had to demonstrate that they, too, were genuinely concerned about the American family and that the conservative idea of family excluded many Americans, such as single-parent, female-headed, or dual-income families.

By the late 1980s, liberals had regained some of what they had lost earlier in the decade "by shifting the debate to the most 'deserving' poor of all, needy children." Dionne viewed the rise of children's issues as part of a "broad but subtle shift in popular attitudes towards government and social programs." It was not a sudden burst of social activism but an endorsement of social spending on certain programs, most notably "education, the environment, medical insurance, programs for the elderly, public works, and day care."[78] This was not a full swing back to the more liberal attitudes toward social programs that had characterized the 1960s. Instead, liberals realized that new approaches and accommodations might be needed to advance important children's policies.

For liberals, the entrance of women into the workforce largely out of economic necessity facilitated the revisiting of family and child-related issues (see figure 1.1 and table 1.3). Conservatives preferred that women stay home to care for their children and continued to oppose any notion of federally subsidized child care.[79]

New Organizations Advocating for Child Care

Certain changes within liberal circles were relevant to child care policymaking, especially the establishment and growth of the CDF and the founding of the Child Care Action Campaign (CCAC). In 1973 Edelman created CDF as "an attempt to create a viable, long-range institution to bring about reforms for children."[80] She wanted CDF to be known for its high-caliber research reports and analyses of federal policies for children, not as a lobbying group.[81] As with many groups, however, a fine line often separates educational and advocacy activities. (CDF has established a separate entity, the CDF Action Council, to fund the lobbying aspects of its work.) Edelman fervently believed in the importance of educating local groups about federal legislation and administrative processes so that they could "educate their constituencies and provide the political muscle" she deemed critical for political success.[82] This was a logical extension of her work with CDGM during the 1960s when she had become aware of how difficult it was to make headway in Washington while simultaneously implementing programs at the local level. Child development and child care were among CDF's first legislative priorities.[83]

CDF has never received any government funding. Its operating expenses are covered by sales of publications and contributions from individuals, corporations, and foundations. CDF's budget, staff, and operating expenses increased significantly over the first fifteen years; by 1988 its annual revenue had exceeded $6 million, and it had an extensive list of individual, corporate, and foundation supporters.[84] CDF had filled a void during the 1970s because there were few, if any, organizations devoted exclusively to children's issues in general or child care in particular. Although the Day Care and Child Development Council, which Elinor Guggenheimer had founded in 1960, still existed in the early 1980s, its reorganizations and financial difficulties hindered its effectiveness.

Organized interests involved with child care underwent other changes in the late 1970s and early 1980s. For example, in response to the enormous growth of family day care providers, the National Association for Family Day Care was formed in 1982. Privately owned child care centers organized under the National Association for Child Care Management in 1972. By 1980 this organization had become the National Association for Child Development and Education (NACDE), composed of seven hundred proprietary child care providers.[85] The National Child Care Association (NCCA) was formed in the mid-1980s as a coalition of more than twenty state associations representing private child care providers.

Child Care Action Campaign Joins the Scene

Elinor Guggenheimer, the well-known child care organizational entrepreneur, launched a new organization in 1983. Looking back on the early 1980s, she explained her disappointment with child care politics:

> In 1983 . . . I examined the scenery and noted that there was no organization representing child care in its broadest sense. So, I called together the heads of women's magazines and organizations, and I said to them, "Look, you've been sitting on your hands." . . . I invited them to my apartment and we had a meeting around my dining room table. I asked them, given the double burden that so many women had of work and child care . . . with the demographics of women in the labor force, where have you been? . . . For there not to be more done for child care was outrageous.[86]

Those at this first meeting held at Guggenheimer's apartment noted the lack of any one advocacy organization for child care. No group was getting the word out about the need for child care for families of all income levels, providing information, and serving as a consciousness-raiser for the public at large. Guggenheimer envisioned a new, action-oriented organization. She held a few more meetings with her core group of consultants, which included leaders of women's organizations and professionals from women's magazines, and then widened the circle to child care policy experts and leaders, such as Edelman; Sheila B. Kamerman at Columbia University; Gwen Morgan at Wheelock College; Evelyn Moore, executive director of the National Black Child Development Institute (NBCDI); and Dana Friedman, former policy analyst at the Conference Board and cofounder with Ellen Galinsky of the Families and Work Institute (FWI). According to Guggenheimer, these organizational leaders and child care experts were not receptive to starting a new organization devoted exclusively to child care activism. Many were threatened by the possibility of a new group competing with the existing ones. "Each organization had a piece of the pie," and they weren't comfortable with the idea of giving it up.[87]

Never one to sit idle, Guggenheimer went to work setting up a new child care organization. There was some talk of moving the organization to Washington, D.C., but Guggenheimer objected because of the importance of reaching the mass media, based primarily in New York, and because, as she said, "I would be raising most of the money, so it needed to be here."[88] The organization, Child Care Action Campaign (CCAC), was founded in 1983, and one of its first goals was to inundate the popular press with articles on child care. Through Guggenheimer's connections, *Parade* magazine carried a feature story on child care by former President Gerald Ford, the honorary chairman of CCAC.

In its first year CCAC's Magazine Committee, under the chairmanship of Myrna Blyth, editor-in-chief and publisher of *Ladies' Home Journal*, contacted more than thirty-eight magazines to encourage them to carry feature articles on child care. Guggenheimer reported that "the results were electrifying. Tens of thousands of letters flooded our small office, bringing us stories from desperate parents, pleas for help from providers, and information about the problems local organizations were having."[89] For a variety of reasons, child care was beginning to attract the attention of the public and the media.

Over the next few years, CCAC gained corporate and individual support. Its board was one of the few forums that brought together educators, employers, labor unions, legislators, women's organizations, academics, proprietary providers, and corporate representatives to focus on child care. Among its members were Helen Blank (CDF), Ronald Blaylock (Payne Webber), Hillary Rodham Clinton (who had been chair of CDF's board), Moore, Ann Muscari (Kinder-Care), Richard Stolley (president, Time Inc., Magazines), and Zigler (Yale University).

Small and Steady Progress on the Child Care Front

The growth of organizations concerned about child care produced a dedicated group of individuals who worked in concert with members of Congress to advance federal child care support. In response to the federal budget cuts to the SSBG and other programs, advocates devoted most of their energies in the early 1980s to recapturing federal funding. This was important because at the time the only sources of federal child care support were Title IV of the Social Security Act (welfare) and the SSBG. They also lobbied for enactment of several child care bills.

In the mid-1980s several child care organizations formed the Ad Hoc Coalition on Day Care as a way of coordinating activities and interest in child care. The NBCDI spearheaded the coalition, with CDF leading the lobbying efforts. The coalition was a short-term predecessor to later and larger advocacy efforts discussed in the next chapter.

Members of Congress also were active on the child care front. Senators Christopher Dodd (D-Conn.) and Arlen Specter (R-Pa.) started the Senate Children's Caucus in 1983. Its first policy forum in June of that year was on latchkey children.[90] In the House, Representative George Miller (D-Calif.) introduced legislation to authorize a House Select Committee on Children, Youth, and Families, which the House passed in 1982.[91] As the committee's first chair, Miller chose child care as one of the panel's top priorities.

As another expression of the growing interest in child care legislation in 1984, Senator Hatch, chair of the Committee on Labor and Human Resources, added an amendment to the Head Start reauthorization bill during conference committee deliberations. His amendment proposed a new Dependent Care Block Grant, which authorized funding for before- and after-school care, dependent care, and information and referral programs. Hatch based his legislative proposal on previously introduced bills, especially Senator Donald W. Riegle's (D-Mich.) legislation (S. 1531) for before- and after-school care and Senator Gary Hart's (D-Colo.) bill for resource and referral programs. Representatives Sala Burton (D-Calif.), Patricia Schroeder (D-Colo.), and Geraldine Ferraro (D-N.Y.) cosponsored a similar measure (H.R. 4193) in the House. Senator Hatch and four other senators opposed S. 1531 as passed by the Committee on Labor and Human Resources because they thought that child care for school-age children should be administered by states, local communities, and the private sector.[92] The creation of the Dependent Care Block Grant with programs for school-age children enabled Hatch to claim credit for such programs through grants to states, as he preferred. Hatch's amendment for the Dependent Care Block Grant was included in the final 1984 Head Start reauthorization bill (P.L. 98-558).[93]

In 1985 a group of senators "formed a loose-knit coalition" in the Senate to address the lack of affordable quality child care. The coalition included senators Cranston, Dodd, Dennis DeConcini (D-Ariz.), Hart, and Riegle. Each senator cosponsored the others' legislation in areas such as increasing Title XX funding (DeConcini), supporting family child care (Hart), and improving the skills of child care workers (Dodd).[94] Although none of these bills passed in its entirety, aspects of each were incorporated into subsequent legislation.

Another factor that affected the politics of child care, though perhaps more indirectly than other events, was the establishment of on-site child care centers in the House and Senate. Each chamber had to pass a resolution approving its child care center. The Senate did so in 1982 and opened the center two years later. The House passed a resolution in 1985 and opened its center in 1986.

Credit for creating the Senate child care center goes to a group of Senate employees who gained the support of several senators' wives. Most of these spouses had adult children, but took an interest in the increasingly popular notion of child care located on-site or near the workplace. One of the most ardent promoters of the Senate child care center was Susan DeConcini, wife of Senator DeConcini. She was joined by Nancy Thurmond, wife of Strom Thurmond; Laurie Riegle; and Marcelle Leahy, wife of Patrick Leahy (D-Vt.). These women fought hard to overcome senatorial resistance to the child care center, especially in the Senate Rules Committee. As Susan DeConcini explained:

> It was quite a struggle just to get a quorum in the Rules Committee. . . . Nobody wanted to be against women and kids, yet it wasn't something everybody was ready to accept. There were a lot of people who needed to be updated in their thinking. . . . They were just not aware of their employees' conflicts about leaving their children at home while they went to work. . . . People were still relying on the old clichés that women should stay home and bake cookies . . . as if everyone had a choice![95]

The Senate passed its child care center resolution on November 14, 1983, by a vote of fifty to thirty, with nineteen abstentions.[96] In 1985 the Senate opened its employee child care center. Many of the senators' wives were on the advisory board, which was chaired by Susan DeConcini.

In December 1985 the House passed a resolution by voice vote to establish its on-site center. The vote followed nearly two years of debate over congressional liability of administering a child care program, which resulted in the center being placed under the auspices of a separate nonprofit entity.[97] The two congressional on-site child care centers and the proliferation of other child care centers in federal office buildings contributed to public officials' growing awareness of child care as a policy concern.

Another component of child care policy that advocates focused on in the early and mid-1980s was the dependent care tax credit (DCTC). Congress first created a dependent care tax deduction for certain employment-related expenses in 1954 and then replaced the deduction in 1976 with a nonrefundable tax credit. (A tax deduction reduces taxable income, while a tax credit lowers tax liability by reducing taxes owed.) But by not being refundable, the DCTC did not help those with the lowest incomes who had no tax liability and therefore could not take advantage of a tax credit. The DCTC was intended to help with costs incurred to enable a taxpayer (or spouse) to work or look for work. As part of the Economic Recovery Tax Act of 1981 (P.L. 97-34) Congress increased the amount of the DCTC that could be claimed to $2,400 for one child and $4,800 for families with two or more dependents, and it replaced the flat rate credit with a sliding scale based on adjusted gross income.[98] Since the early 1980s CDF and the National Women's Law Center (NWLC) had been working with several members of Congress, such as Representative Olympia Snowe (R-Maine), to get Congress to make the credit refundable and extend the sliding scale. In 1982 CDF and NWLC succeeded in convincing President Reagan to issue an administrative order requiring the IRS to include a line for the DCTC on the short tax form, thereby making it accessible to the many low-income families who do not use itemized tax returns.[99]

In 1983 CDF organized the Multigenerational Coalition on Dependent Care, composed of organizations representing children, women, and the elderly that strove to make the DCTC refundable and expand its sliding scale so that more low-income families would benefit. Although they were unable to effect these changes, an offshoot of the coalition lobbied in the summer of 1983 for increases in Title XX funding. Organizations such as the American Public Welfare Association (APWA), National Association of Counties (NACO), AFSCME, and Service Employees' International Union (SEIU) spearheaded efforts to increase Title XX funding. These groups worked on a quick report that highlighted the impact of Title XX cuts on a range of services. Their work was buttressed by CDF's extensive national survey on the impact of Title XX cuts on state child care systems, which showed that despite a growing need, thirty-two states were providing Title XX child care to fewer children in 1983 than in 1981.[100] As a result of the research and lobbying, Congress increased the annual funding for Title XX starting in 1983. Congress periodically increased funding for the Title XX SSBG throughout the 1980s, so that it reached $2.8 billion for FY 1990. However, Congress continually allocated funding below the authorized levels.[101] Senator John Chafee (R-R.I.) introduced the initial amendment to increase Title XX funding in the Senate Finance Committee. Even with the new infusion of support, funding for Title XX in 1983 remained lower than it·had been before the cut instituted in the 1981 OBRA legislation. However, the increases were a sign that Congress was recognizing the importance of child care assistance for low-income families. By the end of the 1980s, Congress was poised to make major changes in child care policy, starting with welfare reform.

Welfare Reform Features the First Federal Child Care Entitlement

In the late 1980s welfare reform again landed on the legislative agenda as part of President Reagan's commitments to reduce the role of the federal government in all social programs and to decrease welfare dependency.[102] Reagan's success at welfare reform followed the failed attempts of Presidents Nixon and Carter. Children, in general, did not figure prominently in any of the welfare debates. But by the late 1980s, child care advocates were able to make the case that for work requirements under welfare reform to succeed, legislators needed to address the child care needs of welfare recipients. Consequently, the FSA of 1988 (P.L. 100-48) established the first federal child care entitlement. The politics of child care under Reagan's welfare proposal repeated themes from a decade earlier under President Carter.

Child Care and Welfare Reform Under Carter

A main goal of Carter's welfare reform proposal, the Program for Better Jobs and Income (PBJI), was to provide up to 1.4 million jobs and wages to those who could work. Individuals incapable of working, including single welfare parents with children under the age of seven, would be eligible for a minimum level of income support.[103] Carter's staff estimated that approximately 150,000 public service jobs could be in child care. One billion dollars would be available to pay for jobs in a wide range of child care settings (including informal baby-sitters), as long as they were filled by women currently on welfare. In addition, each working mother participating in the program would be eligible to deduct a maximum of $150 per child per month for incurred child care expenses from her monthly earnings.[104] Known as the child care disregard, this was a seriously flawed method of subsidizing child care.

Carter's proposal presented several problems. The CWLA and other child organizations complained that $150 a month disregard was insufficient to buy adequate child care. Moreover, there was no assurance that those enrolled in public service jobs would have the training necessary to provide quality care. Expressing a theme that was to be repeated over the next two decades, many women's and welfare organizations argued that mothers of young children should be able to choose whether to work outside the home and not be forced to work.[105] Some organizations argued that the income support levels in Carter's bill were too low and that too many families would lack the cash for child care, removing any incentive to work. As one CDF staff explained, "In crass economic terms, it may make more sense to stay home than to take a job."[106] Some of the biggest controversies were over the quality of child care that would be offered under Carter's proposal. Organizations such as CDF and CWLA complained that Carter's welfare program would provide only custodial care when what was needed was a more developmental approach. All these objections became moot when Senator Long blocked Carter's welfare proposal in the Senate in 1979 because he opposed expanding cash benefits. Long preferred his bill (S. 1382), which would have replaced federal matching payments for welfare with a block grant to states, an idea that came into favor nearly two decades later.[107] The House passed the welfare reform bill in November 1979. Welfare reform did not reappear on the legislative agenda until the late 1980s.

The New Look of Child Care and Welfare Reform in the Late 1980s

By 1987 Democrats had regained control of the Senate (55 to 45) and recaptured some of the House seats they had lost earlier in the decade, giving them an 81-seat margin over Republicans (258 to 177). With a Republican president and a Democratic Congress, the politics of welfare reform inevitably involved compromises that differed from those under a Democratic president and Congress ten years earlier.

In the mid-1980s Senator Daniel Patrick Moynihan (D-N.Y.), then chair of the Senate Committee on Finance Subcommittee on Social Security and Family Policy (and previously one of the major architects of Nixon's FAP),[108] described how increases in labor force participation among young mothers helped make comprehensive welfare reform "a plausible political possibility." According to Moynihan, one area of consensus was that "whether children live with both parents or just one, able-bodied parents have a responsibility to support their children by working . . . poor single mothers ought to work, at least part-time." Moynihan also acknowledged that if policymakers expected single parents to work, then supportive services, such as child care, were a necessity.[109] Moynihan's observations regarding demographic shifts were on the mark. The growth of women's participation in the labor force during the 1970s and 1980s was among the highest in the postwar period, especially for women with young children. Between 1970 and 1985, the proportion of employed married women with children under six increased from 32.2 to 53.5 percent, with higher employment rates for women with older children (see figure 1.1 and table 1.3).[110] Furthermore, by 1990 almost 25 percent of children lived in one-parent families, compared with 9 percent in 1960. The number of families headed by single women who were not in the labor force increased from 2.5 million in 1965 to 4.1 million in 1985.[111] These trends led to a greater interest in requiring welfare mothers to work.

Conservatives argued that welfare dependency drained federal resources and created social and economic problems. In their views, "the discrepancy between the labor force participation of women in recipient families and nonrecipient families ha[d] become less acceptable."[112] However, it was one thing to require poor mothers to work and another to support working mothers in more well-to-do families, something conservatives would not condone. In contrast, liberal groups, such as the CDF and the National Coalition on Women, Work, and Welfare Reform, preferred that welfare mothers with young children work or seek employment on a voluntary basis.[113]

As welfare reform heated up in the mid-1980s, the main goals of child care advocates, such as CDF and CWLA, were to create a federal child care entitlement for welfare families and ensure that those moving from welfare to work had child care assistance. Before the enactment of the 1988 FSA, the child care disregard was the only way welfare families could receive child care assistance. The disregard allowed welfare recipients to deduct a part of their child care expenses from their monthly earnings in determining welfare eligibility. Deborah Phillips, a 1987 midcareer fellow at the Bush Center in Child Development, explained the problems with the disregard in her testimony before Congress: "Families are reimbursed after they purchase child care, with a lag time as long as two months. Poor families simply cannot sustain two months of child care costs."[114] Child care advocates wanted to increase the disregard and let states use Title IV-A child care funds for contracts (which the state grants to eligible providers) or vouchers (which the state grants to parents to purchase child care from eligible providers). They considered contracts and vouchers more expedient and desirable forms of child care assistance than the disregard. Many states were already using vouchers and contracts for child care under the SSBG. Although child care advocates lobbied for these various changes, their main objective, by far, was to establish a guarantee of child care assistance that went beyond the disregard for welfare families with young children whose parents were enrolled in work training or were employed. They also wanted to guarantee child care assistance for an extended period to families making the transition off welfare so that lack of child care support would not force them to give up work and return to welfare dependency.

Given the push for requiring welfare beneficiaries to work, lawmakers on both sides of the aisle acknowledged that the federal government had a legitimate role in providing some type of child care assistance to families on welfare. However, conservatives had reservations about increasing federal spending on child care during an era of federal budget deficits. Longstanding reluctance to investing federal dollars in child care persisted. As Republican members of the Committee on Education and Labor noted:

> We do not deny the need for adequate day care. . . . However, we do not believe that this legislation is the appropriate means by which the overall lack of day care should or can be addressed. . . . The issue is not whether appropriate day care should be available, the issue is at what point does the inability to *guarantee* [emphasis in original] day care become sufficient to justify nonparticipation.[115]

Several lawmakers and witnesses at hearings called for consideration of children's well-being in the context of welfare reform. For example, Representative Pat Williams (D-Mont.) deplored the lack of concern for children throughout the welfare discussions:

> Americans ought to understand that the Congress is about to embark on welfare reform on the cheap. We are about to dump millions of children into inadequate, virtually unfinanced child care centers with this legislation. . . . It seems to me that those most concerned about day care should throw themselves across the tracks to be sure that this bill from the very beginning provides funding for America's children, because when we are all done with welfare reform a generation or so from now, we are going to find out that the important thing we did was not with regard to the parents, it was with regard to the children, and the children are getting short shrift in this bill.[116]

Barbara Blum, president of the Foundation for Child Development, made a compelling case for bringing children back into the discussions of welfare reform. She explained, "It is perverse to expect mothers to work if they cannot be certain that their children will be well cared for."[117] Many witnesses cited a report from the U.S. General Accounting Office (GAO) claiming that although almost every state's Aid to Families with Dependent Children (AFDC) work program offered child care assistance to their participants, "half spent less than 6.4 percent of their 1985 budgets for this purpose."[118]

Testifying before a House committee, Phillips noted, "The question then, is not whether to include a child care component to welfare reform legislation, but rather how to craft and finance an effective child care component." Expressing the views of her colleagues in the child care professional and advocacy community, she explained the importance of quality care and the financial realities that many low-income families faced. If a single mother had an entry-level job that paid the minimum wage, she made $6,700 per year, but her full-time child care would cost at least $3,000 per year. For high-quality care, she would likely pay $5,000 per year and more for infant care. Head Start averaged $2,500 per year, but it runs typically only part time. Phillips and her colleagues argued that the government needed to provide financial support to welfare families for child care, and this support had to be sufficient to allow families to purchase high-quality, regulated care.[119]

As always, Edelman offered some of the liveliest testimony. At hearings in 1987, much of her oral statement was in response to the testimony of James Miller, President Reagan's OMB director. Miller proposed revising the exemption of mothers with children at the age of six and under from work-related activities. He contended that a work gap of six years "makes it difficult for women to be employed." He also called for mandatory participation in work-related activities because it would increase the low self-esteem of welfare recipients. And he claimed that there was a "vast body of information which indicates that informal child care, particularly care by relatives of the child, is not only the usual arrangement but is preferred . . . regardless of the mother's marital status and income level. . . . Most of this informal care is no- or low-cost care."[120] Edelman countered:

> As one parent to another, [I] just want to state my very strong exceptions to his relegating children of the poor to services that he and I wouldn't stand for a minute for, for our children, particularly the informal day care arrangements. . . . Higher income parents are seeking child development programs for enrichment. I do it. He did it. Other middle-class parents are doing it . . . less than 35 percent of the four-year-olds whose families are earning less than $10,000 are enrolled in these preschool programs, and I would submit that they need these programs more than my children need them or Mr. Miller's children need them. . . . I was just outraged, frankly, at his relegation to informal day care arrangements for children of the poor.[121]

Edelman testified in support of a child care entitlement for children in welfare families, which could be administered through contracts or vouchers. She also urged Congress to increase the monthly allowable child care disregard to $225 for children aged two and over and $250 for children under two. She called for language that would specify that welfare-related child care in unregulated settings would not be eligible for reimbursement, and she recommended continued child care assistance on a sliding fee scale after the year of transition off welfare. She urged members "not to go cheap on child care."[122]

As in the past, the position of the nation's governors proved pivotal to the final outcome of the child care discussions. At hearings in the spring of 1987, Governor Bill Clinton of Arkansas, who cochaired the National Governors Association (NGA), explained the importance of child care to mandatory work participation: "You don't want to set up a system and go to all this trouble to change it and then discourage people from taking work because they can't afford to take care of their children properly in child care centers."[123] The NGA and its allies in Congress and among organized interests proposed extending child care benefits beyond when recipients found jobs as a way of helping people shift from welfare dependency to self-sufficiency. The issue was how long after work placement child care benefits should continue. The governors and members of the advocacy community were interested in extending them for more than six months. As Clinton explained, "The provision of day care services for six months following placement in a job might not be long enough to help newly employed clients maintain the stability in those jobs. I would urge you to at least consider whether you want to go to twelve months. The Governors, I think it's fair to say, would strongly support that."[124] The final welfare bill included provisions very similar to the governors' recommendations.

Enacting Child Care Under Welfare Reform

The themes just described were interwoven with welfare negotiations in both chambers of Congress. However, the deliberations focused mostly on work requirements for adults. The major vehicle in the House for welfare reform was H.R. 1720, introduced in March 1987 by Representative Harold E. Ford (D-Tenn.), chair of the Committee on Ways and Means, Subcommittee on Public Assistance and Unemployment Compensation. The bill enjoyed the support of the chair of the Committee on Ways and Means, Daniel Rostenkowski (D-Ill.), and of the House leadership. When Ford was indicted on federal charges of bank, mail, and tax fraud, Representative Thomas Downey (D-N.Y.) became acting chair of the subcommittee and shepherded the welfare legislation through the House.

On June 17, 1987, the Committee on Ways and Means approved welfare reform legislation (H.R. 1720). The states were required to provide child care to families participating in mandatory work programs and to guarantee child care for six months to families who no longer received AFDC because of increased income from employment. This became known as the transitional child care entitlement. Advocates fought hard to ensure that transitional child care was an open-ended entitlement, meaning there would be no limit on federal expenditures. The bill from the Committee on Ways and

Means exempted parents with children under the age of three from mandatory participation in work training programs and required parents with children under the age of six to participate on a part-time basis. States could use vouchers or contracts to finance child care under the FSA. The bill also increased the child care disregard from $160 to $175 per month for children two and older or $200 per month for children under the age of two.[125]

A month later, the House Committee on Education and Labor revised H.R. 1720 by extending child care to families with children up to the age of fifteen. The committee added other language, such as requiring state assessments of existing child care resources, authorizing funds to expand the supply of child care, and requiring that representatives of child care resource and referral agencies or other knowledgeable individuals distribute child care information to welfare families. The education committee's bill lacked any provisions for transitional child care because the transitional child care provisions were part of similar provisions extending Medicaid, but the House Committee on Education and Labor lacked jurisdiction over Medicaid.[126]

The House passed welfare reform legislation on December 16, 1987, by a vote of 239 to 194. Only thirteen Republicans voted for it. Most GOP members opposed it because they thought its price tag of $7 billion over five years was too high, and they feared the bill would promote welfare dependency because it made it too easy for states to increase benefits. The House bill allowed twelve months of transitional child care.[127]

In the Senate, the Finance Committee had jurisdiction over welfare reform. Although Senator Lloyd Bentsen (D-Tex.) was the chair of the committee, Moynihan, because of his expertise, took the lead on many substantive aspects of the deliberations. In July 1987 Moynihan introduced S. 1511, the Senate companion to H.R. 1720. The bill had bipartisan support. But Bentsen's reluctance to approve a revamping of welfare made it difficult for the Senate to act swiftly. He and other Senate leaders wanted to acknowledge the interest of conservative and GOP constituencies. Moreover, Bentsen and his colleagues on the Finance Committee had other legislative priorities, most notably catastrophic health care coverage and an omnibus trade bill.

In February 1988, at the prompting of the nation's governors, Bentsen began to move welfare reform through his committee. On April 20, 1988, the Senate Finance Committee approved S. 1511. The full Senate passed welfare reform on June 16, 1988, by a vote of ninety-three to three. The Senate bill had lower funding levels than the House bill, and its child care provisions were less generous. For example, the Senate approved only nine months of transitional child care compared with the twelve months included in the final House bill. The Senate bill also lacked the House's funding for enhancement of child care quality and supply.[128]

The Senate bill had an important provision that child care for participants in the Job Opportunities and Basic Skills Training Program (JOBS) must be within payment limits designated by the state but not in excess of applicable local market rates, which states would set in accordance with regulations promulgated by the secretary of HHS.[129] Efforts to pass language pertaining to rates in the House were unsuccessful because of concerns that those rates would be too expensive for state and federal authorities. Making local market rates a federal requirement provided a way of raising the rates for child care payments under welfare, and ideally this would also improve the quality of care. Requiring the establishment of local market rates also acknowledged variations in payment and economies across geographic locales. It was a key aspect of child care policy that set a precedent for years to come. CDF and other child care advocates wanted to go even further and give states the option of exceeding local market rates. But just requiring states to establish local market rates was very important, especially because many states were paying child care assistance below the market rate for child care. (Regulations implementing the FSA set the local market rate at the seventy-fifth percentile, which had implications for subsequent child care policymaking, as explained in the following chapters.)

The conference committee on welfare reform legislation, composed of representatives from committees responsible for welfare in each chamber, agreed to a final version of the FSA in late September 1988. States were required to establish a JOBS program enrolling all able-bodied welfare recipients once the recipient's child was at least three years old and as long as state resources were available. States were also required to guarantee child care for each family with a dependent child to the extent that such care was necessary for a welfare recipient to work or participate in the JOBS program. This was the first federal child care entitlement. States were also required to guarantee twelve months of transitional child care once a recipient was employed. Federal funding for transitional child care was open-ended. Similar to welfare-related child care funding, it was based on a formula that took into account the state's AFDC benefit match rate (50 to 80 percent). Families were required to pay a copayment for transitional child care based on a sliding scale determined by each state.

In addition to approving the child care entitlements, the conference committee retained the House provisions to increase the disregard for child care costs from $160 per month to $175 and $200 per month for children under the age of two. The child care disregard was to be applied after other disregards, most notably the standard welfare eligibility disregard, which was increased from $75 to $90 per month. Both of these disregards were intended to provide financial incentives for families to work while easing the transition off welfare because it raised the level at which earnings ended eligibility. But the child care disregard was far lower than the total cost of child care in most locales.

Other aspects of the final bill included increasing the federal matching rate (the rate at which the federal government matched state payments) for child care from 50 percent to a range of 50 to 80 percent, which was the same as Medicaid matching rates. The final bill lowered the age cutoff for child care eligibility from fifteen (as proposed in the House bill) to thirteen. As for standards, the bill required that child care meet applicable standards under state and local law and that states establish ways of guaranteeing that center-based care "is designed to ensure basic health and safety." States were also required "to endeavor to develop guidelines for care provided in private homes."[130] The final bill also provided $13 million for each of the fiscal years 1990 and 1991 so states could improve child care licensing and registration requirements and monitor child care for the AFDC population. States had to match this with 10 percent of the funding.

For those who followed child care policies, the FSA was monumental. As one state children's advocate observed in an interview with the author nearly a decade later, "All we could do for child care under welfare before the FSA was the disregard. . . . With the FSA, all of a sudden we had a federal child care guarantee, the requirement of market surveys, and uncapped funding." But the open-ended funding was beneficial only to the extent that states used the FSA child care guarantee, eventually applied for federal child care funds, and provided a state match. Unfortunately, a number of states failed to allocate sufficient funds for child care under the FSA.[131]

The FSA also made significant changes to the DCTC, based on amendments that Senator Bill Bradley (D-N.J.) proposed to the Senate Finance Committee version of the bill on the Senate floor. The Finance Committee partially financed welfare reform from a phaseout of the DCTC for taxpayers with annual incomes over $70,000. Bradley, working with the NWLC and

Senator Barbara Mikulski (D-Md.), argued that it was unfair to single out child care tax credits without limiting tax benefits for other employment-related expenses. Thus, instead of the DCTC phaseout, Bradley proposed a limit on tax deductions for employment-related business expenses, such as meals and entertainment, for individuals with annual incomes over $360,000. The full Senate sustained the amendment. The House version of the FSA had no such provisions. Members of the welfare reform conference committee were concerned that the business community would be harmed by the Bradley amendment.[132] Therefore, they dropped the Finance Committee's proposal to impose an income eligibility level for the DCTC and instead found other ways to finance welfare reform, such as lowering the maximum age of eligible dependents for the tax credit from under fifteen to under thirteen. They also required parents to offset against the DCTC any benefits they received under a child care plan provided by their employer. And they generally disallowed the DCTC unless taxpayers provided employer identification numbers or Social Security numbers of the dependent care providers. These changes had the cumulative effect of decreasing the number of people claiming the DCTC in 1989.[133] In particular, the requirement that parents disclose information about child care providers, many of whom were illegal immigrants or relatives, led many parents to discontinue claiming the DCTC within months of the bill's enactment.[134]

Members of Congress hailed the welfare law as a major achievement, especially given congressional failure to enact welfare reform under Presidents Nixon and Carter. Child care advocates applauded the child care provisions but remained concerned about adequate child care funding for welfare recipients, the states' willingness to implement the child care provisions, and the quality of child care available to poor and low-income families.

The 1970s were a time of regrouping for child care policymaking as liberals and conservatives developed new ideas and structures that provided the basis for subsequent legislative efforts. As the nation and its elected officials became increasingly conservative, individuals and organizations advocating a federal child care bill faced growing resistance to their legislative proposals. Because of Carter's economic and political priorities, child care was not a major concern to him or his staff. Demographic shifts in the 1970s and 1980s included an increase in the number of employed mothers with young children and single mothers, which substantiated the need for increased federal support for child care. However, conservatives stifled such initiatives and successfully opposed promulgation of federal child care regulations. In 1988 liberals and conservatives reached consensus on welfare reform, including the first federal child care entitlements. These events set the stage for the most contentious round of child care legislation in recent history.

4 Politics of Child Care Legislation, 1987–1990

From 1987 to 1990 the politics of enacting a federal child care program that was separate from welfare or any other federal law constituted the most significant episode for American child care policymaking in the late twentieth century. Disagreement over the responsibility of the federal government in child care policymaking resulted in three arduous and lively years of debate over the shape of child care legislation. Interest in child care in the late 1980s was largely attributed to the dramatic changes in the social and political fabric of American life, some of which were described in the previous chapter. New structures within Congress and shifting political power within the executive branch influenced the course and outcome of child care legislation in the late 1980s. However, the final enactment of child care legislation in 1990 was due largely to budget politics. The outcome of those contentious events were child care provisions that established a framework for child care legislation and regulation that lasted more than a decade.

Launching a Child Care Initiative

The late 1980s were a time of renewed interest in child care, largely because of the influx of mothers with young children into the labor force. In addition, a cadre of state and national child care advocates and experts and several new congressional structures established during the 1980s facilitated the advancement of child care legislation. One of the most important catalysts for setting the child care agenda was the House Select Committee on Children, Youth, and Families, which was established in 1982 and opened its doors in 1983.

As Helen Blank, CDF's director of child care, explained in the early 1990s, "The seeds for all of the current child care activity can perhaps be traced to 1984 when Representative [George] Miller and his new select committee on children and youth held a series of hearings and issued a report on child care."[1] The title of the select committee's first hearing in 1984, "Child Care: Beginning a New Initiative," accurately conveyed the idea that Congress was embarking on new ways of approaching child care. The hearing launched the committee's child care initiative; between 1984 and 1987 this consisted of other hearings in Washington, D.C., and across the country as well as an analytic report on child care.[2] The committee was instrumental in publicizing "the best information available about the need for child care, the importance of quality care to children's development and families' stability and economic security, and the pioneering efforts that states and communities were making to piece together whatever they could to support families and children in their areas."[3] Ann Rosewater, who was the committee's deputy staff director and then staff director (and later held leadership positions in HHS), explained the importance of the committee's work:

> Even the creation of the select committee was important. It was an effort to say that there has to be someone at the federal level watching . . . and asserting that the relationship between kids or families and government was changing. . . . It was a real strategy, a deliberate strategy . . . for the committee to select child care as its first priority issue.[4]

By 1986 a convergence of factors convinced Blank that the timing was right to introduce major child care legislation. Staff for several Democratic lawmakers, such as Senators Alan Cranston and Christopher Dodd and Representative Miller, reached similar conclusions based on the increased attention child care was receiving in the popular press[5] and the rising number of working women with young children (see table 1.1). To launch the legislative campaign, Blank and her colleagues in other organizations invited representatives of about thirty groups to begin drafting a child care bill. Those attending the meeting agreed to a self-selected steering committee, which met periodically and planned larger coalition meetings. To expedite their efforts, the coalition formed work groups in areas such as care for school-age children, infant care, child care under welfare, salaries for child care staff, and standards for child care providers. These early organizers intended to introduce child care legislation in 1987, make it a presidential campaign issue in 1988, and then get a bill enacted in 1989. Those attending the early meetings agreed that it was logical to give CDF the leadership role in organizing the coalition, mainly because it had the resources, including full-time staff, to devote to the issue. As Blank explained and others said in so many words, "CDF is aggressive . . . and we knew we could move things politically."[6]

Within a few months, the coalition had outlined major aspects of a child care bill. The coalition members' goals were to improve the availability, affordability, and quality of child care through federal support to states. Unlike their predecessors in 1971, they agreed that a universal subsidy for child care was too costly and politically impractical. Instead, they designed a program of child care assistance to families with incomes below 115 percent of their state's median income.[7] Prime sponsorship, the issue that had caused such an uproar in 1971, was a moot point because local authority over child care would never survive politically under President Reagan's New Federalism, which gave states the responsibility for administering many social programs. Thus, the coalition members endorsed a federal child care program targeting low-income working families that funded states at $2 billion. They named their bill the Act for Better Child Care, known as ABC.

After lengthy discussion, the coalition members opted for mandated federal standards, meaning that all providers receiving federal funding would have to meet federal requirements. Some members of the coalition were concerned that federal standards would threaten the viability of the bill and decrease its likelihood of passage, especially because Congress had revoked the FIDCR in 1981. But the coalition decided at least to try for federally mandated standards because of overriding concerns about the poor quality of child care. As one lobbyist who participated in the formative stages of the bill explained, "If you don't demand that federal standards are imposed, then the Mississippis and Louisianas of the world will never come around." Once the bill was introduced, standards became one of the most controversial issues. The ABC also targeted money for enhancing the quality and supply of child care.

By the summer of 1987, more than seventy organizations had joined the coalition, now named the Alliance for Better Child Care. On November 19, 1987, congressional supporters of ABC held a joint House and Senate press conference to introduce their bill. Addressing a crowd of two hundred, they proudly claimed 126 representatives and 22 senators as cosponsors, most but not all of whom were Democrats.[8] Senator Dodd, chair of the Senate Labor and Human Resources Committee, Subcommittee on Children, Family, Drugs, and Alcoholism, introduced ABC (S. 1885) that day, cosponsored by Senator John Chafee, a moderate to liberal Republican member of the Finance Committee. Representative Dale Kildee (D-Mich.), chair of the House Committee on Education and Labor, Subcommittee on Human Resources, introduced the companion bill (H.R. 3660) in the House, with bipartisan support from Representative Olympia Snowe. Although not a member of a committee with jurisdiction over child care, Snowe was another moderate Republican with an interest in child care.[9]

Dodd was a tireless advocate for his bill. He spoke often of the shortages of public and private licensed child care for infants and toddlers and lack of after-school programs. He also acknowledged the importance of setting standards and of improving the quality of care in child care settings. Scores of labor unions, women's organizations, public officials, religious and civic groups, children's policy experts, and early childhood professionals offered thousands of pages of testimony in support of ABC and the long-standing need for such an initiative.[10] One Senate staffer described the strength of the coalition's early efforts: "In the ten years I have spent on the Hill, I can't remember a bill with as much consensus before it arrived, with as much input from experts such as Edelman, labor groups, child psychologists, child care experts, education groups, state advocates, and state public officials."

In addition to CDF, many other ardent advocates for child care legislation supported ABC. For example, the CWLA, NCJW, AJLI, and NAEYC featured child care prominently at their annual conferences. Many labor unions issued position statements in support of the bill. CDF operated an aggressive grassroots campaign for the entire time that ABC was on the agenda. Unlike any of the other organizations, CDF had a full-time field representative devoted exclusively to child care who visited twenty to thirty states to help organize local advocates of child care legislation.[11] Although the other alliance members participated and shared in these events, CDF's resources far exceeded those of the other members of the alliance. CDF also worked with the media, running radio announcements on child care during commuter rush hours and printing advertisements in the *Washington Post*. At various points while lobbying for ABC, CDF shared its leadership role with other organizations, in particular, the NWLC and AFSCME.

Child Care Vouchers

Despite the consensus that legislators and organized interests reached in drafting the bill, two issues—vouchers and funding of child care providers with religious affiliations—proved especially problematic as early as 1987. The original 1987 ABC allowed funding of child care services through grants, contracts, or loans, all of which would provide assistance to child care providers, public entities, or private nonprofit agencies. It also authorized distribution of child care certificates (vouchers) to parents of eligible children "to purchase child care services that meet the requirements of the Act." Unlike the Mondale–Brademas child care legislation of the 1970s, ABC authorized proprietary child care providers to receive funding for certain functions.[12] By the end of the 1980s, for-profit programs comprised nearly 34 percent of all early education and care settings; the overwhelming majority of them were run by independent operators, while others were owned by national or local chains.[13] Although allowing federal child care vouchers was controversial because of their links to the furor over educational vouchers, as Blank explained, "Much of child care policy was carried out by states and many states allowed vouchers for child care through Title XX of the SSBG, so it didn't make sense to oppose what was already in place."[14]

For some coalition members, especially those representing public education, the language on vouchers was one of the most contentious features of ABC even before the bill was introduced. They feared that "institutionalizing vouchers through federal law [would] open the flood gates for vouchers for elementary and secondary school certificates."[15] Acknowledging these concerns, the coalition members originally agreed that parents could use child care vouchers for care not under the auspices of an entity that had religious affiliations. While the Senate legislative counsel was reviewing the proposed child care legislation in November 1987, the lobbyist for the National PTA discovered that the bill did not have any restrictions on the use of vouchers for religiously affiliated care. Following the introduction of ABC, the National PTA, NEA, and other education groups tried to get Dodd and Kildee to make the language on vouchers more restrictive.

The Senate Labor and Human Resources Committee approved the ABC on July 27, 1988, without revising the voucher language. The committee specified in its report language that allowing vouchers for child care was "significantly different from the use of certificates or vouchers in this nation's predominantly public system of elementary or secondary education." Child care vouchers were not a "basis for the establishment of a voucher system" for public education.[16] Shortly after the Senate committee passed the ABC legislation, the National PTA withdrew its support for the bill. The NEA took a different course. Although its members strongly objected to the voucher language, they chose to work on revising it once the bill was introduced.[17] Another aspect of the bill was more problematic for NEA than vouchers: the use of funds for religion-based care.

Use of Funds for Child Care Providers with Religious Affiliations

The language on the use of funds for religiously affiliated care generated conflict about whether such funding violated the First Amendment of the Constitution, which states: "Congress shall make no law respecting an establishment of religion, or prohibiting the free exercise thereof." The child care debates, similar to other issues, such as prayer in public school, produced discussion regarding interpretation of the First Amendment.[18]

The draft of the ABC bill that Dodd first sent to the Senate legislative counsel for review lacked any reference to religiously based care. However, in early October when the Senate legal counsel was reviewing the bill, NEA, with the support of the National PTA, submitted to Blank a technical change that severely restricted religious providers' use of funds under ABC. The education groups insisted that they could not support the bill unless these changes were made. Blank, wanting to avoid bickering among the groups that could derail the bill, went along with their request. She mentioned the technical change to a few of her colleagues in the coalition, who advised her to circulate a memo to the other members informing them that she had submitted a technical change, and this she did.

But the changes were more than technical. Basically they said that if churches or synagogues wanted to use ABC funds for their child care programs, they had to "neutralize" the areas by covering or removing all religious symbols.[19] Many education, women's, civil rights, and religious organizations supported these changes because of their contention that without these provisions it would be too easy for religiously affiliated centers to violate the First Amendment by advancing religious goals within child care settings that received public funds. These groups, referred to as the secularists,[20] also did not want to permit providers of religiously affiliated care to give preference to members of their own religion in hiring personnel or admitting children.

Other members of the alliance were furious when they heard about the changes to the ABC bill. Some charged that it was unfair of a few organizations to make changes to a bill that they had agreed to as a group, especially when it had been so difficult to reach any type of consensus in the first place. Others said that the bill they had originally agreed to had been tampered with and that the bill Dodd and Kildee eventually introduced was no longer the same.

U.S. Catholic Conference Joins the Fray

The proposed changes created opposition to the bill among religious groups outside the coalition, most notably the U.S. Catholic Conference (USCC), whose members provide child care in church-based centers throughout the country. In 1990, 28 percent of center-based programs were under the auspices of religious organizations.[21] As Frank Monahan, director of government relations for the USCC at the time, explained, "When we saw the bill's nondiscrimination language, we jumped in with both feet. We could not live with what the coalition was proposing."[22] Practically all the language in ABC that pertained to church–state issues was problematic for the USCC. In particular, the USCC and several other religious groups were opposed to language that prohibited them from giving preference to members of their own religion in hiring personnel or admitting children. They also were against the ABC language that required centers to cover or remove all religious symbols as a condition of receiving federal child care assistance. The situation was aptly summarized by a lobbyist who remarked, "By early 1988, the battle lines were drawn, with secularists, comprised of education groups and some women's and religious organizations, on one side, and the USCC and other religious organizations on the other."

Between late 1987 and April 1988, Marian Wright Edelman, as president of CDF, brokered a series of meetings with organizations on both sides of the issue. These high-level meetings of lobbyists and legal counsels were an attempt to eliminate opposition to the religious discrimination language and the financing of religiously affiliated care that could prevent the bill from going forward. Edelman's solution was to "pursue church–state concerns after the bill is enacted." Noting the mounting conservative opposition to

ABC and the importance of reaching a consensus, she urged the groups to reach a compromise, explaining that

> going into detail on what is and is not prohibited in statute is unprecedented and creates unnecessary political problems. . . . Congress has learned to leave these issues to other forums—particularly the regulatory process and the courts. . . . I hope therefore, that none of us will insist on a Pyrrhic victory at the expense of low-income children and families. . . . We already have enough battles to fight for the money, the standards, and against the right wing who would love to see us battling among ourselves.[23]

Two points are worth noting here. First, for CDF and many of the other alliance organizations (such as the CWLA, AJLI, and NAEYC), the separation of church and state was not as central to their mission as it was for other organizations, such as the NEA, National PTA, NCJW, and NOW. Although many member organizations of the coalition were concerned about separation of church and state, their main priority was the enactment of comprehensive child care legislation. Second, not all education organizations were aligned with NEA and the National PTA. For example, the Council of Chief State School Officers did not oppose funding of religiously affiliated child care providers as long as the federal funding was not used for religious instruction.[24]

On April 18, 1988, trying to reach a middle ground, Blank asked the alliance members to endorse amendments that prohibited the use of ABC funds for sectarian (religious) purposes or activities and allowed religiously affiliated providers to receive vouchers, but not for religious activities that were part of child care programs.[25] Most of the coalition members and the USCC agreed to the changes, except the secularists, who felt that these provisions gave religious providers too much leeway. In July the secularists lost when the Senate Committee on Labor and Human Resources indicated its preference for letting the conflicts over child care providers with religious affiliations be handled through the regulatory process. They changed the wording on the use of funds for religiously affiliated child care providers by "simply prohibit[ing] the expenditure of funds for any sectarian purpose or activity."[26]

The Senate committee's new wording also gave religious institutions some leeway regarding preference in admissions and eliminated the original

ABC's prohibition against employment discrimination on the basis of religion. The members agreed that "this omission should not be interpreted as an indication that the Committee endorses employment discrimination on the basis of religion." Child care providers still had to adhere to discrimination requirements of civil rights and other applicable laws.[27] In August 1988 the Senate Committee on Labor and Human Resources approved the child care bill by voice vote and sent it to the full Senate.

On October 7, 1988, the Senate voted fifty to forty-six to end debate on a package of family legislation, including child care and family leave. Lacking the sixty votes required for cloture (ending debate), none of the bills were voted on. This left a clean slate for legislators and interest groups on both sides of the issue when Congress reconvened for the 101st Congress in 1989 with a new president in the White House.

But first another side of the story must be told.

The Other Side of the Story: Conservatives Offer Competing Proposals

In the late 1980s, unlike in 1971, many alternative legislative proposals to a major child care bill were on the agenda. Most were sponsored by conservatives who preferred tax policies to help low-income working families with children and abhorred the notion of a new federal child care program. Tax policies as a vehicle for helping families had been a GOP theme for decades before the 1988 elections. Republicans argued that since the 1960s married families with children had experienced undue tax burdens as the value of the personal tax exemption failed to keep pace with inflation. Although the 1986 tax reform raised the value of the exemption to $2,000, Republicans argued that it would need to reach over $6,000 to compensate for its erosion in value.[28] One of the mechanisms that Republicans preferred for helping low-income working families was expanding the Earned Income Tax Credit (EITC). The origins of the EITC can be traced to the late 1960s when Senator Russell Long opposed Nixon's FAP and proposed instead a way of offsetting taxes for working poor families. Originally enacted as part of the Tax Reduction Act of 1975 (P.L. 94-12), the EITC provides a refundable tax credit to poor and low-income working families as a way of protecting them from falling into poverty. In the late 1980s only low-income families with children were eligible for the credit. Because its benefits require earnings, the EITC was popular among those who opposed welfare and preferred the EITC as a way to assist low-income families.[29] Another solution the GOP preferred was to create a new child tax credit, which unlike the DCTC would not disproportionately favor middle- and upper-income families with both parents working.[30] These alternatives—expanding the EITC and creating a new tax credit—became the principal components of conservative legislative proposals for helping working families with children during the late 1980s.

In 1988 several legislators introduced bills that expanded tax credits for low-income families with children. One proposal (S. 2187/H.R. 3944), introduced by Senator Malcolm Wallop (R-Wyo.) and Representative Clyde Holloway (R-La.), became the major GOP alternative to the ABC bill. It created a refundable child tax credit that took into account the number of children under the age of four in low-income working families. Holloway claimed that his bill could "accomplish what ABC attempts but fails to do. It offers more assistance, more choice, to more families, with less cost to the Government. Rather than subsidize public day care, [it] enables parents to care for their own children."[31]

Another important Republican initiative was the toddler tax credit (H.R. 4434/S. 2620), which Representative Richard T. Schulze (R-Pa.) and Senator Pete Domenici (R-N.M.) introduced in April 1988. This legislation gave low-income families with children under the age of six a $750 tax credit per child. These bills became the basis for George Bush's campaign platform on child care in 1988, which included a $1,000 refundable tax credit for low-income families with children under the age of five.[32]

Differences between the early 1970s and later 1980s were captured in the 1988 presidential campaign when, for the first time, GOP delegates articulated a position on child care that sought to distinguish them from Democrats.[33] According to a Bush White House aide, child care was one of several important themes for Republicans in the 1988 campaign because it was an issue for which they could identify principles they would support, instead of merely opposing Democratic preferences.[34] The Republican 1988 platform was a far cry from the Democratic call for the federal government to become more involved in building a strong child care infrastructure.[35] Republicans also emphasized their support of federal funding for religiously affiliated care: "Democrats propose a new federal program that negates parental choice and disdains religious participation. Republicans would never bar aid to any family for choosing child care that includes a simple prayer."[36]

By July 1988 the Bush–Quayle campaign outlined its four-point comprehensive child care plan, which included providing assistance to all families with similar income levels, whether or not the parents were working; giving parents the widest choice possible, including care sponsored by relatives or religious agencies; placing priority on low-income families; and providing leadership on quality that was commensurate with changes in the family and workplace. Bush's campaign proposal included a $1.5 billion children's tax credit, making the DCTC refundable, and a $50 million investment in employer-sponsored child care.[37] The Republicans' preference for child care vouchers provided an alternative to what they considered the Democrats' excessive regulation of child care from Washington. In 1986 Representative Nancy Johnson (R-Conn.) introduced one of the first child care bills (H.R. 4787) to include vouchers.[38]

All the discussions about child care in the late 1980s boiled down to philosophical differences between those (mostly liberals and Democrats) who favored a strong federal government initiative that gave money to states to administer child care programs and those (mostly conservatives and Republicans) who opposed such an approach and favored assisting families primarily through tax policies. These differences were the major themes of the political discussions in the late 1980s and characterized child care politics into the 1990s. Schisms between camps reflected differences in how each side defined the problem. Liberals, most of whom were Democrats, tended to see the problem as a crisis in the lack of affordable, accessible child care of high quality. Conservatives, most of whom were Republicans, doubted that such a crisis existed. Instead, they saw the issue as how to assist low-income families with the costs of raising their children, whether or not they used child care facilities outside the home. Most conservatives opposed the ABC bill because they claimed that it discriminated against families in which one parent stayed home to care for children or families that preferred to use religiously affiliated care. Opponents of ABC referred to it as "An 'Attempt to Bureaucratize Motherhood' and 'Government Nannies for America's Children.'"[39]

Those advocating a new federal child care program also supported revisions of the tax credits to help families with children, but they argued that tax credits alone could not resolve the problems of child care quality, accessibility, and affordability. As Edelman explained at a 1989 Senate hearing:

We have two crises in this country, the crisis of low-income families not having enough income, and we think that a tax credit like the

EITC or the Dependent Tax Credit, whose refundability we have supported for a number of years, would be significant supports on this particular crisis and so we favor them as supplement to ABC, but they are not substitutes for creating the child care infrastructure that we think is absolutely essential to meet the needs of the 10½ million preschoolers whose mothers are already in the labor force.[40]

Robert Rector at the Heritage Foundation became one of the leading opponents of ABC and a forceful articulator of conservative viewpoints. He was joined by staff and members of several right-leaning organizations who shared his position, including Gary Bauer and William Mattox Jr. at FRC; Phyllis Schlafly, president of the Eagle Forum; and Beverly LaHaye at CWA. When it came to provisions pertaining to religious providers, the National Association of Evangelicals and other religious right entities joined the fray. Testifying before a House committee, Rector summarized his colleagues' concerns about ABC:

> First, a true pro-family child care policy should rest on the premise that all children are important, not just those using professional day care. . . . Second, a pro-family child care policy would not discriminate against or exclude traditional two-parent families where the mother makes a financial sacrifice to remain at home to raise her own young children. . . . Any policy dealing with child care and low-income families should begin by addressing the needs of traditional families . . . rather than treating such families as an afterthought or ignoring them entirely, as the current ABC bill does.[41]

Addressing the importance of tax policies, Rector explained:

> In many cases mothers of young children are pushed into the work force against their wishes to compensate for the erosion of family income due to excessive taxation. A pro-family child care policy would allow parents to retain a greater portion of their own hard-earned income rather than creating a vast new subsidy system for bureaucrats and social service professionals.[42]

Rector and other conservatives also thought that the voucher provisions in ABC were inadequate. As he explained,

While the ABC bill contains a minor provision allowing states to provide day-care vouchers, which would stimulate consumer choice, no state is required to provide vouchers. Vouchers are mentioned in only two paragraphs of the 63-page bill. In practice, little if any of the ABC funding would reach parents in the form of vouchers.[43]

Schlafly referred to the sections on religiously affiliated child care providers as "the most bigoted, anti-religious sections ever proposed in any legislation." And she complained that under ABC, "any facility where the children say 'Thank you, God, for these cookies,' would be automatically barred from benefits."[44] Conservatives may have overstated the negative impact of the bill. But they had the advantage of being more closely aligned with the White House than their liberal opponents.

Public-opinion polls taken in 1988 to ascertain the public's attitude toward federal child care policies revealed various findings. As one analyst noted, public-opinion data were "being bandied about to prove that . . . Americans prefer one legislative approach over others."[45] Nonetheless, in a January 1988 Louis Harris poll, 65 percent of those sampled endorsed the statement "The federal government should establish and pay for programs to set up child care centers to provide quality day care for children." In the same poll, 85 percent of the respondents concurred that the federal government should establish minimum standards to ensure child care quality, and 28 percent agreed that a $750 tax credit would solve almost all child care problems encountered by working mothers. Almost 75 percent of those surveyed disagreed that most parents could find relatives, friends, or family to care for children while they worked.[46] Of the respondents to a different poll conducted in 1988, 48 percent agreed that a preschool child was likely to suffer if his or her mother was working. In 1989, 1990, and 1991 the identical question produced nearly the same responses.[47] These data show that despite supporting government assistance for child care, the public remained ambivalent about the effect of child care on a young child's development. This ambivalence contributed to the turbulence in the policy arena.

Beyond organized interests and public opinion, the politics of child care legislation were strongly influenced by structural and procedural aspects of lawmaking. In addition, the complex relationships between the president and Congress figured prominently. These themes were illustrated by the twists and turns that child care legislation took through Congress in 1989 and 1990.

1989: Senate Success

In 1987 and 1988 members of Congress and organized interests deliberated child care legislation knowing that the Reagan administration had little interest in the issue and anticipating a new political terrain after the 1988 elections. Bush's presidential election in 1988 and leadership changes in both houses of Congress created new opportunities for child care legislation. But mounting federal budget deficits made lawmakers reluctant to create any new federal programs.

Bush and the 101st Congress

In 1988 George Bush was elected president with 54 percent of the popular vote. Republicans lost seats in both chambers. Democrats maintained an 85-seat margin (260 to 175) in the House and a 10-seat margin (55 to 45) in the Senate. Bush's congressional relations suffered from the outset. He entered office with "fewer Republicans to work with in the House than any other newly elected GOP president in the 20th century."[48]

In 1989 George J. Mitchell (D-Maine) became Senate majority leader, replacing Senator Robert Byrd (D-W.Va.). Mitchell's leadership style was characterized by his ability to establish viable coalitions with Senate Republicans and Bush White House officials. He was committed to negotiating a child care bill because of its importance as a Democratic issue and his desire to claim credit for major domestic legislation.[49]

In March 1989 Bush introduced his child care legislative proposal based on the 1988 GOP platform. He proposed making the DCTC refundable and creating a new child tax credit for low-income working families with children under the age of four as a supplement to the EITC: "For each eligible child, parents could claim the one credit that best meets their needs and circumstances." The cost of the two tax credits totaled $187 million for FY 1990, reaching $2.5 billion by FY 1993. In his statement introducing his proposed legislation, Bush reiterated the themes of his campaign, emphasizing parental choice and the family as the mainstay of any child care policy.[50] Rector at the Heritage Foundation praised Bush's tax credit plan. His main criticism of it was that it did not provide as much tax relief to families with young children as the child tax credit proposals by Holloway and Schulze did.[51]

In May 1989 the White House issued a fact sheet outlining the president's principles for child care policy and how the ABC clashed with them. Specifically, Bush opposed the ABC proposal because it placed too much control in the hands of federal and state governments instead of parents, its federal standards would force some providers to close, it discriminated against families in which one parent stays home to care for the children, and it would not adequately target low-income families most in need because its income eligibility level (115 percent of state median income) was too high.[52] These four points were the major principles that guided Bush's child care policies.

Muddling Through Child Care in the Senate

Child care moved more swiftly through the Senate than through the House. Before taking child care to the Senate floor in June 1989, Mitchell and Dodd brokered agreements on standards and church–state issues. Both were critical for full Senate approval of child care legislation.

Negotiating on standards. The 1987 version of ABC included a National Advisory Committee that would design minimum child care standards for center-based and family-based care. Supporters of federal child care standards thought this was important because although almost every state had some type of standards, especially for child–staff ratios, there was tremendous variation among states in the extent to which they regulated child care.[53] To address these inconsistencies and improve child care quality, the advisory committee would set standards for child care centers and family day care in areas such as child–staff ratios, group size, personnel qualifications, health and safety requirements, and parental access to child care programs. Opposition to this language came from many circles. For example, conservatives at the FRC and Heritage Foundation who advocated "limited government" considered the standards intrusive. The intergovernmental lobby (represented by groups such as the NGA, NACO, and the National Conference of State Legislatures [NCSL]) also vocally opposed federal standards. In February 1988 the NGA, chaired by Governor John Sununu (R-N.H.), who later became Bush's chief of staff, asserted that "the quality and regulation of child care are state responsibilities."[54] In June 1988 Governors Tom Kean (R-N.J.) and Bill Clinton (D-Ark.) represented the NGA at Senate hearings and argued that federal standards could never account for interstate variability. Kean summarized the governors' concerns by asserting that "day care is not like socks or pantyhose—one size doesn't fit everybody."[55] In 1989 as in each juncture when child care landed on the legislative agenda, the governors' influence on child care legislation was significant.

When Dodd reintroduced the ABC package in 1989, he had the cosponsorship of Senator Orrin Hatch, the ranking member of the Senate Committee on Labor and Human Resources.[56] Hatch had shown interest in 1986 as chair of the Senate labor committee when he held hearings on the subject and in 1987 when he introduced his own child care bill.[57] Hatch's endorsement enabled Dodd to claim important bipartisan support for his bill. But it angered Republicans and conservatives who were firmly against ABC. They considered Hatch a traitor to their cause.[58]

According to a Senate staffer, Hatch's decision to support the ABC proposal was based on the strong offers of compromise he received from Dodd and other members of the Senate Committee on Labor and Human Resources, especially Senator Barbara Mikulski. Speaking on the Senate floor in June 1989, Hatch eloquently explained his reasons for joining Dodd in supporting ABC. He also explained why tax credits alone were an inadequate solution:

> If an additional $1,000 to $2,000 in the pockets of families will inspire more people to get into the child care market, that is great. . . . But for parents who need to work for whatever reason, a tax credit will not expand their choice regarding child care. . . . There are other factors that discourage choice in child care which cannot be addressed by simply giving more money to the consumers.[59]

Furthermore, Hatch was concerned about the growing number of women who were forced to work out of economic necessity. As he explained, "With all my heart, I wish that more families had the option of having a full-time parent. . . . But, wishing will not make it so; and, in fact, the two-parent, one-income family has not existed as a majority since 1979, and it is time we recognize that."[60] Acknowledging arguments from critics of ABC, he said:

I do not see that this legislation—with or without a tax component—represents the Sovietization or Swedenization of children that many of the bill's organized detractors have asserted. . . . Nowhere in this bill is it required that children be in child care. Nowhere is it required that they be assigned to a specific type of child care. And, nowhere does it say that government will operate child care programs. So all of that disinformation is wrong. I bitterly resent those who are distorting what this bill says. What exactly, is meant by the Sovietization of children?[61]

One of Hatch's concerns with the original ABC was its language on federal standards.[62] With the ascent of GOP lawmakers who wanted to decrease federal regulations and the legacy left by the FIDCR controversy, federal standards continued to generate opposition. Opponents of federal standards, such as Senator Pete Wilson (R-Calif.), pointed to child care regulations that already existed at the state level.[63] Proponents, such as Professor Alfred Kahn at Columbia University, argued that the federal government had a compelling role to play in ensuring child care quality.[64]

In April and May 1989, recognizing that mandatory federal standards had become a potential obstacle to the bill's progress, the alliance revised its position. By June 1989, using the alliance's recommendations, Dodd, Hatch, and Senator Edward Kennedy (D-Mass.) had reached an agreement on standards with the NGA, other members of the intergovernmental lobby,[65] and most of the alliance members. They replaced ABC's mandatory federal standards with language requiring states to have standards in place for certain key areas of health and safety three years after ABC became law. At that time, states with standards above the national recommended ones would be eligible for a reduction in their state match under ABC. Those with standards below the recommended level would be eligible for a special incentive grant for improvement of standards. A twenty-member national committee of experts would set recommended standards that states could use in developing their own standards in areas such as group size, child–staff ratios, health and safety, and parental involvement.[66] The revised language on standards helped make the bill more palatable to Hatch and others who firmly opposed mandated federal standards. While Dodd and his staff were negotiating on standards, he and others in the Senate also negotiated an agreement on church–state language.

Church–state language.   In early 1989 Dodd instructed his subcommittee staff director, Richard Tarplin, to meet with key groups to resolve the controversial church–state language.[67] In March, Tarplin, Shirley Sagawa (legislative counsel for Senator Kennedy), and Jeff Blattner (legal counsel for Kennedy from the Judiciary Committee) brokered an agreement with the relevant interest groups, which was generally acceptable to all at the bargaining table. Compared with the 1988 committee agreement regarding religiously affiliated facilities, which had caused such furor among the religious groups, the 1989 compromise allowed child care programs with religious affiliations more flexibility in their hiring and admission policies based on religious preferences. Organizations such as the National PTA, Americans United for Separation of Church and State, and the American Civil Liberties Union (ACLU) opposed these changes. NEA reluctantly went along with the agreement. According to interviews with Senate staffers, it was clear to Dodd and Kennedy that they could not simultaneously satisfy both the ACLU and the USCC. But the support of the USCC was more critical in getting the bill past the full committee and the Senate, so they drafted their legislation accordingly.

On March 15, 1989, the Senate Labor and Human Resources Committee passed the ABC legislation, which included church–state language based on the negotiations among organized interests. However, the deal collapsed just a few days after it had been completed. Different sources attribute its demise to different causes. According to Monahan at the U.S. Catholic Conference, Dodd and his staff failed to appreciate the tentative nature of the USCC's agreement to the new language regarding religious discrimination and prohibiting the use of funds for sectarian activities.[68] The NEA and American Jewish Congress (AJC) were furious that the USCC had reneged on what they understood to be a "done deal." They accused the USCC of sabotaging the negotiations and the bill and not being a team player. From another perspective, one Senate legislative staffer involved in the negotiations commented in an interview, "You can't say that the USCC reneged. We did leave things rather ambiguously."

Upon learning of the USCC's opposition, Tarplin and Sagawa tried to salvage what was left of the agreement. But their efforts were in vain. In the end, the committee's report language was supported by the CDF, NEA, AJC, and other members of the Alliance for Better Child Care but not by the USCC, which sought support for an amendment to ABC elsewhere.

In the spring of 1989, USCC began working with Senator Wendell H. Ford (D-Ky.) to draft an amendment that would allow vouchers for religious child care programs without any of the limitations of earlier legislative proposals. Senator David Durenberger (R-Minn.), who represented a state with a child care voucher system, cosponsored the legislation. In a short time, Ford and Durenberger proposed an amendment that allowed vouchers for child care sponsored by religious organizations without the restrictions of the pending ABC bill. Monahan figured that if Ford, a staunch opponent of elementary and secondary school vouchers, approved vouchers for religiously affiliated child care, then other legislators skeptical of child care vouchers might be inclined to endorse the amendment. Ford and other legislators who endorsed child care vouchers viewed child care as an issue distinct from education. Many of them also thought it was important to recognize and accommodate the large number of child care providers with religious affiliations.

The political influence of the USCC, joined by many right-wing fundamentalists who had support from the Bush White House, made the Ford–Durenberger amendment difficult to defeat. Civil rights groups and some religious organizations saw it as a violation of the First Amendment. CDF, NWLC, unions, and most other members of the alliance originally lobbied against the amendment. Senate Majority Leader Mitchell's role in the handling of the Ford–Durenberger amendment was critical to its outcome because, according to one Senate aide, "the amendment was so controversial, it could have brought the entire bill down." Mitchell decided not to oppose the amendment. He wanted a child care bill to pass under his watch, and if opposing this amendment (and the USCC) meant that there might not be enough support for the child care legislation, then he had to go along with the amendment. Furthermore, many senators thought the secularists asked for too much and were unrealistic. As one legislative aide said, "The ACLU and others were upset and obsessed with the idea that if a child care center was in a church basement, even with nuns not wearing habits and no crucifixes on the wall, if there was a choir singing next door, they would still be in violation of the law. . . . So, then where do you draw the line?"

Not wanting to face the uncertainties that could arise from a floor vote on the Ford–Durenberger amendment, Mitchell decided to broker a compromise between the various constituencies and then fold the Ford–Durenberger amendment into a Mitchell child care package. Dodd, Kennedy, and the alliance members were faced with a "take it or leave it" decision. They either could oppose the amendment and risk losing the entire ABC bill, or could go along with the amendment in the interest of getting a bill passed. Ultimately, Dodd, Kennedy, and other senators supported the Mitchell package, including the Ford–Durenberger amendment, because they wanted the child care bill to move forward. CDF and many other members of the alliance made a similar choice, despite their previous opposition to the amendment.

Mitchell incorporated the Ford–Durenberger language into his substitute bill, along with a Senate Finance Committee package, which included expansion of the EITC; a new young child supplement to the EITC, making the DCTC refundable; and a new child health tax credit for low-income families with children, which Senator Lloyd Bentsen, the committee's chair, had proposed.

With the governors on board in terms of the language on standards and the USCC finally supporting the bill's language on church–state issues and vouchers, Mitchell was able to take child care legislation to the Senate floor, confident that the most problematic areas had been resolved. Some Republicans still opposed the bill. For example, Senator Daniel Coats (R-Ind.) argued in favor of tax credits alone and referred to the ABC bill as "a $2.5 billion boondoggle that will primarily benefit bureaucracies, not individuals."[69]

On June 22, 1989, after four days of debate, the Senate approved Mitchell's package by a vote of sixty-three to thirty-seven. Mitchell's success was undoubtedly due to his skillfully combining the child care program with the tax package from the Senate Finance Committee. The popularity of a combined tax credit and block grant approach was catching on.

1989: The House Imbroglio over Child Care Legislation

Once the Senate had passed child care legislation, the ball was in the House's court. Compared with the Senate, the House was characterized by more jurisdictional conflicts among committees. House members also faced many leadership changes in June 1989 with the resignations of Speaker Jim Wright (D-Tex.) and Majority Whip Tony Coelho (D-Calif.). Former majority leader Thomas S. Foley (D-Wash.) replaced Wright as Speaker, and Representative Richard A. Gephardt (D-Mo.) became the new majority leader. Child care legislation was also impeded by tension between

Edelman and key players in the areas of child care policy and a stronger constituency for conservative positions on child care. Secularists, too, found more support for their positions in the House than in the Senate, although their views were still very much in the minority. Representative Augustus Hawkins (D-Calif.), chair of the Committee on Education and Labor and one of the most senior members of Congress, was closely aligned with the education community and had opposed the compromise language of the Senate Labor and Human Resources Committee on church–state issues in 1988. Kildee, as subcommittee chair and a cosponsor of ABC, wanted to move his bill forward, but also did not want to alienate Hawkins. However, without Hawkins's support, it would be difficult, although not impossible, to move child care legislation out of committee.

In 1989, with the support of the NEA, National PTA, other members of the education community, and groups such as NOW, NCJW, and AAUW, Hawkins introduced the Child Development and Education Act (H.R. 3). The organizations supporting him preferred this bill because ABC's provisions for vouchers and funding of religiously affiliated providers no longer represented their interests. Moreover, they favored giving public schools the responsibility of administering child care programs because this would promote the universal availability of child care. They worked with Edward Zigler at Yale, who had conceptualized the Twenty-First Century School program, which relied on public schools to provide a variety of services, including all-day child care for preschoolers and before- and after-school care for older children.[70] Many alliance members, such as the CDF, NAEYC, CWLA, NBCDI, AFSCME, ILGWU, and SEIU supported both ABC and H.R. 3, hoping that legislators would reach a compromise between the two bills.[71]

President Bush was adamantly opposed to H.R. 3 placing child care programs under the "traditional educational bureaucracy" because it was "evident that in many states, child care dollars were being steered toward publicly financed, center-based care." Bush also opposed placing responsibility for child care in the public school systems because so many of them were having difficulty "fulfilling their current missions."[72] He disliked what he considered H.R. 3's excessive bureaucracy, discrimination against religiously affiliated services, and federal mandates that would limit parental choice.

Several organized interests also were against H.R. 3. For example, the National Association of Evangelicals was against any type of federal government child care program that would detract from parents' "God-given responsibility for child care." The NCCA, representing 30,000 small-business proprietary child care centers, complained that the bill would "legislate a virtual public-school monopoly over care for three- and four-year-olds, impede diversity and thwart parental choice options."[73]

Hawkins prevailed over these objections, and on June 27, 1989, his Committee on Education and Labor passed H.R. 3 after combining it with ABC (H.R. 30), which Kildee had introduced earlier in the year. However, jurisdictional conflicts between the Committee on Education and Labor and the Committee on Ways and Means blocked the smooth sailing of H.R. 3 to the House floor.

Downey Enters the Ring

In February 1989 Representatives Thomas Downey and Miller introduced an alternative child care measure (H.R. 882/S. 354), cosponsored by Senator Al Gore (D-Tenn.). Although Downey was a supporter of ABC, he began to have doubts about the bill's likelihood of enactment. As he explained,

> [T]he idea that you could have new authorization and get any money for it . . . just flew in the face of recent history and recent budget battles. That's why it seemed as if it would be better to have a guaranteed source of funding. . . . Miller and I were both dissatisfied with ABC. I remember turning to him one day and asking, "Why not just do tax credits and Title XX?"[74]

Downey's bill can also be seen as an extension of his leadership in enacting the FSA when expanding the EITC and making the DCTC refundable were discussed.[75] The Downey-Miller-Gore bill expanded the EITC for families with low incomes, adjusted it for families with more than one child, and made the DCTC refundable for families with incomes below a certain level. Compared with Bush's tax credit proposals, Downey's would reach more families and provide them with more assistance. The bill also featured increases in Title XX earmarked for child care and required states to set minimum health and safety standards. Given the difficulty ABC was facing in Congress at the time, Downey's proposal in early 1989 had some merit.

However, the Downey–Miller bill came as a total surprise to Blank and other alliance members. From their perspective, if Downey had wanted to emphasize tax credits, he could have proposed combining them with ABC, as the Senate did. The EITC expansions of Downey's bill were not problematic for the alliance members (unless considered the only solution to child care, exclusive of a direct subsidy such as ABC). But they objected to Downey's use of Title XX as the vehicle for increasing child care funding because Title XX was a capped entitlement, and its funding levels do not keep pace with need. In addition, Title XX had a poor funding history, having suffered severe cutbacks in the early 1980s. Moreover, CDF, NAEYC, and the other alliance members objected to earmarking funds for child care because this "[put] valuable services like foster care and elder care in competition with child care."[76] Most important, CDF and the other alliance members resented Downey's proposal because it diluted their child care solution. They thought it would impede the progress of child care legislation as it would not result in a federal program devoted explicitly to child care.

Edelman's reaction was that Miller and Downey had betrayed her, even though in 1989 both candidates had received top ratings from CDF for their voting records, and in 1988 Miller had been named CDF's man of the year.

Conservatives, such as Mattox at FRC; William Tobin, government affairs director at the NCCA; and *Wall Street Journal* columnist Paul Gigot, complimented Downey for changing the course of the legislation in the House and offering a more palatable alternative to H.R. 3 and ABC.[77] They especially liked the Downey–Miller EITC provision and the absence of new federal bureaucratic structures. But when it came time to vote, most Republicans and conservatives opposed Downey's bill because they thought it didn't go far enough in requiring states to offer vouchers for any new child care program or in ensuring that funds could be used for religious instruction. They preferred proposals that focused exclusively on tax credits. Despite those objections, the Committee on Ways and Means voted twenty-six to ten to insert Downey's bill into its reconciliation recommendations. (Reconciliation is explained in more detail later.) A week later, on July 26, the Committee on Education and Labor attached Hawkins's bill (H.R. 3) to its reconciliation recommendations. On September 3 the Committee on Ways and Means approved an amended version of H.R. 3, replacing Title III (which had the closest resemblance to ABC) with the Downey bill it had just passed. Thus, by September 1989, the Committee on Ways and Means's version of child care was Downey's bill replacing ABC, and the Committee on Education and Labor's version was Hawkins's H.R. 3.

CDF and the other members of the ABC coalition were outraged by the maneuvering of the Committee on Ways and Means. They urged representatives not to allow the substitution, but to forge an agreement between the two committees. The politics of child care legislation became characterized by stalemate, rivalry between House committees, and divisiveness among Democrats. The future of child care legislation was in limbo.

Conservatives Gather Steam

While the groups in favor of some type of federal program—whether ABC, H.R. 3, or Downey–Miller—battled among themselves, organizations such as Eagle Forum, FRC, Heritage Foundation, and CWA pushed for bills that, similar to President Bush's proposal, provided a tax credit to low-income families with young children. By the spring of 1989, several legislative proposals featuring tax credits and other alternatives to ABC were on the table. In October 1988 Tobin convened a coalition of organizations representing primarily business, certain religious interests, and proprietary child care providers to draft an alternative to H.R. 3 and ABC. Other groups involved were the Chamber of Commerce, the National Federation of Independent Businesses, and the National Association of Evangelicals.[78] Tobin and his colleagues worked with Representative Charles W. Stenholm (D-Tex.), who was the leader of the Conservative Democratic Forum. However, Stenholm was not a member of a committee with jurisdiction over child care, so he enlisted the support of Representative E. Clay Shaw Jr. (R-Fla.), ranking Republican on Downey's subcommittee. Stenholm and Shaw drafted what later became known as "Stenholm-Shaw One (SSI)." CDF, AFSCME, and other alliance members opposed SSI because of its lack of minimal health and safety standards, inadequate funding, and reliance on tax credits, which would not address the issues of affordability, availability, and quality child care.[79]

In October 1989, when the House leaders brought child care legislation to the House floor as part of the reconciliation package, the Rules Committee allowed two amendments: SSI and an amendment offered by Representative Mickey Edwards (R-Okla.). The Edwards substitute, backed by the Bush administration, expanded the EITC and phased out the DCTC for high-income families. SSI lost by a vote of 195 to 130. It lacked the support of major conservative interests, such as Eagle Forum and FRC, which wanted tax credits only. Their bill, the Edwards substitute, lost by a vote of 285 to 140.

After the demise of SSI, the House passed as part of its reconciliation bill what one lobbyist described as "an inelegant mixing together of the Hawkins and Downey bills." The leadership relegated to the House–Senate reconciliation conference committee the responsibility of resolving differences between the two House versions of child care legislation. By October 1989 the House leadership had decided not to force a decision between Hawkins and Downey. Instead, Foley and Gephardt inserted both bills into the reconciliation legislation (H.R. 3299), expecting to resolve the differences in conference committee. The reconciliation committee had two subconference committees on child care. One focused on programmatic concerns and was composed of members of the Senate Committee on Labor and Human Resources and the House Committee on Education and Labor. The other, a tax subconference committee, included members of the Senate Committee on Finance and the House Committee on Ways and Means. The subconferees from the labor conference committee eventually agreed to a $1.7 billion child care authorization package, with most of the funding going for an ABC-like program. The tax conferees remained deadlocked on whether to support child care through Title XX or through a new ABC-type program. They also were unresolved about how to proceed with the various tax proposals relating to the EITC and DCTC.

In the last few weeks of the reconciliation negotiations, with both parties posturing on tax issues, the Senate went along with Majority Leader Mitchell's suggestion to pass a reconciliation bill stripped of any extraneous measures. Consequently, the Senate prohibited any nonbudget items, such as child care, while the House retained its reconciliation bill, laden with many measures including the two versions of child care legislation that Representatives Hawkins and Downey had separately introduced.[80] On November 16, 1989, Foley announced that he was postponing all action on child care until the next session.[81] The stalemate between the House committees and the tension between Edelman and some of the leading Democrats (in particular, Downey and Miller) created more hurdles for child care legislation.

Edelman versus Downey and Miller

On August 7, 1989, Downey and Miller sent Edelman a letter expressing their "dismay over some of the materials" sent out by the alliance during the child care debates. They took issue with materials distributed at an alliance meeting calling for opposition to any actions that would replace or weaken H.R. 3 and ABC. According to Downey and Miller, "The more important question is this: can we expect *any* funds to be appropriated for Title III of H.R. 3 as reported by the Education and Labor Committee? The answer—at least for FY 1990—seems to be no." They reiterated their position that relying on Title XX was the best mechanism for increasing child care funding when budget resources were tight.[82] In a six-page reply to Downey and Miller, Edelman expressed her "disappointment" with their assessment of her position and their lack of support for ABC, which they had both cosponsored. She wrote, "In numerous conversations and communications over the past two years, neither of you raised concerns to me about ABC— its purpose, design, funding level or mechanism."[83] The relationship between Edelman and Downey deteriorated further when Miller and Downey supported a motion, offered by Representative Tom Tauke (R-Iowa), ranking minority member on Kildee's subcommittee, that instructed the child care conferees to replace ABC with increases in Title XX. This was in direct opposition to the alliance's recommendation that both ABC and increases in Title XX be enacted.

Downey and Miller's support of the Tauke proposal followed by Foley's decision to pull the bill was more than Edelman was willing to tolerate. She immediately sent Downey and Miller an angry memo regarding what she called their "continuing private guerrilla war to kill child care legislation this year and to defeat ABC." She accused them of blocking child care legislation and explained:

> This memo is for the record. Without doubt, it is the saddest memo I have written in 20 years of lobbying on behalf of children. Its purpose is to let thousands and thousands of child care and Head Start advocates, women, and working parents all around the country— who have worked unceasingly for years to push child care to the top of the national agenda . . . know that if child care legislation is not enacted this year, the two of you will deserve the full blame for this tragic and unnecessary outcome. . . . The Tauke Amendment . . . offered yesterday with your active encouragement and support . . . is only the latest in a series of efforts you have engaged in to sabotage groundbreaking child care legislation all year for petty jurisdictional and power reasons.[84]

On November 17 all members of Downey's subcommittee and Representative Daniel Rostenkowski, chairman of the Committee on Ways and Means, signed a letter to Edelman defending Miller and Downey. They wrote, "Tom Downey and George Miller are no enemies of children or child care; you know that as well as we do. . . . The Ways and Means proposal may not square with your vision for child care. However, . . . we ultimately must choose to support the policy which we think will serve the public best."[85]

Edelman's memo jolted the entire child care political community. Some members of the coalition were upset that she would resort to such tactics, and several lobbyists were concerned that her memo could provide an excuse for legislators who were undecided on ABC to vote against it. According to others, Edelman's memo did not detract from the bill's success because child care legislation was already dead by the time she wrote it, which was what prompted her to send the memo in the first place. Some advocates defended Edelman's actions, saying that somebody had to do something to shake people up and move things along. Certainly, the memo and its publicity enhanced the visibility of child care legislation when Congress reconvened in 1990 and gave it one last try.

Thus, 1989 ended with Congress still unable to pass a child care bill. No single reason emerged. According to some sources, Foley pulled the bill because of the irreconcilable committee disputes; others pointed to the Senate's insistence on a clean reconciliation bill, stripped of extraneous measures.

1990: The Last Chance

By mid-1990 the alliance had become very fragmented; many resented CDF's (and Edelman's) style. Jurisdictional problems within the committee persisted, and conservatives introduced new legislative alternatives for child care. By the fall of that year, federal budget politics turned the situation around, and child care appeared in a new light to congressional and White House officials.

One More Time

In 1990, responding to pressure from conservative groups, Stenholm and Shaw revised their bill by strengthening language on vouchers and intro-

ducing a new child tax credit for low-income families. They introduced the
Family Choice and Child Care Improvement Act (H.R. 4294), referred to
as Stenholm-Shaw Two (SSII), on March 15, 1990. It also included earmarked increases for child care under Title XX, totaling $2.25 billion over
five years. Of all the child care bills on the table, the principles embedded
in SSII were closest to what President Bush could support, despite his concerns about the bill's costs.[86]

On March 27, 1990, House Speaker Foley combined aspects of Downey's
and Hawkins's bills into a leadership child care bill (H.R. 4381). Right before
the House was to vote on child care, Representative William Grey (D-Pa.),
the majority whip, sent a letter to House Democrats reminding them that "the
leadership had promised last fall that it would move toward the church–state
language contained in a bill already approved by the Senate."[87] Thus, the
House measure was the same as the 1989 Senate-approved bill in that it
allowed funding of religiously affiliated providers. This outraged the nearly
fifty organizations that opposed federal financing of religiously affiliated
child care. Among them were long-standing opponents, such as the NEA,
National PTA, and Americans United for Separation of Church and State.
Other groups—such as the Presbyterian Church, American Federation of
Teachers (AFT), SEIU, and United Auto Workers (UAW)—joined in opposing the language on funding of child care providers with religious affiliations. The AFT, SEIU, and UAW decisions were significant because each
were AFL-CIO affiliates opposing the main AFL-CIO position in favor of
allowing federal funding of religiously affiliated child care providers.
AFSCME also chose not to oppose the Senate language and went along
with phrasing that allowed federal funding of religiously affiliated child care.
Thus, child care legislation created divisiveness among labor unions. With
every month child care remained on the agenda, the links among the organizations involved became more tenuous.

During the last week in March, when child care was scheduled for debate
in the House, all the groups mobilized their resources. The Alliance for
Better Child Care was the most fragmented it had ever been, but its remaining approximately one hundred members continued to fight for direct
federal assistance for child care. Blank worked closely with Gerald Klepner
at AFSCME and Nancy Duff Campbell at NWLC. Their goals were to get
the House leadership bill passed and to block SSII.

From the other side of the issue, the FRC activated its grassroots network
and flooded the Capitol's switchboard with phone calls in favor of SSII. The

organization used its popular radio show *Focus on the Family*, featuring psychologist James C. Dobson, to urge listeners to contact their legislators. Of all the groups, the USCC very skillfully established a win–win situation in the House because it supported both the leadership and the SSII bills. But it preferred the leadership bill over SSII because it was broader in scope and offered more direct assistance to child care providers.[88]

On March 29 the House passed the leadership child care bill after rejecting all the proposed amendments, including SSII. A conference committee was convened to resolve the differences between the chambers. As in 1989 the conference committee had two subcommittees. One, composed of members of the House Committee on Education and Labor and the Senate Committee on Labor and Human Resources, focused on programmatic issues. The other included members of the Senate Committee on Finance and the House Committee on Ways and Means and handled tax-related child care issues and child care entitlements.

Organizations seeking strict separation of church and state felt they had little choice but to oppose the bill passed by the House as well as that passed by the Senate because of the language on religiously affiliated providers. This was a tough decision for groups such as AJC, NCJW, NOW, NEA, and National PTA that had been ardent supporters of child care since the late 1960s. Other groups, such as CDF, AJL, NWLC, and NAEYC, were not as concerned about the language on providers with religious affiliations.

Following passage of child care legislation by the House in 1990, CDF's publicity campaign for child care exceeded any previous efforts in the organization's history. Starting in April, according to Blank, CDF "went for broke" in activating the state and local grassroots networks and raising publicity for child care legislation. In June ten cities held rallies displaying paper chains made by local advocates of child care legislation. In September 1990 these groups sent the paper chains to Washington, where staff from organizations that were members of the alliance stretched the chains from the Capitol steps to the White House. Continuing its ongoing field and publicity activities, CDF activated its religious networks. CDF staff regularly sent editorial memoranda to the press and helped legislators and advocates draft op-ed pieces for local newspapers. They held press conferences and devoted enormous resources to the child care issue, making it a priority for the organization. Since the beginning of the ABC legislative campaign in 1987, CDF's grassroots operations, especially its role in building state-level coalitions, contributed to the advancement of child care legislation at critical junctures. CDF had a staff person who worked exclusively with state organizations and taught them how to organize and rally other groups in support of ABC. By the fall of 1990, these state and local child care advocates had acquired skills in advocacy, including working with the media, and had become politically savvy as they fought for their cause. Lobbyists from both conservative and liberal groups, often reluctantly, admitted that none of the other organizations on either side of the issue had the extensive field operations of CDF or as "slick" a system for keeping up contacts with the media. But the lobbying could not force the conferees to reach a final agreement on child care.

A turning point came in June 1990 when Sununu, Bush's chief of staff, sent a letter to Representative Bill Goodling (R-Pa.), ranking minority member of the Education and Labor Committee. Before Sununu wrote the letter, he, Goodling, and Thomas A. Scully (associate director for human resources, veterans, and labor at OMB) had a detailed conversation during which Goodling outlined what he wanted in the letter.[89] Republicans in Congress and the White House were showing a willingness to make a deal. When Sununu wrote his letter, the conference committee on child care was meeting, and House members were feuding over whether the House conferees should accept a bill similar to the ABC one, and if so, under what conditions. Sununu's letter was a way of placing Bush's terms on the bargaining table, even though he was not a formal participant in the conference committee discussions. In the letter Sununu wrote:

> The President strongly prefers a tax credit approach to child care policy. . . . In the spirit of compromise he is willing to accept a carefully crafted grant program. If there is to be a grant component of the bill, the President's preference would be for a "clean" earmarked increase in the Title XX Social Services Block Grant program. By clean, I mean that the bill should not contain any federal standards, model or otherwise, nor should it require the States to establish standards. . . .
>
> As a second choice, the President would be willing to accept a "clean" block grant under the jurisdiction of the Labor Committee that is consistent with the guidelines stated above. . . . A stand-alone grant program for school-based care, such as Title II of H.R. 3 is unacceptable.[90]

Basically, Sununu was explaining that a child care block grant program would not automatically draw a veto, that certain issues were nonnegotiable, and that other items were open for discussion.

Over the summer of 1990, Sununu and Downey met several times to discuss child care. Dodd and Kennedy also met privately with Sununu and Richard Darman, the director of OMB. Although none of these meetings produced any substantive results, they showed that some of the players had realized that backdoor negotiations might be necessary to move child care forward. By the end of July, the education and labor conferees agreed to authorize approximately $1.8 billion for child care in FY 1991, including a yet-to-be determined portion for a program like the one envisioned by the ABC proposal. But the tax conferees remained deadlocked. The conferees of the House Committee on Ways and Means wanted increases in Title XX, but their Senate counterparts would have no part of that. In August the Senate Committee on Finance conferees, led by Bentsen, offered a compromise in the form of a new capped child care entitlement for families at risk of going on welfare (the At-Risk Child Care Program).[91] In the meantime, child care took a back seat to federal budget negotiations.

Failed Budget Agreement Opens Window for Child Care

The 1974 Budget Reform and Impoundment Act (P.L. 93-344) established the framework for the 1990 budget process, including the use of budget reconciliation. Although budget reconciliation had been available since 1974, Congress did not use it until 1980. Reconciliation is the process used by Congress to get its committees to comply with budget targets set by previous budget resolutions. When striving to reduce federal spending, reconciliation requires committees to produce cuts in entitlements and discretionary funding. Because reconciliation is a large bill that legislators must accept or reject in its entirety, they often use it as a vehicle for enacting laws with policy goals other than deficit reduction.[92] However, legislators need a reason to add other provisions to reconciliation. In 1990 the politics of the failed budget summit provided the impetus for adding child care provisions to the reconciliation bill.

For most of 1990 child care was a minor aspect of the budget deliberations that were among the most contentious in recent history. In May 1990, wanting to move stalled budget negotiations forward, Bush invited congressional leaders to the White House for preliminary budget talks. On June 26, with Congress and the public criticizing the president for his inability to lead the country out of the federal budget deficit crisis, Bush made one of the most critical decisions of his term. He endorsed tax increases by saying that deficit reduction could be reached only through a combination of measures, such as entitlement reform, discretionary spending decreases, and tax revenue increases. His move, which reversed his popular campaign pledge of "no new taxes," angered fellow Republicans who were staunchly against any type of tax increase.[93]

Over the summer of 1990 budget negotiations continued, to no avail. They resumed in September when White House and congressional leaders met in seclusion at Andrews Air Force Base. Budget negotiators were motivated to reach some type of agreement by the fear of facing across-the-board budget cuts, which would automatically set in if deficit targets could not be reached. Their interest in concluding budget talks grew as Election Day was approaching. Neither party wanted to be blamed for unresolved budget issues. The main point on which the negotiators remained stuck in a deadlock over was tax policy, specifically how to distribute taxes across income levels.

On September 30, at the eleventh hour before FY 1991 began on October 1, Bush announced that a core group of eight negotiators had agreed on a budget deficit package that reduced federal spending by $500 billion over five years.[94] When reporters asked House Speaker Foley if child care was "officially disengaged from the budget package" and, if so, would there still be a child care bill this year, he replied that he expected there would be a bill. However, he was unsure if it would be part of the final budget package.[95]

The budget summit agreement contained many controversial provisions that ruffled the feathers of members of both parties.[96] The most disturbing aspects of the budget summit agreement, and a catalyst for the subsequent child care negotiations, were its regressive effects. According to staff for the House Committee on Ways and Means and the Joint Committee on Taxation, under the budget agreement families earning under $30,000 would face a larger tax burden than those earning over $200,000.[97]

Given the conflict surrounding the tax increases in the budget summit, it was not surprising that the House rejected it on October 4 by a vote of 179 to 254. Political observers considered the rejection of the summit package one of Bush's most severe domestic policy defeats. It was the first time in ten years that Congress had turned down such a major piece of budget legislation.[98] The delay in the budget process provided an opportunity to shift child care from the authorization to the reconciliation track.

The Committee on Ways and Means showed that the burden on low-income families in the failed budget agreement could be offset by EITC expansions. Moreover, if one combined such expansions with pending child care proposals, then the redistribution shifts in favor of the lower income groups were even more pronounced. Armed with these findings, legislators in both chambers and parties showed unsurpassed enthusiasm for the EITC although there was no guarantee that Congress would enact freestanding child care legislation with provisions expanding the earned income tax credit before it adjourned for the year.[99] Lawmakers also showed renewed interested in child care legislation because it was the vehicle to which the EITC was attached and because it was a way of offering something to low-income families in the context of the budget summit agreement. Child care was beginning to take on a new meaning because of its importance to an audience that extended beyond those heretofore involved with legislative negotiations regarding child care.

On October 9 both houses passed a revised budget resolution; although not a law, this resolution set the course for subsequent reconciliation legislation. The next step was for each chamber to pass a reconciliation bill based on the recommendations of each committee on how revenues would be increased or spending decreased to meet the reconciliation targets for reducing the deficit. Budget committees in each chamber were to compile the committee recommendations and draft the reconciliation bills. Following floor passage in each house, a conference committee would resolve the differences between the House and Senate versions of the reconciliation package and return the revised bill to each chamber for final approval, after which it would be sent to the president for his signature.

White House and Senate Reach Accord on Child Care

With the White House eager to enact EITC expansions to offset some of the damage from the new taxes included in the FY 1991 budget legislation, Senate Majority Leader Mitchell (also a member of the Finance Committee) ventured that the timing might be right to negotiate a child care agreement that would include the EITC provisions and be included in the Finance Committee's reconciliation recommendations. According to an interview with a Senate legislative assistant,

> Mitchell called Dodd and Kennedy, as chairs of the full and sub-committees with jurisdiction over child care, and asked them what they wanted to do. Their choices were to let [child care legislation] take its course in conference committee, which wasn't going well, or they could place child care legislation in reconciliation, where they ran the risk of it being stripped from the bill, because legislators could consider it extraneous.

Technically, reconciliation legislation is to include only deficit reduction provisions. Hence, the child care provisions could have been considered extraneous and been subject to a point of order. That is, any member could have raised a parliamentary objection to the inclusion of the child care provision on the basis that it violated the 1974 budget act's language, which allowed legislators to include in reconciliation only measures that would reduce the deficit. If a senator raised the point of order, then sixty senators would have to vote to waive it so that the child care provisions could be retained. It was a gamble: nobody knew if the separate child care conference would ever complete action, or if someone would raise the point of order, and if so, if there were enough votes to overturn it and retain the child care provisions.

Despite the uncertainty, Dodd and Kennedy decided to go the reconciliation route. Mitchell met with Bentsen, who agreed to place child care legislation in the Senate Finance Committee's reconciliation recommendations, along with the EITC expansions, his health care credit for low-income families, and his proposed At-Risk Child Care Program under Title IV-A of the Social Security Act, which he had already recommended to the child care tax conferees.

According to a Senate staff member, the next step was to bring on board Senator Robert Dole (R-Kans.), the minority leader. Dole wanted to see if the White House objected to including child care legislation in the reconciliation bill. White House staff responded that they definitely had problems with child care as passed in the Senate, especially with its mandated standards, effect of "regulating grandmas," lack of parental choice about vouchers, and failure to fund child care in religious organizations. White House staff claimed that if child care were to be included in the reconciliation bill as currently packaged, they would oppose the entire bill. However, some Senate staff saw a chance for success. Given the changes the Senate had already made in the bill immediately before it was brought to the floor in June 1989, there was good reason to believe that consensus could be reached with the White House. After all, based on negotiations with the NGA and religious organizations, standards were no longer mandatory, vouchers were included, and the bill allowed funding to go to child care programs run by religious institutions.

Mitchell discussed this with White House officials, who eventually agreed to give negotiations a try. He knew that the expansions of the EITC were important to Bush. They were a way of satisfying conservatives' demands and offering something to low-income working families. One OMB official explained, "I can't say enough how popular the EITC was, it was overwhelming, and there was this sense that you had to take the EITC with child care." Commenting on the linkage between the tax credit and child care legislation, OMB's Scully recalled, "It seemed as if Mitchell would have held on forever" in his insistence that any EITC expansion also include a new child care program.[100] In essence, the child care legislation became a quid pro quo for the EITC provisions. In addition, both the EITC and the child care provisions redistributed income to low-income families, which was important for budget negotiations.

Eventually, the White House figured that the importance of the EITC expansions warranted agreeing to some sort of child care legislation as long as it satisfied Bush's major conditions. OMB staff also estimated that they were in a good position to compromise because, as one OMB official noted, "Dodd was 'hell-bent' on getting child care, and would be open to negotiating." Scully explained that although child care was the most important social policy issue for the administration, "President Bush would have vetoed the entire reconciliation bill if it had a child care block grant without vouchers." This was in part because he wanted child care vouchers as a precedent for education vouchers, and because he saw vouchers as a way of promoting parental choice.[101]

Over the weekend of October 13 and 14, representatives from the White House domestic policy staff and OMB met with staff for Mitchell, Dodd, Kennedy, and Hatch to salvage child care legislation and work out a compromise that Bentsen would insert into the Finance Committee's reconciliation recommendations. They were under an extremely tight deadline because all committees had to submit their reconciliation recommendations to their respective chamber's budget committees no later than October 15. House delegates were deliberately excluded from the meeting, mostly because of concern from those on the Senate side that the House's unresolved jurisdictional conflicts over child care would impede negotiations.

On October 16 Dole and Mitchell announced that a compromise had been reached between the White House and the Senate leaders on child care.[102] In a landmark decision, Bush agreed to a new child care block grant, the Child Care and Development Block Grant (CCDBG). However, the agreement, which would be inserted in the Senate reconciliation bill, still had to go through the rest of the reconciliation process before being enacted.

Basically, White House and Senate negotiations approved the CCDBG with 75 percent of its funding allocated to direct services and 25 percent to a reserve fund for quality improvement and other purposes. Addressing Bush's emphasis on parental choice, lawmakers agreed that under the 75 percent for direct services, parents would be free to choose from a wide range of child care arrangements such as relatives, neighbors, schools, employers, family child care homes, and child care centers. Funds would be provided through grants, contracts, or vouchers, but all child care would have to meet state and local standards and be licensed, regulated, or registered to qualify for funding under the new legislation.

Lawmakers designated a portion of the reserve fund for quality improvement and another portion for before- and after-school care and early childhood education. While vouchers could be used for the 75 percent allocated for direct services, they were not allowed for these provisions. This was a major concession for OMB and the White House officials who had wanted vouchers for all types of care. The Senate–White House package required that each state receiving funding under the new CCDBG develop a child care plan, which would be administered by a lead state agency. To be eligible for assistance, a family would have to earn less than 75 percent of the state median income (the original ABC set eligibility at 115 percent of the state median) and have children under the age of thirteen. Eventually, the OMB and congressional leaders agreed to a $750 million authorization level for FY 1991, $825 million for FY 1992, and $925 million for FY 1993, totaling $2.5 billion over three years.

Child Care and Reconciliation: Win Some, Lose Some

The Senate and White House negotiations on child care were completed in time for Bentsen to include them in the Finance Committee's reconciliation recommendations to the Senate Budget Committee.[103] The Finance Committee also recommended increases in the amount of the EITC and adjustments in the credit for families with two or more children. It also made the DCTC refundable and approved Bentsen's child health tax credit.[104] On October 18 the Senate approved the budget reconciliation bill, including the Finance Committee's recommendations, by a vote of fifty-four to forty-six.

Before passing the reconciliation bill, the Senate voted sixty-nine to thirty-one (with the necessary three-fifths majority) to waive a procedural rule known as the Byrd rule, which could have limited the addition of extraneous provisions to the reconciliation bill. Waiving the procedural rule allowed senators to add nonrelevant amendments to the reconciliation bill without being subject to a point of order.[105] The decision reflected one of the important differences between the 1989 and the 1990 reconciliation bills. In 1990 the Senate had a more open and flexible approach that enabled the child care "entrepreneurs" to build their initiatives into the bill. With child care in the Senate reconciliation bill, it now awaited action by the House.

On October 15 the House Budget Committee, chaired by Representative Leon Panetta (D-Calif.), reported a budget reconciliation bill (H.R. 5835) that included an expansion of the EITC by $5 billion over five years.[106] However, before the House voted on the bill, Panetta introduced an amendment that "stripped the child care bill" because he felt it "should be dealt with outside of reconciliation."[107] Hawkins was outraged and urged members to oppose the reconciliation bill unless it included child care.[108] Panetta told Hawkins that the House leadership would protect child care in the reconciliation negotiations. On October 17 the House passed its budget reconciliation bill by a vote of 227 to 203, with only 10 Republicans voting for it. Although child care was not included, Foley stated that he thought it would be part of the final reconciliation package.[109]

By this point, both houses had passed reconciliation bills, but only the Senate version included a new block grant program for child care. Both houses had included provisions to expand the EITC in their reconciliation bills, with the Senate allowing adjustments for families with more than one child. The Senate had provisions to make the DCTC refundable for families with incomes below $28,000 and also included Bentsen's new At-Risk Child

Care Program and child health tax credit. It was now up to conferees on reconciliation to work out the differences.

The nagging issue of how to distribute taxes among various income levels was paramount at this point. Democrats on the House Committee on Ways and Means were acutely aware of the distribution charts for the budget summit agreement that showed how people in the lowest quintile carried most of the burden of the budget summit plan. Wanting to avoid this with the reconciliation bill, Rostenkowski, chair of the Committee on Ways and Means, and Bentsen, chair of the Senate Finance Committee, sought to redistribute as much of the tax burden as possible away from the lower quintile.[110] As a congressional aide explained in an interview with the author, "The vehicle that redistributes money the best to the lower quintile is the earned income tax credit, . . . so they [legislators] went for it big."

In the last minutes of reconciliation negotiations, Rostenkowski and Bentsen single-handedly expanded the EITC beyond what anyone had heretofore imagined, increasing it by nearly $18 billion over five years by raising the amount of the credit and adjusting it for family size. As a result of Bentsen's and Rostenkowski's decision, the income distribution charts showed a handsome redistribution to the lowest quintile.[111] The costs of the tax credits and At-Risk Child Care Program were to be covered by a permanent extension of the telephone tax, which was included in both the House and Senate versions of reconciliation. In the face of the failed budget summit agreement, the EITC took on more importance for both parties, as did its "sidekick," child care legislation.[112]

According to those involved in budget reconciliation negotiations between Bentsen and Rostenkowski, at the last minute Sununu called and insisted on a new supplemental tax credit for families with infants. With this credit on the books, the conferees dropped the Senate's request to make the DCTC refundable. As one Senate aide explained, "With the agreement to expand the EITC adjusting for family size, and the insistence on the [infant] credit from Republicans, there were too many refundable tax credits, and something had to go."

By October 20, based on discussions among Dodd, Kennedy, Hatch, Hawkins, and the White House, the reconciliation conferees had made some minor adjustments in the child care provisions, mostly to satisfy House conferees who were angry at being excluded from White House–Senate talks. To appease Hawkins, they increased the proportion of reserve funds allocated for before- and after-school care and early childhood development. To compensate, they decreased the allocations for quality improvement.

On October 27 the House approved the reconciliation bill by a vote of 228 to 200. The Senate passed it by a vote of fifty-four to forty-six. Bush signed it into law (P.L. 101-508) on November 5 (for a summary of the final bill, see table 4.1).

TABLE 4.1 Summary of Child Care Provisions in
1990 Omnibus Budget Reconciliation Act (P.L. 101-508)

Provision	Authorization	Eligibility	Description
Child Care and Development Block Grant	$750 million in fiscal year 1991 (FY91), $825 million in FY92, $925 million in FY93, such sums as necessary in FY94–95	Children below age thirteen in families with working parents and family income below 75% of state median	75% of funds were for child care services available through grants, contracts, or vouchers, including care by relatives or in churches; parents receiving vouchers could select any licensed or regulated provider. 25% was reserved for quality improvements, early childhood development, and before- and after-school child care.[1] Funding to states was based on a formula that took into account number of children below age five and number receiving assistance through School Lunch Program.
At-Risk Child Care Program (expanding Title IV-A of the Social Security Act)	$1.5 billion over five years; plus an additional $50 million starting in FY92 to help states improve licensing and training	Families at risk of becoming welfare-dependent	Capped entitlement, permanently authorized at $300 million annually. State allocations were based on the number of children under age thirteen in a state relative to the total number of all such children in the U.S. The program ran under guidelines similar to the Aid to Families with Dependent Children child care programs.
Earned Income Tax Credit (EITC) expansion	$12.4 billion over five years	Working families with children under age nineteen; amount of credit varies according to family income; new law also allowed for number of qualifying children in a family	For FY94, projected income eligibility ranged from approximately $8,030 to $23,890 (with a phaseout for families with incomes above $12,650).
Supplemental Credit for Infants	$0.7 billion over five years	Working families with child under age one	Same income limits and phase outs as the EITC; credit rate was 5% of income.

[1] States were required to allocate 75 percent of their reserve funds for early childhood development and before- and after-school care, 20 percent for quality improvement activities, and 5 percent for their own discretionary use.

Source: U.S. House, Committee on Ways and Means, 1992 Green Book, 102d Cong., 2d sess., 5 May 1992, 949–52, 969–74, 1015–19.

Thus, the reconciliation bill with landmark child care legislation met Democratic and GOP goals of helping low-income working families with children. It was not the comprehensive legislation of 1971, but it was a breakthrough in many ways.

Upon enactment of the bill, CDF and the other alliance members claimed victory for getting Congress to pass major child care legislation after nearly twenty years. Blank and her colleagues were quick to note the similarities between the final CCDBG and the original ABC drafted in 1987 in that both were grants to states for a new child care program. Conservatives were pleased that the 1990 bill included tax revisions, parental choice through the mandated use of vouchers, and no discrimination against parents choosing to stay at home to care for their children. The USCC and NGA were satisfied because their recommendations were incorporated into the final bill. The strict secularists opposed the final legislation because it allowed vouchers and religious preference in employment and admissions. Although the CCDBG had a small set-aside for school-based programs, it was not nearly as much as Hawkins and the education organizations would have liked.

Comparing 1971 and 1990

Why was child care legislation enacted in 1990 and not in 1971? Certainly, the rise in the proportion of working women with young children gave a competitive edge to those advocating a new child care program.

By the mid- and late 1980s, several measures of women's participation in the labor force passed the fiftieth percentile. For example, by 1985, 53 percent of married women with children under the age of six were in the labor force. In 1988, for the first time, more than 50 percent of married women with a child under the age of one were in the workforce.[113] Moreover, compared with the 1970s, there were more single mothers who needed child care assistance. Thus, between 1971 and 1990, women's participation in the labor force was more than a rising trend; it had become a way of life for many American women, including those with young children. However, the major increase in working women, which was so frequently mentioned during child care deliberations, had occurred almost a decade before the enactment of the 1990 child care legislation, illustrating that a lag time may be needed before social policy catches up with demographic trends.

While advocates of federal child care legislation had female participation rates in the workforce on their side, opponents of a federal child care program could still point to the large numbers of children who received most of their care from relatives or through other informal arrangements. In 1988 approximately 44 percent of all children under five years of age whose mothers were employed were cared for by relatives.[114] Families with annual incomes under $25,000 relied on relatives for care more than those with incomes above $40,000 (46 compared with 26 percent).[115] Thus, conservatives had a valid point in calling attention to the large number of low-income families that might not benefit from federally subsidized center-based care. But some families could not afford high-quality child care, so they were forced to rely on relatives and other forms of informal care. If out-of-home care were more accessible, affordable, and of better quality, then perhaps more low-income families would use it.

Another difference between 1971 and 1990 pertained to the politics of the presidency. Unlike Nixon, Bush had strong reasons to enact child care legislation. These included the advantages that child care legislation offered in the wake of a failed budget summit, his reversal of his campaign pledge not to raise taxes, his commitment to low-income working families with children, and his need for a domestic policy success in the face of dropping approval ratings among members of Congress and the public at large.[116] Furthermore, Bush was the first president who did not have to contend with child care as it related to welfare reform. The enactment of the FSA of 1988 took care of child care under welfare, at least for the time being.

Moreover, by the time Bush was in office high-level OMB staff had assumed centralized roles as policy negotiators for the president. Continuing the trend that had begun under President Reagan, OMB became the focal point for negotiating not only budget policies but other domestic policy issues as well.[117] Thus, Scully and his staff assumed major responsibility for child care policy, including negotiating with staff on Capitol Hill. The centralization of power within OMB enhanced Bush's ability to present a united front to the various constituencies involved with child care legislation, and it facilitated the final negotiations that folded child care into the reconciliation bill. This was a distinct difference from Nixon's presidency, during which OMB had played an influential but less visible role and had sparred with Elliot Richardson at HEW.

The reconciliation bill itself was another major difference between 1971 and 1990. In 1971 there was no alternative vehicle for child care legislation, nor did budget politics figure as prominently in domestic politics as in the late 1980s.

Another aspect of the legislative process that distinguished the course and outcome of the child care debates in the late 1980s was multiple referral of House bills. In 1975 the House revised its rules to permit review of legislation by multiple committees as a way of breaking up "committee fiefdoms" and enhancing coordination among committees. Before that, both chambers had employed single referral to committees as a way of permitting "each committee to be the sole arbiter of legislation within its jurisdiction."[118] Between the 94th (1975–1976) and 101st Congresses (1989–1990) the proportion of measures assigned to more than one House committee increased from 6.0 to 18.2 percent.[119]

In 1989 House Speaker Wright referred ABC jointly to both committees. Representative Hawkins, chair of the Committee on Education and Labor, felt that the Committee on Ways and Means should limit its scope to indirect child care subsidies in the form of tax credits. But members of the Committee on Ways and Means countered that federal child care entitlements, such as those under Title XX and Title IV-A of the Social Security Act, fell under their jurisdiction. Hence, they had a legitimate interest in all aspects of child care policy.

These jurisdictional disputes delayed the progress of child care legislation. Several congressional staffers and lobbyists commented that the final decision to approve both the At-Risk Child Care Program and the CCDBG reflected jurisdictional as much as substantive concerns. Giving a piece of the pie (the At-Risk Child Care Program) to the Committee on Ways and Means was important as a way to get the committee to support the final agreement.

Although multiple referral has always been an option in the Senate, it is rarely used because there is a "relative ease with which senators can exert leverage on a wide range of issues, even those that lie outside of their committee's jurisdiction."[120] Therefore, committee turf battles were less of an issue in the Senate's handling of child care.

Finally, other congressional structures contributed to the politics of child care legislation. For example, few would dispute the importance of the House Select Committee on Children, Youth, and Families, especially for the agenda-setting phase. When the House approved a resolution (H.R. 107) in March 1993 to discontinue funding for its four select committees, legislators and organized interests devoted to child care and other children's issues were left with a void.

Another important committee in the agenda-setting process was the Subcommittee on Human Resources of the Committee on Ways and Means. It was one of many subcommittees formed as a result of the congressional reforms of the mid-1970s aimed at diluting the entrenched seniority system and loosening the hold of the powerful chair of the full committee, Representative Wilbur Mills (D-Ark.), on his colleagues.[121] These changes signaled a "new participatory politics" and an attempt to shift the concentration of power from the hands of a small group of senior members.[122] These changes were relevant to the politics of child care in that as acting chair of the Subcommittee on Human Resources, Downey had a podium for presenting his bill in the House. It enabled him to influence the agenda-setting for child care by holding hearings and to promote his legislative proposal as a formidable alternative to the ABC proposal.

In both 1971 and 1990 Edelman offered "intellectual and organizational leadership."[123] Even if her persistence in the later years was due to her desire to avoid another personal defeat, her role in enacting child care legislation was unique and pivotal. CDF's mobilization of state child care coalitions, leadership on legislative strategizing, rallying of groups in Washington, and success in working the media gave the Alliance for Better Child Care a presence and influence that far surpassed those of national organizations involved with child care decades earlier.

One might have expected women's groups to be in the forefront of the debate about child care in the late 1980s given the tremendous influx of women into the workforce, but they were not. Nonetheless, a few national women's groups, such as NWLC, AJLI, and YWCA/YMCA, were active members of the alliance. Other women's groups, such as AAUW, NOW Legal Defense and Education Fund, the Girls Club of America, and LWV, were also alliance members. For some women's groups, most notably NCJW and NOW, the final bill posed too strong a threat to the Constitution's separation of church and state. Consequently, they opposed it, even though they had been ardent and long-standing advocates of a federal child care program.

The proliferation of conservative organizations and think tanks enabled Bush and congressional Republicans to offer proposals that became integral to the final legislative outcomes. These organizations' well-funded advocacy activities, launched in the 1970s, made them a force to be reckoned with in the late 1980s when child care politics were under debate.

The battle over child care legislation between 1987 and 1990 resulted in the enactment of the first federal child care program—the CCDBG—not connected with an existing program such as welfare. The block grant, combined with the At-Risk Child Care Program, marked the first time politicians in the executive and legislative branches of government reached an agreement about the role of the federal government in the child care arena. The 1990 child care package also illustrated the importance of combining tax and programmatic initiatives.

As always, child care was a lightning rod for a host of issues, including the role of women, balance between church and state, and relationships between federal and state government. These controversies did not end with the enactment of the 1990 bill. They erupted again with the promulgation of the regulations for the block grant and the At-Risk Child Care Program in 1991 and 1992.

5   Regulations, Implementation, and High Expectations, 1991–1993

Following the enactment of the CCDBG and the At-Risk Child Care Program in 1990, the focus shifted to the executive branch for the promulgation of regulations to implement both programs. The battles over the regulations were nearly as contentious as those surrounding the legislation. The difference was that the setting was primarily the executive branch, in particular the newly created Administration for Children and Families (ACF) in HHS. By mid-1992 ACF had issued final regulations for each of the programs, and the states launched child care programs using new federal funds. The 1992 election of President Bill Clinton signaled to some that a unified government with Democrats controlling both the legislative and executive branches of government would provide new opportunities for making child care policy. In his first term Clinton promoted changes in many aspects of family policy. But child care took a back seat to other presidential and congressional priorities. Thus, federal child care policymaking in the early 1990s was characterized by regulatory conflicts and transitions in the executive branch that produced modest changes in policy outcomes.

Placing Child Care Regulations in Context

Controversies surrounding federal child care regulations in the early 1990s focused on the balance between state and federal governments and how far government should go in ensuring high-quality, accessible, and affordable child care. Underlying these themes were the persisting ideological conflicts over nonparental care for young children. Before 1990, federal regulation of child care had a "checkered history."[1] In the absence of federal regulations, the states had become the "cornerstone of government child care policies in the United States."[2] Federal regulations for the CCDBG and the At-Risk Child Care Program were imposed on a regulatory system characterized by differences among federal child care programs and tremendous variation among states. Regulatory battles over child care pitted conservatives, who favored devolution of social programs to state governments, against liberals, who continued to push for a strong federal presence in child care policymaking.

Regulating Child Care

Before discussing the politics of child care regulations, certain key concepts warrant explanation. Typically, states develop regulatory policies for each type of early childhood program (i.e., child care centers, family day care, or group home care). States differ in their definitions of these terms, but usually *child care centers* serve ten or more children from infancy to school age under a variety of auspices, including local governments, employers, religious institutions, national child care chains, and independent providers.[3] *Small family child care* is defined as "care of no more than six children by a single caregiver in [that person's] home, including the caregiver's children age twelve or younger." *Large family child care* (also referred to as group child care) is "care in the caregiver's residence employing a full-time assistant and serving 7 to 12 children, including the caregiver's children age twelve or younger."[4] However, states may deviate from these parameters. For example, as of 1999 South Dakota exempted family child care providers from regulation if they were not receiving public funds and cared for twelve or fewer children.[5]

According to the NAEYC, "the fundamental purpose of public regulation is to protect children from harm, not only threats to their immediate physical health and safety but also threats of long-term developmental impairment." The emphasis on development is based on extensive research showing the linkage between early childhood development and later learning.[6] The regulation of child care is a state function aimed at protecting the safety and well-being of children in child care settings. States vary in their "methods and scope of regulation," using processes such as licensing, registration, and certification, which can differ in meaning from state to state.[7]

Licensing is a government function that establishes and enforces "minimum requirements for the legal operation of programs available to the public."[8] Typically licensed facilities must pass an on-site inspection as a prerequisite to licensing and must undergo periodic inspections thereafter. Approximately 102,000 child care centers were licensed or certified in 1999, representing a nearly 16 percent increase compared with the number in 1991.[9] Although most child care centers are licensed, the majority of family child care providers are not.[10] Either they operate illegally, or the number of children they serve falls below the one for which the state requires them to be regulated in any way.[11]

Some states use other regulatory mechanisms, such as registration or self-certification, for family child care providers. *Registration* differs from licensing in that inspections are usually not required before a provider can open for business. In some states registration of family child care providers entails only their completing a health and safety checklist or other forms of self-reporting.[12] The terms "licensing" and "registration" may be used interchangeably for family child care providers. As of 1999 more than 290,000 family child care homes were regulated. Most were small family child care providers.

In recent years, the use of family child care has decreased among preschoolers with employed mothers. This may reflect parents' uneasiness about relying on a minimally regulated arrangement with providers who lack substitute staff in case of illness or vacation. The decrease in the reported use of family child care may also be due to changes in some states' regulatory procedures and systems of data collection.[13]

In contrast to licensing, which is a mandatory government function, *accreditation* is a voluntary procedure under the auspices of the private sector, which ensures that programs have met standards beyond competency and offer high-quality care. It complements, but does not replace, licensing. A small but growing proportion of child care programs are accredited. Moreover, many states are using CCDBG quality-improvement funds to help programs become accredited or are providing higher reimbursement rates for accredited facilities than for those that lack such credentials.[14] A number of child care programs are accredited by entities affiliated with national organizations, such as the NAEYC, the National Association for Family

Child Care, and the National Early Childhood Program Accreditation Commission. Many providers are accredited by organizations that serve private schools, religiously affiliated programs, care for school-age children (i.e., the National School-Age Care Alliance), or other social service agencies.[15]

Three variables comprise the cornerstone of debates on child care quality: group size, child–staff ratios, and the caregivers' qualifications. Researchers have consistently identified how these "structural factors" affect the quality of care and children's development.[16] Small groups, low child–staff ratios, and well-trained caregivers all contribute to high-quality programs. Children in high-quality programs demonstrate better outcomes in areas such as cognitive functioning, language development, and social skills. However, research has shown that the quality of care among informal caregivers, such as family child care or child care by relatives, is often mediocre either because the caregivers serve a small number of children, which exempts them from state regulation, or because they are not regulated and operating illegally. Although not all unregulated care is of poor quality, the quality of care in regulated programs is usually better than that in unregulated ones.[17]

Because of the importance of health and safety in child care settings, the American Academy of Pediatrics and the American Public Health Association developed voluntary health and safety performance standards to prevent injury and illness in child care settings.[18] These are often considered model standards for states and child care providers. However, despite widespread knowledge of what is required to provide high-quality early childhood programs in terms of child health, safety, development, and education, many programs fail to do so.[19] This is true for child care centers as well as for family child care and for children of all ages. Furthermore, many states fail to set regulations that reflect scientific evidence.[20]

Some states exempt or partially exempt certain types of child care providers from state regulations. For example, three states exempt child care centers run by religiously affiliated centers, and eleven states exempt school-based preschool programs. Many states exempt child care facilities run by or on the property of federal, state, or local governments from licensing.[21]

Several court rulings have supported the right of states to exempt religiously affiliated providers from state child care regulations.[22] Other decisions by state courts have upheld a state's rights to apply the same standards to religious child care programs as to secular ones. William T. Gormley Jr., an expert on child care regulation, succinctly described the judicial and policy implications of exempting religiously affiliated child care facilities:

Thus, the question is not whether states have the right to apply all regulations to church-run day care centers (they do), or whether they have the right to exempt church-run centers (they do), but whether it is wise to do so. Answering that question requires shifting from legal arguments to policy arguments. Policy analysts might ask, What are the consequences for young children?[23]

Gormley concluded that if the state's role is to guarantee the health and safety of children in child care, then state child care regulations do not diminish the rights of church-based child care programs, but rather guarantee a certain minimum level of care for families and children using those services. Moreover, exemptions and partial exemptions make it too easy for church-based centers (and other providers) to overlook their responsibility to care for disadvantaged children who benefit most from the safeguards resulting from regulations.[24]

Child Care Regulations Ignite Feuds over Congressional Intent

With these issues in the background, the proposed regulations for child care, issued in 1991, sparked controversy over whether HHS was following the intent of the 1990 statute. HHS officials remained firm in their claims that parental choice was paramount in the final legislation. They repeated the familiar refrains of conservative organized interests and President Bush that any new federal child care policy must not impose burdensome requirements that could have the effect of decreasing the availability of child care providers and thereby diminish parental choice. In contrast, some members of Congress, state legislators, public welfare officials, and organizations representing children and family advocates felt "that the regulations inappropriately emphasize[d] parental choice at the expense of other priorities established in the law," such as "improving the quality of child care and granting States broad discretion in program operation and regulatory activities."[25] Many lawmakers who worked on child care legislation and members of the Alliance for Better Child Care thought that HHS failed to acknowledge the compromises that had been made in enacting the 1990 law. They argued that the regulations seriously restricted the states' flexibility, which was a cornerstone of the legislative negotiations. From their perspective, the Bush administration had endorsed the 1990 law giving states flexibility and then undermined that process in the regulations by showing preference for parental choice.

Representative Thomas Downey was the most outspoken critic of HHS. At the hearings he held in September 1991, he lambasted HHS officials for the liberties they took in drafting the regulations. As he explained:

> Apparently the Department of Health and Human Services ha[s] proposed rules for the administration of this program that ignore the details and the outcome of last year's debate. They have ignored the clear intent of Congress which was expressed throughout its deliberations over child care. They have written regulations that replace legislative intent with misguided ideology.[26]

Representative Dale Kildee made a similar point, adding concerns about the well-being of children:

> But I can't recognize where the administration found authority for those regulations in the bill. . . . But if you do find any ambiguity, resolve that ambiguity in favor of the most vulnerable element here, the child. They are the most vulnerable ones. We will all survive here. You will all survive out there, but children really depend upon a government that is very concerned about their health and safety. Resolve your doubts that way. You didn't resolve your doubts that way. You resolved your doubts really in favor of choice.[27]

Jo Anne B. Barnhart, the newly appointed head of the ACF, defended her agency's position:

> In relation to the issue of congressional intent . . . I think that that is clearly an issue where . . . there appears to be no absolute consensus among the Members of the Congress what congressional intent was. . . . Certainly, as the person with responsibility for administering the Aid to Families with Dependent Children program with a caseload of over 11 million people and 90 percent of those being single-parent families headed by women, I am well aware on a daily basis that Ozzie and Harriet is not the predominant situation. But I still believe . . . that the legislation and the conference report provided for us to afford

those women . . . the same equity, the same options, the same range of choice as any other American parent.[28]

Downey was unrelenting:

> Your job, Ms. Barnhart, if I may have the last word, is to faithfully execute the laws as we write and intend them. It is not to serve in some crusade about poor women or about what you believe to be the intent of the Congress. The clear unadulterated language of the legislation, if followed scrupulously, would not by any stretch of any imagination have allowed you to write the regulations that you have.[29]

Groups and legislators on both sides of the issue launched extensive lobbying efforts in response to the proposed regulations. Many in the child care advocacy community argued that the proposed regulation for the CCDBG used the parental choice language as a way of evading state child care regulations and standards. Helen Blank at CDF and her colleagues at other organizations from the alliance had a sense of "here we go again" as they reconvened to lobby HHS regarding the regulations. Although the alliance never came back with the same strength it had had during the legislative battles, the regulatory battles entailed an all-out effort among many of the same groups. CDF worked closely with other organizational partners from the alliance, in particular APWA, NCSL, NWLC, and an array of state and federal child care advocacy organizations. Using similar strategies as during the legislative phase, CDF launched a three-pronged approach focusing on the media, Congress, and grassroots child care activists. Their efforts resulted in articles and editorials published in the *New York Times*, the *Washington Post*, and *Newsday* and in letters from advocates across the country to HHS officials expressing opposition to aspects of the proposed regulations. An editorial in the *New York Times* said that the proposed regulations gave child care for families at-risk of being on welfare "a green light to be lousy."[30] A *Washington Post* editorial described the politics surrounding the proposed regulations as a "contest of imagery versus reality that reality should easily win" and asked that the proposed regulations "be rescinded."[31] Barnhart responded by speaking out against what she called the government stepping in as a "national nanny to tell the poor what is 'appropriate' for them."[32] Nancy Amidei, a professor of social work at the University of Utah, published an opinion piece in the *Los Angeles Times* claiming that the regulations "read like political documents written chiefly to please two groups — religious fundamentalists, who operate child care that is exempt from standards in some states, and right-wing groups, who can't get past the fact that women, including mothers, are in the workforce to stay."[33]

But the media were not the ones settling the political battles. So, once again, the champions of a federal child care program clashed with those wanting to minimize the federal government's role in child care policymaking. This time, they fought their battles in the regulatory arena.

Executive Branch Politics and Policies

In the late 1980s and early 1990s, conflicts over federal regulations were not limited to child care programs. "Bureaucratic foot-dragging, complex directives from Congress, and in some cases ideological hostility" characterized the regulatory process for many important laws enacted in the late 1980s. Because of ideological disagreements between a Democratic Congress and a Republican president, Congress often wrote "highly prescriptive laws" that were arduous to implement, and agency officials often wrote rules that "distort[ed]" or "thwart[ed]" the intent of Congress.[34]

Other bureaucratic delays emanated from requirements that President Reagan had initiated through a series of executive orders. These orders called for executive branch officials to evaluate proposed regulations for their affect on areas such as family well-being, federalism, and regulatory impact.[35] But the delays from these requirements paled in comparison with the delays from OMB staff wanting to ensure that the child care regulations adhered to the Bush administration's policy preferences. An official at HHS, who was closely involved with the child care regulations, explained in an interview:

> OMB was not involved in the formulation of the regulations, but intimately involved in changing the regulations to meet the political needs of the Bush administration. . . . I recognize that an administration has a right to try to influence policies, but this went to the extreme. . . . We had the final regulations written in no time, but the negotiations with OMB slowed things down.

Final regulations for the child care provisions in the 1990 budget reconciliation law were issued in August 1992, more than a year after the initial rule for each program. This delay left the child care policy community quibbling over the details of the regulations, while states went as far as they could to establish new child care programs according to the letter of the law and to the proposed rules.

A final aspect of HHS that warrants noting is that staff who handled child care regulations were reorganized in April 1991 when the ACF was formed and Barnhart was appointed its director. She had previously directed the Family Support Administration, which administered AFDC, child support, and other social service programs. Before that, she had been a consultant to the Reagan White House on welfare reform. Programs under the ACF included the CCDBG, administered by the Child Care Division, and the At-Risk Child Care Program, administered by the Office of Family Assistance, which had authority over all AFDC programs. Other programs under ACF were Head Start, child abuse, child support, and community services.[36]

Reasons for establishing ACF varied from internal HHS politics to legitimate concerns about the importance of increasing the visibility of policies for vulnerable families and children. However, because the At-Risk Child Care Program and the CCDBG had different statutory authorities—At-Risk under Title IV-A of the Social Security Act and the block grant as a separate discretionary program—ACF staff had to coordinate across program agencies in its efforts to provide "seamless service" to families and providers participating in federal child care programs.[37]

CCDBG Regulations Spark Feuds over Standards and Other Concerns

Witnesses at congressional hearings often referred to the regulations as if there were one set for both programs. But ACF issued separate regulations for the At-Risk Child Care Program and the CCDBG. Each set of regulations raised different yet overlapping concerns. Both sets of rules raised questions regarding the ability of states to establish different standards and payment rates for regulated versus unregulated federally subsidized child care. Many policymakers argued that regulated care guarantees a minimum level of quality and may impose additional costs on providers, and that such providers should be offered incentives for striving to attain a certain standard of care. In contrast, HHS and other interest groups and legislators argued that regardless of whether a provider was regulated, parents had a right to use federal funds to select their provider of choice.

On June 6, 1991, HHS issued an interim final rule for the CCDBG. Interim rules are binding until final rules are published. In justifying issuing an interim rule instead of a proposed rule, HHS noted that "Congress only allowed ten months between the passage of the Act [November 1990] and the availability of the appropriation [September 1991] and thus the start of the program." This did not allow enough time for review of a proposed rule, its revision, and the publication of a final rule. States needed a regulation in place to develop their child care plans.[38]

Federal officials explained that they were going into more detail in issuing regulations for the CCDBG than for other block grant programs because of the need to use the regulations to strike "the right balance between family and federalism as embodied in the Act." They were concerned that the "broad State discretion" under the law might "be exercised at the expense of parental choice." Furthermore, because the CCDBG was new, it was important "to establish Federal policy with regard to the program at the outset."[39]

The CCDBG interim rule generated 1,475 comments, 62 percent of which supported the interim rule as published. Another 15 percent agreed with the general thrust of the rule, but cited specific suggestions for change. Most of the organizations and individuals supporting the rule were affiliated with religious institutions or conservative interests that agreed with the regulations' emphasis on parental choice. Conservatives who pushed for parental choice during the legislative battles were pleased with the interim rule but urged HHS to place more emphasis on vouchers, parental choice, and families in which a parent stayed home to care for the children. Robert Rector at the Heritage Foundation applauded HHS for allowing all parents assisted under the grant to receive a voucher, giving them the right to use the voucher in child care "programs that offer religious worship," and for prohibiting states from attaching extra regulations to the use of vouchers that would restrict parental choice. Rector also considered it appropriate that states were exempting religious providers from "building and health requirements beyond those already pertaining to the operation of the church itself."[40] The CWA and Eagle Forum took similar positions.[41] Gary L. Bauer, president of the FRC, expressed concern "that the regulations explicitly promote every child care option except the best — care by a child's own parents." He called on states to "protect the interests of parents who prefer, for whatever reason, informal home-based arrangements or religious programs."[42]

In contrast to conservative groups that embraced the focus on parental choice, organizations such as the CWLA, NEA, NWLC, NCJW, and NOW Legal Defense and Education Fund opposed the regulations' giving greater weight to parental choice than to what they thought was the more important goal of allowing states to impose requirements that promoted the safety and well-being of children in federally funded child care settings.[43] Similarly, NCSL argued that the language on parental choice in the regulations "would preempt state authority to establish or enforce standards for health and safety."[44] But NCSL, CDF, and their allies on this issue among labor unions, education, and women's and many other groups were outnumbered. Less than 20 percent of the comments opposed the regulations or argued that they "put too much emphasis on parental choice."[45]

Health and Safety Requirements

Of the proposed regulations, the CCDBG rules pertaining to standards generated the most vehement protests. The 1990 legislation authorizing the CCDBG required all child care providers funded under the law to be licensed, regulated, or registered. The law allowed states to impose more stringent standards and regulatory requirements on providers funded under the block grant than on other child care providers. It also required states to have health and safety procedures in place for the prevention and control of infectious diseases as well as procedures ensuring building and premise safety and health and safety training appropriate to the setting. These health and safety requirements applied to all providers funded by the block grant, except to the children's grandparents, aunts, and uncles. The states were required to establish procedures for monitoring the health and safety practices of providers that were exempt from state licensing rules.[46]

The interim CCDBG rule took this language one step further. It called for an "effects test," wherein states were prevented from implementing requirements pertaining to standards, registration, and other issues if they resulted in restriction of parental choice, exclusion of categories of care (i.e., center-based, group home, or family care) and types of providers (i.e., nonprofit, religiously affiliated, or relatives), or reduction of significant numbers of providers in any category or type of care. In the preamble to the regulation (which is not legally binding but emphasizes key priorities), HHS explained that this language was needed to balance "competing principles" in the law and the legislative history, in particular the tension between respecting maximum parental choice and allowing the states flexibility in setting child care requirements. According to an analysis of the situation by the Congressional Research Service, "The regulation aim[ed] to prevent States from establishing 'excessive and ill-designed requirements or procedures' that could limit providers' willingness to participate in the program."[47]

CDF complained that the "regulatory provisions on health and safety fail[ed] to comply with statutory requirements" and urged HHS not to deny states "the tools they need to provide" needed protection.[48] HHS remained firm in its emphasis on parental choice. It explained that all child care providers, even those exempt from regulation under state law, had to meet some minimum health and safety standards. But the standards for exempt providers funded under the grant could vary from (and be more lax than) those nonexempt providers had to meet.[49] For many child care advocates, the fact that CCDBG did not require exempt providers funded under the law to adhere to the same standards as other providers was disturbing because of its potential to compromise the health and safety of children in subsidized child care settings. Representative Downey and other legislators expressed similar dismay over the language in the proposed rule for the At-Risk Child Care Program, as discussed later.

The section of the interim block grant regulations concerning registration of providers who were not licensed or regulated raised similar protests. The NGA was one of many organizations that opposed this aspect of the final rule. It "urge[d] HHS to give states maximum flexibility to establish meaningful registration processes and to maintain or establish minimum health and safety requirements." It argued that "compliance with parental choice provisions can be monitored through state plans to ensure that overburdensome provisions are not implemented."[50]

Despite these arguments, HHS made very few changes to the sections of the regulations pertaining to state and local regulatory requirements. It tried to clarify the confusion that the interim regulations had generated in this area. The final rule reiterated that states could not impose standards that would limit parental choice.

Use of the 75 Percent Funds for Quality Improvements

Another controversial aspect of the regulations pertained to the block grant's statutory requirement that states spend 75 percent of their allotted funds on child care services and activities designed to improve the supply and quality of care. The remaining 25 percent were to be spent on early childhood development services, before- and after-school programs, and quality improvements.[51] In the conference report, Congress specified that a "preponderance" of the 75 percent of funds be spent on "child care services" and a "minimum amount on other authorized services."[52] This was an attempt to ensure that most of the funding went to services and not administrative costs. HHS interpreted this in the regulations by placing a 15 percent cap (falling to 10 percent after the second year) on the 75 percent funds that a state spends on activities to improve the availability and quality of child care and all other nonservice expenditures. This meant that at least 90 percent of the 75 percent allocated for child care services had to be spent directly on child care.[53]

One of the most ardent critics of the provisions pertaining to the allocation of funds was Bernest Cain, a state legislator from Oklahoma, who testified on behalf of the NCSL at congressional hearings in 1991. His words illustrated the intensity with which he and others opposed the proposed rule:

> We went to the National Conference on State Legislatures, down in Florida, . . . and they asked us how many of the State legislatures approve of these regulations? There was one person and 150 people spoke out against it. . . . We spoke out strongly because these regulations rape the bill that was passed. . . .
>
> Let me tell you in our State we pay more for zookeepers and dog-catchers than we do for child care workers and this legislation says that we can't use money for improving the quality on this; it has go to be used for new slots. Now, that's absurd. . . .
>
> Let us have some flexibility. If we mess it up, you come back and put these regulations on us. Tell us we have to open up all of these slots. If we are not dealing with quality, come back and deal with us.[54]

State and local officials generally wanted more flexibility in how they could use funds, especially to allow states with programs of poor quality to use CCDBG funds to raise the level of care. As Peter M. Weinstein, majority leader of the Florida Senate, explained:

> If we are to serve all children equally, additional training for child care workers . . . and enhanced resource and referral services . . . are vital.

By requiring that 90% of the funds set aside for direct services/administration/quality improvements be spent on the purchase of child care slots, Florida's ability to utilize these new dollars to ensure that critical initiatives are adequately funded will be greatly diminished.[55]

The NGA registered similar concerns. Because of the influence of the governors and their role in implementing the block grant, their concerns carried considerable weight. Ray Scheppach, executive director of the NGA explained:

States have reported that they anticipate their administrative costs to be somewhere between 8–15 percent. A 10 percent cap will leave virtually no funds in this category for quality improvement or to expand availability.

We encourage the Administration to remove the proposed cap on expenditures for administrative costs, quality improvements and availability and allow states to determine the use of the 75 percent of the overall funds. This would be consistent with existing block grants which allow states maximum flexibility in spending.[56]

In urging HHS to review the allocation of funds under the grant, David Liederman at CWLA referred to the JOBS and Transitional Child Care (TCC) programs in which states found that the costs of administering certificate programs exceeded 15 percent.[57] Senators Orrin Hatch, Christopher Dodd, and Edward Kennedy also were concerned with this aspect of the regulations. They wrote,

Nothing in the legislative history of the statute suggests a set-aside as high as 90 percent. To the contrary, the final statutory language . . . was designed to give states maximum flexibility to allocate these funds for a variety of activities based on the needs of individual states. . . . Thus, unless [states] are given greater flexibility, virtually none of the funds under this portion of the block grant will be used to improve availability and quality, thus nullifying our intent.[58]

Among the comments submitted to HHS in response to the interim CCDBG rule, 26 percent wanted an increase in the percentage of funding for quality improvement and other activities in the 75 percent "services" component of the grant. In the final regulations, HHS made some concessions to those concerned about the allocation of funds. The department allowed states to petition for spending up to 15 percent for administrative and other authorized activities, as long as the states could document that the expenditures for operating vouchers and related consumer education comprised at least 10 percent of funds under this section. In addition, HHS expanded the definition of activities that could be included in the quality component.[59]

Other Payment and Administrative Issues

The interim CCDBG regulations allowed states to set different payment rates for different categories of care (i.e., center-based, family, or in-home care) but not for different types of providers (i.e., licensed or accredited programs) within those categories. Therefore, payment rates could not differ for licensed and unlicensed providers within the same category. This outraged many who felt that it prevented states from setting higher rates for care that may cost more due to licensing. They argued that eliminating the payment differential for licensed or other forms of regulated care seriously reduced the incentives to states and providers to improve child care through licensing and other mechanisms. The NWLC was one of the many groups opposing the interim regulations in this area. As it explained:

> This policy is not only inconsistent with the statute, but is ill-advised as well. Many states currently pay higher rates for licensed or high-quality care than for other care. Such policies provide an incentive for providers to meet licensing standards and accommodate the higher costs of higher quality care. . . . The statute clearly contemplated— even required—that states would vary payment rates based on such factors as quality and regulatory requirements to which they are subject.[60]

In the final CCDBG regulation, HHS eased these constraints by permitting states "to establish different payment rates within a category of care" as long as the differential did not exceed 10 percent. States also had to document that their payment rates were based on actual market rates.[61] These changes were welcomed by child care advocates.

Finally, under the 1990 law states had to give parents funded under the block grant the option of enrolling their child with a provider paid for by a state grant or contract or receiving a certificate (voucher) to purchase care from eligible providers. The regulations required states to make certificates available at any time and not allow parents to be placed on a waiting list or be told that state funds for certificates were depleted.[62]

Many organizations and child care providers opposed the CCDBG requirement that certificates (vouchers) be available to parents throughout the year. They wanted more emphasis placed on contracts, which they thought offered a certain stability to child care providers. According to Bruce Hershfield, director of child day care and HIV/AIDS at CWLA, contracts offer "a stable base to serve populations most at risk . . . and if you take contracts away, then it is harder to serve troubled or subsidized kids because as a provider, you lose a source of stability that offers flexibility. . . . It also takes away states' ability to control how they target money."[63] Predictably, the NEA and other organizations that had opposed vouchers in the original ABC bill also were against the regulatory language on vouchers.[64]

The NEA, National PTA, and NWLC were among the organizations that claimed that the regulations went too far in allowing the use of funds for sectarian activities and in permitting providers to discriminate on the basis of religion in admissions and employment.[65] Senators Hatch, Kennedy, and Dodd raised similar concerns.[66]

In sum, according to most state legislators and child care advocates, the final regulations' emphasis on parental choice seriously restricted the ability of states to set policies that would increase child care quality and impeded the flexibility that had been called for throughout the legislative negotiations. Ironically, some legislators and other individuals favoring the regulations' directives regarding parental choice were among the same constituencies who opposed federal mandates in other areas, such as health and safety standards. HHS staff did their best to follow the letter of the law and arrive at reasonable policies that were consistent with President Bush's priorities. The regulations for At-Risk Child Care Programs generated similar debates.

At-Risk Child Care Regulations Add More Fuel to the Fire

On June 25, 1991, HHS issued a proposed rule for the At-Risk Child Care Program. As with the CCDBG, the most disputed aspect of the proposed At-Risk Child Care regulation pertained to standards. The proposed regulations stated that child care funded under the at-risk program had to meet applicable standards of state and local law, "regardless of the source of funding for the care." This meant that if parents selected providers that were exempt from state regulation, such as religiously affiliated child care in some states or certain family child care providers in other states, they would still be eligible for federal at-risk child care funding.[67] In such circumstances, the federal government had no way of ensuring that care provided with federal dollars met any type of minimum standards. However, the regulations' emphasis on parental choice over standards of care was explicitly stated in the proposed at-risk regulations:

> If a State has standards which affect only publicly-funded care, and a caregiver of that type of care does not meet them, for title IV-A purposes . . . that care is still "legal," and the State must pay for that care. In proposing this policy, we believe that "parental choice" must be a paramount consideration. . . . Furthermore, it would be antithetical to our overall goal of supporting the family in its quest to remain independent and self-sufficient to interfere in so personal and critical a decision as who will take care of one's children.[68]

The regulations went against policies in many states of setting higher standards of care for publicly funded care than for nonsubsidized care based on the premise that taxpayers' money should be spent with some accountability. Many state and federal lawmakers and child care advocacy groups felt that prohibiting states from setting separate standards for Title IV-A child care (and other publicly subsidized care) violated states' rights, went against the notion that public dollars should be spent in a responsible manner, and was counter to the intent of the negotiations leading to the 1990 law. The intensity with which the players engaged in discussion over these issues is illustrated by excerpts from an exchange between Representatives Downey and Charles Stenholm at the 1991 hearings Downey held on the regulations:

ACTING CHAIRMAN DOWNEY: Charlie, . . . let me quote from your statement last March. You said, "I do not argue against standards. There's nothing in my bill that says there are not going to be standards. What we argue against is having them federally mandated." What made you change your mind?

MR. STENHOLM: I beg your pardon?

ACTING CHAIRMAN DOWNEY: What has made you change your mind? The child care regulations that are in this bill specifically say to the State of Texas, when it comes to the at-risk program, that Texas can't have two sets of standards. You wanted to leave it to the States? I didn't want to, you are correct. I wanted the Federal Government to have standards. I compromised and I said, "All right, we'll leave it to the States."

Now, these regulations say we're not going to leave it to the States. We are going to tell the States what sort of regulations they can and cannot have. What has made you change your mind from when you wanted to turn it over to the States?[69]

Stenholm offered a vague answer, but was clearer when Downey later asked him if he thought it was fair to allow a state to have more stringent regulations for subsidized care than for nonsubsidized care as a way of demonstrating the state's interest in protecting the interests of taxpayers. Didn't the state have a legitimate right to protect children from unsafe publicly funded care? Stenholm's response illustrated how he and others, including executive branch officials, relied on parental choice as the basis for child care policy:

Now, what I am trying to emphasize is parental choice. If parents are making various decisions regarding the safety of their children, I think that parental choice carries greater weight than anything that you, and this committee, and we, together might do in the creation of regulations as to what's safe and what's not safe in any shape, form, or fashion of child care and the regulations thereon.[70]

In another twist on the same theme, Stenholm and others argued that families whose child care was funded under Title IV-A (welfare) should not have their options regulated more than other families:

What we are talking about is not, in any way, prohibiting, and the regulations do not and certainly the statute does not prohibit the States of Texas, Connecticut, Iowa, New York or Florida from coming up with its own standards. It just says, don't keep two sets of books. Apply what you are going to [apply] against subsidized as well as to unsubsidized care and apply them equally.[71]

Representative Jim McDermott (D-Wash.), a former state senator elected to Congress in 1990, also pursued the parental choice versus states' rights debate with Barnhart:

MS. BARNHART: What we are saying is that regardless of whether or not that care meets the standards the State has, if the mother chooses to put her child [in her neighbor's care], then the State has to reimburse it under the IV-A program. That is what we are saying. . . .

MR. MCDERMOTT: So if I can distill that all the way down, what you are saying is that these regulations were written with the basic principle that what a parent decides for children is preeminent above everything. If a parent makes the wrong choice, too bad, the child got burned. . . . [72]

If you would say in your regulation, you must bring your regulations up to the level of the State for all places where this money goes, I would be cheering for you. But you don't. You let the States make the choice, and you know politically they can't bring them up or they would have done it a long time ago.[73]

On the issue of standards, Downey was joined by many of his colleagues and like-minded organizations, including the NCSL, CDF, APWA, and other state and national groups that argued that rather than expanding parental choice, the regulations had the effect of limiting the availability of safe care that could be purchased with funds from the at-risk program.[74] According to an interview with one HHS administrator who was closely involved with the at-risk program, "The child care advocates felt that you had to have rules that applied across the board. And we said that if a parent chose another kind of care [that was not regulated] that they were entitled to it."

The proposed regulations for the At-Risk Child Care Program also stipulated that all providers not required to meet applicable standards and giving care to other than family members must be registered with the state. The proposed registration procedures allowed only for collecting information needed for the state to make payment or provide information to the provider.[75] Many groups opposed this limitation on the type of information that states could collect for purposes of registration. CDF's position was that under the proposed rule, registration would not ensure that informal caregivers met the most minimal health and safety standards. A Republican state senator from Indiana made a similar point in testimony on behalf of the NCSL.[76]

When HHS officials published the final regulations for the At-Risk Child Care Program on August 4, 1992, more than a year after issuing the proposed rule, they noted that by far the largest number (559) of comments were on standards; 90 percent of those opposed the proposed rule, and 28 percent offered suggestions for change. One-quarter of all the comments submitted to HHS in response to the at-risk program were on the registration requirements, mostly opposing the provision that registration procedures had to be simple and not include minimum health and safety requirements.

After considering all the comments on quality of care, HHS revised the language to specify that states could deny payment for any care that failed to meet health and safety requirements applicable to child care providers in the same category. However, the final regulations specified that these changes must not exclude or have the effect of excluding any categories of child care providers.[77] As one HHS official noted, "The change was a way of saying that if a provider wanted to receive funding under the act, then in the areas of health and safety, he or she had to adhere to certain minimal requirements." For At-Risk Child Care, as with the CCDBG, the final regulations also allowed states to set separate standards for publicly subsidized care. That is, if a state required providers of federally or state-subsidized care to pass a criminal background check, the same standard could apply to Title IV-A care, but not to providers not receiving public funds. The regulations also specified that such provisions were in force as long as they did not have the effect of excluding any categories of child care providers or restricting parental choice.[78] These were important changes in ensuring a certain minimal standard of subsidized care. However, child care advocates acknowledged that these changes still did not address their concerns about the 1990 statute's failure to ensure that federally funded care meet some type of minimum standards even if such care was exempt from state regulation. Similar changes were made to the regulations pertaining to registration procedures. The final regulations allowed states to obtain information regarding health and safety measures of registered providers as long as such procedures did not "exclude or have the effect of excluding any categories of providers."[79] Thus, even with these revisions, the emphasis on parental choice prevailed.

Payment and Eligibility Criteria

Another contentious provision in the At-Risk Child Care regulations pertained to federal payments for child care. The provisions for payment under the at-risk program followed precedents established for AFDC and TCC under the 1988 FSA, which called for the establishment of local market rates. The states' Title IV-A agencies established these rates based on a representative sample of providers queried in a survey. Regulations for both the FSA and the At-Risk Child Care Program required states to pay eligible child care providers at 75 percent of the local market rate for a specific type of care (i.e., center care, in-home, or family child care).[80] An HHS official who worked on child care regulations for both the FSA and the at-risk program explained in an interview with the author how they arrived at the seventy-fifth percentile, given funding constraints and the need to come up with a fair solution:

> Where did we get the 75th percentile? Actually we spent a great deal of time considering various options, such as using the median, the mean, etc. We settled on the 75th percentile because it seemed like a good compromise between something like the average, which would have meant a rate that was below the rate of a good portion of the providers, and a 100 percent rate, which we believed would have had the effect of driving up the rates, even for nonsubsidized care. And because the available funding was less than the need, we were trying to be sure that the money went reasonably far.

Many child care advocacy groups, such as CDF, APWA, and CWLA, were opposed to the local market rate being set at the seventy-fifth percentile and urged HHS to allow states "to pay rates above the 75th percentile if they choose to do so."[81] The CCAC expressed the sentiment of many child care policy leaders:

> It is difficult to recruit providers to serve poor families when they can get higher rates for children of other families. In half of the states CCAC has surveyed, advocates and/or state administrators have stressed that the 75th percentile cost limitation hinders the ability of families to find any child care at all—regardless of quality.[82]

The NCSL explained that in some states the lower payment rate for JOBS child care "has discouraged providers from serving subsidized families." Furthermore, unless the At-Risk Child Care Program had the same payment structure as the CCDBG, a two-tiered system would persist, with block grant programs funded at a higher rate than At-Risk Child Care and TCC.[83]

Almost all those commenting thought that the rate was set too low. Many urged HHS to revise also the AFDC and TCC rules pertaining to market rates. Nonetheless, in the final regulations HHS left the seventy-fifth percentile of the market rate unchanged. Although many might have preferred that states be given more flexibility, the inclusion of market rates and payment at 75 percent of that rate at least ensured minimum funding of child care providers for low-income families. Welfare reform in 1996 changed the market rate provisions (see chapter 6).

Regarding eligibility, the proposed regulations for the At-Risk Child Care Program allowed funds to be used only for children in low-income families (as defined by each state) who met certain other eligibility criteria, including needing child care assistance so the parent(s) could be employed. CDF, APWA, the NACO, and others opposed the eligibility language and preferred language that used only income as the criterion for eligibility.[84] Most of those commenting on the proposed rule said that having a low income ought to be sufficient to be eligible and that any additional definition was an administrative burden.[85] In the final regulations, HHS noted, "Based on the comments, we agree that low-income alone as defined by the States is a good predictor of a family's being at-risk. We have, therefore, clarified the regulations to permit States to define at risk in terms of low-income alone." In addition, families must not be receiving AFDC and must need child care in order to work. A parent not working but engaged in education, training, or job search activities would not qualify for at-risk child care assistance. Many child care advocates continued to oppose this definition because of its exclusion of those engaged in education or training activities.[86]

In sum, the final rules for the CCDBG and At-Risk Child Care Program included modest changes, especially regarding the differential payment rates under the CCDBG and the requirements for health and safety in the At-Risk Child Care Program. These were important successes for child care advocates. Those in favor of strong parental choice provisions, in the White House, Congress, and among conservative groups, were pleased with the regulations' emphasis on parental choice. ACF officials could claim credit for upholding parental choice and formulating what they considered reasonable language regarding payment, standards, and other aspects of the programs.

The issues just described were the major points that organized interests, child care providers, and government officials identified in their responses to proposed rules for both the at-risk and block grant programs. However, as one HHS staff person observed, people on both sides of the issue tended to narrow their focus to just a few concerns. In so doing, they overlooked many important aspects of the rule, such as grievance procedures, monitoring, and state reporting requirements.

The final regulations added new structures to federal policymaking for child care. They gave providers, advocates, and government officials the guidelines needed to implement the child care programs enacted in 1990. But without annual congressional appropriations for the CCDBG, states lacked critical resources needed to run their state child care programs.

Implementing the 1990 Child Care Package

Child care advocates at federal and state levels of government monitored and lobbied Congress regarding appropriation of funds for the CCDBG. With many different child care programs on the books, the need for federal and state coordination increased. Following the enactment of the 1990 law with its EITC expansion, several organizations launched an important outreach campaign regarding the tax credit.

Appropriations for Child Care

Because the 1990 reconciliation law created the At-Risk Child Care Program as a capped entitlement program authorized at $300 million annually, its funding levels were set and not on the legislative agenda. In contrast, the 1990 law authorized the CCDBG for $750 million in FY 1991, $825 million in FY 1992, $925 million in FY 1993, and such sums as may be necessary for each of FY 1994 and 1995.[87] But authorization levels represent only the ceilings and parameters for funding; Congress must annually appropriate funds for discretionary programs such as the CCDBG. This means that each year child care advocates both in and outside Congress lobbied the appropriations committees in both chambers for full funding of the CCDBG. Thus, it wasn't enough to win the legislative battles or lobby for changes in the regulations; once enacted, the block grant posed formidable political challenges in the annual appropriations process.

For FY 1991, which started on October 1, 1990, Bush proposed approximately $750 million for the CCDBG, a significant portion of which would be forward funded in the next fiscal year (that is, legislation would allow funds for a specific purpose to be committed in a given year for programs that would not be implemented until the following fiscal year). In October 1990, House and Senate conferees for the FY 1991 appropriations bill accepted the $750 appropriations level, based on the White House and Senate agreement. The appropriations committee also approved a late start date, September 1991, for appropriating the first CCDBG funds. In the spring of 1991, during deliberations for the FY 1992 appropriations bill, the House cut FY 1991 funding for the CCDBG by $165 million. The Senate retained the FY 1991 CCDBG appropriations at approximately $750 million. A lengthy fight ensued while House and Senate conference committee members for the FY 1992 appropriations bill worked out their differences, including the proposed cuts in CCDBG appropriations for FY 1991. Once again, CDF took the lead in enlisting the support of child care advocates across the country. In the end, their efforts paid off, and the CCDBG was fully funded for FY 1991 at $731 million, which included a 2.4 percent across-the-board cut for FY 1991 that the appropriations committees had previously approved. In exchange for restoring full funding for the CCDBG, Congress delayed the FY 1991 start date a few more days into mid-September, saving a small amount of money, and did not appropriate funds for the child care quality improvement grants. The latter were authorized at $50 million for FY 1991 and funded at $13 million in FY 1990 under Title IV-A from the FSA.[88]

For FY 1992, Congress appropriated $825 million for the CCDBG as a result of relatively uneventful deliberations compared with the tumultuous arguments over CCDBG funding for FY 1991. With steady annual increases, the CCDBG appropriations reached $935 million for FY 1995 and FY 1996.[89] The increases were due to the growing popularity of the program, its bipartisan support, and President Clinton's interest in domestic social programs, such as child care. Given the concerns about the federal budget deficit during those years, the CCDBG funding increases were important accomplishments for child care advocates.

CCDBG Services and Expenditures

HHS allocated child care funds to states with federally approved block grant plans. The first HHS report to Congress on the CCDBG described services provided from September 7, 1991 (when funds were first available), through September 30, 1992. During that period, more than 571,000 children received child care under the block grant. According to HHS, this "met only a fraction of the estimated need for child care."[90] Of the children served, about 90 percent came from families with incomes at or below 150 percent of the federal poverty level; 65 percent were cared for in child care centers, and 17 percent in family child care homes. Another 4 percent were cared for in the child's home by a person not related to the child. More than 33 percent of the children were four to five years old; 25 percent were two to three years of age; approximately 20 percent were below one year of age; and another 20 percent were between six and twelve years old. More than 75 percent of the FY 1991 expenditures were for child care services, and the remaining funds were for activities to expand and improve the availability and quality of child care programs. Almost every state and territory and 159 tribes were allotted funds, but 21 of the tribes were unable to use the allotment because the federal government did not approve their child care plans.[91]

According to an HHS official, working with the Indian tribes to implement their child care programs was a big challenge. Unlike states, which had some type of structures in place, tribes typically lacked the infrastructure needed to run their programs. Moreover, there was tremendous variation among tribes. Large tribes, such as the Navajos, typically had a designated person in charge of child care. But there were also many small tribes with just a few hundred people, none of whom was familiar with child care policy.

The funds allocated in the 25 percent set-aside for improving the quality of child care services were spent in every state on training providers for early childhood care. This was a significant change from before the block grant when many states lacked such programs.[92] Other major investments were in child care resource and referral agencies, programs that assist families in finding affordable quality care in their vicinity.[93]

As a result of the CCDBG regulations' requirement that states establish health and safety standards in order to be eligible for block grant funding, a number of states strengthened their child care licensing requirements. In 1995 CDF issued a report that found "a mixed picture regarding the extent to which states adequately protected children in child care." In areas such as immunization requirements, most states had "adequate protections for children in their licensing requirements." Almost all states required children in licensed centers and family homes to have all the basic immunizations.[94]

But in other areas, such as requiring child care staff to be trained in CPR or first aid, many states fell short. States also varied in their requirements for periodic fire drills or smoke detectors in child care centers and family child care homes.[95]

Another feature of the 1990 CCDBG law was the quality set-aside, which enabled states to improve the quality of child care for all children, not just for those subsidized under the block grant. States used those funds for increasing staff training and preparation or for hiring staff so that they could lower child–staff ratios.[96] Thus, despite having to overcome impediments in funding and coordination, once implemented, the block grant proved to be a catalyst for improvements in the quality of care for all children in child care settings.

Coordination and Aiming for Seamless Services

One of the biggest obstacles the new child care programs posed was how to coordinate across programs, especially because many families, depending on their work and income status, were eligible for more than one program. For example, low-income working families could be considered at-risk of becoming dependent on welfare and thereby be eligible for At-Risk Child Care funds. But if their annual income placed them below 75 percent of the state median income level, they also qualified for the CCDBG. According to a 1994 study by the GAO, the major federally funded early childhood programs targeted different populations, had different eligibility criteria, and offered a different mix of services to children and their families, all of which created obstacles to an integrated system. Moreover, many programs reported serving only a portion of their target population and maintaining long waiting lists. Furthermore, in 1990 most disadvantaged children of preschool age were not enrolled in any type of preschool program.[97] Finally, administrative and organizational aspects of the various types of AFDC-related child care programs varied. Under the 1990 law, for example, unlicensed child care providers serving families under the At-Risk Child Care Program had to be registered. The other welfare-related child care programs lacked such a requirement.

Financing arrangements also varied across child care programs. Many states had difficulty coming up with the matching funds required for the Title IV-A child care programs.[98] Some used CCDBG funds intended for low-income and working poor families to pay for child care for AFDC families participating in welfare-to-work programs. They did this to avoid having to use state matching funds required in the Title IV-A programs and instead served AFDC families by first using "free dollars" when their state budgets were tight.[99] In 1993 fifteen states reported using CCDBG funds to pay for child care expenses of AFDC parents who were in education or training programs or were eligible for TCC programs. Another five anticipated using funds this way in the future.[100] In FY 1993, 1994, and 1995, federal payments to states for At-Risk Child Care totaled $216 million, $275 million, and $296 million, respectively, which was less than the $300 million authorized annually.[101] Of those states not using their entire At-Risk Child Care allotment for 1992, more than half had waiting lists of families they were unable to serve.[102] In addition, states differed in how they exercised certain options for providing At-Risk Child Care. Forty states used certificates, twenty-one purchased child care through grants or contracts with providers, ten offered cash or vouchers in advance, and nine provided cash reimbursement to families. (States often used more than one option.)[103] Variations across programs also contributed to the eventual restructuring of federal child care programs in 1996. But that is another story, explained in the next chapter.

Child Care Tax Credits Outreach Campaign

As discussed in the previous chapter, the child care package enacted in 1990 included significant expansions of the EITC. Even though the EITC was not expressly a child care policy, many low-income working families used it to help cover child care costs. As Nancy Duff Campbell, copresident of the NWLC, explained:

> After 1990, there was a big influx of child care money, broadly defined, if you include the EITC and the CCDBG. . . . We decided to help with the tax credits. We worked with child care groups across the country to get them to include information on the expanded EITC and the DCTC. Even though the DCTC was not expanded in 1990, it was changed in some aspects and people in child care communities needed to know it existed and was available to low-income families.[104]

In 1991, building on its earlier advocacy on tax issues, the NWLC led a tax credits outreach campaign, targeting the child care community. It worked in strong partnership with the Center on Budget and Policy Priorities, which led a broader EITC campaign, and with CDF. The idea behind the campaign was to use the EITC expansions as an opportunity to educate the child care community (parents and providers) about the EITC and DCTC. The three-year NWLC campaign included training staff at state organizations to help eligible low-income families apply for and use the EITC and DCTC. Hundreds of thousands of posters, designed by CDF's advertising agency, and materials developed by NWLC were distributed to child care advocates and providers. Well-established contacts with child care community leaders, developed by CDF during its fieldwork for child care legislation and by NWLC in its work with both child care and women's organizations, facilitated the campaign's success.

The NWLC, as part of the campaign, for three years published its *Advocate's Guide to the Child Care Tax Credits Outreach Campaign*, which included extensive information on the two tax credits and media strategies and, in 1994, information on ways for recipients to update the information annually. Other activities with national and local television and printed media were featured in the campaign. The NWLC also worked closely with IRS officials.

The outreach campaign was successful, especially considering the modest resources it required. By the end of 1992, for example, the number of families claiming the EITC had increased by 21 percent over the previous year and the amount of the tax benefits rose by 68 percent.[105] DCTC usage held steady, which was a significant accomplishment given that other tax policies at the time could have lowered the number of DCTC claimants. Of course, it is impossible to ascertain how far to attribute these changes to the campaign. However, as Campbell explained, "This was the beginning of the child care field becoming more educated and engaged about tax issues that affected them."[106] Throughout the 1990s the NWLC continued to offer detailed analyses and expert advice on tax credits for low-income families.

1993: A New Political Era

While working on the implementation of child care policies, child care advocates and policymakers also kept their eyes on the national elections. Bill Clinton's presidential victory in 1992 introduced a new era of child care policymaking. Clinton won with 43 percent of the popular vote; Bush received 37 percent; and Ross Perot, running as an Independent, obtained nearly 19 percent. In Congress, Democrats lost 9 seats in the House but still maintained a lead over Republicans (258 to 176). In the Senate, Democrats gained a seat and retained their margin (57 to 43) over Republicans.[107] For the first time in over a decade, the Democrats controlled both the legislative and executive branches of government. Many of them had high hopes that this unified government would shift domestic policymaking in their favor. Child care activists were optimistic that Clinton would support their policy preferences, especially because of Hillary Rodham Clinton's long-standing commitment to children's policies, including her role as chair of the CDF board during the 1980s.

However, Clinton offered a mixed bag in this regard. He was not a "tax-and-spend" liberal Democrat. Instead, he "had come from the Democratic Leadership Council (DLC), a centrist group that he had helped found in 1985 in order to search for a way to break the Democrats' presidential losing streak and change the party's image as too liberal for the country."[108] Members of the DLC "wanted government to design and implement programs that would . . . help people while staying as much out of their lives as possible." They envisioned an "activist" government that was not "intrusive."[109] Clinton often explained that he was not a traditional liberal or a conservative Democrat, but one who would find a "third way" by bridging these two camps.[110] His words foreshadowed his subsequent positions on child care and other social policies.

As outlined in their book *Putting People First: How We Can All Change America*,[111] Clinton and Al Gore's campaign platform emphasized the need to redirect economic policies to help low-income and middle-class families. Claiming that "the working poor had the door of opportunity slammed in their face," Clinton embarked on a campaign that centered on "strengthen[ing] families and empower[ing] all Americans to work." He endorsed increasing the EITC and enacting the Family and Medical Leave Act, which Bush had vetoed in 1990. As a New Democrat, he focused on tax policies instead of new programs as a way of helping middle-class families. As such, he recommended giving middle-class taxpayers a "choice between a children's tax credit or a significant reduction in their income tax rate."[112] He also proposed creating a "child care network as complete as the public school network, tailored to the needs of working families; establish[ing] more rigorous standards for licensing child care facilities and implement[ing] improved methods for enforcing them."[113] He offered to "put an end to welfare as we know it by making welfare a second chance, not a way of life; empower people on welfare with the education, training, and child care they need, for up to two years, so they can break the cycle of dependency . . . and ensure that their children are cared for while they learn."[114] In addition, Clinton advocated fully funding Head Start,[115] which contributed to heightened interest in other federal early childhood and child care programs.

Clinton won the election by appealing to certain social groups. In addition to the "core Democratic constituency," which included the disadvantaged, nonwhites, and ethnic minorities, he garnered support from women and the "oft-derided 'Bubba vote' comprised of white male southerners and born-again Christians who overlap the economically poor and less educated."[116] Clinton also appealed to a diverse group of constituents composed of wealthy Americans, male college graduates, suburban professionals, and others who were drawn to his campaign themes of job security and the economy.[117] He also drew support from what some had referred to as Reagan Democrats—a group that included "working-class and ethnic whites in the industrial Midwest" and suburbanites who were looking for a president who offered a different approach from the Democratic liberalism of the 1960s and 1970s.[118] Bush won the majority of votes among "highly religious participating whites in general and religious conservatives, in particular."[119] Thus, Clinton entered office with the support of a more diverse constituency than the traditional liberal Democratic following. But his lack of an electoral mandate necessitated policies that would be palatable to many groups. He also would have to win over the Perot voters as he looked ahead to reelection in 1996.

Once elected, Clinton placed other issues ahead of child care. He focused on keeping his campaign promise of stimulating the economy and broadening his support beyond the 43 percent of voters who had cast ballots for him. Health care reform preoccupied him for most of 1994, followed by welfare reform. During Clinton's first term, as he devised legislation in both of these areas, he had to contend with the nagging federal budget deficit and with budget hawks from both parties, including his OMB director, Leon Panetta, and deputy director, Alice Rivlin. He faced a Democratic Party that was splintered in many ways, making domestic policy a challenge for this centrist president.[120]

Child Care Yields to Other Issues During the Early Clinton Years

Because of budget realities, political considerations, and Clinton's own ambivalence, child care was not a major point on Clinton's agenda during his first two years in office, other than to deal with the "nannygate crisis" surrounding his nominees for attorney general. His first nominee, Zoë Baird, had hired illegal immigrants as nanny and chauffeur in 1990 and had not paid Social Security taxes for them until January 1993. The publicity surrounding her nomination generated a class conflict. As columnist Elizabeth Drew explained, "Baird, who earned over five hundred thousand dollars a year, was seen by less affluent people to have bought her way out of a difficulty many working mothers faced."[121] Clinton's next nominee, Kimba Wood, had employed an illegal immigrant as baby-sitter, even though this was before the law was enacted that "made such employment illegal." Unlike Baird, she had paid the woman's Social Security taxes. But this "perturbation" was too much, and eventually Wood withdrew her name.[122]

Although the nanny issue brought attention to the general issue of child care, its focus on well-to-do families with chauffeurs and hired help was a far cry from the target of most federal child care legislation: low-income working families with children. It did little to reverse what one New York City official called "the poor person's nannygate."[123] Some people thought that the attorney general fiasco would prompt Congress to take a comprehensive look at the child care system and propose reform.[124] But in the absence of presidential leadership on this issue, it was unlikely that Democrats would pick up the cause.

Keeping with his campaign pledge, one of Clinton's first actions was signing into law the Family and Medical Leave Act (P.L. 103-3) on February 5, 1993. This legislation required employers with fifty or more employees to grant them "unpaid leave of up to 12 weeks for the birth or adoption of a child or the illness of a close family member." It was practically the same legislation that President Bush had vetoed in 1992. Some Democrats thought it was a sign that Clinton would bring an end to gridlock on Capitol Hill after twelve years of divided government.[125] Child care advocates anticipated that this would lead to new support for their policy preferences in child care. But this was not the case, at least not right away. Settling the economy and moving tax legislation through Congress took priority over other social policy issues.

Clinton's major domestic policy proposal in 1993 was his economic package aimed at "laying the foundation for long-term growth"[126] This three-part initiative included an economic stimulus plan, investment spending, and deficit reduction. The economic stimulus part included expanding the EITC by increasing the income level at which families would qualify and extending it to low-income childless couples. Under investment spending there were proposals for child care, job training, and health care. But by child care, Clinton meant Head Start, a program with broad support even among Republicans. Although the goals of Head Start and many early education programs overlap, in most locales, Head Start is not a viable alternative to child care. Head Start's programs are usually part time and do not run in the summer. Moreover, most Head Start programs serve only children aged three and four years and do not reach infants and toddlers. But some aspects of Head Start, especially the parental involvement requirements, are models for many child care providers. Riding the wave of popularity surrounding Head Start, Clinton's investment in "lifelong learning" included increasing the funding for Head Start so that it would reach more children in summer programs and eventually achieve full funding for an estimated 1.4 million children by 1999. As part of Clinton's efforts to reverse what he called the Republicans' "investment deficit," he proposed increasing Head Start funding by $3.8 billion over five years. He also proposed investing in two other popular children's initiatives: childhood immunizations and the Special Supplemental Nutrition Program for Women, Infants, and Children (WIC).[127]

Clinton's proposed investments in domestic policy, including his goals for children and families, were limited by fiscal constraints and political realities on Capitol Hill. His 1993 requests to increase spending on social programs were scaled down due to opposition from Republicans and divisiveness between Democrats who wanted discretionary spending and those who wanted to "limit the tax increases and cut more spending." The 1993 budget reconciliation bill, which included the remnants of Clinton's stimulus package, passed by a two-vote margin (218 to 216) in the House, with Gore breaking the tie in the Senate. It included the EITC expansions and several new initiatives for children and families. It also eliminated the infant tax credit that had been enacted with the child care package in 1990. Clinton signed these provisions into law (P.L. 103-66) on August 10, 1993.[128]

Clinton's Head Start proposal was not part of the reconciliation bill. On May 18, 1994, Clinton signed into law the Human Services Amendments of 1994 (P.L. 103-252). The law expanded Head Start by offering full-year, full-day programs, creating a new program (Early Start) for infants and toddlers from birth to the age of three, and instituting quality-control mechanisms, such as developing updated federal Head Start standards.[129] The reauthorization of Head Start enjoyed strong bipartisan support as legislators acknowledged its importance in child development.

Many child care advocates supported Clinton's Head Start proposals, but they were disappointed that he didn't do more for child care. Clinton revealed how he perceived child care within the context of other issues:

> We have focused our child care efforts basically on trying to increase the incomes of working parents with modest incomes. . . . So we're focusing on that. In our welfare reform bill, we plan to also do more to try to help parents with modest incomes afford their child care. Beyond that, of course, there is the Federal child care tax credit, and most States do the same thing. Have we done as much as we should? I don't think so. But I think if we can help cover the health care expenses of all working parents and their children and help to deal with the income tax structure, I think that would go a long way toward helping you afford child care. And we're doing as much as we can with the money we have.[130]

When asked to explain his child care policy at a different event, Clinton responded that he supported "partnerships with states to help them to develop high standards for child care" and increases in the EITC and DCTC.[131] His words echoed the themes of moderate and conservative lawmakers during deliberations on child care in the late 1980s. Because of Clinton's need to toe the middle line and keep in mind upcoming congressional and presidential elections, this approach made sense.

The Clinton Administration and Child Care, Revisited

At first glance, it appears that Clinton's positions on child care were lackluster during his first two years in office. But a closer examination reveals how they deviated from those of his predecessor, President Bush. First, many of his high-level appointees in HHS and the White House were people with previous political experience advocating for an expanded federal role in child care. Among them were Rich Tarplin, Ann Rosewater, Shirley Sagawa, and Mary Bourdette. Joan Lombardi, whom Clinton appointed head of the Federal Child Care Bureau, was another well-known expert on child care and early childhood. These were among the many individuals who helped Clinton develop child care policies that distinguished him from Bush. Even a *Wall Street Journal* reporter noted a fresh perspective on family policies, including child care, within the White House. She attributed this in part to an increase in working couples with young children within the high echelons of the Clinton White House and across the federal government.[132]

Another example of new directions in child care policymaking under Clinton was the proposed revision to the regulations for the CCDBG[133] issued under the leadership of Mary Jo Bane, Clinton's assistant secretary for children and families. The proposed changes illustrated Clinton's willingness to reverse the tone and stance of the regulations issued under Bush.

Many of the revisions in the proposed regulations were based on input from Blank, state child care administrators, and other experts on child care and welfare, such as Mark Greenberg with the Center for Law and Social Policy (CLASP). In April 1993 Blank suggested to Bane how HHS might rewrite the regulations and strengthen strategies for improving child care licensing. She explained that "a major re-write of the regulations including a shift in the tone concerning quality would be terrific. It would send an important signal about the Administration's commitment to improve the quality of child care." She also suggested building immunization requirements into the regulations, which would dovetail nicely with Clinton's immunization initiative and address the gaps in coverage among children in child care programs that were exempt from state regulation.[134]

One of the goals of the proposed regulations was to enhance coordination among the federal child care programs for welfare recipients and low-income families. In addition, the regulations proposed eliminating the "effects test" and the 10 percent ceiling on payment differentials within categories of care for the block grant. The new proposed rule also allowed states to pay more than the seventy-fifth percentile of local market rates for Title IV-A child care that exceeded the level of quality required for licensing. The proposed regulation also increased to 15 percent (from 10 percent) the proportion of block grant funding that grantees could use for program administration and for improvements in the quality and availability of child care. Child care providers, state administrators, and other members of the advocacy community were pleased with these suggested changes, in particular the elimination of the cap on the CCDBG payment differential.[135]

As could be expected, religious groups, conservative entities, and proprietary providers were among those opposing the proposed changes. For example, William Tobin, representing licensed, private, and religious child care centers, asked ACF to "leave the effects test intact." He argued that "the proposed rules [were] unnecessary, premature, and antithetical to both the letter and spirit of the original statutes and their implementing regulations." He urged Bane to allow vouchers to parents as the "preferred mode of payment" for all child care programs under the ACF.[136] The NCCA, a confederation of state associations representing private center-based child care providers, argued that ACF lacked compelling arguments for making many of its proposed changes.[137] HHS never issued final regulations partly because of pending welfare reform legislation, but above all because the midterm elections of 1994 changed the terrain of child care policymaking under Clinton. Child care advocates' hopes were dashed when midterm elections gave the Republicans control of Congress. Suddenly child care advocates were warding off attacks against federal child care programs from the new Republican majority in Congress. This dramatic shift of power created a new playing field for the politics of child care under welfare reform.

The years from 1991 to 1994 were characterized by a continuation of the ideological clashes between those for and against a strong federal presence in the area of child care regulation. Unlike the late 1980s, when the legislative branch was the hub of child care policymaking, the early 1990s centered on the executive branch and its regulatory functions. Final regulations for the CCDBG and the At-Risk Child Care Program became new structures for child care policymaking that shaped state and federal child care policies for years to come.

Difficulties coordinating across programs and levels of government created a complicated maze of federal child care policies. Many eligible children from low-income families remained unserved. Child care of poor quality and unregulated child care still existed. Ensuring adequate appropriations for the block grant was an annual challenge for state officials and child care advocates.

During his first two years in office, Clinton often viewed child care in the context of other issues, even though under his watch there were some important policies formulated for children, families, and child care. The GOP takeover of Congress in 1994 put a damper on any subsequent changes as the Republicans escalated their crusade to balance the budget and reduce spending on domestic social programs, including child care.

6 Child Care and Welfare Reform, 1994–1996

The midterm elections in 1994 ushered in a new era of governance as the Republicans gained control of both chambers of Congress. Changes in congressional structures and procedures affected how Congress worked and shaped the politics of child care legislation. For the first part of 1995 the Contract with America strongly determined what landed on the congressional agenda. Welfare reform was a high priority for both parties in Congress and for President Clinton. Although each party had a different vision of welfare reform, a consensus prevailed in Washington, supported by popular opinion, that welfare needed to be revamped. The politics of welfare reform were closely linked to the politics of child care legislation in that the CCDBG was due to be reauthorized at the same time that welfare reform landed on the agenda. Moreover, President Clinton's proposal for welfare reform included funding increases for child care as he and other lawmakers increasingly realized that mandatory work requirements for mothers with young children would succeed only if child care assistance was part of the package.

The anticipated increased need for child care under welfare reform did not automatically translate into broad federal support for child care legislation. Thus, champions of child care in Congress and beyond engaged in the familiar debates regarding the balance between state and federal authorities and the allocation of federal funds for areas such as quality improvement. In contrast to earlier rounds of child care deliberations, by the mid-1990s the CCDBG had established a framework that facilitated legislative negotiations. The politics of child care in the mid-1990s also differed from those of earlier periods in that across the political spectrum the organized interests were not as tightly organized as in the past. By 1996 growing interest in the well-being of children added a new twist to child care policymaking.

1994: Elections Set a New Stage for Child Care

The 1994 change to Republican majority rule was important in setting and controlling the agenda and in determining political behavior, organization, and outcomes for a host of issues,[1] including child care. John H. Aldrich and David W. Rohde explained how after the 1994 elections the Republicans reorganized their "partisan and leadership institutions" with the goal of enacting outcomes that the party "collectively sought to achieve." Under Aldrich and Rohde's model of conditional party government, political parties provide an organizational structure for advancing the policy views of the majority party. This is especially true when there is homogeneity of policy preferences within the majority party and such preferences are distinct from those of the minority party. Under conditional party government, the majority party allocates power and resources to produce institutional changes in areas such as selection of committee chairs, power of committee chairs, and size of congressional staff. These changes are intended "to strengthen the ability of the party leadership to shape the House agenda . . . and to increase party cohesion on policy."[2] Aldrich and Rohde's model of conditional party government can be applied to the politics of child care policymaking after the GOP takeover of Congress.

Some of the congressional changes that created the context for legislative deliberations about child care were the direct result of the new Republican majority in Congress. Others had been brewing but heated up considerably with the change in power. Thus, to understand the impact of the changes in Congress after 1994 some of the preceding events warrant explanation.

Prelude to 1994

The leader of the Republican revolution was Representative Newt Gingrich (R-Ga.), Speaker of the House in 1995. Elected to Congress in 1978, Gingrich was part of "new breed of Republicans" in the House who were "staunch conservatives" out to change "the institutional status quo." National media described them as "partisan fire-eaters," "guerrilla warriors," and "bomb throwers."[3] In March 1989 Gingrich orchestrated a stunning campaign and came from far behind to be elected minority whip by his Republican colleagues.[4] In his new role Gingrich stepped up his aggressive campaign to "undermine the Democratically controlled House" and, in particular, to oust Speaker Jim Wright. In the spring of 1989, faced with a series of ethics violations, Wright stepped down, and Representative Thomas Foley, who had been majority leader, was elected Speaker. Wright's downfall was due to a combination of factors, including the Republican push to thwart Democratic control, which Gingrich led.[5] The success of the Republican takeover in 1994 was partly due to the party's ability to form coalitions around certain conservative themes and make the internal governance of Congress one of many national issues in local elections.[6] Even moderate Republicans, such as Representatives Olympia Snowe and Nancy Johnson, supported Gingrich. They were interested in strategies that would enable Republicans to gain legislative influence.

While Republicans pushed for a reordering of public policies, the public was expressing a new level of mistrust in government and a desire for change.[7] In one 1994 poll, disapproval of congressional performance reached 79 percent. As Roger H. Davidson explained:

> Hovering over Congress like a vast storm cloud in the 1990s was an unprecedented level of public discontent and even anger—what one member of Congress called a "civic temper tantrum." It reflected not only generalized distrust of politicians and outrage at widely reported scandals, but also a feeling that government was not working well and that the nation itself had strayed off course. . . . This sour mood found concrete expression in the 1992 and 1994 elections, which reconfigured membership and party control at both ends of Pennsylvania Avenue.[8]

Political discontent was also accompanied by—and some claimed due to—an economic malaise emanating from the stagnation of middle-class income between 1973 and 1992.[9] The same "economic discontent" that helped elect Clinton in 1992 persisted in 1994 and contributed to the ousting of the Democrats from Congress, especially insofar as voters perceived Democratic candidates as symbols of Clinton and his policies.[10] Between 1993 and 1994, dissatisfaction with Clinton rose as he failed to deliver legislatively in areas such as health care and campaign finance reform. Moreover, he had not acted on his promised tax cut for middle-class Americans because it was "inconsistent with his primary goal of deficit reduction."[11] In the months before the 1994 elections, Clinton's approval ratings were among his lowest, hovering between 44 and 50 percent.[12] Thus, the 1994 elections reflected disapproval of not just Clinton but also his "administration's approach to public policy."[13]

Gingrich helped Republicans maximize their opportunities to make the 1994 elections a "referendum on the Democratic party."[14] As such, the GOP sought to distinguish itself from the Democrats on social policy issues. The shift in Congress also represented a victory for conservatives in their efforts to destroy any "remnants of the Great Society programs of the 1960s" and other forms of what they called "social engineering."[15] Republicans preferred deregulation for a host of issues, including child care. They wanted to restore the role of parents in raising children and opposed large federal child care programs. To achieve their goals, they proposed tax credits to help low-income and middle-class families with children.[16] Any type of new federal investment in child care was out of the question, at least for the time being.

Contract with America

The Contract with America, originally designed as an election strategy, was a list of ten platform planks that called for policy changes and congressional reforms.[17] Aspects of the contract relevant to the politics of child care legislation were a new tax credit for families with children, proposals for welfare reform, and changes in congressional structures and procedures.

On September 27, 1994, 367 Republican House candidates agreed to a detailed description of the contract, including its proposals for structural and legislative change in the House. The key groups behind the contract were small business organizations, the National Rifle Association, those advocating term limits for lawmakers, and the Christian Coalition. The last was formed in 1989, following Pat Robertson's unsuccessful presidential bid in the 1989 elections. Under the leadership of Ralph Reed, the Christian Coalition continued the themes of Robertson's campaign. After the 1994 elections, Christian Coalition leaders pledged to spend $1 million lobbying for the contract.[18] Thus, in many ways, the contract reflected some of the most extreme conservative social policy positions. However, Republicans carefully worded the contract so as to avoid moralist conservative issues, such as abortion and school prayer, and replaced those themes with economic and political concerns.[19]

Welfare reform was a key feature of the contract. The Christian Coalition and other conservatives viewed rising illegitimacy rates as the root of welfare dependency.[20] Along with many Republicans, they wanted time limits on welfare and work requirements as a condition of receiving benefits. The Republicans' welfare reform proposals were silent on child care as they sought to consolidate social welfare programs through a large block grant that encompassed welfare, child care, nutrition, and other social services. The contract's major initiative for families with children was the $500 per child tax credit. GOP leaders would willingly have dismantled child care and other social policy programs in favor of the tax credit and other contract provisions.

Conservatives viewed the contract's child tax credit as its "crowning jewel." It met their call for "pro-child tax relief," which had been on their agenda for many years. Although the child tax credit had bipartisan support, its initial proponents were conservatives, such as the Christian Coalition and FRC, who saw it as a way of strengthening the American family. In particular, it would address the failure of the child tax exemption to keep pace with inflation.[21]

Conservatives also saw the child tax credit as a way to reduce the "bias against parental child-rearing," which they claimed was a result of the growth in federal support of nonparental care.[22] They argued that because the DCTC was available only to families who required child care to enable parents to work, it discriminated against families that did not use paid child care. In contrast, the child tax credit would be available to all families, including those with "stay-at-home moms." Providing tax relief to families with stay-at-home parents was a theme that grew in popularity throughout the 1990s. The original contract had a $500 per child tax credit for families with annual incomes of up to $200,000.

1994 Elections Generate Structural and Procedural Changes in Congress

These themes were the backdrop to the 1994 midterm elections, which resulted in the GOP gaining control of Congress. The effects of this "new historical era"[23] were felt in political discussions across the country. The elections marked the first time in forty years that Republicans controlled both chambers. They gained 52 seats in the House, for a 230 to 204 lead over Democrats. In the Senate, Republicans gained 9 seats (including Senator Richard Selby of Alabama, who switched parties), for a 53 to 47 margin over Democrats. The elections brought 110 new members to Congress, making it the largest freshman class in forty-four years. Indicative of the upheaval, even House Speaker Foley lost his bid for reelection, making it the first time in more than 130 years that a Speaker was not reelected.[24] At the state level, Republicans also fortified their hold on government. There were thirty Republican governors in 1995, eleven more than in the previous year. The number of state legislatures controlled by Republicans increased from eight to nineteen; that of Democratic-controlled state legislatures dropped from twenty-four to eighteen, and twelve legislatures were split between both parties, compared with seventeen before.[25] All these disruptions demonstrated the cataclysmic impact of the elections.

One of the first items on the GOP congressional agenda was to reform House organization rules. Even before the Republican takeover, congressional staff and members from both parties had supported reforms such as reducing committee size and eliminating jurisdictional overlap.[26] But prior to 1995, legislation calling for reform barely got beyond the House Rules Committee. As C. Lawrence Evans and Walter Oleszek explained, "In the end, the Democratic majority rejected reform because reform did not appear to be worth the trouble. Following the November 1994 elections, a new majority made a different calculation."[27]

By changing the rules of the game, the House Republican majority enhanced its ability to impose its political will on the rest of the chamber. The new rules also had the effect of undermining the power of committees while strengthening the power and influence of the Speaker.[28] For example, the new House rules, approved in January 1995, decreased committee staff by at least one-third and required all committee chairs to hire subcommittee staff, eliminating the prerogative of subcommittee chairs to do so. As Ronald J. Peters Jr. noted, "The reduction in committee staffs struck at the heart of committee power because the scope of committee activity is delimited by its resources."[29] Gingrich also took control of appointing committee chairs to ensure that they shared his perspectives. He often overlooked members with seniority and instead chose committee chairs who would toe the conservative line.[30]

Gingrich also established party task forces to outline legislation in key areas such as welfare reform. This "effectively supplanted the committees as drafters of Contract legislation." Although Congress had used ad hoc committees in the past, Gingrich's reliance on them surpassed previous efforts.[31] Among the new Republican procedures, joint referral of bills, which had plagued child care in the late 1980s, was eliminated and replaced with the Speaker's ability to designate "lead committees" and direct committee referrals. The result of these changes was the "relative absence of jurisdictional infighting between committees." They "worked in private to settle their jurisdictional differences, and the Republican leadership stepped in quickly to help resolve any differences." Gingrich also went about changing committee names "to reflect GOP priorities." For example, the Committee on Education and Labor became the Committee on Economic and Educational Opportunities to avoid any association with organized labor.[32]

The Senate's smaller size and more informal style made the need for reform less compelling. Nonetheless, partisan motives prompted the Senate Republican Conference to approve a few reforms aimed at "promot[ing] the policy agenda of the conservative-oriented majority." These reforms, such as limiting terms of committee chairs, did not have an immediate effect.[33]

The changes in the House made it more difficult for Democrats to get their options on the table. Although Republicans had voiced the same complaints when the Democrats were in control, Democratic members of Congress and their staff felt that after forty years of minority status, Republicans had gone to far greater extremes than Democrats had to ensure that their views prevailed. For issues such as child care, Democrats would have to find a middle ground, identify alternatives with bipartisan appeal, and enlist the support of moderate Republicans if they wanted to capture a majority of votes.

Child Care and Welfare Reform Legislation

The story of child care under welfare reform shows child care becoming a major negotiating point in the final welfare bill after barely being mentioned at all in the original GOP proposals.[34] Underlying the deliberations for welfare and child care was a consensus among lawmakers and organized interests that the CCDBG had established a workable structure for child care legislation. The CCDBG and its regulations enabled members of Congress to sidestep certain issues, such as providing vouchers and funding religiously affiliated child care providers, that had been so contentious a decade earlier.

Early Linkages Between Welfare and Child Care

Starting in 1993 Republicans attacked what they considered the "two fundamental causes of welfare": nonwork and illegitimacy. Robert Rector at the Heritage Foundation had a major influence on the development of Republican welfare proposals.[35] In the late 1980s Rector had been the chief strategist for conservative organized interests as they tackled child care legislation. At his prompting, Republican proposals now eliminated AFDC, "lumped it with nearly all other major poverty programs [including child care] . . . and turned the money over to the states to do with as they please—provided they followed certain federal guidelines."[36] Rector called for "strings-attached welfare reform." As he explained: "The [legislation] would end sixty federal welfare programs and fold them into a block grant. We . . . get rid of sixty feet of regulations and instead attach ten or thirty pages of firm federal requirements that come with this money. Those requirements basically say, 'We want work, not dependence. We want marriage, not illegitimacy.'"[37]

In June 1994, almost eighteen months into his first term, Clinton introduced the Work and Responsibility Act of 1994 (H.R. 4605). In contrast to GOP provisions for welfare under the Contract with America, Clinton kept welfare as an entitlement and invested in support services, such as child care. His bill required welfare recipients to work within two years of receiving welfare benefits. He also included $2.7 billion over five years to pay for child care for those enrolled in mandatory education and training programs and to continue to extend child care for one year after welfare recipients joined the workforce. Clinton's 1994 welfare proposal maintained a guarantee of child care for welfare recipients and added another $1.5 billion for child care for working poor families.[38] Other Democratic welfare proposals on the table at the time also emphasized job training and invested more than Clinton did in support services, including child care.[39] But between 1993 and 1994, health care reform dominated most of the congressional agenda, leaving little room for anything else other than some initial legislative activity and hearings on the welfare and child care fronts.[40]

With a Democratic Congress, hearings had focused on President Clinton's welfare proposal and related issues. In July and August 1994 the House Committee on Ways and Means, Subcommittee on Human Resources held seven days of hearings on welfare reform.[41] Child care did not figure prominently in the testimonies and discussion. Representatives Snowe and Patricia

Schroeder testified at hearings before the House Committee on Education and Labor, Subcommittee on Human Resources. Both were members of the Congressional Caucus on Women's Issues, which had requested congressional hearings on child care and commissioned the GAO to investigate the linkage between child care subsidies and women's employment.[42] Moreover, despite billions of federal and state dollars invested in child care, only 6 percent of the AFDC caseload received child care subsidies.[43] Gaps in child care service were due to variations among states in eligibility criteria, limits to employment-related child care assistance, and the states' unwillingness to invest in child care for low-income and poor working families, especially if it required a state match, as with the At-Risk Child Care Program. Consequently, state funding for welfare-related child care often took priority over assistance for low-income families.[44] One of the GAO's most important findings was that the number of poor and low-income women who could be working would increase significantly with higher subsidies for child care.[45]

At the same hearing, Nancy Ebb of CDF described the impact of welfare reform on children. She explained that "welfare reform doesn't only mean helping parents work. It also means helping children thrive and grow and turn into productive citizens so they have an alternative to welfare when they are adults."[46] But sentiments about the well-being of children were few and far between at this point. Instead, discussions on child care focused on its role in promoting employment for welfare recipients.

Public opinion revealed support for child care as a part of welfare reform. A 1994 Gallup poll reported that 90 percent of those surveyed thought that "the government should help provide child care so a parent on welfare can work or look for work."[47] But it took months before Congress arrived at a final solution incorporating these views.

Getting Welfare off the Ground

The GOP ascent to power created changes in committee leadership. Representative Bill Archer (R-Tex.), the new chair of the House Committee on Ways and Means, was a "quiet" and "true conservative" with "an explosive agenda" and an appreciation for consensus building.[48] Representative Clay Shaw, who had cosponsored the major Republican alternatives to the ABC in 1989 and 1990, became chair of the Committee on Ways and Means, Subcommittee on Human Resources.

Representative Bill Goodling became the chair of the Committee on Economic and Educational Opportunities. He had been the ranking minority member of the committee when the child care bill was enacted in 1990. Goodling presented a mixed profile when it came to child care. As a former teacher and principal, he had a long-standing interest in the education of young children. He was interested in family literacy and Even Start (a program that offers adult basic education and parent–child activities) but was not very involved with child care. The education committee's Subcommittee on Human Resources, which Dale Kildee had chaired in the late 1980s, was eliminated. Child care now fell under the Subcommittee on Early Childhood, Youth, and Families, chaired by Representative Randy Cunningham (R-Calif.).

Because of the new House rules pertaining to committee jurisdiction, rivalry between the Committee on Ways and Means and the Committee on Economic and Educational Opportunities, which had stymied the 1990 child care legislative process, was no longer an issue. The new House rules eliminated simultaneous multiple referral of bills to more than one committee, but they allowed for sequential referral.[49] In 1995 GOP leaders in the House agreed that the Committee on Educational Opportunities would take the lead on child care while the Committee on Ways and Means took the lead on welfare legislation.

In the 104th Congress, which began in January 1995, the Republican majority ensured that devolution and block grants dominated welfare reform. According to one GOP legislative staff person, immediately upon winning the majority, House Republicans asked the Congressional Research Service to complete a report on all domestic programs and policies in areas such as child care, welfare, nutrition, education, and health. The report revealed over 300 programs in various sectors. Republicans then developed a proposal for one block grant to states that would enable them to administer these various programs as they saw fit. This was in line with the GOP intent to diminish the federal government's involvement in state programs. Although the proposal never materialized, it demonstrated Republicans' intent to consolidate many federal programs in their subsequent deliberations.

In early 1995, Speaker Gingrich and Representative Archer formed a work group on welfare composed of staff for Republican members, congressional committees, and Republican governors. The group drafted what became Title I of the leading GOP welfare reform bill, which included time limits on welfare eligibility and stringent work requirements. As someone involved with the discussions explained in an interview, "When it came to day care, it was surprisingly easy . . . we ended a bunch of programs . . . and put all the money into one place . . . and basically what we did was somewhat modify the CCDBG."

But Republicans did more than just modify the block grant. They eliminated the child care entitlements under the At-Risk Child Care Program, TCC, and AFDC Child Care. They also repealed CCDBG language on standards and all its set-asides for improvement of quality and supply. GOP proposals also included structural changes to several child nutrition programs, including block granting WIC with the Child and Adult Care and Food Program (CACFP). The latter subsidizes meals for children at child care centers and in family child care programs. Democrats, including President Clinton, were quick to complain that GOP welfare reform proposals would unfairly punish children. In the words of Senator Christopher Dodd:

> House Republicans would eliminate the school lunch program, gut child care funding just when it will be more desperately needed than ever before, and tear apart our basic safety net for children. I believe they will find that any money saved from these measures will be lost many times over when ill-nourished, deprived children reach adulthood completely incapable of participating in our economy.[50]

Child care advocates were demoralized by the GOP proposals. In an interview with the author, one lobbyist noted, "We had a sense that we were losing everything we ever did. . . . We were just trying to keep bad things from happening. February 1995 was one of the lowest points in my career."

In January 1995 the House subcommittee on early childhood held a hearing on the Contract with America's child welfare and child care provisions. A month earlier, the GAO had released a report on the importance of child care subsidies in promoting the employment of low-income women.[51] At the hearing, Jane L. Ross from GAO explained how consolidation would streamline administrative responsibilities and "offer states the flexibility to tailor their child care assistance programs to their particular mix of low-income families."[52] However, many witnesses warned against the pitfalls of consolidation. As Ross explained, "Some states might take advantage of the opportunity to divert money that otherwise would have gone to child care for other purposes."[53]

In February 1995 the House Subcommittee on Human Resources and the Subcommittee on Early Childhood, Youth, and Families held joint hearings on welfare and child care.[54] Helen Blank from CDF explained the importance of investing in child care resources while also supporting consolidation:

> There is nothing wrong with consolidating several programs with certain safeguards for children, but it won't fix the resource problem. Some type of block grant is fine, but there has to be some reality testing about what it is going to do given the kind of need there is for child care, and that you don't end basic national commitments.[55]

Witnesses from conservative and liberal camps supported consolidating federal child care programs to eliminate the overlap and complications that arose from differing programmatic guidelines and eligibility levels. In efforts to block the dismantling of the CCDBG, witnesses from state and county child care offices, HHS, and national advocacy groups described the positive aspects of the block grant, such as its ability to increase assistance to eligible families, its quality enhancements, the states' authority over standards for health and safety, and its emphasis on vouchers and parental choice.

One of the national commitments that Blank and other child care advocates wanted to protect was the CCDBG's quality set-aside. At another hearing, Patty Siegal, one of the first grassroots organizers of child care in the late 1960s and the executive director of the California Child Care Resources and Referral Network, described the CCDBG quality set-aside as

> the little island of infrastructure that attempts to hold this whole shaky, evolving child care world together. . . . It's the island of consumer protection. It's all the pieces that it's easy to take for granted because they may seem invisible. But, in fact, we must protect these resources. . . . Because the States are simply facing great odds.[56]

The Senate also addressed child care in the context of welfare reform. With Republicans in control of the Senate, Senator Nancy Kassebaum (R-Kans.) became chair of the Committee on Labor and Human Resources. Kassebaum was a moderate Republican with a record on domestic issues that blended conservative and liberal themes. Senator Dan Coats (R-Ind.) became chair of the Subcommittee on Children and Families. He had a conservative voting record, with the exception of his support for the Family and Medical Leave Act of 1993.[57]

In February 1995 Coats's subcommittee held hearings on the CCDBG.[58] Douglas Besharov from the American Enterprise Institute (AEI) called for "free[ing] localities from the straitjacket of federal bureaucracy without unreasonably cutting financial support."[59] Child care advocates emphasized the importance of protecting funding for low-income working families. The CCDBG targeted such families, but approximately sixteen states used CCDBG funds to subsidize welfare-related child care. As Senator Edward Kennedy noted, "[W]elfare reform threatens to become a battle between families trying to get off welfare and families trying to stay off welfare—a battle with no winners."[60]

Other witnesses at the Senate hearing included Mayor Cardell Cooper of East Orange, New Jersey, who testified in support of the CCDBG as the base for child care consolidation. He described the Conference of Mayors' positions in support of policies that enhanced the supply and quality of child care and increased funding. Administrators of child care programs for low-income families in Indiana, Massachusetts, and Florida all spoke about the importance of federal child care assistance.[61]

Senator Dodd, ranking member of the Senate Subcommittee on Children and Families, was one of the most ardent advocates for children in the context of welfare reform. He commented, "Instead of putting children at the center of the welfare reform debate, as they should be, in my view, some people on the other side are treating them as nuisances to be swept under the rug."[62]

Mary Jo Bane, HHS assistant secretary for families and children, described the steps her agency had taken to make the CCDBG and Title IV-A (welfare-related) child care programs consistent with each other. Administration of the four major child care programs was now under one entity, the newly formed Child Care Bureau, directed by Joan Lombardi. Establishing the Child Care Bureau in late 1994 was a structural change that, combined with Lombardi's dynamic leadership, was critical in advancing child care as a national issue and elevating the priority ranking of child care within the federal government. Bane also cautioned the committee about a welfare reform that forced people to go to work without proper regard for the safety of children in child care settings. She described the hundreds of thousands of children on state waiting lists for subsidized child care across the country.[63]

In March 1995 Kassebaum chaired hearings on the impact of welfare reform on children and families. The second day of the hearings focused on child care. Lead witnesses were Deborah Phillips from the National Research Council and Sandra Hofferth from the University of Michigan. Phillips emphasized emerging research findings regarding child care quality and the importance of protecting the health and safety of children in child care settings. Hofferth also addressed the quality issue in her testimony:

> Even action as seemingly minor as the five percent quality set-aside in the CCDBG has served to increase the number of states that offer systematic child care training from half of all states to virtually every single State. . . . Rather than restricting States, this set-aside gives them the opportunity to make a very broad range of enhancements in their child care infrastructure.[64]

Another major concern of child care advocates was that Congress not eliminate the child care entitlement under Title IV-A (welfare) established in 1988 under the FSA (see chapter 3). A child care entitlement posed problems to legislators preoccupied with balancing the federal budget and limiting the role of the federal government. However, without a child care entitlement, there was no guarantee that Congress would annually appropriate enough money to meet the need. As Blank explained, "The number of programs was not an issue. . . . We said it was fine if you wanted to consolidate. . . . But the real problem was giving up child care slots and losing it as an entitlement."[65]

Congressional committees worked quickly in drafting welfare bills. On February 21, 1995, Goodling introduced the Welfare Reform and Consolidation Act of 1995 (H.R. 999), which the Committee on Economic and Educational Opportunities promptly amended and approved by a vote of twenty-three to seventeen. Title I of this bill called for consolidation of the four major federal child care programs: AFDC child care, TCC, At-Risk Child Care Program, and the CCDBG. In the committee report, members quoted the NGA 1995 policy statement calling for a "seamless child care system . . . incorporating all child care programs and making the CCDBG the foundation . . . to form a single child care system operated by the states."[66]

The Democrats on the committee were outraged at how the Republicans ran the bill through committee. They were annoyed that the bill eliminated the three child care entitlements and replaced them with a single discretionary program subject to the unpredictable annual appropriations process. They complained that the bill made no allowance for the anticipated increased need for child care due to mandatory work provisions under welfare. Democrats also opposed allowing the states to transfer up to 20 percent of child care funds to other block grants, fearing that this would reduce funding for child care. And they opposed elimination of the CCDBG's health and safety standards and quality set-aside. They pointed to Goodling's statements, published in the *Washington Times*, expressing concern about a lack of funding for child care under his welfare bill.[67] After all, if the Republican chair of a committee with jurisdiction over child care had such concerns, wasn't there cause to reconsider the funding levels?

Goodling's bill also consolidated several food and nutrition programs for children into two block grants, one of which combined funding for WIC and the CACFP. Those in favor of the provisions claimed that the consolidation would streamline burdensome regulations for these programs. H.R. 999 also limited CACFP benefits for family child care to families with incomes below 185 percent of poverty. GOP committee members explained that such changes would "assist the Committee in achieving budget savings without reducing benefits to low-income children."[68]

CDF, CWLA, and other child care groups worked with a coalition of organizations opposing these changes to children's nutrition programs. They argued that block granting the CACFP with WIC would diminish the availability of funds for important nutritional services, restrict benefits to low-income families, and force many family child care providers that relied on these subsidies to go out of business. Moreover, the CACFP had provided an incentive to family child care providers to become licensed or registered. Without such an incentive, many would go underground and the quality of care could be compromised.[69] Donna E. Shalala, secretary of HHS, sent a letter to the leaders of the Committee on Economic and Educational Opportunities explaining the Clinton administration's objections to H.R. 999, which were similar to the concerns expressed by Democrats on the committee.

On March 13, 1995, chairs of the House committees with jurisdiction over major social welfare programs—Representatives Archer, Goodling, and Pat Roberts (R-Kans., and chair of the Committee on Agriculture, which was responsible for food stamps and federal nutrition programs)—introduced a "sweeping conservative bill" (H.R. 1214) that gave states unprecedented authority to run their own social programs. It required adults receiving cash assistance for more than twenty-four months to engage in work activities.[70] The bill, based on the recommendations of the Republican welfare task force, became the new version of H.R. 4 (Personal Responsibility Act from the Contract with America). On March 24, 1995, the House debated H.R. 4 and approved it by a partisan vote of 234 to 199. Nine Democrats voted for it, and five Republicans opposed it. Regarding child care, H.R. 4 folded the three Title IV-A child care programs into the CCDBG, along with other federal child care programs, for a total authorization of $2.1 billion over five years. This was a significant cut in existing child care funding. Similar to Goodling's bill, the House measure repealed all the CCDBG health and safety requirements and set-asides (including the one for quality improvement) and allowed states to transfer up to 20 percent of child care block grant funds to other block grants, such as the Title XX SSBG. The bill had provisions for block granting and restructuring child nutrition programs similar to those of H.R. 999.[71]

Before the final House vote, four Republican representatives—Nancy Johnson of Connecticut, Deborah Pryce of Ohio, Jennifer Dunn of Washington, and Enid Greene Waldholtz of Utah—had offered an en bloc amendment prohibiting the requirement that an individual engage in work activities unless affordable child care is provided. The Rules Committee had blocked the amendment, but the House had approved Representative Johnson's amendment to increase child care funding by $150 million over five years, bringing the total child care funding to $2.1 billion.[72] A Democratic alternative (H. 1267), introduced by Representative Nathan Deal (D-Ga.), had the support of both liberal and conservative Democrats. The Deal substitute, which Clinton "quietly" supported, restored some of the child care funds that Republicans had cut and retained a child care entitlement. Members engaged in a partisan floor debate over the differences between the Deal substitute and the GOP welfare bill regarding child care. But in the end, the Deal bill was defeated by a partisan vote of 205 to 228.[73]

Opposition from the Democrats to H.R. 4 was strong. Minority Leader Richard Gephardt explained: "Everybody knows you're not going to get people off welfare if you don't have child care."[74] Protesting that the bill would leave many children without benefits, Democrats wore "Save the Children" ties and scarves and "charged that the Republican bill was mean-spirited." According to Elizabeth Drew, "The House debate on welfare was uglier than any in memory. . . . The last shreds of civility were gone."[75] Clinton opposed the bill, explaining that the "legislation contains no incentives or requirements for States to maintain their own funding for cash assistance or for child care or work supports."[76] Senator Kassebaum responded to the

House bill by promising to take care of child care in the Senate's welfare package.[77]

Two Senate Committees Approve Child Care Legislation

Senate actions on child care in 1995 provided the basis for later negotiations with the House and a framework for the final child care provisions under welfare reform. The two Senate committees with jurisdiction over welfare and child care, the Committee on Finance and the Committee on Labor and Human Resources, each passed child care legislation, thereby creating the need to reconcile their differences over funding, organization of federal child care programs, and committee jurisdiction.

The Finance Committee's new chair, Senator Bob Packwood (R-Ore.), had been one of the main opponents of child care legislation in 1988 because of his uneasiness with federal child care standards.[78] On May 26, 1995, the Senate Finance Committee approved Packwood's Family Self-Sufficiency Act by a vote of twelve to eight, with all Republicans in favor and all Democrats, except Senator Max Baucus (D-Mont.), opposed. Packwood's bill merged AFDC, JOBS, and the Title IV-A child care programs to create a new grant to states called Temporary Family Assistance Grants. Packwood allowed a provision that "if a state required participation by the parent of a child under six, the state must provide child care." But his bill lacked a specific child care funding stream and did not define what constituted child care. It also eliminated the requirement first enacted in 1988 under the FSA that states set market rates for Title IV-A child care payments. Deleting language on market rates would allow states to set very low rates, which could make it difficult for providers to sustain an adequate level of quality. CDF opposed Packwood's bill, arguing that it required states to "choose between child care subsidies and basic cash benefits, job training, or other services to families on welfare."[79] In September 1995, faced with charges of sexual harassment, Packwood resigned from office. Senator William Roth (R-Del.) became the new chair of the Finance Committee. His "visceral distaste for high taxes and excessive government spending"[80] made him an unlikely proponent of investing in child care programs.

Senator Kassebaum and the Senate Committee on Labor and Human Resources took a different approach from the Finance Committee's. Kassebaum and the next highest Republican on the committee, Senator Jim

Jeffords of Vermont, were more liberal than most GOP members. The committee also had some of the most ardent Democratic child care champions, in particular Dodd, Kennedy, and Barbara Mikulski (as well as staunch conservatives, such as Senator John Ashcroft [R-Mo.]). On May 24, 1995, Kassebaum, joined by Senators Dodd, Kennedy, Jeffords, Coats, and Daniel Inouye (D-Hawaii, who was not on the committee), introduced the CCDBG Amendments Act of 1995 (S. 850), which reauthorized and amended the CCDBG. The 1990 CCDBG was due to be reauthorized at this time. According to Kassebaum, "The primary goal of this bill is to ensure that there is a seamless system of child care where it counts—at the point where the parent, child, and provider meet."[81] Kassebaum's bill was not the first one in the Senate to consolidate child care programs. In February 1995 Dodd and Kennedy introduced a bill (S. 472) that consolidated child care services for low-income families, increased funding, and left child care as a capped entitlement. On May 26, 1995, the Senate Labor and Human Resources Committee unanimously approved Kassebaum's bill and sent it to the full Senate for consideration as an amendment to welfare reform.[82]

Unlike the House bill, Kassebaum's legislation retained the health and safety standards from the 1990 CCDBG. Kassebaum also combined the set-aside for care for school-age children and the early childhood set-aside into one quality set-aside and lowered it to 15 percent of a state's allocation from the 25 percent total set-aside under the 1990 law. The bill extended eligibility to families with average annual incomes at or below 100 percent of the state median (compared with 75 percent in the 1990 CCDBG law). It also required a "representative distribution of funding among the working poor and recipients of federal welfare assistance." This was to ensure that the low-income and working poor families were not cut out of federal child care programs altogether. No more than 5 percent of state allocations could be spent on administrative costs. However, the committee made it easier for states to comply with the 5 percent allotment by allowing many expenses that were previously considered administrative to be counted under the costs of service delivery.[83]

One of the most controversial items in the Kassebaum bill was the requirement that "any federal funds used by states for child care services must comply with the regulations, standards, and criteria of this act."[84] This stipulation angered conservatives and some Republicans who preferred to give states flexibility and reduce federal regulations. Kassebaum kept the language from the 1990 law pertaining to funding of religiously affiliated child care providers. As one Senate staff person explained in an interview, "Republicans were concerned that legislation for child care have parental choice and allow funding for religious providers. . . . There were dead bodies all over the place with this issue in 1990, so we left the wording as it was in the CCDBG."

Kassebaum's bill also created a jurisdictional problem because it required that welfare-related child care, which was under the jurisdiction of the Committee on Finance, fall under the CCDBG, which was in the purview of the Senate Committee on Labor and Human Resources. Neither committee wanted to relinquish control over child care. According to a Senate staff member, this jurisdictional conflict "was an important, but not an overriding factor" in the final negotiations. Some House participants in the child care deliberations thought otherwise and claimed that the jurisdictional conflicts in the Senate over child care delayed progress on the bills.

On June 8, 1995, Senate Minority Leader Tom Daschle (D-S.D.) introduced Work First, which was the Senate Democratic leadership's major welfare reform initiative, cosponsored by Senators Dodd, Kennedy, Mikulski, and John Breaux (D-La.). It kept child care as an entitlement for welfare recipients and created a new child care entitlement targeting low-income working families with incomes below the poverty level. Democrats proposed a $15 billion increase in new child care funds over seven years. Daschle, speaking on behalf of his fellow Democrats, called child care the "linchpin between welfare and work." And he commented, "If child care is not going to be provided for, then what real expectation is there that somehow these mothers are going to be forced to go out that door and expect the system to work? It is not going to happen."[85] Clinton was squarely behind Daschle's bill because "it really heavily emphasize[d] the importance of child care."[86] But CDF and others knew that the Democrats' increased funding levels for child care and maintenance of existing welfare programs would never pass muster in a Republican Congress.[87]

On August 11, 1995, Senate Majority Leader Robert Dole introduced the Work Opportunity Act of 1995 (S. 1120) to replace Packwood's Family Self-Sufficiency Act.[88] The child care provisions in Dole's bill were almost the same as those in Kassebaum's bill, except that Dole eliminated the controversial provision that applied CCDBG rules to all federal child care programs. Like Packwood, Dole also combined all federal child care assistance initiatives with other welfare programs into one block grant, which lacked specific funding for child care. In contrast, Kassebaum's bill, as a reauthorization of the CCDBG and not a welfare reform bill, focused only on child care. Dole's bill also eliminated Packwood's guarantee of child care for children under the age of six. Given Dole's "very stringent work requirements," which CDF and others claimed would "trigger extraordinary child care costs," this was a significant change. HHS estimated that by 2000 the new work requirements in Dole's bill would require over $4.1 billion in child care spending above federal and state expenditures at the time.[89] President Clinton opposed Dole's bill for many reasons, including its shortcomings regarding child care.[90]

In mid-August, Dole postponed floor debate on welfare claiming that there was insufficient time to resolve partisan differences in the weeks remaining before recess. The postponement increased the likelihood that welfare would be part of reconciliation legislation when the Senate reconvened after Labor Day.[91]

Senate Republicans Change the Course of Child Care Legislation

In addition to Kassebaum, other moderate Republicans (such as Senators Snowe, John Chafee, Jeffords, Ben Nighthorse Campbell of Colorado, Arlen Specter, and William Cohen of Maine) opposed their more conservative party colleagues on several welfare-related issues.[92] Armed with a sense of unity and knowing that the Senate GOP could not pass welfare reform without their votes, these Republicans succeeded in getting many of their views included in the final Senate welfare bill, including an expansion of the child care provisions. In an interview with the author, a staff person for one of these moderate Republicans in the Senate explained:

By May 1995, there were thirteen people from Senate moderate Republican staffs . . . and we became a policy group. . . . Across the months we met three to four times a week and pulled together an agenda of about twelve issues for our bosses. It fell out that each person had some issue . . . and our bosses met on a fairly regular basis. . . . The senators went to the leadership and told Dole that unless changes were made, there would be no [welfare] bill. . . . So in the Dole bill that went to the floor . . . basically, we got the Labor and Human Resources Committee bill on child care intact, along with a provision that parents with children below age six cannot be sanctioned off welfare because access to child care was unavailable.

Senator Snowe (one of the original sponsors of ABC when she was a House member in 1987) championed the provision to accommodate parents with children below the age of six.[93]

As in the late 1980s, Senator Orrin Hatch was again pivotal in influencing the course and outcome of child care legislation. Concerned about the lack of adequate funds for child care under welfare reform, he preferred a separate funding stream for child care under welfare. Working with the NGA, CDF, NCSL, NWLC, and APWA, Hatch drafted an amendment to carve out $5 billion for child care over five years from Dole's welfare block grant.[94] As Hatch explained, "I believe we need to delineate funds for child care under the welfare program, and the reason we do is because if you just block grant them to the governors . . . it becomes too easy to use those funds for other children's programs."[95]

According to a Senate staff person, Hatch felt his approach was feasible because "states had a structure [CCDBG] with which to work . . . that did not exclude the woman next door who stayed home with her kids . . . or your kids . . . and it still had church-based care as an option." Another staff person made a similar point:

> In a sense, we had fought these battles in 1990 and did not have to revisit them. . . . If we had to fight these battles under welfare reform, I'm not sure that we would have had success in enacting child care under welfare. . . . CCDBG offered sufficient flexibility to parents and states, so the idea of putting more money into this was not problematic.

Child care, thus, had become a critical bargaining chip for Hatch and other Senate Republicans in their negotiation with their leadership over welfare. Dodd and Kennedy supported Hatch's proposal to carve out child care funding but did not think it went far enough because it lacked additional child care funding. Consequently, lively debate ensued when Dole brought welfare reform to the floor.

Home Alone with Child Care in the Senate

In the summer of 1995, Senate Democrats stepped up their publicity on child care. By fall, child care had become an important issue even for Dole. He knew that he needed moderate Republicans to get welfare through the

Senate. On September 8, 1995, Dole revised his welfare bill by including Snowe's proposed revision, which exempted from work requirements welfare recipients who had children under the age of six and could not obtain child care.[96] Kennedy's amendment, guaranteeing that no preschool child be left alone under welfare, lost by a vote of fifty to forty-eight. Two Republicans, Senators Campbell and Jeffords, voted with the Democrats.

Kennedy was one of the harshest critics of Dole's welfare legislation, which he referred to as the "home alone bill" because of what he considered its shortcomings in regard to child care. Kennedy and Dodd preferred investing more in child care so that parents could engage in work activities. To that end, they introduced an amendment that increased funding for child care beyond the $5 billion that Hatch had carved out from the block grant. Dodd and Kennedy offered $6 billion more, for a total of $11 billion of new child care funding over five years. Careful to avoid calling it an entitlement, they also created a guarantee of child care for those funded under the new welfare block grants. Dodd defended his amendment on the Senate floor, saying, "All we are saying here is that to really make our welfare reform program work, to really make the Dole bill work, you have to have some feature to this that makes it possible for people to be able to leave their home in the morning, knowing full well that their most important asset, the thing they care about the most, their children, are taken care of."[97]

Dodd and Kennedy were initially joined by moderate Republicans who supported this funding increase. Hatch opposed it. He questioned where the additional $6 billion would come from. Dodd planned to fund it with "reductions in corporate welfare" but was vague as to the specifics. Hatch also opposed the creation of a separate child care *program*, in contrast to a separate funding *stream*, which he endorsed. As he explained: "This is not to disparage the efforts of my friends, because . . . if the moneys were there, . . . if we really could go out and find them somewhere, certainly I would be very much in favor of trying to do that. But I am not in favor of creating an additional program to be run by HHS."[98]

For reasons that are unclear, at the last minute the moderate Republicans dropped their support for Dodd's amendment. As one Senate staff person put it in an interview with the author,"For whatever reason . . . Republican members who had endorsed the amendment before started to feel uneasy and looked as if they wouldn't go along with Dodd. . . . So one by one Dodd crossed their names off the amendment and introduced it anyway."

Several congressional staff speculated that the NGA exerted influence here. Although the governors wanted more money for child care under welfare, they were not willing to endorse Dodd's amendment, with its requirements that money be spent a certain way. The NGA was in a difficult situation regarding welfare reform because of the bipartisan makeup of its membership. Republican governors supported stringent work requirements and time limits. Democratic governors opposed the loss of welfare as an entitlement. These partisan differences made it difficult for the NGA to take a firm stand on many aspects of welfare legislation.[99]

On September 11, 1995, the Senate approved a motion offered by Senator Rick Santorum (R-Pa.), who had drafted the GOP welfare bill when he was a member of the House, to kill the Dodd amendment. The Santorum motion to defeat Dodd's amendment won by a vote of fifty to forty-eight; only two Republicans (Senators Jeffords and Campbell) voted with Dodd.[100]

Although Dodd's amendment failed, eventually Dole, Daschle, and Dodd, with input from Snowe, other moderate Republicans, and Hatch, negotiated to set aside $5 billion over five years for the CCDBG and add $3 billion over five years as an entitlement, to be distributed to the states based on their current Title IV-A child care spending.[101] Kassebaum's amendment to strike the provision that would have allowed states to transfer up to 30 percent of their CCDBG funds to other programs won by a vote of seventy-six to twenty-two. Daschle's Democratic alternative lost by a vote of forty-five to fifty-four, with all Democrats except Baucus voting for it. On September 19, 1995, the Senate approved welfare reform, H.R. 4, by a vote of eighty-seven to twelve. Its child care provisions differed from the House bill by protecting single welfare recipients with children under the age of six from having to participate in work requirements if they were unable to find child care. The Senate also had earmarked more funding for child care than the House. Based on the Kassebaum bill, the Senate's legislation maintained the CCDBG and its health and safety provisions as well as a quality set-aside. At this point, it was still unclear if there would be enough time to enact a freestanding welfare bill that year. So congressional leaders anticipated that they might have to fold it into their reconciliation bill.

Welfare Reform and Reconciliation

On October 26, 1995, by a vote of 227 to 203, the House approved reconciliation legislation (H.R. 2491), which included the full text of H.R. 4

as approved by the House in March. The Senate approved its reconciliation bill two days later by a vote of 52 to 47. The conferees for reconciliation created a single child care program with two funding streams totaling $18 billion over seven years. They maintained the same total dollar amount of funding as in the Senate bill but decreased the annual allocations by stretching it across seven instead of five years. One funding stream was a capped entitlement (mandatory spending) funded at $11 billion, and the other was a discretionary program funded at $7 billion. Of the capped entitlement funds, 70 percent were targeted to welfare families, the rest to low-income families. The conferees eliminated all language that required providers to meet minimum health and safety standards and set aside 3 percent of the funds for consumer education to parents and the public, which was a decrease from the 15 percent set-aside in the Senate bill for activities enhancing child care supply and quality. The reconciliation bill set family income eligibility at 85 percent of the state median income and prohibited states from transferring funds out of the CCDBG for other purposes, which had been one of Kassebaum's concerns.

Opposition to the overall welfare bill ran high among Democrats in Congress and among organized interests representing children and welfare recipients. They continued to decry the detrimental effects the bill would have on children. Marian Wright Edelman, with friends at high levels in the Clinton administration (Hillary Rodham Clinton was a past president of CDF's board, and HHS Secretary Shalala had been a CDF board member), wrote a stinging open letter to President Clinton in the *Washington Post*. In her own words:

> I am calling for your unwavering moral leadership for children and opposition to Senate and House welfare and Medicaid block grants which will make more children poor and sick. . . . As you well know, these block grants are not designed primarily to help children . . . they are Trojan Horses for massive budget cuts and for imposing an ideological agenda that says that government assistance for the poor and children should be dismantled.[102]

For a combination of reasons, on December 6, 1995, Clinton vetoed the reconciliation bill. Among his concerns were its cuts in "child care that helps mothers move from welfare to work."[103] The demise of the budget bill was a stinging hit to Republicans because it pointed to weaknesses in their ability to govern. Some political observers claimed that the budget defeat, not the Contract with America, "was the defining event of the 104th Congress." Frequent government shutdowns at the end of 1995 because of delays in enacting budget bills, ethics charges against Gingrich related to his fund-raising activities, and congressional failure to enact major legislation did not work in the Republicans' favor.[104]

In the meantime, welfare legislation proceeded on its own track. In December the House and Senate each passed a conferenced version of H.R. 4, the Personal Responsibility and Work Opportunity Act of 1995 (PRWORA), which was very similar to what had been passed under the reconciliation package. Lawmakers thought that as a freestanding bill welfare might not be burdened with the other problematic aspects of the reconcil-iation bill. The House passed welfare reform by a vote of 245 to 178, and the Senate by a vote of 52 to 47.[105] On January 9, 1996, Clinton vetoed the welfare legislation because, among other things, it failed to protect children adequately in areas such as child care.[106] By now, Clinton had vetoed welfare legislation twice, once as part of reconciliation legislation in December 1995 and again as a freestanding bill in January 1996. In both versions, he singled out the inadequacies of the child care provisions.

Governors Give Welfare Another Chance

One of the most important events that helped jump-start welfare legisla-tion after Clinton's vetoes occurred on February 6, 1996, when the nation's governors reached a unanimous agreement on welfare. For child care, the governors recommended adding $4 billion to the child care funding in the vetoed welfare legislation. According to one person involved with the gov-ernors' deliberations, this was " a threshold issue for Democratic governors." The NGA also recommended exempting from work requirements parents of children under the age of one and giving states the option to limit work requirements to twenty hours per week for parents with a child under the age of six.[107] The NGA welfare proposal provided a road map for Congress after the twice-vetoed welfare bill.

CDF and other child care advocacy groups opposed the governors' plan because many aspects of it were unchanged from earlier versions of welfare reform, including its repeal of health and safety requirements. Moreover, its more stringent work requirements and cuts in the Title XX SSBG (a major source of child care funding) diminished the significance of the increased child care funding. CDF complained that the NGA proposal would "gut health and safety protections for children" and not do enough for improving child care quality and supply.[108]

Regrouping in early 1996 with the benefit of the NGA plan, both chambers went to work on welfare reform, which would be folded into budget reconciliation legislation. On June 12, 1996, the House Committee on Ways and Means and the Committee on Economic and Educational Opportunities each passed separate versions of welfare legislation that included child care. The House Budget Committee was to combine the measures into one bill for a full House vote. The Committee on Ways and Means approved its welfare bill (H.R. 3507) by a vote of twenty-three to fourteen, with only one Democrat joining all the GOP members of the committee in support of the bill. The legislation included nearly $14 billion for the reconfigured CCDBG over five years, a $4 billion increase over the vetoed welfare bill of 1995 (H.R. 4). The Committee on Ways and Means restored the health and safety requirements as they had been in the 1990 CCDBG, based on an amendment offered by Representative Pete Stark (D-Calif.) during the subcommittee's markup of the bill. As a House staff person explained in an interview, "We got rid of the health and safety standards in the original draft and after that put them in due to the Senate Labor and Human Resources Committee wanting them. We didn't have any problem with that." The Committee on Ways and Means rejected (by a tie vote) an amendment offered by Representatives Johnson and Barbara Kennelly (D-Conn.) that would have exempted mothers with children under the age of ten from the five-year time limit for welfare benefits if they could not find suitable child care. The bill allowed states to exempt from work requirements parents with children aged six or younger.[109]

The Committee on Economic and Educational Opportunities approved its welfare bill by a vote of twenty-three to eleven; five Democrats joined the Republicans in voting for the bill. The committee funded the reconfigured CCDBG at $22 billion over seven years. Members adopted an amendment offered by Representative Lynn Woolsey (D-Calif.) that exempted a single parent of a child aged ten or younger from work requirements if child care was not available.[110] Goodling also restored the health and safety standards for the CCDBG. In addition, the committee accepted an increase in the quality set-aside. That decision was spurred by Representative George Miller's proposal to increase the quality set-aside from 3 to 5 percent. Goodling countered with 4 percent, which Miller accepted. Even this change kept the committee's funding of quality enhancements lower than in the 1990 CCDBG law. The committee defeated by a vote of twelve to twenty-one an amendment that Representative Patsy Mink introduced to exempt single parents of a child under one from work requirements.[111]

The final House welfare bill combined both committees' versions of child care legislation. It retained the education committee's language on exempting parents with children below the age of eleven if child care was unavailable. It also kept the child care health and safety standards and the 4 percent quality set-aside. On July 18, 1996, the House passed its welfare reform (H.R. 3734) by a vote of 256 to 170. One hundred sixty-five Democrats and four Republicans voted against it.[112]

On June 26 the Senate Finance Committee passed its welfare bill (S. 1795) by a vote of eleven to nine; members voted strictly along party lines. The bill was very similar to the House version. However, regarding child care, it eliminated minimum health and safety standards, perhaps as a nod to the governors, and left the quality set-aside at 3 percent.[113] When the full Senate debated welfare reform in July, Senator Dodd offered a floor amendment, which was passed ninety-four to zero, restoring the child health and safety standards. After all, if the conservative House had accepted them, they should no longer be problematic. Senate Republicans also went along with Dodd's amendment to increase the quality set-aside from 3 to 4 percent of total child care funding. On July 23, 1996, the Senate passed the Republican welfare bill by a vote of seventy-four to twenty-four. Many, including CDF, pointed to a study by the Urban Institute released on July 25, 1996, in the midst of the welfare controversy, which showed that if Congress passed welfare reform, the number of children in poverty would increase by 1.1 million.[114]

The House and Senate conference committees met in late July. In regard to child care, there were few differences between their bills. However, presumably yielding to pressure from the NGA, the conferees deleted language that both chambers had accepted and that would have exempted parents with children under the age of eleven who could not find suitable child care. The final bill lowered this limit to children under the age of six.[115] On July 31 the House passed the conferenced welfare bill by a vote of 328 to 101, with only 2 Republicans opposing it. Ninety-eight Democrats supported it, and an equal number opposed it. Technically, this was a reconciliation bill to reduce spending over six years, mostly through ending the federal guarantee of welfare and eliminating federal support to legal immigrants in areas such as food stamps.[116] On July 31, 1996, Clinton announced at a news conference that he would sign welfare reform legislation. He mentioned that the new child care provisions were among those that would help families become better off.[117]

On August 1 the Senate approved the conference report on welfare reform by a vote of seventy-eight to twenty-one. All fifty-three Republicans and twenty-five Democrats voted in favor of it. On August 22, 1996, Clinton signed the PRWORA into law (P.L. 104-193).

New Welfare Law Significantly Changes Policies for Families with Children

The new law abolished AFDC and other programs and replaced them with a new block grant of federal funds to states, Temporary Assistance to Needy Families (TANF), which went into effect on July 1, 1997. To receive federal funds, states had to operate a welfare program but unlike in the past, states had great flexibility in how they designed and implemented it. As a condition of receiving federal funds, states had to have a certain proportion of their TANF recipients meeting work requirements, reaching 50 percent by 2002. The law did not require states to subject to work requirements parents with children younger than one year. Parents working twenty hours per week and with children under the age of six also were considered working for purposes of receiving TANF benefits. Furthermore, adults could not be penalized for failure to meet work requirements if their failure was due to an inability to find or afford child care for a child under the age of six.[118]

Regarding child care, the 1996 welfare reform bill eliminated the guarantee from the 1988 FSA that the federal government would provide child care assistance to families on welfare that needed such care to participate in work or training programs. It eliminated AFDC child care, TCC, and the At-Risk Child Care Programs and replaced them with the new CCDBG. Of the $22 billion authorized for child care over seven years, $7 billion was discretionary funding, an increase over the 1995 CCDBG funding levels. The remaining $15 billion was a capped entitlement from which states could draw if they maintained child care spending at certain levels of funding. Seventy percent of the capped entitlement funds were to target families receiving or moving off welfare or at risk of becoming dependent on welfare. Most of the rest of the capped entitlement was for low-income working families (table 6.1 summarizes child care provisions under P.L. 104-193).

TABLE 6.1 Child Care Provisions in the Personal Responsibility and Work Opportunity Reconciliation Act of 1996 (P.L. 104-193)

Repeals previous programs	Eliminates child care as an entitlement for families on welfare, repeals Transitional Child Care and the At-Risk Child Care Program
Funding	Replaces AFDC Child Care, Transitional Child Care, At-Risk Child Care, and Child Care and Development Block Grant (CCDBG) with a new CCDBG composed of two funding streams as follows:

1. A capped entitlement to states
   a. Requires state match of federal funds, based on Medicaid formula
   b. Funded at $15 billion over seven years
   c. In order to maintain their portion of capped entitlement, states are required to maintain child care funding at level of FY 1994, FY 1995, or the average of FY 1992–94 (whichever is greater)
   d. Funds distributed based on a state's percentage of the nation's population under age thirteen (which was the formula for the At-Risk Child Care Program)
   e. Funding implemented October 1, 1996

2. Discretionary program
   a. No state match required
   b. Authorized at $7 billion over seven years
   c. Funding distributed to states based on previous formulas for state allocations under the CCDBG
   d. Funding implemented August 22, 1996

States may transfer up to 30 percent of the Temporary Assistance for Needy Families (TANF) Block Grant funds to the CCDBG; states may not transfer funds from the CCDBG to TANF but may finance child care directly out of TANF.

Administrative costs	Limits CCDBG administrative costs to 5 percent but has a broader definition of services defined as nonadministrative than the 1990 CCDBG statute.
Eligibility	States may define eligibility for child care assistance at 85 percent of state median income. States must require both parents in a two-parent family to work, except for certain exceptions related to parental or child disability.

States have the option of allowing mothers with children under age six to work only 20 hours per week. States may exempt mothers with children under age one from work requirements.

	Prohibits states from withholding or decreasing assistance to mothers who cannot obtain child care within a reasonable distance from their home or job and have children under age six.
Quality and standards	Retains the 1990 CCDBG health and safety protections in the areas of prevention and control of infectious diseases, building and physical premises safety, and minimum health and safety training for providers.
	Sets aside a minimum of 4 percent of total child care funding for improving quality, expanding supply, and providing consumer education. This replaces the 25 percent set-aside in the original CCDBG reserved for quality improvements, early childhood development, and before- and after-school care.
	Requires states to distribute consumer information concerning child care.
	Eliminates language in the Family Support Act and the regulations for At-Risk Child Care that required states to pay market rates for child care, but requires states to ensure that eligible children are provided the same access to child care as those not eligible for subsidies.
Work provisions	For FY 1997 and 1998, 20 percent of a state's welfare population must be participating in a work related activity; increasing to 30 percent for FY 1999, 35 percent in FY 2000, 40 percent in FY 2001, and 50 percent in FY 2002.

Sources: Personal Responsibility and Work Opportunity Reconciliation Act of 1996 (P.L. 104-193); Sheila B. Kamerman and Alfred J. Kahn, eds., *Report 4: Child Care in the Context of Welfare Reform* (New York: Cross-National Studies Research Program, Columbia University School of Social Work, 1997), appendix 1.

One of the most significant changes was the decrease in the quality set-aside to 4 percent of CCDBG funding, which constituted a considerable decrease from the 1990 CCDBG's allocations for quality improvement.

In addition to changes in child care, the bill made serious revisions in other related areas. For example, the Title XX SSBG, which many states use for child care programs, was cut by 15 percent. In addition, the CACFP was reduced by $2.3 billion over six years. For CDF and other organizations that opposed cuts and block granting of child nutrition programs under welfare reform, the CACFP issues were worrisome. The final welfare law lowered the reimbursement rates for meals and snacks to family child care providers that failed to meet strict eligibility requirements in terms of per capita income of the areas in which they are located. The 1996 law also eliminated the option of subsidizing an additional meal or snack for children spending more than eight hours in child care centers.[119]

Reflections on the Final Outcome

Child care advocates were proud of their accomplishments. Given the low level of interest in child care under the House GOP welfare proposal in 1995, they had accomplished much. Most attributed their success to the effectiveness of linking child care with welfare reform, the consistency of their message, and the precedent of the CCDBG. Public opinion was also on their side. A May 1996 Yankelovich poll reported that 85 percent of respondents thought that child care programs for poor children so their parents can work was one of the highest or an important priority in helping the nation's children.[120]

But despite their achievements, child care advocates remained concerned. According to Bruce Hershfield of the CWLA:

The perception of child care under welfare was that child care was a big winner. . . . But child care was a half victory. We got people to understand the link between welfare and child care, but we couldn't link it to what kind of care. Quality was an issue that was not talked about enough. . . . We lost money on the quality side.[121]

Joan Lombardi, the first director of the Child Care Bureau, reflected on the 1996 welfare law some three years later:

On the one hand, consolidation of the child care funding and streamlining was helpful. However, losing the entitlement to child care was a set-back. Just as women were required to go to work, they lost the assurance that they would have child care support. Since they now competed for the same pot of money with other families, this had an impact on the amount of funds available for low-income working families. At the same time, there was less emphasis on quality—with only a limited amount of funds targeted for improvements and fewer safeguards on reimbursement rates. . . . The states have had to balance the increasing demands to serve more families with assuring adequate rates and co-payments. At the same time, we now know more than ever, that quality child care—particularly for at-risk children—is important for overall child development and later learning.[122]

Many liberal Democrats and organizations criticized the final welfare bill because of the hardships they claimed it would impose on children. Bane and Peter Edelman (Marian's husband), both high-level HHS officials, resigned in protest over the bill, citing its sharp cuts in social services. Thus, welfare reform gave many policies for children a new face.

The Changed Face of Political Action for Child Care and Children

Missing from the description of the politics of child care under welfare reform is the role of organized interests. Compared with the late 1980s, when the Alliance for Better Child Care enhanced the ability of organized interests to speak in one voice, in the mid-1990s interest groups involved with child care were less cohesive. This is attributable to the dynamics among the groups and the new pressures they faced under a Republican Congress generally not sympathetic to their causes. By 1996 public opinion and political activism pointed to a new interest in children's causes, which coincided with growing support for child care under welfare reform.

Changing the Scope of Child Care Advocacy Activities

In the early 1990s the core national organizations involved in federal child care policymaking met sporadically but did not come together as a formal coalition to lobby on child care issues. Many of them collaborated in responding to the proposed child care regulations, as discussed in the previous chapter. But after that, without a specific bill to focus on other than annual appropriations for the CCDBG, they channeled their energies in other ways. For example, in 1994 CCAC established the Media Strategies Group, which consisted of about twenty national organizations that met every other month to plan strategies for child care advocacy. Groups involved included the National Head Start Association, CDF, NAEYC, CWLA, National Association of Child Care Resource and Referral Agencies (NACCRRA), National Center for the Early Childhood Workforce, National Council of Chief State School Officers, and YWCA. The Media Strategies Group, with funding from private foundations, worked with the Communications Consortium Media Center in Washington, D.C., to train child care advocates on how to use the media to disseminate information about child care.[123] Funding for the Media Strategies Group ended in 1996. But groups were also meeting regularly under the auspices of another entity.

On April 19, 1993, representatives of major national child care advocacy organizations started to meet on an informal basis. Not wanting to get entangled with the politics of creating a new organizational identity, they simply called themselves the April 19th Group. The group was formed to "explore the development of a collaborative effort to strengthen all child care/ early education at a national level."[124]

From the outset, members of the April 19th Group decided that no organization would take the lead. Many were leery of CDF's tendency to dominate, even though the reality was that no other group had CDF's financial resources or political expertise. The April 19th Group was intended to promote open discussions among national nonprofit organizations working on child care policy. Its aim was to minimize the competition among these groups and enhance collaboration while working to increase the visibility of child care among policymakers.

The April 19th Group hired Ann Mitchell, a well-regarded early childhood education professional, as facilitator. For their first order of business, the group members agreed to fifteen "Guiding Principles for a Child Care/ Early Education System." After issuing a resource guide for state policymakers,[125] the organizations decided that they no longer needed to meet. After all, child care was receiving national attention, and the groups had plenty of work to do explaining their key concerns to policymakers. It was unclear if the April 19th Group had reduced competition among organizations, but it had enabled them to work together in a way that facilitated their subsequent advocacy efforts.

Organized Interests and Welfare Reform

When the Republicans took control of Congress, things changed dramatically for the child care advocacy community. The Democratic policymakers with whom CDF and the other organizations were in regular contact were no longer calling the shots, either because they were not reelected, or if still in office, they were relegated to minority status. There was talk in Washington's policy circles that Edelman and CDF had lost some of their clout.[126]

CDF, though, attracted millions of dollars annually from foundations, individuals, and some corporate sponsors. Moreover, Edelman had utilized the skills of a "full-time director of religious affairs to build relationships with religious groups." As a result, despite changes in the congressional and political environments in the mid-1990s, CDF held its place as a strong leader in children's advocacy circles.

Blank and her colleagues at CDF arduously advocated for changes to child care under welfare. They wrote frequent and detailed communications to child care advocates across the country, urging them to fight for child care funding and oppose the proposed changes to the CCDBG. CDF and about ten other national organizations held biweekly conference calls to plan their strategies.

In response to proposed changes to the CCDBG, child care advocates launched a well-publicized doll campaign. The first part coincided with the February 1995 NACCRRA annual meeting in Washington and the House Subcommittee on Early Childhood, Youth, and Families markup of welfare legislation related to welfare child care. NACCRRA members brought their life-size, handmade dolls to the subcommittee markup to protest proposed changes to the CCDBG. In the morning NACCRRA used the dolls at a press event outside the Capitol. Later that day the House GOP leadership banned the dolls from the House. The dolls offered a visual cue about child care provisions in welfare reform and the constituency that opposed them. Five years later some House staff and members still referred to the spectacle the dolls created.

Child care advocates knew that the dolls were too big to mail to legislators, so advocates from across the country sent thousands of small paper-doll Valentines to congressional offices in protest of the proposed changes to the CCDBG. The campaign was a collaborative effort among CDF, NACCRRA, NAEYC, YWCA, YMCA, and other organizations. The exact number of paper dolls received in Washington is unknown. However, it was reported that about 30,000 were received from advocates in Pennsylvania alone.[127]

One of the major differences between the advocacy efforts of the late 1980s and those surrounding welfare reform in the mid-1990s was that in the later years, with the CCDBG channeling millions of dollars to state authorities, state legislators had a vested interest in federal child care funding. Consequently, the NCSL was a major player in championing funding for child care under welfare reform. Congress was hard-pressed to ignore calls for increases in child care funding under welfare reform from intergovernmental groups such as the NCSL and NGA.

Despite the efforts of the child care and other advocacy groups, many members of Congress, such as Senator Daniel Patrick Moynihan, felt that liberal organized interests were amazingly silent on welfare reform.[128] This was understandable because, as one of them explained, "we were all fighting so many battles, that we couldn't amass all the fighters in one place." National organizations involved with child care each focused on different aspects of welfare reform, such as cash assistance, work requirements, child nutrition, and child care. Even if their efforts were invisible in the halls of Congress, their work resulted in some important changes.

Finally, what can be said of the organizations aligned with conservative interests? In contrast to previous legislative episodes, these groups and individuals were relatively quiet on child care. This was because the 1990 CCDBG had settled the score on what were important issues for conservatives, most notably, vouchers, standards, parental choice, and funding of religiously affiliated child care. The CCDBG reauthorization retained most of these provisions. In the mid-1990s conservatives' main concern was the streamlining of federal child care programs. They eventually acknowledged that their mandatory welfare work requirements would require child care assistance to succeed. Ironically, welfare reform called new attention to the importance of federal child care legislation. However, in implementing child care under welfare, new challenges regarding quality and affordability arose, as did questions regarding equity between welfare and low-income families.

Standing for Children

The child care advocates' success in obtaining increased funding for child care under welfare reflected more than a focused lobbying effort, although that was definitely a factor. It was also a sign of a new interest in children's issues. As welfare legislation made its way through Congress, upcoming presidential and congressional elections were a reality for every politician. No candidate wanted to be portrayed as hurting children.

Hillary Rodham Clinton's book *It Takes a Village* also was part of the rising salience of children's issues and achieved several other goals.[129] In addition to resurrecting a positive public image for the First Lady after her health care reform debacle, it helped spread the word about her expertise on children's policy. But the book also had another, perhaps unintended effect. It reignited the public discourse on the role of parents and government in helping families with children. Those on the right were quick to interpret her "takes a village" theme as the relinquishing of parental responsibility. Others saw it as a rallying call for public and private sectors and communities to join in developing policies that made children a priority. Most important, her book helped move the discussions about the need to create supportive policies for children beyond the hallways of Congress and academia to the discourses of everyday life.

Building on the growing concern about children, CDF, working with other national groups, became the organizer of what has become an annual nationwide event on June 1, "Stand for Children." In early 1996 CDF began its planning for a day when people from every state would come to the Lincoln Memorial in Washington, D.C., to "demonstrate the strength of support for children."[130]

CDF portrayed "Stand for Children" as a nonpartisan event and did not invite any politicians to speak. More than 3,000 national and local groups signed on for the march, ranging from the Girl Scouts to Catholic Charities.[131] CDF raised significant funds for the "Stand for Children" march and sponsored a fundraiser the Friday before, featuring Rosie O'Donnell, which was partially subsidized by Warner Brothers.[132] Through "Stand for Children," a variety of powerful people and corporations began to take an interest in children's issues.

Conservatives opposed the march. Gary Bauer, head of the FRC, called it "the liberal agenda being repackaged. . . . [And] another way to push the sort of big-government approach that doesn't work." Representative Shaw also opposed the march and criticized CDF for its "vested interest in the problem rather than the solution."[133] Even if the impact of "Stand for Children" on legislation and policy was minimal, it raised the visibility of children's issues in some circles.

As they advanced their respective agendas, liberals and conservatives shared a growing interest in putting children first, although this was not voiced in the initial welfare reform discussions. President Clinton featured children and families prominently in his 1996 State of the Union address.[134] Having enacted welfare legislation, both the president and congressional candidates headed for the 1996 elections confidently claimed that they had reformed welfare. They could point to increased funding for child care to defend themselves against criticism that the bill might harm children.

The GOP takeover of Congress changed the balance of power among individuals and ideas. Although Republicans had a majority of seats in both chambers, their narrow leads and the veto power of a Democratic president made bargaining and compromise inevitable parts of the legislative process for welfare reform, including child care. Reforms in the House enhanced the influence of the Republican leadership and diminished the power of subcommittees and their chairs. However, relationships among House committees involved with child care were characterized by cooperation compared with the tension that had characterized their relationship in the late 1980s. Changes in Congress also shifted the balance of power among organized interests and their access to congressional leaders, giving conservative organizations an edge over their liberal counterparts. Nonetheless, CDF and its partners in the child care advocacy community held their own and could claim credit for some important gains for child care in the midst of welfare reform.

Finally, and perhaps most important, divided government restrained the legislative process. But, ironically, it was under a divided government and a GOP Congress that welfare reform resulted in significant changes and increases in funding for federal child care programs. Similarly, in 1990 a GOP president and a divided government had made landmark child care policies. The significance of these events is discussed in the last chapter of this book.

Certain other structural and institutional features enhanced the ability of policymakers to make strides in child care policy under welfare reform. In particular, a well-established legislative framework from the 1990 CCDBG promoted bipartisan consensus on the CCDBG reauthorization. Furthermore, creation of the Child Care Bureau streamlined the administration of programs, thereby facilitating the legislative restructuring under the 1996 law, and it promoted a unified voice to child care issues within the executive branch. Legislatively, several Democrats and Republicans, especially in the

Senate, introduced important amendments that survived to final enactment. Although the coalition of organized interests was not as tightly knit as in the past, it rode the crest of the new wave of interest in the well-being of children and kept its message as focused as possible. As in the past, the nation's governors proved to be critical in shaping child care legislation. The NCSL also provided important input. Conservatives and Republicans generally wanted a child care block grant rather than a child care entitlement. They eventually accepted some of the proposed changes, given the precedent of the 1990 CCDBG and the need for child care assistance under a revamped welfare system.

Federal budget politics also influenced the course of events for child care in the mid-1990s, as they had in 1990. Both times budget deficits constrained options and provided the vehicle—the reconciliation legislation—for the final bill. The handsome increase in child care funding under welfare, combined with a new interest in children, were necessary ingredients for the era following the 1996 elections when President Clinton introduced the greatest presidential child care initiative in history.

7   High Hopes, 1997–2000

After welfare reform, other opportunities arose for expanding federal child care initiatives. Among them were new interest in early brain development, a president with a commitment to child care, and the first federal budget surplus in decades. Despite these developments, enacting federal child care laws remained difficult. Without a major child care bill to rally around, advocates for increases in federal child care assistance proposed child care as a solution to many different problems. Consequently, child care became part of tobacco settlement legislation, crime prevention initiatives, and federal budget bills. By the beginning of the twenty-first century, most members of Congress agreed that the federal government had a legitimate role in the child care arena. However, the size and shape of that investment still stirred debate. President Clinton's child care proposals prompted interest but failed to produce anticipated changes. Using Frank Baumgartner and Bryan Jones's punctuated equilibrium framework,[1] the years after 1996 were a time of reorganization when those involved with child care legislation redefined the issue to attract new interest. Compared to the dramatic changes of 1990 and 1996, the late 1990s were characterized by moderate shifts in federal child care policies.

1997: New Opportunities for Child Care

After 1996, child care policymaking featured new efforts to link research on early brain development with legislation. President Clinton capitalized on these developments as he demonstrated a commitment to child care that surpassed that of his predecessors. He and other lawmakers were increasingly aware of the importance of child care for many American families. Members of both parties introduced child care bills, many of which included extending the DCTC to families with a stay-at-home parent. For child care and other issues, Clinton faced a Congress that experienced only a few structural changes after the 1996 elections.

1996 Elections Create Subtle Shifts

Clinton won the 1996 presidential election with 50 percent of the popular votes. GOP contender Bob Dole received 42 percent, and Reform Party candidate Ross Perot, 8 percent. Most analysts saw the economy as the critical issue in the election. However, unlike in 1992, when Clinton won largely on his pledge to improve the economy, by 1996 he won because voters were satisfied with the economy or considered their family's financial situation to be better than it had been four years earlier.[2] By many accounts the 1996 elections were a call to retain the status quo. Voters reelected most members of Congress, the president, and governors of both parties.[3] One result of the 1996 elections, potentially relevant to child care, was the addition of thirteen female members of Congress—eleven in the House and two in the Senate. This brought the number of women in the House to an all-time high of fifty-one. In the Senate, the number of women (nine) remained unchanged.[4]

Republicans retained control of the House but with a smaller margin (227 to 207) than their 32-seat lead after the 1994 elections. As the majority party they still held the upper hand on most issues, including child care. In the Senate the GOP net gain of 2 seats gave the Republicans the largest Senate majority (55 to 45) since 1929. Senator Trent Lott (R-Miss.) became majority leader when Senator Robert Dole stepped down in June 1996 to campaign for the presidency. Lott was conservative on most economic and social issues. As the 105th Congress began in 1997, the Senate was less conservative than the House,[5] which partially explains its subsequent ability to move more speedily than the House on child care legislation.

As in the past, the Senate Committee on Labor and Human Resources provided a focal point for child care policy deliberations. Following the retirement of Senator Nancy Kassebaum, Senator Jim Jeffords became chair. He often "ruffled some Republicans" with his liberal leanings.[6]

The newly elected legislators in both chambers were less strident and more interested in compromise than the "firebrands" who had entered Congress in 1995.[7] Even Newt Gingrich expressed his desire to minimize confrontation.[8] But as the 105th Congress unfolded, these initial calls for collaboration faded, especially with the partisan clamor surrounding Clinton's potential impeachment. In the child care arena, several organized interests and legislators remained vociferous in their opposition to an expanded federal role in the child care arena because it would promote a model of child rearing (nonmaternal care) and family life (mothers working outside of the home) that they considered wrong. Federal support of child care conveyed a misguided message to conservatives and others intent on preserving a notion of family life that relied on two parents, with one, typically but not always the mother, at home caring for young children. However, this image of family life clashed with reality. It ignored that many families could not afford to forgo one spouse's salary, and it did not take into account the increased need for child care under welfare reform. It also overlooked the benefits that many children received from early child care programs.

Budget Surpluses and the Balanced Budget Act

In 1997 one of the first orders of business for Congress and the president was reaching an agreement on the federal budget as they strove to eliminate the budget deficit. On May 2, 1997, Clinton and Republican congressional leaders announced that they had reached a budget agreement for the next fiscal year. After much political wrangling, both chambers passed legislation based on the initial plan. On July 30, 1997, the House passed the Balanced Budget Act by a vote of 346 to 85, with 32 Republicans, 52 Democrats, and 1 Independent opposing it. The Senate passed the bill the next day by a vote of 85 to 15. President Clinton signed both the Balanced Budget Act (P.L. 105-33) and its accompanying tax bill (P.L. 103-34) into law on August 5, 1997.[9]

By the time the Balanced Budget Act was enacted, the deficit for FY 1997 was projected to be $75 billion, a sharp fall from the Congressional Budget Office's (CBO) estimate of $124 billion earlier in the year.[10] According to those who followed the budget deal closely, "budget gurus of all stripes" acknowledged that success in lowering the federal budget deficit was attributable to the 1990 reconciliation law (which included landmark child care legislation) and the 1993 budget act (P.L. 103-66), both of which generated tax revenues, lowered federal spending, and helped create a strong economy.[11]

One of the most expensive items in the tax bill was the child tax credit, originally pushed by House Republicans under their Contract with America. The 1997 Balanced Budget Act granted the credit to single taxpayers with annual incomes of up to $75,000, with a phaseout for couples with incomes between $110,00 and $130,000.[12] The $400 child tax credit went into effect in 1997, increasing to $500 in 1998. Another important provision of the Balanced Budget Act granted $24 billion to states to provide coverage to uninsured children of low-income families. Led by Senators Edward Kennedy and Orrin Hatch and financed partly by an increase in the cigarette tax, it was the largest investment in child health since the enactment of Medicaid in 1965.[13] In the months that followed, Kennedy and others proposed using cigarette tax increases to subsidize increased federal spending on child care and after-school programs.

Many child care advocates thought that the discretionary spending caps embedded in the 1997 budget bill blocked increases in federal child care funding. Others, including congressional staff from both parties, disagreed, arguing that with ample political will, Congress would find a way to expand discretionary programs such as child care. Regardless of which side was right, discretionary caps certainly limited opportunities to increase federal spending on child care at least for 1997 and 1998. Nonetheless, other events prompted an increased interest in child care policies.

The Politicization of Research on Early Brain Development and Child Development

One of the major promoters of agenda-setting for child care legislation in the late 1990s was "new research" on early brain development. Within the disciplines of child development, child health, and neuroscience, many of these findings had been known for at least ten years.[14] What changed was how organizations and advocates interested in child development marketed the information.

In 1994 the Carnegie Foundation issued its report *Starting Points: Meeting the Needs of Our Youngest Children*.[15] The authors described the "quiet crisis" facing children under three and their families:

Across the United States, we are beginning to hear the rumblings of
a quiet crisis. Our nation's children under the age of three and their
families are in trouble, and their plight worsens every day. To be sure,
the children themselves are not quiet; they are crying out for help.
And their parents' anxieties about inadequate child care and the
high cost of their child's health care can be heard in kitchen's play-
grounds, pediatricians' waiting rooms and workplace cafeterias across
the nation.[16]

Starting Points generated public and private discussions regarding the link
between early childhood development and policymaking. In 1996 the FWI
convened 150 experts of brain science, child development, early education,
business, policy, and the media for a meeting in Chicago.[17] The scientific
evidence presented at the conference focused on the first three years of life
as a unique time of rapid formation of brain synapses, establishing the basis
for subsequent brain development. Research showed that these synapses
were formed in response to environmental stimuli, implying that lack of
such stimulation placed children at developmental and learning disadvantages. Moreover, new medical technology, in particular, positron-emission
tomography (PET), offered clinicians details on brain development.

In 1996 the director Rob Reiner and his wife, Michelle Singer Reiner,
in collaboration with the FWI, launched the "I Am Your Child" Early Childhood Public Engagement Campaign. The campaign's theme was simply,
"The crucial groundwork for a person's emotional and intellectual life is laid
between birth and age three, and parents should have access to support
services, if they need them, to help their babies develop."[18] The Reiners'
efforts were funded by philanthropic foundations and corporate support.[19]
Zero to Three, a national organization dedicated to disseminating research
on infants, toddlers, and their families, fueled the campaign with data showing that most parents did not know what signs to watch for regarding their
children's social, emotional, or intellectual development.

The "I Am Your Child" campaign resulted in a prime-time ABC-TV
special, which aired in April 1997, and a special edition of *Newsweek* focusing on young children and their families.[20] Reiner's work and the "I Am
Your Child" campaign also led to a study by RAND that showed how early
interventions could "result in compensatory decreases in government expenditures" for costs such as welfare and criminal justice.[21]

The media assiduously spread the message about the importance of the
first three years of life.[22] Simultaneously, organized interests used research

findings in their calls for increased government investment in high-quality programs that could enhance brain development. The fervor of the message reached Congress, where legislators joined the fray by sponsoring hearings and introducing legislation. Some state legislators also captured the message and used it as a rationale for investing in early childhood and child care programs.

However, a few scientists grumbled that the neuroscience used to advance attention to early brain development was "selective, oversimplified, and interpreted incorrectly." One of the most outspoken critics was John T. Bruer, Ph.D., president of the James S. McDonnell Foundation. He wrote, "Indeed, to get from the brain science to the supposed policy implications requires some leaps of faith and interpretation. These leaps are so long and perilous that we might do more for children by questioning than by accepting this popular claim."[23] In his book, *The Myth of the First Three Years*, published in 1999, Bruer explained the fallacies surrounding the emphasis on the first three years.[24] Bruer bluntly stated that "there [was] no such new brain research" and argued that the "myth of the first three years" created misunderstandings that "can contribute to poorly informed policy and legislation."[25] He argued that in emphasizing the first three years, the media and policymakers undermined the importance of development in older children.

Zero to Three posted a response to Bruer's book on its Web site.[26] It countered that Bruer had astutely noted in a 1997 article that research findings had been "blown out of proportion" and that the "neuroscience of early childhood [was], in a sense, in its own infancy." But it claimed that Bruer's book went too far in denying the importance of early interventions, especially for children at risk.[27]

Even if the advocates overstated their claims regarding the importance of the first three years, the publicity surrounding the new interest in early brain development had the intended effect of mobilizing legislators and policymakers to action. It led on April 17, 1997, to the White House Conference on Early Childhood Development: What New Research on the Brain Tells Us About Our Youngest Children,[28] at which Clinton announced the White House Conference on Child Care, scheduled for later in the year.

In addition to the attention surrounding early brain development, several large and important studies provided new evidence about the relationships between child development and child care. As in the past, the interpretation and dissemination of the research findings became politicized. Each side highlighted the results that furthered its cause. The most prominent research, launched in 1991, was a longitudinal study, sponsored by the National Institute of Child Health and Human Development (NICHD), that examined the effect of child care on children's development and attachment through age seven. The researchers studied 1,364 families at fourteen universities, taking into account variables such as characteristics of the child care setting and family environment. In April 1998 researchers concluded that by the time a child is fifteen months old, "child care in and of itself neither adversely affects, nor promotes, the security of children's attachment to their mothers." However, certain factors, such as care of poor quality, spending more than ten hours per week in care, and multiple child care arrangements, when combined with "maternal insensitivity to infant needs," tended to affect attachment adversely. Moreover, researchers found that "characteristics of the family were stronger predictors of children's behavior than their child care experience."[29] Other major studies linked the quality of child care with child development and prompted interest in improving the quality of care for poor children.[30] These studies strengthened child care advocates' arguments about the need for initiatives in the public and private sectors to enhance the quality of child care.

Those opposed to child care because of its alleged negative impact on children used the same studies to substantiate their claims that parents should stay home with their children. The *Wall Street Journal* commented that the media's "chirpy attitude toward very early childhood" failed to reveal the more "uncongenial" things reported in the NICHD study regarding the relationship between child care and child development. According to the editors, the message that needed to be heard was "Mom and Dad matter most. Mom and Dad are the best teachers. Bill and Hillary's $21 billion of subsidies, credits, public-private partnerships and day trainers won't get your kid into Stanford."[31] In addition, several books in the popular press called attention to the difficulties families faced in balancing work and home and the potential harm of this juggling routine on children's well-being.[32]

Child Care Activity Escalates in the 105th Congress

Many child care bills introduced in the 105th Congress (1997–1998) emphasized child care quality and revisions to the DCTC. Some measures focused on tax credits alone, but most, including Clinton's 1998 child care legislative proposal, were a combination of tax measures and programmatic initiatives. Most of the child care action was in the Senate, where moderate Republicans continued to support child care initiatives. A few outspoken members of the House, mostly Democrats, championed child care legislation. However, the House leadership was too conservative to give child care much consideration.

Senator Christopher Dodd introduced one of the first child care bills in 1997. His Working Families Child Care Act (S. 19) increased CCDBG funding by $10 billion over five years, added support for low-income working families, and provided funding to enhance the child care supply.[33]

In June 1997 the Senate Subcommittee on Children and Families held the hearing "Pre to 3: Policy Implications of Brain Development." The purpose of the hearing was to "review the status of medical and scientific understanding of prenatal and postnatal brain development and to explore some of the policy implications that arise."[34] One of the leading witnesses was Dr. Harry Chugani, of the Detroit Children's Hospital, who had developed positron-emission tomography to study the biochemical processes in the brain. Chugani explained the importance of brain development during the first years of life:

> There are many children who do not really get much in terms of enriched environment until 5 years of age—some 3, but very few from zero to 3. So we are really not making use of what Mother Nature has provided us as a unique opportunity, when our brains are able to learn relatively easily . . . this really affects all socioeconomic classes . . . and we must, I believe, as a society, ensure that all children are given the opportunity of an enriched environment in order to maximize their potential.[35]

Edward Zigler of Yale University, a familiar witness at congressional hearings, lamented the lags in policies for children:

> In response to the new scientific knowledge about the growth of the brain, the question for Members of Congress and other policymakers is this: Does American society today support the optimal development of children in the critical early years? The answer, unfortunately, is no. . . . To date, social policy in America has done little to help families deal with conflicting responsibilities toward work and childrearing. Children are suffering.[36]

Coincidentally, the magazine *Working Woman* had just selected Zigler and Senator Dodd for their 1997 "Men of the Year" awards. In contrast to Chugani and Zigler, who called for increased investment in child care programs, several witnesses recommended tax policy revisions that would assist families with a parent staying home to care for children. For example, Diane Fisher of the Independent Women's Forum, which supports women who interrupt their careers to stay home with their children, complained about the bias toward care outside the home:

> The new day care and brain research is being used as a springboard to persuade Americans of the need for higher taxes, new Federal programs, expanded day care. . . . I would like to ask for subsidies for all parents, so that they can make that choice. When day care is presented not as an option, but as the model for the future, we have to ask ourselves why.[37]

In July 1997 Senator Jeffords introduced CIDCARE (Creating Improved Delivery of Child Care: Affordable, Reliable and Educational, S.R 1037/ H.R. 2213) cosponsored by Senator Dodd. Representative Benjamin Gilman (R-N.Y.) introduced the House companion bill. Because of the bipartisan support behind CIDCARE, many legislators hoped that it would be a vehicle for moving child care legislation forward. CIDCARE covered almost every aspect of child care policymaking, from tax credits and employer benefits to quality enhancement and federal child care facilities. Around the same time that Jeffords introduced his bill he held a hearing, "Improving the Quality of Child Care."[38] The star witnesses were two parents whose infant had died at a licensed family child care home. The theme of the hearing was the importance of child care quality, beyond licensing, in ensuring safe and nurturing child care environments.

CIDCARE was in the drafting stage when Jeffords decided to attach all its tax provisions[39] to reconciliation legislation. But his amendment fell four votes short of the sixty votes needed for procedural purposes to amend budget bills. Instead, the Senate passed Senator Herb Kohl's (D-Wis.) amendment, which provided a tax credit to employers who extended their child care services for employees.[40] Kohl's amendment also never got beyond the Senate floor. Other Senate bills introduced in 1997 included the Child Care Access Means Parents in School Act (known as the CAMPUS Act, S. 1151). Senators Dodd and Olympia Snowe sponsored the measure, which authorized $60 million to support campus-based child care for low-income students. Senator Paul Wellstone (D-Minn.) introduced a bill (S. 2489) offering loan forgiveness to eligible child care providers who completed degrees in early childhood education and worked in low-income communities. Both the campus-based child care initiative and the loan forgiveness bill were enacted in 1998.

White House Conference on Child Care Kindles Activity

On October 23, 1997, six months after the White House Conference on Early Childhood Development, President Clinton and the First Lady hosted the White House Conference on Child Care. A new sense of hope and excitement spread across the child care community as representatives of national child care groups, business leaders, and government officials gathered at the White House. Some observers rightfully wondered if the conference would result in meaningful action. Jonathan Alter of *Newsweek* accurately predicted that Clinton and his fellow Democrats were skating on thin ice unless they defined child care as a problem for all families, including those with stay-at-home parents, and unless they handled their initiative with "serious money." Alter captured the mood surrounding the conference when he wrote, "The question that hung in the East Room chandeliers last week was whether the White House Conference on Child Care, chaired by the First Lady, was the beginning of a big 1998 idea—a bid to finally catch up to every other industrialized country in the world on this front—or just another gabfest for the faithful."[41]

The White House Conference on Child Care featured an impressive array of representatives from academia, government, and organized interests.[42] Hillary Rodham Clinton, as the official conference convener, marked her return to the public "spotlight" after the health care debacle a few years earlier. The president credited his wife with articulating the importance of investing in child care, explaining that she had been talking to him "about all of these things for more than 25 years now."[43] The publicity she gave the issue bolstered the president's initiative and also made it vulnerable to attack from social conservatives.

One of Hillary Clinton's major concerns was the need "to increase the income, the training, the status" of child care providers. Helen Blank of CDF explained to a *New York Times* reporter that "child care workers, on average, earn less than bus drivers, garbage collectors and bartenders."[44] Marcy Whitebook, codirector of the Center for the Child Care Workforce (formerly the National Center for the Early Childhood Work Force), reported that with almost one-third of all child care workers earning the minimum wage, turnover among staff made it difficult for children to establish stable relationships with their child care providers. The First Lady was careful to promote her vision for child care policy as one that entailed strong public and private partnerships across all levels of government.[45] Neither a bold large federal program nor federal child care standards were included in the president's preliminary child care proposals, undoubtedly because of the antagonism such ideas would generate, especially in conservative circles.[46]

Child care policy experts gave high praise to Joan Lombardi, the first head of the Child Care Bureau, for her efforts in organizing the White House conference. They recognized her indefatigable commitment to strengthening the federal government's role in child care as an important force behind the president's initiative. As Lombardi explained:

> The Child Care Bureau was important because it elevated child care as a children's service. It created an agency involved with child care that was not inextricably linked with welfare. We also had an incredible level of readiness within the executive branch to address this issue . . . and to address it in a way that made it a children's issue. This came through at the White House Conference.[47]

With the announcement of the White House Conference on Child Care, CDF and more than thirty other organizations signed a letter to President Clinton urging him to introduce "a major child care initiative when Congress convenes in January." They explained that welfare reform had left many gaps in child care support for low-income working families. Their recommendations included increasing funding for the CCDBG, revising the DCTC by making it refundable and increasing the amount families could claim, strengthening state licensing requirements, and enhancing compensation and education of child care staff. They also called for increased support for care for school-age children, Head Start, and the CACFP.[48]

Some child development experts and policymakers took a different tack. Stanley I. Greenspan, clinical professor of psychiatry and pediatrics at George Washington Medical School and a participant of the White House Conference on Child Care, argued that Clinton relied too much on child care facilities that lacked proper staffing and quality. He thought that federal policies should focus on restructuring family and work life.[49]

As child care took off in December 1997, organized interests, led by CDF, came together under the banner Child Care Now! Their coalition was more loosely structured than the late-1980s Alliance for Better Child Care. Once again, child care became an organizational priority for CDF. Blank and her staff worked closely with a handful of key groups, in particular the NWLC, Fight Crime: Invest in Kids (discussed later), and some of the large labor unions. By the late 1990s CDF's Child Care Division worked closely with approximately two hundred advocates on the state level with extensive state-wide networks. In addition, CDF had strengthened its own Child Care National Network, which included more than one hundred national organizations dedicated to working on child care, many of which joined Child Care Now! By 1998 CDF's child care listserv, combined with CDF's other listservs and networks, enabled the organization to reach thousands of interested individuals across the country. CDF also published exemplary reports on the status of child care that the media and government officials frequently cited.[50]

One of CDF's strongest partners was the NWLC. While favoring increases in federal spending on child care for low-income working families, the NWLC also acknowledged the importance of supporting stay-at-home parents.[51] NWLC's analyses of proposals to revise the DCTC were detailed and well written. It also rallied other women's groups around child care legislation by disseminating information and obtaining signatures for letters to public officials.[52]

By late 1997 the major bill that CDF, NWLC, and their allies in the advocacy community focused on was Senator Kennedy's Smoke-Free Children Act (S. 1492). Representative Rosa DeLauro (D-Conn.) introduced the companion bill (H.R. 3028) in the House. DeLauro was knowledgeable about child care policymaking, having been Senator Dodd's chief of staff from 1980 to 1987. The Kennedy–DeLauro bill relied on money from the pending settlement between state attorneys general and major tobacco companies and an additional $1.50 tax on cigarettes, half of which would support child care programs. (The other half would support biomedical research.) The $10 billion in their bill for children's programs in one year alone included increased funding for Head Start and the CCDBG. Kennedy and DeLauro reasoned that if the tobacco industry had aimed so much of its advertising at America's youth,[53] some type of compensation or payback was warranted. Moreover, research showed that increases in cigarette prices were likely to reduce smoking among youth.[54] Thus, the increase in the cigarette tax both was a disincentive to teen smoking and offered new ways of financing children's programs in areas such as child care. The Kennedy–DeLauro bill never went far. Child care advocates never officially endorsed it, allegedly because it wasn't bipartisan enough. However, its use of tobacco money for child care legislation and linkage of smoking prevention with child care were important themes that other lawmakers, including President Clinton, used in advancing child care proposals.

Right after the White House Conference on Child Care, Senator Dodd led a bipartisan task force on child care, joined by Senators Hatch, Jeffords, Kennedy, Patty Murray (D-Wash.), Snowe, and Arlen Specter. Many senators were interested in child care, and some even asked to be on the task force. The task force took a two-pronged approach of increasing CCDBG funding and expanding the DCTC. But members of the task force split along party lines; Republicans opposed Democrats' recommendations for CCDBG set-asides that required states to spend certain percentages of their funds on specific activities, such as quality enhancement. They questioned how Democrats planned to pay for their proposal to increase CCDBG funding. Furthermore, Republicans were opposed to the Democrats' wish to make the DCTC refundable, although members of both parties expressed interest in expanding the DCTC benefits for low-income families. Eventually the members of the task force reached a tentative agreement.[55] According to a staff person involved with the discussions, Democrats gave up their efforts to make the DCTC refundable and Republicans went along with CCDBG funding increases, at least for the time being. But the task force's efforts were derailed with the introduction of Clinton's child care initiative.

1998: New Twists for Child Care Legislation

A few months after the 1997 White House Conference on Child Care, President Clinton announced a bold child care initiative. However, for a number of reasons, it did not result in the immediate gains that many child care advocates had anticipated. Policymakers sustained interest in child care through several other vehicles, making 1998 a tumultuous year for child care advocates.

Clinton Sprints Forward with Child Care

On January 7, 1998, Clinton presented his proposal to spend an additional $21 billion over five years for child care. He referred to it as "the single largest national commitment to child care in the history of the United States." His proposal included increased funding for the CCDBG by $7.5 billion over five years, an Early Learning Fund for local programs to improve child care training and safety, expanding the DCTC by targeting families earning less than $60,000, and creating a new tax credit for employers who provide employee child care assistance. He also recommended "the expansion of before- and after-school programs to help some 500,000 children say no to drugs and alcohol and crime and yes to reading, soccer, computers and a brighter future for themselves."[56]

Clinton proposed financing approximately one-third of his proposal from the anticipated settlement between state governments and tobacco companies, with the understanding that, if the tobacco settlement failed, he would seek other ways to fund his child care initiative. He assumed that the remaining two-thirds of the costs of the child care bill would come from federal funds generated by the budget surplus.[57] But when Clinton later declared his preference that any budget surplus be devoted to Social Security,[58] lack of a designated funding source became an obstacle to the advancement of child care legislation.

Initially, Clinton was an ardent promoter of his child care proposal.[59] In his State of the Union address, he referred to child care as "the next frontier we must face to enable people to succeed at home and at work." He explained, "Not a single American family should ever have to choose between the job they need and the child they love."[60] Clinton engaged high-level officials and agencies across his administration on child care. The Department of the Treasury and Department of Labor each issued reports in April 1998 that featured the importance of child care for businesses and employees.[61]

Most Democrats and others interested in extending federal child care programs enthusiastically welcomed the president's child care initiative. However, a closer look revealed some unsettling effects, especially in the Senate, where Dodd's bipartisan task force on child care was making steady progress. Immediately after Clinton announced his child care initiative, GOP members of the task force told their Democratic colleagues that there was no way they could work together on the issue. One explanation for this change of heart was that the Senate Republican leadership did not want to help make it possible for Clinton to claim a child care victory during an election year. As one Senate staff person explained in an interview, "It was seen so much as the president's own initiative that the Republicans felt there was no way they would be able to reframe it and be part of it all." Moreover, according to other sources, Clinton failed to acknowledge the contributions of the Senate bipartisan task force to his proposal. Another Senate staff person from a different party made a similar point: "We were working on the bipartisan child care bill and were close to consensus when the President announced his initiative two weeks early . . . at which point everything blew up . . . smash, bang, no bipartisan child care. . . . Clinton wanted the issue but not the legislation."

Republicans and conservatives sharply criticized Clinton's child care initiative. Not wanting to portray themselves as opponents of programs for children, they emphasized the importance of helping all families with children, whether or not they used formal child care. Two GOP women, Representatives Deborah Pryce and Jennifer Dunn, emphasized their party's preference to "return money to taxpayers rather than spend it." Pryce criticized the proposal for its "glaring omission" of not supporting "stay-at-home moms." Representative Bill Goodling complained that Clinton's proposal was unnecessary given the existing array of federal child care programs and recent child care expansions under welfare reform. Representative Clay Shaw expressed the sentiment of many of his party members in accusing Clinton of sustaining an "era of big government."[62] Conservatives remained opposed to any expansion of federal child care programs and favored tax credits to assist families with children. They hoped that Congress would enact a tax bill before the end of 1998 that would eliminate the so-called marriage penalty[63] and extend DCTC benefits to families with a stay-at-home parent. Robert Rector and his colleagues at the Heritage Foundation called Clinton's proposal "irrational and unfair." They preferred that Congress use the coming budget surplus for tax relief and not "discriminate against families who make a financial sacrifice so that one parent can remain home."[64]

The FRC published a report entitled *Emptying the Nest: The Clinton Child Care Agenda*, which attacked many of the assumptions underlying Clinton's proposal. Its author, Charmaine Crouse Yoest, denied that any type of child care crisis existed and reported FRC-sponsored polls indicating that most women would prefer to work part time or stay at home with their children instead of leaving their children in the hands of others. An editorial in the *Wall Street Journal* commented on Clinton's child care proposal:

> Now it is important to understand that the Clintons and their allies in the multibillion-dollar child care industry have a specific idea in mind when they talk about "quality care." They don't mean finding better baby-sitting in the home, or even, heaven forbid, staying home one's self with a lovely child from time to time. No, they envision building great numbers of brightly lit centers where child experts stimulate infant brains by waving flash cards before their cribs.[65]

The *New York Times* expressed concern about Clinton's child care proposal, claiming that it did not adequately target low-income families. Furthermore, when the economy slowed down, cuts in discretionary spending for programs such as child care could place many of the components of Clinton's plan at risk.[66] Thus, from the outset, Clinton's proposal met with skepticism. But this criticism failed to detract from the positive reception that Clinton's proposal enjoyed among most Democrats and children's advocates across the country.

Republicans responded to Clinton's proposal with bills that typically focused on tax credits. Senator John Chafee and Representative Nancy Johnson introduced a Republican alternative, the Caring for America's Children Act (S. 1577/H.R. 3144), which enhanced the DCTC benefits for low- and middle-income families and allowed families with a "stay-at-home" parent taking care of a child under the age of four to receive it. Chafee's bill also provided $5 billion over five years for increased discretionary funding in the CCDBG and had several provisions aimed at enhancing child care quality.[67]

Dodd took a slightly different approach. On February 4, 1998, he introduced the Affordable Child Care for Early Success and Security Act (ACCESS, S. 1610). Dodd's bill increased the benefits for the DCTC for low- and middle-income families and made it refundable for families without any tax liability; however, his bill had lower annual payments to families than Chafee's.[68] ACCESS also extended the DCTC to families with a stay-at-home parent. Unlike Chafee's bill, which increased the CCDBG *discretionary* funding, Dodd's proposal increased its *mandatory* funding by $15 billion over five years. Pushing for mandatory instead of discretionary funding increases under the CCDBG was an important distinction between

Dodd's and Chafee's proposals at this time. Together with CDF and others in the child care advocacy community, Dodd reasoned that without mandatory funds, it would be difficult to ensure sufficient child care funding in the years ahead. Dodd's bill included other provisions to increase funding for quality child care.

By May 1998 more than forty bills were on the table representing an array of options.[69] The divisive nature of child care as a policy issue emerged at the Senate Finance Committee's "Hearing on Child Care" in April 1998.[70] In addition to partisan differences, the hearing brought to light fragmentation between moderate Republicans (such as Chafee), who were willing to invest federal dollars in child care programs, and their conservative GOP colleagues (such as Senator Don Nickles of Oklahoma), who were not. The disputes within Republican ranks illustrated the extensive negotiating that would have to take place for Congress to reach an agreement on any major child care initiative. However, apart from these differences, one aspect of child care policy was becoming increasingly popular and showed promising signs of bipartisan consensus.

*Care for School-Age Children Shifts the Terms
of the Child Care Debate*

Among the many components of Clinton's child care proposal, after-school child care resonated with the public and drew strong bipartisan support. A 1998 opinion poll funded by the Mott Foundation found that 94 percent of polled Democrats and 90 percent of polled Republicans thought such programs should be available daily to all children.[71] Compared with early childhood care, which spurred ideological debates over family values and the role of women, few legislators or organized interests opposed care for school-age children. In addition, care for school-age children was not as expensive to operate as early childhood care.

In 1996 nearly 77 percent of women with children between the ages of six and thirteen worked outside the home.[72] In 1995, 24.7 million children between the ages of five and fourteen had parents in the workforce or in school. Approximately 5 million of these children (20 percent of all children in this group) cared for themselves while their parents were engaged in work or school activities.[73] One out of six low-income parents indicated that their children between the ages of four and seven regularly spent time alone or in the care of a sibling under the age of twelve.[74] The number of school-age children left alone was probably higher than reported because parents were ashamed to admit leaving children without supervision. The demand for care for school-age children was also expected to rise because welfare reform required more mothers with school-age children to work.

Although after-school programs were popular in many locales, some critics were concerned about "the notion of the government, rather than families, being responsible for children for more hours each day." Given the "shortcomings of public schools," they questioned if more time in such facilities would "just produce more failure." Some experts on education and child development were concerned about overprogramming children or placing them in after-school settings that lacked stimulation or supervision.[75]

One of the most compelling reasons for supporting after-school care was its role in providing activities for children that prevent at-risk behavior and encourage positive aspects of development. For example, children left on their own are at greater risk of substance abuse, truancy from school, and poor grades than are their peers who receive adult supervision.[76] Juvenile crime was another significant problem, as law enforcement officials were making nearly 2.8 million arrests of children under eighteen in 1997.[77] The Department of Justice documented that the peak hours for violent juvenile crime were between 3:00 P.M. and 8:00 P.M., with 12 percent of such crimes committed around 3:00 P.M., right after the school day ends. Nearly half of all juvenile crime occurred between 2:00 P.M. and 8:00 P.M. After-school hours were also the most common time for adolescent sexual activity.[78] After-school care offered safe alternatives to crime, teen pregnancy, and substance abuse, thereby making it a priority for President Clinton and other federal officials.[79]

Organized Interests Help Shape the Scope of Child Care Discussions

Some of the impetus in support for after-school programs came from organizations such as the National Institute on Out-of-School Time (NIOST, formerly the School-Age Child Care Project). Founded in 1979 by Michelle Seligson and Jim Levine and located at the Center for Research on Women at Wellesley College, NIOST's mission was to improve the quantity and quality of programs for school-age children. It worked closely with other education groups, in particular the National School-Age Care Alliance, composed of state affiliates and professionals involved with programs for school-age children.

An interesting development among organized interests involved with child care, especially care for school-age children, was the founding in 1996 of an organization called Fight Crime: Invest in Kids (Fight Crime). The president and founder of Fight Crime, Sanford A. Newman, was an attorney who became interested in crime as "an issue that progressives and conservatives need[ed] to take seriously." He arrived at that point after he and his wife woke up one night to find an intruder crouching between their bed and their newborn's crib. Realizing that if something had happened to his family, the intruder's going to prison wouldn't have undone the damage, he began examining research to see what approaches had been proved effective in "helping kids turn out to be good neighbors instead of criminals." Newman consulted with Elliot Richardson (former secretary of HEW and attorney general under Nixon) and Patrick Murphy (former police commissioner of New York, Detroit, Washington, D.C., and Syracuse) about the feasibility of support among police chiefs for an "organization that would help the public understand that our most powerful weapons against crime were investments in programs that could help kids get a good start . . . programs such as child care."[80]

In 1996, with grants from individuals and foundations and an advisory committee that read like a "Who's Who" of experts on child care policy, Newman launched Fight Crime. Its goal was

> to help Americans understand that the public policies that give children and families a fair shot at life—from prenatal care and early childhood education, to effective youth development and after-school programs—are the same policies that reduce crime and restore public safety. It was designed to create a paradigmatic shift in the way Americans understand both the fight against crime and their self-interest in investing in helping all of America's children and youth achieve their potential.[81]

Fight Crime's members (who by 2000 included over 500 police chiefs, prosecutors, and crime survivors) had expertise in crime and the factors that lead to it. As Newman explained:

Moderate and conservative Americans understand that law enforcement and crime victims are hard-nosed representatives of traditional values. Because they find it surprising that we are speaking out for increased public investments in kids, the press and the public sit up and take notice.

Groups like CDF, the CWLA, and other national, state, and local advocates have educated millions of Americans, and there is no substitute for the terrific, critical work they are continuing to do. We aim to supplement their army with troops who have until now been outside the fray—troops who are in a unique position to persuade many of those who have been unreceptive to supporting government help for disadvantaged kids, or who just haven't made it a top priority. Helping at-risk kids get the right start moves way up the priority list when people realize it's the best way to protect their own families from crime.[82]

One of Fight Crime's successes has been to greatly increase understanding by policymakers that after-school programs can play a key role in reducing juvenile crime. Fight Crime's after-school effort took off in September 1997 when it held a press conference and presented Attorney General Janet Reno with its report *After-School Programs or After-School Crime*. The event generated broadcast and print coverage and caught the attention of federal and state policymakers, including President Clinton, who referred to the data in support of after-school programs in his 1998 State of the Union message. Fight Crime sponsored other reports and initiatives.[83] As Newman explained, "Our thinking is that, while the link between early childhood investments and crime prevention isn't quite as intuitive to the public and press as the after-school link has become, with enough repetition and saturation, we'll get there."[84] Fight Crime helped shift the definition of the problem of child care from welfare reform and the pros and cons of non-parental care to crime prevention. In so doing, it helped win bipartisan support for aspects of child care policies, particularly, after-school child care.

Care for School-Age Children Goes to Capitol Hill

Interest in care for school-age children extended to Congress, where several legislators introduced bills featuring expansion of care programs for school-age children. For example, Senator Dodd's 1998 child care legislation (S. 1610) increased CCDBG funding for care for school-age children and raised funding for it through Twenty-first Century Community Learning Centers (21st CCLC) Programs. Clinton also proposed financing the component for school-age children of his child care initiative through 21st CCLCs.[85]

Twenty-first CCLCs became increasingly relevant to child care as other options for funding after-school care diminished. Administered by the Department of Education, 21st CCLCs were initially authorized under a 1994 amendment to Title X of the Elementary and Secondary Education Act. Congress originally intended 21st CCLCs to enable rural and inner-city schools to provide a broad range of activities, such as literacy education, senior citizen programs, or child care services. Funding for 21st CCLCs was a modest $1 million in FY 1997.[86]

That year, the Department of Education issued guidelines specifying that the money for 21st CCLCs would go to "public schools to establish or expand after-school programs." The new "absolute priority" was to serve children and youth, with the understanding that "applicants *may* propose projects that also serve and involve other members of the community" (emphasis in original).[87] This was in contrast to the original legislation, which had *required* that programs serve a broad range of community needs. In seeking ways to finance after-school child care under the FY 1999 budget, Clinton proposed $1 billion over five years for the 21st CCLCs, which was a handsome increase over the $40 million that Congress had appropriated in 1998.

In February 1998 Senator Jeffords, an original designer of the 21st CCLCs, held a Senate hearing to help identify problems and barriers related to providing after-school care.[88] Also in 1998 the Charles Stewart Mott Foundation pledged up to $55 million to provide technical assistance for Clinton's proposed expansion of 21st CCLCs.[89] Thus, in a short time, 21st CCLCs became one of the most popular ways to expand after-school care. Other options, such as increasing funding under the CCDBG and enacting freestanding legislation on after-school programs, were not politically viable in the late 1990s, mainly because of political obstacles under a Republican Congress. Care for school-age children was only one component of federal child care policymaking. Those seeking an expanded federal investment in all aspects of child care, from early childhood to quality enhancements, had to work other channels.

Looking in All the Wrong Places

Support for child care for school-age children was strong, but the rest of Clinton's child care proposal faded from sight by the end of March 1998. Some attributed its demise to the Monica Lewinsky scandal, which became news right after Clinton had announced his child care initiative. Others pointed to a lack of public support for child care as a pressing national priority.[90] Some people thought that lack of funding made Clinton's child care proposal a political impossibility. Whatever the reasons, child care advocates now had to seek other ways to increase funding for federal child care programs. One option was to amend budget legislation. The other route was to increase funding for child care through the tobacco settlement. Both created notable but insufficient victories for child care.

In late February 1998, concerned about the need for increased funding for child care, Senator Dodd introduced an amendment to the Senate budget resolution that would establish a reserve fund for child care under subsequent budget legislation. Dodd explained the purpose of his amendment, which had the support of many of his fellow Democrats:

All I want to do is create a reserve fund to leave open the possibility of dealing with the issue of child care. I can't imagine anybody here, regardless of ideology or party, would say I should not be allowed, in a budget resolution, to address a priority we all agree is pretty high on the list. . . . A reserve fund . . . is simply a mechanism that allows legislation, in this case child care legislation, to be offered later in the year without the threat of a budget point of order being brought against it.[91]

Dodd contended that the amendment was needed in case he or another member of Congress wanted to use federal revenues from the tobacco settlement or other sources to increase federal child care support. Senator Pete Domenici, chair of the Budget Committee, opposed Dodd's amendment. He claimed the federal government already spent $13.8 billion on child care programs, and the 82 percent increase in federal child care expenditures since 1990 was "not too shabby." Domenici wanted to use money from the tobacco settlement to restore Medicare funds, and he cautioned against easing budgetary constraints in the face of looming budget surpluses: "I think we are in an era of balanced budgets and surpluses. You will not stay there very long if you return to the day that whatever the Government is spending, it is not spending enough."[92] In fact, by 1998 the federal budget ran a surplus of $69 billion, the first surplus in three decades.[93]

In defending the need for the child care reserve fund, Dodd and his colleagues, with strong support from CDF and other child care advocates, argued that "welfare reform did not take care of child care" as demonstrated by the states' inability to serve most eligible children. Moreover, funds were needed to strengthen after-school care and the quality of care, which Congress had not adequately addressed under welfare reform.[94] On March 31, 1998, a majority of voting senators approved Dodd's reserve fund by a vote of fifty to forty-eight. All forty-four Democrat senators present that day supported it and were joined by six Republicans.[95] But the amendment lacked the sixty votes needed to waive certain procedural requirements. It was another sign of strong interest in child care being still insufficient to enact legislation.

The Rocky Tobacco Road

Advocates continued to work on obtaining child care funding linked to tobacco revenues even though the Dodd amendment had failed. This time, the train leaving the station that everyone jumped on was the tobacco settlement bill. In 1997 forty-one state attorneys general and five of the largest tobacco corporations reached an agreement to settle lawsuits brought by the attorneys general against the tobacco companies. The attorneys general sued the tobacco companies for health care costs resulting from tobacco-related illnesses, arguing that states had to pay for the costs of these illnesses through Medicaid and other public health programs. The settlement required the tobacco companies to pay nearly $370 billion over twenty-five years in compensation to state governments, private litigants, and an array of public antismoking and health education campaigns. In exchange, the state attorneys general agreed to drop all lawsuits against the tobacco companies and grant immunity against future cases. The agreement was sent to Congress with the understanding that force of federal law would enhance its enforcement and because it included many contentious issues that fell under federal purview.[96] Proceeds from the pending settlement presented a treasure chest of potential funding for public health advocates and others seeking to increase federal and state spending on programs that enhance children's well-being, including child care.

In late 1997 Congress set to work on legislation that would enforce and modify the original tobacco deal. Much of the discussion focused on preventing young people from smoking, since the rate of teen smoking had soared since 1992.[97] Because increasing the price of a pack of cigarettes contributed to decreases in teen smoking,[98] many of the negotiations centered on how much to raise the price per pack and how to spend the proceeds from the settlement.[99] Furthermore, the tobacco companies had targeted youth in their advertising campaigns, which "relied heavily on giveaways and youngster-friendly cartoons like Joe Camel."[100] These disturbing trends justified devoting large portions of the settlement money to smoking prevention programs for youth and child health.

In the Senate, where most of the tobacco action occurred, several committees claimed jurisdiction over the tobacco settlement. Among them were the Senate Committee on Labor and Human Resources, the Committee on Agriculture, and the Committee on Finance. But the Republican leadership gave the Committee on Commerce, Science, and Transportation full responsibility for tobacco legislation, even though some of the issues did not routinely fall under its scope. Legislators with an interest in how the proceeds from the tobacco settlement should be used testified at hearings and introduced various bills.[101] President Clinton was slow to present his tobacco settlement terms, but when he did, reducing smoking among youths was one of his priorities, funded by a $1.50 increase in the price of cigarettes. (The original settlement called for an increase of approximately 62 cents per pack.)[102]

On November 5, 1997, Senator John McCain (R-Ariz.), chair of the Senate commerce committee, introduced the National Tobacco Policy and Youth Smoking Reduction Act (S. 1415), which mostly followed the original settlement between the attorneys general and the tobacco giants. Senator John Kerry (D-Mass.) managed the bill for the Democrats, which was significant because earlier in the year Kerry had introduced legislation (S. 756) that increased federal spending on early childhood programs. Kerry had difficulty obtaining GOP cosponsors for his early childhood bill because few were willing to endorse legislation with a high price tag and an agenda that was not central to the priorities of the Republican leadership. Eventually, Kerry enlisted the support of Senator Christopher Bond (R-Mo.). In November 1997, with Bond as cosponsor, Kerry introduced a scaled-down version of his original early childhood bill. The Kerry–Bond legislation (S. 1309) invested $11 billion over five years for increases in the child care block grant, Head Start, and other early childhood initiatives.

McCain's bill as introduced in the commerce committee had vague priorities as to how the tobacco settlement funds should be used. When the committee revised the bill, its members accepted an amendment from Senator Kerry that proceeds from the settlement be used to expand CCDBG funding. The committee adopted the amendment with the understanding "that good quality child care is key to the healthy development of children and constructive after-school activities are an important part of keeping school-age children from smoking."[103] Kerry's committee amendment was a step in the right direction, but it offered no guarantee that Congress would appropriate funds for child care.

Before being sent to the full Senate, the McCain tobacco bill included a carefully negotiated agreement between the White House and the NGA that half of the funds from the settlement would be unrestricted in use. The other half would be spent on six health and education priorities, which included child care. The other five areas were child health, substance abuse and mental health, child welfare, safe and drug-free schools, and professional development for teachers.

This agreement infuriated child care advocates who had worked hard to ensure that tobacco revenues would be allocated for child care. If child care was only one of six priorities, there was no guarantee of any funding increases for it. Even though President Clinton had relied on tobacco revenues to subsidize his proposed increases in federal child care programs, the McCain bill promised nothing when it came to child care.

In May 1998 Senators Kerry and Bond drafted a floor amendment for Senate consideration of McCain's tobacco bill. Their amendment required states to spend half of the federal share, which was 25 percent of their settlement money, on child care. This would have boosted funding for child care by several billion dollars over five years.[104]

The Child Care Now! Coalition activated its grassroots networks in support of the Kerry–Bond amendment, which was scheduled for a floor vote in late May 1998 and then postponed to early June. Actually, Child Care Now! had been working on the tobacco–child care connection since November 1997 when Kennedy and DeLauro introduced their Health and Smoke-Free Children Act, which Kerry cosponsored. CDF organized a nationwide telephone blitz on Congress between May 11 and June 12 to support the Kerry–Bond amendment. Anyone could call a toll-free number, hear a message about child care, and then be connected with his or her legislator's office to urge support of the Kerry–Bond amendment. The long-distance telephone company Working Assets covered the costs of all the calls made over that period as part of the Child Care Now! campaign.

National organizations representing women, children, and child care interests lobbied in favor of Kerry–Bond. The NWLC wrote letters to each senator endorsing the amendment, cosigned by fourteen other women's organizations, such as the AAUW, NOW Legal Defense and Education Fund, 9 to 5 National Association of Working Women, and NCJW.[105] CDF ran Child Care Now! advertisements in the *Washington Post* and *Congress Daily*. One ad was partially subsidized by Fight Crime.

This linkage between child care and smoking prevention presented a new spin on child care, a new way of framing the issue. One child care advocate referred to the matching of child care and smoking prevention as "voodooism." Another described it as a "marriage of convenience." Regardless of the merits of the arguments, linking smoking and child care was a necessary venture, especially given the scarcity of other options for increasing child care funding. So child care became part of the tobacco legislation, forcing child care advocates to roll with its ups and downs.

The Tobacco Deal Sparks Intergovernmental Feuds

A major stumbling block to the tobacco bill was opposition from the NGA and NCSL. Under the terms of the large tobacco agreement, Congress would decide how to grant states half of the proceeds, based on formulas from Medicaid law. Senator Bob Graham (D-Fla.), a former governor of Florida, sided with the governors in complaining that federal authorities had offered no help to states in fighting the tobacco companies. And "now the federal government, without having lifted a finger to assist the states, is claiming the right to a portion of any settlement funds."[106] The NCSL had similar complaints.

Opposition from the NGA and NCSL created large gaps in the wall of solidarity for child care. These groups opposed decreases in the amount of money available to states and restrictions on the states' flexibility in spending tobacco revenues, both of which resulted from various amendments to the McCain bill.[107] The NGA opposed the Kerry–Bond amendment because it dictated how states should spend their tobacco settlement funds. The governors argued that "by locking states into a specific child care requirement, the Kerry–Bond amendment would prevent states from meeting other compelling needs as their particular circumstances dictate."[108]

The NCSL opposed the Kerry–Bond amendment for similar reasons. NCSL generally opposed any type of earmarking of federal dollars. Thus, it could not support legislation that required states to set aside part of their tobacco settlement proceeds for child care. Because members of the NGA and NCSL would be implementing the tobacco settlement, their opposition was significant.

Despite opposition from the intergovernmental lobby, on June 11, 1998, all forty-five Senate Democrats and twenty-one Republicans voted for the Kerry–Bond amendment.[109] The official vote (sixty-six to thirty-three) was to defeat a motion from Senator Nickles to kill the amendment, after which the Senate approved Kerry–Bond by voice vote.[110] Opposition to the amendment came from conservative Republicans, most notably Senator Nickles, who saw the entire tobacco bill as a "tax-and-spend" initiative. Speaking on the Senate floor, he argued that "this amendment is not about curbing smoking. It has nothing to do with curbing smoking—nothing, not one thing. It is not going to reduce consumption by teenagers one iota, but it will spend $50 billion." Support from moderate GOP senators, in particular Chafee, was important in passing the amendment. Speaking on the Senate floor, Kerry read a letter supporting his amendment from well-known pediatrician T. Berry Brazelton of Harvard, former surgeon general Dr. Julius Richmond, and other leading experts on child health and development. Senators Dodd, Kennedy, and Wellstone were among those who joined Kerry and Bond in speaking for the amendment.[111]

But the entire tobacco settlement unraveled in late June because McCain's bill lacked the sixty votes needed for procedural purposes to move it forward in the Senate.[112] The bill had little likelihood of enactment because of congressional squabbling over how to use the settlement to fund legislators' pet projects, objections from state officials, and quarreling among organized interests over the pros and cons of the deal.[113] According to some policy analysts, the defeat of tobacco legislation was the most stinging defeat of the year for Clinton and his fellow Democrats because they had expected to use the cigarette tax increases to finance many programs, including child care. The downfall of the tobacco settlement symbolized yet another episode in the 105th Congress when child care advocates won an impressive victory (the Kerry–Bond amendment) but could not achieve enactment of a major child care bill.

In November 1998 the attorneys general of forty-six states and the District of Columbia reached another tobacco settlement, worth $206 billion over five years. Each state was to determine how to use its windfall from the settlement, which triggered a new round of skirmishes at the state level.[114]

The Last Hurrahs of the 105th Congress

Despite the defeat of the tobacco bill, by the end of 1998 several funding measures for child care were enacted. Under the Higher Education Reauthorization Act (P.L. 105-244), Congress authorized $45 million for campus-based child care, based on the initial bill proposed by Dodd and Snowe in 1997, and $115 million for Wellstone's loan forgiveness bill for child care providers. Demonstrating the popularity of after-school programs, Congress increased FY 1999 appropriations for 21st CCLCs (targeting after-school programs) by $160 million, bringing the total annual funding to $200 million.[115] In addition, Congress appropriated $182 million in new discretionary funding for the CCDBG, $172 million of which were earmarked for quality enhancement. This was a significant increase over the 4 percent quality set-aside in the 1996 welfare reform bill. Congress set aside an additional $10 million for research and maintained the $50 million already on the books as a set-aside for infant and toddler care.[116] When combined with the $2.17 billion in CCDBG mandatory funding (through the capped entitlement portion enacted under welfare reform), total FY 1999 funding for the block grant was $3.35 billion. Head Start was also reauthorized during the last days of the 105th session, with new provisions that emphasized quality enhancement and the linkage of child care and Head Start services on the state level (P.L. 105-285).

On the downside, funding for the Title XX SSBG, which many states use to fund child care, fell from nearly $2.3 billion to $1.9 billion.[117] On another front, Congress reauthorized the Child Nutrition Act (P.L. 105-336). These changes gave community-based organizations, child care providers, and schools increased resources for snacks for children in after-school programs.[118]

Many child care advocates were disappointed that the 105th Congress ended without enactment of a major child care bill. Neither a presidential initiative nor possible windfalls from the tobacco settlement had resulted in favorable outcomes. But the funding increases for child care in 1998 symbolized a growing presidential and congressional interest in child care, especially because the gains came only two years after Congress increased funding for child care under welfare. Some people claimed that the Clinton–Lewinsky scandal was responsible for the demise of major child care legislation in 1998. Others argued that the defeat of the tobacco bill "killed those initiatives."[119] It was tempting to wonder if without Monicagate, Clinton would have been more tenacious with his child care commitment. Although he might have had a freer agenda, it is unclear if he would have remained steadfast in his dedication to child care. In addition to waning presidential interest, lack of a secure funding source and of a consistent message impeded the enactment of child care legislation. The 106th Congress (1999–2000) brought new issues and challenges.

Ushering Federal Child Care Policy into the Twenty-first Century

The 1998 midterm elections were a call for moderation. Republicans held the slimmest lead in the House (223 to 211, and 1 Independent) in more than forty-five years, while holding their 55 to 45 margin in the Senate. Congressional Republicans touted a third session of majority status. Democrats pointed to their party's gains in the House, which were rare in an off-year election for the party controlling the White House. Moreover, Democrats won their House seats despite the Clinton–Lewinsky scandal, which many had thought would give Republicans a political edge.

After the elections Republicans blamed their electoral losses on Gingrich's waning influence and his inability to lead the party, which led to his resignation. After the derailed nomination of Representative Robert Livingston (R-La.), House Republicans elected Representative Dennis Hastert (R-Ill.) as Speaker. Hastert had a strong probusiness, antitax voting record, and a more conciliatory manner than Gingrich.[120] But he found it difficult to achieve legislative successes for his party. The turmoil within the Republican leadership and the party's narrow lead over Democrats indicated that the Republican revolution was "running out of steam."[121]

In 1999 Representative Michael Castle (R-Del.) became chair of the Subcommittee on Early Childhood, Youth, and Families of the House Committee on Education and the Workforce (formerly the Committee on Education and Economic Opportunities). Castle had a reputation for attracting a bipartisan coalition of moderates, especially on social policy issues.[122] Representative Johnson, also a moderate Republican, replaced Shaw as chair of the Subcommittee on Human Resources of the Committee on Ways and Means, and Shaw became chair of the Subcommittee on Social Security.

With Senator Dan Coats not running for reelection, Senator Judd Gregg (R-N.H.) replaced him as chair of the Subcommittee on Children and Families of the Committee on Health, Education, Labor, and Pensions (formerly the Committee on Labor and Human Resources). Gregg had a moderate to conservative voting record and was a leading proponent of extending the DCTC to stay-at-home-parents.

Despite the moderating influences of the elections, by 1999 the two congressional parties had become highly polarized. Enacting laws, therefore, required tedious negotiations between parties and between Congress and the White House. Partisan conflict often centered on how to handle the growing federal budget surplus. By February 1999 OMB estimated a FY 2000 budget surplus of $79 billion, which eventually reached approximately $167 billion.[123] Clinton remained firm in his preference for using the surplus to protect Social Security and Medicare.[124] Republicans wanted to use the surplus for tax cuts. A July 1999 *Wall Street Journal*/NBC News Poll revealed that 46 percent of those polled preferred spending the surplus on social programs and 20 percent chose tax cuts. The rest chose paying down the federal debt or other options.[125] In January 1999 and the months that followed, polls showed that the public ranked education, crime, and ethics as the most important problems facing the nation.[126] Thus, the challenge for child care advocates was to turn the budget surplus, concerns about education, and growing interest in social programs into legislative gains.

Familiar Refrains and New Hope

In the first few months of 1999, Congress and the nation were preoccupied with Clinton's impeachment. Nonetheless, in January 1999 Clinton delivered a well-received State of the Union message in which he repeated his calls for substantial increases in funding for child care, early childhood initiatives, and working families.[127] Clinton's budget proposal for FY 2000 included an increase of $3.6 billion in child care expenditures and tax incentives over 1999. He proposed a $200 million increase in the CCDBG, $600 million for an Early Learning Fund to improve the quality of care for children under five, $183 million for the set-asides for quality improvements and research, and a $400 million (200%) increase for 21st CCLC after-school programs. Total FY 2000 funding for the block grant would reach $4.5 billion, including the mandatory $2.4 billion for child care entitlements to states that had been enacted in 1996. Clinton also proposed expanding the DCTC for families with incomes below $59,000 and extending it to families with parents who stay at home with children under one.[128]

As in 1998, in 1999 various child care measures were on the table. Senator Dodd and his Democratic cosponsors reintroduced their ACCESS legislation (S. 17), which the White House supported.[129] Representative Ellen O. Tauscher (D-Calif.) introduced a similar bill (H.R. 1139) in the House. Senator Chafee with cosponsors Hatch, Snowe, and Specter introduced legislation (S. 599) that made the DCTC available to parents who stay home to care for children aged three or under, expanded the credit for low-income working families, and increased spending for the CCDBG. As in the past, Chafee's tax credit provisions were more generous than Dodd's, and Chafee's CCDBG increases were lower.[130] The combination of tax and programmatic provisions in both bills suggested a possible bipartisan consensus on child care legislation. Senators Kennedy and Ted Stevens (R-Alaska) introduced the Early Learning Trust Fund (S. 749), which provided states with flexible matching funds to support the expansion of prekindergarten programs. Senator Jeffords's Caring for America's Children Act (S. 810) was a comprehensive measure that included various tax and programmatic initiatives. In the House, legislators introduced similar measures. Representative Johnson was the lead House proponent of revising the DCTC by expanding it to low-income families and offering it to parents staying home to care for children.[131]

Republicans were generally reluctant to increase child care funding when many states were running TANF surpluses. In early 1999 the Congressional Research Service reported that states had approximately $6.3 billion in unspent TANF funds, although states had obligated (or committed to spend) half that amount. In March 1999 Representative Johnson's Subcommittee on Human Resources held a hearing at which she and her GOP colleagues urged governors to spend their TANF money on child care and other welfare-related services.[132] Johnson also wrote a letter to the nation's governors urging each to spend the TANF money to help as many TANF and low-income working families as possible.[133]

But many states were leery of spending their TANF surpluses. They anticipated needing the funds in lean economic times when their TANF caseloads were likely to rise.

Olivia Golden, assistant secretary for children and families, expressed the sentiments of many experts on child care policy when she explained that welfare was only one piece of the child care puzzle. TANF funds alone could not solve the unmet child care needs of many low-income working families.[134] In August 1999 front-page stories reported that declining TANF caseloads left states with large amounts of unspent federal dollars.[135] Many economists and politicians explained that it was too soon to know how long states would sustain their TANF surpluses and how the surpluses would affect welfare, child care, and other services for poor or low-income families. An October 1999 HHS report pointed out that only one out of ten eligible children received federal child care assistance, thus confirming the importance of publicly subsidized child care. The report documented variation in child care expenditures between the states and the gaps in federal and state child care policies for low-income families.[136]

With Congress focused on the budget, child care advocates sought new ways of increasing federal spending on child care. As in the past, the Senate was the forum for child care debates while the House remained too divided and conservative to muster support. Furthermore, Senators Dodd and Jeffords had an exceptionally strong commitment to child care legislation. As a result of their efforts, the Senate approved four measures in 1999 that increased child care funding for FY 2000, but none of them survived to enactment.

First, on March 24, 1999, Dodd and Jeffords introduced a budget resolution amendment that provided an additional $5 billion in mandatory CCDBG spending over five years. They proposed subsidizing the amendment by offsets in the pending tax-cut bill. The Senate passed the amendment by a vote of fifty-seven to forty-two. Second, on April 13, 1999, the Senate instructed members of the House and Senate budget conference committee to support a $5 billion increase in CCDBG mandatory funding over five years. The nonbinding vote passed by a vote of sixty-six to thirty-two. The House version of the budget resolution lacked any such provision. The House and Senate budget conference committee replaced Dodd's amendment with a $3 billion increase in new mandatory CCDBG spending over ten years and $3 billion in additional tax credits for families with children.[137] Both houses approved the conference report for the budget resolution, which included the Senate language.[138] But the amendment had limited influence because budget resolutions lack the force of law.

The third time the Senate approved increases in the CCDBG was on July 30, 1999, when it passed an amendment by Dodd and Jeffords to Senator William Roth's tax bill (S. 1429). The amendment increased the CCDBG by $10 billion over ten years. The Senate also approved Senator Gregg's amendment, which extended the DCTC to stay-at-home parents with a child under one.[139] But all of this became a moot point in September 1999 when Clinton vetoed the tax bill (H.R. 2488), claiming that its tax cuts were too large and that it left little room for other priorities, such as protecting Social Security and Medicare.[140]

Dodd and Jeffords had one last chance. By the fall of 1999, child care advocates were no longer insisting on increases in mandatory CCDBG because it was not politically viable. On September 30, 1999, the Senate approved a Dodd–Jeffords amendment to the appropriations bill for the Departments of Labor, HHS, and Education that increased CCDBG funding for FY 2000 by $818 million. Officially, the Senate voted fifty-four to forty-one against a motion to remove the Dodd–Jeffords amendment from further consideration and then approved the amendment by voice vote.[141]

On November 3, 1999, Clinton vetoed the FY 2000 appropriations bill for the District of Columbia, which included the conference report for the Departments of Labor, HHS, and Education appropriations bill. In his veto message, Clinton identified Congress's decrease in SSBG funding and its failure to increase the CCDBG funding.[142] In the final version of the FY 2000 spending bill for the Departments of Labor, HHS, and Education, Congress froze CCDBG spending, restored some of the SSBG cuts, and appropriated an additional $250 million for 21st CCLC before- and after-school programs. Head Start received increases, too. Senator Specter, chair of the Appropriations Committee, Subcommittee on Labor, HHS, and Education promised to increase the CCDBG funding by $818 million in the next year's appropriations bill.[143] As an aside, Senator Chafee died in October 1999, leaving a legacy of bipartisan leadership on child care and other children's issues.

Clinton's last State of the Union address in January 2000 included the now familiar refrains of increased support for child care. His FY 2001 budget proposed increasing the CCDBG by $817 million in discretionary funding. He also proposed $1 billion for 21st CCLC after-school programs. His recommendations for the Early Learning Fund and DCTC expansions were nearly identical to his proposals the year before. However, in 2000, he also proposed making the DCTC refundable. As in the past, he supported the creation of a child care tax incentive for businesses providing child care services for their employees.[144] Senator Specter's pledge to increase CCDBG funding, coupled with Clinton's similar proposal, boded well for the enactment of such legislation in 2000.

But enactment of the FY 2001 labor appropriations bill, which included child care, proved to be difficult. In June 2000 the House passed an appropriations bill (H.R. 4577) that increased CCDBG funding by $400 million for FY 2001, which was $417 million below the president's budget request. When the bill landed on the House floor, GOP conservatives complained that its forward funding (obligating money in FY 2001 for spending in FY 2002) would exceed their previous limit on forward funding for all thirteen appropriations bills under the House budget resolution (H. Con. Res. 290). To keep forward spending in line, House Republicans pushed through a provision that, in short, limited FY 2002 funds for the CCDBG to the FY 2000 level of $1.2 billion. Approximately sixteen other programs in the labor appropriations bill had forward funding, but Republicans eliminated only the CCDBG increases, ostensibly because these forward funding increases were the largest. Before the floor vote on the appropriations bill, an amendment offered by Representative David Obey (D-Wis.), ranking Democrat on the House Appropriations Committee, to reinstate the CCDBG funding increases lost by a vote of 212 to 219, with members voting primarily along party lines.[145] The Senate restored the $817 million increase in CCDBG funding (for a total of $2 billion) to be made available in FY 2001, included set-asides for child care quality improvement, care for school-aged children, infant and toddler care, and increased funding for 21st CCLCs. In July the House and Senate conferees for the labor appropriations bill followed the Senate's lead and retained the $817 million increase in CCDBG funding for FY 2001 along with the CCDBG set-asides and increases in funding for other child care programs.

By October 2000 members of Congress and Clinton had reached a tentative agreement on the FY 2001 appropriations bill, which included an $817 million increase in the CCDBG for FY 2001 and the various CCDBG set-asides. It also provided increases in 21st CCLCs, Head Start, and other programs, such as campus-based child care. Congress and the president also agreed to a establish an Early Learning Trust Fund, which would enable communities to develop early childhood development programs, and an Early Childhood Education and Development Program. However, in an unusual course of events, the appropriations bill was not enacted before the November elections. As a result, the final negotiations for the labor appropriations bill became entwined with partisan bickering over funding for education, a controversial rider pertaining to ergonomics in the workplace, and postelection politics as the country anxiously awaited the final results of the presidential elections well into December 2000. President Clinton and Secretary of HHS Donna Shalala urged Congress to pass the labor appropriations bill with the increases in child care funding that Congress and the White House had agreed to in late October. They cited new HHS data showing that millions of children were not receiving federal child care assistance even though they were eligible.[146]

Finally, in mid-December 2000, right before adjourning, lawmakers reached agreement on the FY 2001 labor appropriations bill, which included handsome increases in child care funding. The final FY 2001 appropriations law included the long-sought-after $817 million increase in CCDBG funding, bringing the total discretionary stream for FY 2001 to $2 billion. Of the $2 billion, $173 was set aside for quality enhancement, $100 million for infant and toddler care (double the amount from FY 2000), $10 million for child care research, $19 million for care for school-age children and resource and referral programs, and $1 million for a toll-free child care hotline. Moreover, 21st CCLCs received a $392 million boost for after-school programs, bringing that total to $846 million. Campus-based child care was increased by $20 million, for a total of $25 million. Head Start received its largest increase ever, $933 million, bringing its total FY 2001 funding to over $6 billion. The Early Learning Trust Fund was also established under the appropriations bill, starting with a $20 million authorization for demonstration grants to states to fund local councils that administer various early childhood and family support activities.[147]

Child care advocates exulted in their victory. After three years of trying to get Congress and the president to approve a sizable increase in child care funding, they had finally succeeded. The FY 2001 labor appropriations bill was another juncture in the history of child care policymaking that set the stage for subsequent activity at the federal and state levels. Although not as major a shift as the previous three episodes (1970, 1990, or 1996), it was a significant episode in the history of child care legislation. Moreover, it demonstrated that even a Republican Congress, opposed to expanding domestic programs, can approve increases in federal child care assistance. Perhaps this was because the provisions were part of an omnibus appropriations bill that Congress was eager to pass. It might also have been due to the growing acceptance of child care as a federal initiative.

As another example of federal action pertaining to child care, in October 2000 Congress and Clinton approved the Children's Day Care Health and

Safety Improvement Act (S. 2236), sponsored by Senator Bill Frist (R-Tenn.) and cosponsored by Senator Dodd. The law authorized $200 million for grants to states to establish programs to improve the health and safety of children in child care settings. It included activities such as strengthening licensing and regulation of eligible child care providers and educating them about illness and injury prevention. The legislation was enacted as part of a children's public health bill, the Children's Health Act (P.L. 106-310). Framing child care as a public health measure enabled Frist and Dodd to circumvent GOP opposition to any type of new spending on child care. Frist was able to fold the child care bill into the public health legislation because he was the main cosponsor of both initiatives. But because the child care bill was enacted late in the session, there was not enough time to secure its appropriations for FY 2001.

The 2000 elections presented interesting choices for child care advocates. Vice President Al Gore, the Democratic nominee for president, featured child care and early education prominently in his campaign. He proposed increased funding for after-school programs, making the DCTC refundable, extending it to families with a parent at home caring for children, and encouraging states to provide universal preschool. Governor George W. Bush of Texas, the GOP nominee, made education a campaign priority, but his platform did not highlight early childhood education or child care. He did voice strong concerns about parental choice in the context of education, reminiscent of his father's positions as president a decade earlier.

In a landmark national contest, Gore won the popular vote by over 500,000 votes, while Bush narrowly won the electoral votes. Bush's calls for a scaled-back federal government presented challenges to those favoring federal child care assistance. But his calls for education reform could create opportunities for injecting child care and early education into policy discussions. Bush's campaign pledge to "leave no child behind," using the exact four words that constitute CDF's motto, sparked lively commentary among observers of child-related policies.[148] However, it was unclear if his policies, once he was in office, would match his campaign rhetoric.

Initially, Bush faced a divided Congress for the 107th session, with the Senate evenly split (50 to 50) between Democrats and Republicans. In May 2001, Senator Jeffords left the Republican Party and became an Independent, thereby giving the Democrats an extremely narrow ruling majority (50 to 49 to 1). In the House, Republicans hold a narrow 220 to 211 lead over Democrats, with 2 Independents. With such close margins in both houses, reaching consensus on any issue is difficult. Moderates of both parties will be important in obtaining majorities. Committees also changed as both parties designated new chairs for several key panels. When the Democrats gained control of the Senate, Max Baucus became chair of the Finance Committee. Senator Kennedy assumed the chair of the Health, Education, Labor, and Pensions Committee. His long-standing commitment to increasing government spending on child care means that such positions will be given more visibility than in the past. In the House, the resignation of Representatives Bill Archer and Goodling left openings at the helm of two major House committees with jurisdiction over child care. Representative Bill Thomas (R-Calif.) is the new chair of the Committee on Ways and Means, and Representative John Boehner (R-Ohio) is the new head of the Committee on Education and the Workforce. Both Thomas and Boehner have reputations for voting along conservative lines. Neither has been very active on child care issues.

In the 107th Congress, which began in January 2001, 13 percent of the seats in both chambers are held by women, an all-time high, but still not a large enough proportion to enact laws on many of the issues, including child care, that are priorities for some female legislators and women's organizations. Hillary Rodham Clinton, as Democratic senator from New York, may call attention to child care and other children's issues, but she will have to work her agenda in a Congress that is highly polarized along party lines. Early education received attention in Congress from debates over the reauthorization of the ESEA, especially because its Title I includes services for preschoolers who are economically and educationally disadvantaged. With the CCDBG due to be reauthorized in 2002, child care will definitely be part of the congressional deliberations in the years ahead. But its politics will be very different from those of the late 1960s and 1970s, when Senator Walter Mondale and Representative John Brademas first tried to enact their bills.

Growing Consensus and New Developments

By late 1999 and into the next millennium, a consensus had emerged about the importance of federal child care support. As many observers of child care politics have noted, the focus of federal child care debates shifted. It was no longer a question of whether Congress should invest in child care. Instead, it was a matter of what shape the investment should take and how much should be spent. Except for those on the extreme right, most legislators were in favor of increasing spending on child care in some way. The controversy centered on what the rate of increase should be and how best to invest federal dollars in helping parents care for their children.

One explanation for the acceptance of federal child care funding was that the 1990 CCDBG set an important precedent for subsequent legislation. It resolved many contentious issues. For example, even though school vouchers remained one of the most heated aspects of educational policymaking, child care vouchers were accepted under the CCDBG and other federal programs. Parental choice for child care was a prominent component of state and federal child care policies, largely because of the CCDBG. And hardly anyone wanted to disturb the delicate balance that the 1990 CCDBG had established regarding health and safety standards.

Outside Congress, interest in child care gathered momentum. Ongoing research on the impact of child care quality on child development continued to capture media attention. For example, a 1999 study found that as children in preschools of higher quality progressed through elementary school, they did better in math and, to a lesser extent, in language skills than children in low-quality care.[149] In 2000 the National Research Council and the Institute of Medicine released a report on the state of the science of early childhood development and its implications for policy, practice, research, and professional development. The report called for a presidential task force to review the entire array of public investments in early childhood education and child care. It also called for the President's Council of Economic Advisors and the Congress to review tax, wage, and income support policies with regard to working families with young children.[150] Many communities and states devoted resources to child care, in recognition of its importance for the economic and social well-being of their residents. Reports depicting the inadequacies of child care funding under welfare reform identified the need to invest in child care for low-income working families (see chapter 8).

Within the federal government, the Child Care Bureau provided technical assistance and support to states and child care providers across the country. Its purview expanded as federal child care funding increased to encompass research projects, coordination with Head Start, and other initiatives. Linking child care and child health programs was another important development that HHS spearheaded through its Healthy Child Care America campaign, which had been launched in 1995.[151]

Much of the credit for the increases in funding for child care lies with CDF and the rest of the child care advocacy community. Among organized interests lobbying for child care, CDF remained the lead organization while others filled important niches. Fight Crime added new dimensions on linking child care with crime prevention. NAEYC's hiring of a professional lobbyist in 1999 held promise for strengthening early childhood education and child care advocacy on Capitol Hill. The Center for the Child Care Workforce drew attention to the importance of well-qualified staff receiving adequate wages. Scores of other child care and children's advocacy groups, too numerous to identify by name, increased the size and strength of the child care advocacy community.

In 1998 and 1999 women's groups, in Congress and beyond, showed renewed interest in child care after a lull (at least among some groups) in the 1980s and early 1990s. Within Congress, the Congressional Caucus for Women's Issues included child care and child care tax policies as part of its legislative agenda for the 106th Congress.[152] In February 2000 the NCJW officially issued a report on child care. The issue was once again a priority for the national organization.[153] The board of the NOW Legal Defense and Education Fund adopted language in 1998 that confirmed its commitment to securing high-quality, affordable, and accessible child care for all families.[154] In 1998 the National Council of Women's Organizations, representing more than one hundred national women's groups, designated child care as one of its official agenda items. It developed a child care task force, co-chaired by the NCJW and the NOW Legal Defense and Education Fund, with strong input from the YWCA and the National Center for the Child Care Workforce.

Another event that breathed life into women's organizations' interest in child care was Lifetime Television's campaign "Caring for Our Kids: Our Lifetime Commitment." In March 1998 Lifetime partnered with leading women's and children's organizations and the Congressional Caucus for Women's Issues to heighten awareness of child care as a policy concern.[155] By mid-1999, more than one hundred national organizations had joined Lifetime's initiative.

These and other child care activities on behalf of women's groups evolved from a serendipitous meeting. The often-told story was that in January 1998 several leaders of women's groups were stuck at New York's LaGuardia Airport. Because of bad weather, their trip to Washington for the announcement of Clinton's child care initiative was canceled. While waiting at the airport and sharing a taxi back to New York City, they talked about the importance of major women's groups being more actively engaged in child care. Meredith Wagner, senior vice president for public affairs at Lifetime, took the lead in convening a steering group of women's organizations. Lifetime's direct impact on federal policymaking was probably minimal. But enlarging the involvement of women's groups was a critical change in child care advocacy.

As the twenty-first century began, child care was not a prominent agenda item for conservatives. Instead, their family policy priorities included decreasing the tax burden on families, reducing or eliminating the marriage penalty, providing parents with school vouchers, and lobbying for policies that promoted traditional family values.[156] Conservative legislators and policy analysts denied that a child care crisis existed. They cited the numerous federal child care programs, which together totaled over $14 billion in FY 2000, as proof that the federal government handsomely invested in child care and did its share. Preferring a minimal role for the federal government, they argued that market forces adequately provided for America's child care needs. Individuals and groups in this camp pointed to "alternatives to government largesse" in child care policymaking, especially if employers, employees, families, and voluntary organizations worked together.[157] Furthermore, they contended that if any level of government was to be responsible for child care policymaking, it should be the states, not federal authorities.

Although many legislators and organized interests sympathized with such sentiments, economic and political realities led some of them to acknowledge the importance of federal child care assistance, especially because many of the same lawmakers lobbied for mandatory work requirements under welfare reform, which increased the need for child care. Nonetheless, conservatives have contributed to child care debates since 1980 by defining alternatives, such as tax credits and policies for stay-at-home mothers. Their positions are often part of final compromises on child care issues.

Following the 1996 welfare law, federal child care policymaking experienced few structural changes. The most significant shifts were the growth in CCDBG funding, including increases for quality enhancements and research under the CCDBG, and the soar in funding for school-age children under 21st CCLCs, reaching more than $840 million in FY 2001. Comparing the child care debates of the late 1990s and 2000 with those of earlier decades reveals one major trend. Child care advocates no longer had to justify the federal government's involvement in child care, and the debates now focused on what that involvement should be.

Applying Baumgartner and Jones's framework, in the late 1990s and 2000 policymakers worked at redefining the issue, so as to expand support. Members of the child care advocacy coalition engaged in new activities and created structures that shaped subsequent periods of child care policymaking. Research on early brain development restructured the debates by introducing new themes. President Clinton helped put child care on the agenda with the White House conferences and his repeated budget requests for increased federal spending for child care. Republicans countered with their emphasis on tax policies and measures that helped families with stay-at-home parents. The latter became an increasingly important theme in federal child care policymaking. The Child Care Bureau created a high-level federal presence for the issue. It created a focal point for advancing accessible, affordable child care while recognizing the importance of developmental aspects of child care. Research findings from NICHD, academia, and other public and private entities provided data that contributed to child care policies. Organized interests published reports, attracted the media, and collaborated with one another. In the meantime, as detailed in the next chapter, states moved ahead in implementing the CCDBG and linking it with other early childhood initiatives.

8   A View from the States, 1996–2000

At first glance, it might seem odd for a book on federal child care policy to include a chapter on state issues. However, the synergy between federal and state child care policies makes it necessary to explain how states implemented federal child care laws. In the late 1990s child care policymaking on the state level relied on growing devolution from federal to state authorities. Thus, this chapter places state child care policies in the context of the shifting sands of intergovernmental relations. It describes the importance of governors in state child care policymaking, implementation of child care under welfare reform of 1996, variation among states' child care policies, and the overlap between child care and other early education, health, or social service programs.

Child Care and American Federalism

In the early 1980s President Ronald Reagan's New Federalism shifted control of many programs to state governments and created a resurgence of interest in state policies. Most notably, President Reagan signed into law the 1981 Omnibus Budget Reconciliation Act (P.L. 97-35), which converted fifty-seven federal health and social categorical programs into nine state block grants.[1] This followed President Nixon's version of New Federalism, which featured revenue-sharing and block grants.[2] Both Nixon and Reagan were interested in diminishing the role of the national government in domestic issues and granting states greater influence. Nixon's New Federalism also aimed to strengthen local governments, while Reagan's version focused on state authority.[3]

During the 1970s political conservatives were the main advocates of a strong state and reduced federal presence in many programs. By the 1980s organizations such as the NGA, NCSL, and National League of Cities had taken the lead among those favoring devolution to state and local entities.[4] Over time, both Republicans and Democrats showed a propensity for granting states a strong say in running social programs.[5] But Democrats were generally less willing than Republicans to relinquish the federal government's role as a major funder and supporter of social policy in areas such as child care.

The rationale for dividing responsibilities between state and federal authorities can be found in both the Constitution's Article I, Section 8, which lists the specific responsibilities of Congress, and in the Tenth Amendment, which states that all powers not specifically assigned to the federal government are reserved for the states. Some scholars claim that the Constitution's intentional ambiguity in this regard gives state and federal lawmakers flexibility to meet the economic and political needs of their time. From their perspective, "the Framers . . . inaugurated a permanent American argument over what version of federalism—at each particular time, in each particular set of circumstances—would be truest to the nation's bedrock values."[6] Richard Nathan, noted expert on American government and former undersecretary of HEW in the Nixon administration, made a similar observation when he said, "American federalism is not, and never has been, intrinsically liberal or conservative. The ideological character of centripetal forces in American federalism has varied over time." According to Nathan, the New Deal created a "shift to a social activist role for the federal government," which "conservative social policies advanced by the Republican-led 104th and 105th Congresses in Washington" then repudiated.[7]

Proponents of granting states a strong say in social policymaking hold to the idea that "the government closest to the people is the best government."[8] Other factors contributing to a "resurgence" or "ascendance" of states included lack of confidence in the federal government, appreciation of states as policy innovators, the states' reform efforts that enhanced their effectiveness in implementing programs, and a strengthening of the intergovernmental lobby, consisting of organizations and individuals representing state and local interests.[9] Federal budget deficits, which loomed large over all policy discussions of the late 1980s and early 1990s, also contributed to a growing appreciation for the limits of the federal reach in many aspects of social policy, including child care.

Some experts on state policy contend that federalism fosters competition among states, which engenders innovation in policymaking as states "race to the top." Others fear that giving states substantial leeway without federal enforcement or oversight produces a "race to the bottom." For child care, the question is not whether devolution is inherently good or bad. Rather, it must focus on how devolution affects children and families relying on publicly subsidized care. How do states use federal and state funds and coordinate child care with other programs? How can government authorities collaborate to promote the well-being of children in child care settings?

In the mid-1990s public opinion polls conducted by the Gallup Organization, *Wall Street Journal* and NBC News, and the Harris Group, to name only a few, illustrated a "striking consistency" in support for "enlarging the role of the states." For example, in 1995 a poll taken by the Princeton Survey Research Associates found that 61 percent of those responding declared state governments to "do a better job of running things," whereas 24 percent generally favored the federal government.[10] In a 1999 poll, 29 percent of those responding thought that they got the most for their money from state governments, the highest percentage ever reported for this question in decades. Lack of comparative data for the preceding five years makes it difficult to ascertain if this was a trend or a fluke in reporting. (In the same 1999 poll, 31 percent of respondents thought they got the most for their money from local governments, 23 percent ranked the federal government highest, and 17 percent did not know or did not answer the question.)[11]

Several trends accompanied devolution to states. Between 1960 and 1995, state and local sectors composed a growing proportion of all public employees, while the proportion of federal employees dropped.[12] This enabled states to develop and administer many programs that increasingly fell under their domain. Most of these programs, including child care, entailed shared responsibility for funding and administration among federal, state, and local authorities.

Historically, child care has been a state issue, and states have selected different agencies (i.e., education, social service, or public health) to administer child care programs and determine eligibility, regulatory requirements, and funding. The 1990 CCDBG and At-Risk Child Care Program infused new federal funding to states for child care, and this was further increased in 1996 through TANF legislation. But despite new federal dollars flowing from these federal developments, the main responsibility for administering child care programs and developing policies was, and continues to be, with the states.

Even though responsibility for child care lies mostly with state authorities, the federal government's influence endured because it could allocate funds for states to run their programs and could approve the states' plans. One analysis of state and federal spending in 1993 and 1994 showed that federal expenditures per capita exceeded state spending per capita in practically every state.[13] The same is probably true for child care in the late 1990s and into the twenty-first century, given the increased federal funding for child care through CCDBG and TANF funds.

In addition to offering a source of financing, nationally administered programs were justified as necessary to protect the safety net. Thomas J. Anton summarized this tenuous balance between federal and state roles when he wrote, "Proposals to limit spending and devolve authority over programs such as welfare or health care to the states challenges a sixty-year understanding that the national government is the appropriate source of a social safety net to assist those unable to help themselves."[14] Federal child care and early childhood programs, such as the CCDBG and Head Start, that entail shared responsibility with other levels of government are a type of safety net for many families with children. Without such assistance, many of them would face serious economic hardships.

Child care is one of many issues illustrating the dynamic nature of federalism. Other issues interwoven with the complexities of federalism and related to child care were the tobacco settlement, welfare, and education. On these and other areas the nation's governors have had considerable influence. Their "plea" can often be summed up as "leave us alone."[15] In discussing federalism and welfare, Nathan noted that "one of the surprising things about the present moment is that not only is federal-to-state devolution occurring, but there are also indications of a parallel trend of state-to-local devolution."[16] This second-order devolution pertains also to child care policymaking.

Governors' Interest in Education Boosts Attention to Child Care

The governors' influence on national child care policymaking was evident as early as 1971 when many of them opposed comprehensive universal child care legislation (see chapter 2). Governors also influenced the outcome of the 1988 FSA (see chapter 3), the 1990 child care legislation (see chapter 4), and the 1996 welfare reform (see chapter 6). However, they did not always define the problem as child care per se. Instead, they often focused on child care in the context of other issues, such as welfare and education reform. Gubernatorial interest in education was sparked by the Reagan administration's 1983 report A Nation at Risk, which described the deficiencies of American education and its consequences.[17] In 1990, following the 1989 Education Summit, President Bush and the NGA identified six national education goals. Their Goal 1 was, "By the year 2000, all children in America will start school ready to learn."[18] It became a rallying point for those involved with early childhood education and child care.

In the early 1990s "the state-led education reform movement gained momentum." Several federal initiatives spurred activity on the state level too. The 1994 Goals 2000: Educate America Act (P.L. 103-7) was the "first education initiative specifically designed to help states and communities to initiate, improve, and coordinate their own reform efforts."[19] In 1996 President Clinton signed into law several amendments to an omnibus appropriations bill (P.L. 104-4), which enhanced the flexibility of states and communities in implementing school improvements. By 1999 every state was referring to Goals 2000 to support ways of improving education.[20] Even though most of the Goals 2000 legislation focused on elementary and secondary education, the first of the national educational goals, enhancing school readiness, involved child care as part of early education and remained an important policy objective for state and local officials.

However, not all state and local lawmakers equated child care with early childhood education. Some of them viewed child care as an issue for welfare or low-income families and not as a component of education policymaking. Public officials rarely included infants and toddlers in school readiness programs. Furthermore, child care continued to be burdened with other controversies, in particular about whether mothers of very young children should be working out of the home.

But the realities of everyday life for millions of low-income families pointed to the importance of state child care policies. Child care advocates at the state level became increasingly savvy at calling attention to the needs of families with children under welfare reform. Moreover, no education initiative at the state level would be complete without an early childhood component, which often included child care providers. Thus, state officials became increasingly interested in child care, if only because they needed to spend a certain amount of money on it to quality for federal matching funds under the CCDBG.

NGA Delineates State and Federal Roles for Child Care and Early Education

Aside from actions by individual states regarding child care policymaking, governors collectively took an interest in child care and early education. In 1996, under the leadership of Governor Bob Miller of Nevada, a Democrat, the NGA identified the first three years of life as its priority issue.[21] Some of this interest was sparked by publicity surrounding early brain development, as discussed in chapter 7. The next NGA chairman, Governor George Voinovich of Ohio, a Republican, was well known in child policy circles for his state's initiatives in early childhood care and Head Start.[22] Under Voinovich's leadership, the NGA Center for Best Practices sponsored a 1997 conference, "Achieving Results for Young Children: What Works," and a survey of state child care activities, conducted from 1996 to 1998. The NGA Center for Best Practices sponsored other research and programmatic initiatives aimed at sharing innovative activities by various states and providing technical assistance to states in many aspects of public policy, including child care. When the Democratic governor of Delaware, Thomas Carper, assumed the NGA chairmanship in 1998, he made education his top agenda item,[23] which also drew attention to child care.[24]

The NGA's 1998 *Policy Statement on Child Care and Early Education* called for a "seamless child care and early education system that provides a safe, nurturing, and developmentally sound environment for all children." It identified parents as "children's first and primary nurturers" and outlined family, local, state, and federal government responsibilities in "the coordination of programs serving children through links at all levels of child care, health care, and education systems."[25]

The governors listed fourteen options for states, covering a wide range of ideological and partisan interests, such as exploring incentives for one parent in a two-parent family to stay home to care for children, at least in the first year; improving quality through setting statewide standards and credentialing; and encouraging public schools to provide after-school care and full-day kindergarten. They stated that "the federal government should support state activities in child care and early education, not control them." Options for federal roles and public–private partnerships were also included in the statement.[26] The NGA statement on Head Start emphasized the importance of linking Head Start with other early care and education programs,[27] which was a concern of many state officials and early education specialists, as discussed later. Many of the NGA's policies were aimed at influencing federal policy debates.

In the late 1990s, as governors and state leaders learned about research on early brain development, they endorsed statewide programs that addressed the quality of early education.[28] One of the most widely publicized was the request by Georgia's Democratic governor, Zell Miller, for appropriations to "purchase and distribute classical music tapes and CDs for newborns." Using the research on early brain development, Miller explained that "listening to music, especially at a very early age, affects the spatial-temporal reasoning that underlies math, engineering and chess." He never needed the state support because private interests came forward to fund his proposal.[29] Actually, Miller's interest in early education preceded the excitement over early brain research. In 1992 Georgia voters approved Miller's proposal for a constitutional amendment establishing a state lottery, the proceeds of which went to fund Georgia's prekindergarten (pre-K) program and other education assistance programs. In 1999 Georgia's pre-K initiative became the nation's first publicly financed voluntary and universal pre-K program.[30]

Although few governors went as far as Governor Miller, most child care policy experts agree that having a sympathetic governor is important for influencing a state's child care policy.[31] According to a state official involved with children's programs, another important role for governors, even if they are "not the drivers of the policy options," is to encourage budget officials to figure out how to subsidize the program.

In some states, governors are among the many state officials who lead on children's issues. A children's advocate working at the state level noted that changes in children's policies can originate with officials other than the governor. If engaging and dynamic individuals are in positions such as majority leader, Speaker, or appropriations chair, they can be extremely effective in championing children's issues. One of the strongest proponents at the state level of investing in early childhood programs was Thomas Ritter, a Democrat and former Speaker of the House in Connecticut, who said, "I did not come into this as an early childhood expert or advocate. . . . But it was clear from study after study that every dollar you spend now saves seven dollars down the road. And it levels the playing field for children and gives them an opportunity to succeed."[32]

Finally, although interest on the state level in early childhood education and child care was a rallying point for many governors, at the national level it was one of many issues that generated partisan debate over the role of the federal government. As one NGA staff person noted in an interview:

Because the NGA is bipartisan . . . everything we do has to be agreed to across the board. And, there is a sense among many Republican governors that this [child care] is not a place for the federal government to step in. . . . Governors prefer block grants, no unfunded mandates, and more discretion in overall federal funding. . . . These are their mobilizing issues.

Thus, discussions about gubernatorial interest in child care must acknowledge the governors' ongoing concerns that they be given sufficient latitude to implement programs in accordance with the needs and resources of their individual states.

Federal Child Care Regulations Revisited

Against this backdrop of evolving federal–state relations and the growing salience of child care as a state issue, HHS issued proposed regulations for the reauthorized CCDBG under the 1996 welfare law. The proposed rule generated discussion about intergovernmental relations in the child care arena and demonstrated how executive branch officials could alter and enforce public policies.

Child Care Advocates and State Administrators Respond to Proposed Rule

On July 23, 1997, HHS issued proposed regulations for the 1996 CCDBG.[33] The new rule was well received within the child care community, especially compared with the ruckus that the proposed regulation for the 1990 law had generated (see chapter 5). Much of the credit for the positive reaction to the proposed rule was due to Joan Lombardi, head of the federal CCB. She appreciated the needs of families affected by the 1996 law and promoted policies designed to safeguard quality while ensuring adequate payment rates for federally subsidized child care providers.

Lack of controversy over the new rule was illustrated by the smaller number of comments it elicited compared with the 1991 CCDBG proposed rule. In 1997 approximately 160 organizations and individuals commented,[34] whereas HHS had received nearly 1,500 letters in 1991. The goals of the proposed 1997 child care regulations were to amend the rules in light of new legislation, "achieve a balance between program flexibility and accountability, assure the health and safety of children in child care, recognize that child care is a key support for work, as envisioned in TANF, and clarify, streamline, simplify and unify the Federal child care program."[35] Concerns over several of the proposed rule's provisions mirrored ongoing political controversies over how far the federal government should go in requiring states to take certain measures.

In preparing the proposed rule, ACF took every opportunity to establish supportive, cooperative relationships with state administrators and child care groups[36] and avoid the friction the regulations had generated after the 1990 law. Somewhat predictably, a Democratic president and his political appointees within the executive branch were more sympathetic to the views of the organized interests within the largely nonprofit child care advocacy community than President Bush's Republican and conservative-leaning administration had been.

States had a vested interest in sustaining their investments in child care in that it enabled them to promote self-sufficiency among TANF recipients and to meet TANF work participation rates set by the 1996 law.[37] If states failed to maintain a certain level of child care funding, they risked losing federal matching funds for child care.

Proposed Rule Prompts Questions About Federal and State Roles

The delicate balance between federal and state governments was reflected in the debates over federal child care regulations for the CCDBG. State officials and others protective of states' rights were easily threatened by any hint of federal mandates to states, especially unfunded ones.[38]

Tension between state and federal authorities was most evident in discussions pertaining to payment rates (section 98.43). ACF required states to demonstrate that they took into account features, such as payment, in determining that their program guaranteed equal access to child care for all eligible families. If payment rates were too low, then eligible CCDBG families might be excluded from access to certain child care providers. In short, as ACF explained, "the [federal] payment rates should reflect the child care market."[39]

In determining payment rates, ACF required states to use a market rate survey conducted no more than two years before the effective date of the state plan. ACF explained that the only way to determine if payment rates provided equal access was through such a survey. States were already familiar with this process because they had been required to conduct market rate surveys for JOBS child care, TCC, and At-Risk Child Care (see chapters 3 and 5). Many states used the same surveys in determining CCDBG rates.[40] However, in 1996 Congress eliminated the requirement that states pay at the market rate (see chapter 6). In the proposed rule in 1997 ACF recommended that states set their child care payment rates at 75 percent of the market rate, in accordance with previous regulations for the At-Risk Child Care Program. The requirement for the market rate survey in the proposed regulations of 1997, along with the recommendation that states pay at the seventy-fifth percentile, generated considerable controversy.

Most of the comments in response to the market rate provisions were favorable,[41] especially those submitted by national organizations that had been disappointed when Congress deleted the child care market rate provision in 1996. These groups, representing primarily nonprofit and private, for-profit child care providers, applauded the reinstatement of market rate surveys in the proposed 1997 rule.[42] Several of them wanted ACF to specify that states had the option of paying rates above the seventy-fifth percentile of the market survey rate, especially for care that was of high quality or located in an area with a child care shortage. In contrast, many administrators at the state level argued that the market rate survey provisions in the proposed rule exceeded federal statutes and imposed strict requirements on states.[43] In the final rule ACF specified that it was not requiring payment rates to be set at the seventy-fifth percentile. Rather, the seventy-fifth percentile was a "reference point against which [states] can judge if [their] payment rates afford equal access." States had the option of setting higher rates if they so desired.[44] The reinstatement of the market rate survey in the CCDBG rule illustrates how HHS used the regulatory process to make an important child care policy change.

Another aspect of the proposed rule that many national and state organizations and state administrators applauded was the elimination of the 10 percent limit on payment differences within a category of care (i.e., center, family, or in-home). Both at the national and the state level, child care advocates had strongly opposed the cap on payment differentials set in the regulations six years earlier because it prevented them from promoting high-quality care (see chapter 5). They reasoned that if such care is more costly to provide, then reimbursing it at a lower rate was a disincentive for those providers to participate in publicly subsidized programs and this could lower the number of slots available to eligible children. In the 1997 proposed rule, ACF explained that payment differentials allow states to recognize and reward high-quality care or to address shortages of certain types of care, such as care provided for families working evening or night shifts or weekends.[45] These new quality incentives were among the most well received aspects of the proposed rule.

Another part of the rule that raised discussion about the balance between federal and state authorities pertained to health and safety provisions (section 98.41). The 1996 law required states to certify that they had set health and safety requirements applicable to child care providers for the prevention and control of infectious diseases, including immunizations, building and physical premises safety, and minimum health and safety training of staff. States had to certify that they enforced such requirements for regulated and non-regulated providers funded under the block grant. Section 98.41 of the child care rule allowed states to exempt from the immunization and health and safety requirements grandparents, great-grandparents, and siblings (living in separate residences) as well as aunts and uncles who cared for children under the CCDBG. The regulation stipulated that states had to ensure that children funded under the CCDBG were immunized as appropriate for their age. In so doing, states had to rely on the recommendations of their respective public health agencies. Thus, the onus of setting immunization policies for children whose care was funded by CCDBG fell to states as a condition of receiving federal funds. Some respondents argued that ACF's language on how states might implement the health and safety requirements exceeded the intent of the statute. The American Academy of Pediatrics took one of the most extreme positions, calling for strengthening the health and safety requirements through federal standards,[46] a position that many others might endorse in principle but considered politically impossible. Basically, ACF encouraged states to use child care enrollment as a way of lowering the number of children under the age of two who were not immunized as appropriate for their age.[47] This overlap between child health and child care systems grew in importance in subsequent years.

Another section of the rule that generated discussion included the requirement that families subsidized under the law pay a copayment of no more than 10 percent of their income for child care. Some child care advocates argued that this was too much for families below the poverty level to pay. Other respondents wanted flexibility in setting copayments.[48] Despite these concerns, in the final rule ACF left the 10 percent copayment unchanged. Finally, in response to concerns expressed by national child care groups and some administrators at the state level, ACF required that states make their child care plans available to the public in advance of required hearings.[49]

Requirement for Collaboration Generates Questions About Funding and Turf

The regulation also required lead child care agencies to coordinate child care services in four areas: TANF, public health, employment services, and public education. Some groups suggested that states should be required to consult with other entities, such as state child welfare agencies or private early education programs.[50] In the final rule, ACF did not enlarge the list of entities with which states had to collaborate.[51] As will be discussed, state interagency coordination was a major challenge to child care providers and policymakers.

To enhance access to early child care programs and encourage coordination among programs at the state level, the new rule allowed states to use private contributions and state pre-K funds to demonstrate that they had met the requirements of maintenance of effort that had to be met to qualify for federal matching funds for child care. States could use public pre-K funds for up to 20 percent of the funds serving to demonstrate maintenance of effort. Some organizations expressed concern that "an overly broad approach to counting pre-K expenditures might result in a real reduction in full-day child care services to potentially eligible working families."[52] Those protective of states' rights thought that the regulation did not give states enough latitude in the use of pre-K funds for matching purposes. For example, the NCSL opposed what it considered "arbitrary caps placed on the use of pre-K funds for matching or [maintenance of effort] purposes." It argued that this aspect of the rule failed recognize the efforts on behalf of states "to merge early childhood education during the critical years of a child's development."[53]

In the final rule ACF kept the 20 percent cap, which gave states new sources of matching funds, albeit without the flexibility that some of them wanted. As a nod to the concerns expressed by several child care advocates, ACF explained that "as a matter of balance," for purposes of demonstrating maintenance of effort, states could not reduce their level of effort in full-day/full-year child care services if they used pre-K expenditures to meet the requirement of proving maintenance of effort. States had to explain how they adhered to this aspect of the rule. Thus, here, as in other sections of the rule, ACF continually balanced state administrators' preferences for flexibility with child care advocates' interests in the well-being of publicly subsidized child care providers and their families.

State Child Care Policies Assume a New Look

State child care policies were always characterized by tremendous intrastate variation,[54] but by the end of the 1990s states had more options than in the past as they integrated child care with other services, such as health or education. The greater variability among states in recent years was partially attributable to elimination of the federal requirement that states guarantee child care to eligible welfare families, the new TANF money available to states, and the growth in local and state child care and other early childhood initiatives. All states faced similar challenges as they implemented child care programs and tried to create a seamless system of care while meeting new child care demands emanating largely from welfare reform. Many public and private organizations produced extensive reports that evaluated how states fared in meeting the new needs for child care in the era after 1996.[55] It would be impractical to summarize or augment the findings of these studies. Instead, this section describes some of the choices states made in implementing federal policies and linking them with state and local initiatives.

New Infusion of Federal Child Care Funding
Gives States New Options

In the 1990s, states benefited from a growing influx of federal child care funds. In FY 1997, total mandatory funding for child care was nearly $606 million over what would have been available for the CCDBG and Title IV child care in 1996 had the PRWORA not been enacted.[56] In FY 1998, states received an increase of about $100 million in mandatory CCDBG funds. Although the 1996 law repealed a small 1994 bill for care for school-age children and resource and referral agencies, for the years 1997 to 2000 Congress annually earmarked an additional $19 million in discretionary CCDBG funds for these programs. In FY 1998 and FY 1999, Congress appropriated a separate earmarked amount of $50 million to increase the supply and quality of infant and toddler care. For FY 1999 and FY 2000, Congress appropriated an additional $182 million in discretionary funds for child care ($172 million for quality improvements and $10 million for research). For FY 2001, federal funding for state child care programs increased considerably. As another source of child care support, the 1996 PRWORA allowed states to transfer up to 30 percent of their TANF funds into the CCDBG, provided they spent the money according to the CCDBG rules. States could also use TANF funds for child care without formally transferring the funds, and thereby they did not have to abide by CCDBG policies.[57] In 1998 more than half the states earmarked TANF funds for child care.[58] In FY 1999, states transferred approximately $2.4 billion of TANF block grant funds to the CCDBG.[59] It is unclear how much the states' TANF funds supplanted state money for child care.

In addition to federal money, states invested their own funds in child care programs. In 1997, 1998, and 1999 almost every state reported allocating enough money to draw down its share of new federal matching child care funds.[60] A number of states allocated significant new state funds for child care beyond their CCDBG match and TANF money. For example, in 1999 California increased its state spending on child care by $26 million and transferred $257 million from its TANF block grant to its CCDBG.[61] From 1997 through 1999 Illinois increased its state child care funding by approximately $284 million, earmarked an additional $148.2 million of TANF funds for child care assistance in 1999, and increased funding for its pre-K initiative. New York transferred $120 million from its TANF block grant to its CCDBG, earmarked an additional $42 million in TANF funds to expand child care assistance, set aside an additional $200 million of its TANF block grant for a Child Care Reserve Fund, and increased state funding by $60 million for various child care and early education projects. In 1999 Wisconsin transferred $6.4 million from its TANF block grant and earmarked an additional $52 million of TANF money for child care. It more than doubled outlays for various child care and early childhood programs, while reducing parents' copayments and broadening family eligibility for subsidies.[62]

Some states created new and "unconventional state revenue sources for child care and early education."[63] For example, by relying on proceeds from riverboat gambling, Missouri expected to generate $21 million annually, starting in 1999. South Dakota dedicated funds to child care from the proceeds of its closed-circuit broadcasts of horse and dog racing. Maine used proceeds from its state tobacco settlement to help subsidize an increase of $11 million in child care funding over two years.[64] In 1998 Californians approved a ballot initiative that included a 50-cent tobacco tax per pack of cigarettes and was predicted to yield about $700 million per year in funding for the state's new Families and Children First Initiative. Rob Reiner and the Reiner Foundation launched the initiative's linking of tobacco tax revenues with the healthy development of children. On March 7, 2000, California voters overwhelmingly defeated another ballot initiative, backed by tobacco interests, that would have eliminated the tobacco tax allocation for children's programs.[65] Despite these investments, as of 1998, California had more than 200,000 families, mostly nonwelfare, low-income working families, on its waiting list for state-subsidized child care.[66]

Although many states increased their overall spending on child care, no state had adequate funding to support quality and affordable child care for all low-income families. Moreover, a large proportion of states transferred funds from their TANF block grant to their CCDBG fund rather than use state subsidies to finance their increased child care spending. This means that most states lack a firm foundation for state child care funding.

In addition to differences in aggregate spending, states varied with regard to policies for parental copayments, income eligibility, and reimbursement for providers. Several states increased their income eligibility criteria. Rhode Island was among the most generous states, expanding its guarantee of child care assistance to families with children up to the age of sixteen with incomes at 250 percent of the federal poverty level as of July 1, 2000. As another example, in 1999 Delaware expanded eligibility for child care to families earning up to 200 percent of the federal poverty level and increased reimbursement rates. Wisconsin raised initial eligibility for child care assistance to 185 percent of the federal poverty level. Once receiving assistance, families remain eligible until their income reaches 200 percent of the federal poverty level. But despite these developments, as of March 2000, only five states have set income eligibility at the maximum amount allowed under federal law (85 percent of state median).[67]

Regarding reimbursement rates, in 1999 thirty-eight states improved their reimbursement rates. Most states reimbursed child care providers at or near

75 percent of a market rate. However, approximately one-third of the states based their rates on surveys that were several years old.[68]

States also varied with regard to the copayments they required of families receiving child care subsidies. For example, California required no copayment; Wisconsin and Ohio enacted legislation in 1999 to limit the maximum copayments to 12 and 10 percent, respectively, of a family's gross income. Other states varied considerably in monthly copayment requirements.[69]

Despite investments in child care, many states lacked a sufficient number of qualified providers. New York State is a case in point. In 1999 the state budget included $800 million in child care funding. At the same time, 82 percent of New York families eligible for child care subsidies did not receive assistance. Despite this documented need, New York was unable to spend much of its budgeted child care funding because of a shortage of licensed providers. Other factors contributing to the state's failure to spend the money were lack of interest in child care among local public officials and a large proportion of eligible families who were unaware that subsidies were available to them.[70] Seven states covered in a 1998 GAO study reported that they had an adequate child care supply for the near future. But they acknowledged that as they complied with future work participation requirements, additional providers might be needed.[71]

In FY 1999, an average of 1.8 million children were served per month under the CCDGBG, a slight increase from the 1.5 million children served in FY 1998. In 1999 the CCDBG reached only 12 percent of all eligible children. States varied in the proportion of eligible children they reached under the block grant from a low of 3 and 5 percent in the District of Columbia and Connecticut, respectively, to a high of 25 percent in West Virginia and 19 percent in Michigan, Missouri, and New York.[72] Thus, millions of families lacked child care despite being eligible for it under federal law.

State reports filed with the federal Child Care Bureau offer other perspectives on implementation of the CCDBG.[73] In 1998, 27 percent of children funded under the CCDBG were younger than three years old, 37 percent were between three and six years old, and 35 percent were between six and twelve years of age. This distribution demonstrates the importance of publicly subsidized care for children of all ages. Eighty-four percent of children served under the CCDBG were funded by certificates (vouchers), 10 percent were covered by grants or contracts, and care for 7 percent was paid directly to the parents in cash. More than fifteen states relied exclusively on vouchers, while others had a blend of payment methods. On average, 55 percent of children funded under the CCDBG in 1998 received care in centers; 34 percent, in family or group homes; and 11 percent, in the child's home. Seventy-two percent of the children funded under the CCDBG received care from licensed or other forms of regulated providers, while 28 percent were cared for by providers operating legally without regulation. Of the providers operating legally without regulation, 53 percent were relatives. The rest probably were nonrelative providers exempt from state regulation. This large percentage of unregulated providers can be traced to language in the CCDBG statute and regulation that emphasized parental choice over regulation and raised concerns about the federal government's ability to protect children in unregulated subsidized settings (see chapters 4 and 6).

Using the provider as the unit of analysis, the largest number of providers receiving CCDBG funds in 1998 were family homes (359,039), followed by relatives or nonrelatives in the child's home (194,493), centers (99,676), and group homes (18,706).

In sum, states used a combination of mechanisms (copayments, subsidies, and payment rates) and other initiatives to craft their child care policies. Some states were strong in one aspect (such as copayments) and less generous in others (such as subsidies). Patterns of usage and payment mirrored variations in state policies and the choices available to parents under the CCDBG. This mixed profile of states' investments in child care will inevitably characterize child care policymaking for years to come.

New Interest in Quality

A distinguishing feature of state child care policymaking in the late 1990s was a strengthened interest in quality.[74] In explaining the increased attention to quality, one child care advocate at the state level noted in an interview:

> The stuff on brain research lit the lightbulb for quality. . . . Several reports came out documenting that kids in child care were doing no worse than kids [cared for by parents alone]. . . . But the reports also made the point that it has to be high quality care. . . . People need to understand it is not just access . . . but access to what?

States had several strategies for advancing high-quality child care. Among them were increasing subsidies for care that met national accreditation standards, expanding child care resource and referral activities, launching public awareness campaigns about early childhood development, improving the quality and supply of family child care providers, and increasing compensation for education of child care workers.[75]

Research linking high-quality child care with school success and important developmental outcomes spurred state legislatures to invest in measures designed to enhance quality. Some states developed innovative ways of funding quality initiatives. Approximately 40 percent of states used their 4 percent quality set-aside from the CCDBG to create comprehensive training systems for child care providers. At least nineteen states developed variable rate structures offering higher reimbursement for providers offering child care of better quality.[76]

Child care policy analysts frequently referred to North Carolina's Smart Start program as one of the best state-sponsored initiatives, especially for promoting quality in child care. Smart Start, a statewide initiative for all children under six, encompassed a range of comprehensive services, including child care, health care, parent education, and counseling. In 1998 Smart Start was one of ten programs selected from 1,500 nominations to receive an Innovations in American Government Award from Harvard University and the Ford Foundation.[77]

The North Carolina law that established Smart Start in 1993 gave communities responsibility for designing and administering programs.[78] For 2000/2001, North Carolina is projected to spend approximately $230 million on Smart Start direct services. The legislation establishing Smart Start requires 10 percent of its funding to come from private contributions. Each year millions of dollars donated from corporations and individuals have enabled Smart Start to exceed the 10 percent requirement.[79]

Smart Start also pioneered the T.E.A.C.H. (Teacher Education and Compensation Helps) program, which grants scholarships to eligible child care teachers and family child care providers to complete college courses in early childhood education. By 1999 at least thirteen states used T.E.A.C.H. or a version of it to enhance quality in child care or were in the planning process of doing so.[80] T.E.A.C.H. addresses three critical issues affecting child care quality: professional development of the staff, compensation, and turnover. Early childhood teachers who reach their educational goals receive additional compensation, arranged through an agreement between T.E.A.C.H. and the teachers' employers. In return, the T.E.A.C.H. participant commits to staying with the same employer for up to one year after completing the course work. North Carolina also used state and federal funds to help cover the costs of health insurance for staff at eligible T.E.A.C.H. programs.[81]

Rhode Island was the first state to link health care coverage to child care providers. In 1998 Rhode Island's Starting Right raised payment rates for child care and authorized many other changes that moved the state toward a comprehensive early care and education program. It first expanded health care coverage to family child care providers, and shortly thereafter center-based providers were also able to buy coverage. This creative solution, advanced by Rhode Island's head of social services, Christine Ferguson (former staff to Senator John Chafee), simultaneously addressed the retention of child care staff and the lack of health care insurance among low-income workers.[82]

CDF, NGA, NCSL, and other organizations documented these and other efforts by states in the child care arena. Further discussion here would unnecessarily duplicate their thorough descriptions. The major point is that after 1996 the states' responses varied widely as they used federal and state child care funds. Welfare reform prompted much activity in child care policymaking at the state level and generated new concerns.

Impact of Welfare Reform on Child Care

From January 1993 to June 2000, the number of AFDC/TANF recipients plummeted by 59 percent, a drop of approximately 2.7 million families (table 8.1).[83] Strong state economies contributed to much of the decline between 1993 and 1995. Other factors, such as state welfare waivers approved before 1996, federal EITC expansions enacted in 1993, and changes in welfare benefits under the 1996 law, contributed to the decline in welfare caseloads since 1993.[84]

The 1996 law gave states considerable flexibility in implementing welfare programs.[85] The result, as one journalist noted, was "a system evolving from a national safety net into a series of state trampolines; they are better equipped to lift the needy into the job market, but much less certain to catch them during the inevitable slips and falls."[86]

Difficulty arranging child care was one cause of such "slips and falls." For many women on welfare, finding a job was easier than keeping it. Mothers receiving TANF faced hurdles of child care, transportation, health care, and the daily travails of managing a household of young children while

TABLE 8.1 Change in TANF Caseloads, as of June 2000

Total TANF families and recipients

	Jan. 93	Jan. 94	Jan. 95	Jan. 96	Jan. 97	Jan. 98	Jun. 99	Jun. 00	Percent change (93–99)	Percent change (93–00)
				(thousands)						
Families	4,963	5,053	4,963	4,628	4,114	3,305	2,536	2,208	–49%	–56%
Recipients	14,115	14,276	13,931	12,877	11,423	9,132	6,889	5,781	–51%	–59%

Source: U.S. Department of Health and Human Services, Administration for Children and Families, available at: www.acf.dhhs.gov/news/stats/caseload.htm, accessed 11 December 2000.

maintaining a steady job. Shift work, infant care, and finding child care in rural areas posed particular obstacles to mothers motivated to establish self-sufficiency. Their problems were aggravated by what Sue Shellenbarger, a *Wall Street Journal* columnist, referred to as the "upside-down economics of child care." Parents who most needed high-quality, flexible child care with off-hour care were typically the least able to afford it. Furthermore, the supply of child care tended to grow most in affluent areas, creating a tighter supply in working-class neighborhoods. Government subsidies helped but did not totally alleviate the problem.[87] Moreover, states' reimbursement rates for child care often did not cover the fees, creating significant financial burdens for welfare parents who typically earned low wages.[88]

Families making the transition off welfare relied on various child care arrangements and payment mechanisms, reflecting differences in state supply and reimbursement policies. One three-state study of single mothers moving off welfare reported that the majority of children were in home-based care, composed of regulated family child care or relatives. In the same study, 70 percent of mothers in Florida selected center-based care compared with 13 percent in Connecticut. Some of the greater usage of center-based care in Florida was due to that state's larger number of available child care slots. Quality of care for welfare families also varied by state. For example, the quality of California's child care centers surpassed the quality of care in the other states. However, regardless of location, poor children are more susceptible to receiving inferior care than are children from families with higher incomes.[89]

Another challenge that former TANF recipients faced was that they often landed jobs that lacked health coverage, paid vacation, flexible hours, or sick leave.[90] This made it difficult for them to care for their children while working. In one study, approximately 30 percent of mothers had difficulty buying enough food for their family.[91] These disturbing trends led liberals and conservatives to acknowledge the importance of ensuring that benefits for Medicaid and Food Stamps reached eligible families, especially those making the transition from welfare.[92]

States with TANF surpluses in the late 1990s could have spent those funds on child care for poor and low-income families. But TANF funds alone could not address child care shortfalls. Other funds from the state and the private sector were needed. Moreover, most state officials preferred saving some of their TANF surpluses for economic downturns, which they felt were inevitable at some point.[93] Some state officials were reluctant to increase the child care expenditures of their state, claiming that they had already invested state funds, from TANF or elsewhere, in child care or early education.

Child care policy analysts cautioned that economic recessions or downturns would change the face of child care policies. As one child care advocate at the state level remarked, "If this is what it looks like in good economic times, what happens when we return to the recession of past years?" Demand for subsidized child care could increase in a weak economy. Moreover, states that depended on TANF money to subsidize child care would have more low-income people relying on government support, and the base of funding for child care would no longer be available. Thus, child care policies were inextricably linked to welfare legislation and economic fluctuations.

Child Care Needs of Low-Income Working Families Often Receive Short Shrift

Because the 1996 law required states to incrementally increase the proportion of TANF recipients meeting work requirements as a condition of federal funding, states tended to target welfare families in allocating child care funds. Often this was at the expense of low-income working families. All seven states (California, Connecticut, Louisiana, Maryland, Oregon, Texas, and Wisconsin) surveyed in a 1998 report by the GAO were able to meet "immediate" child care needs of welfare families and of some, but not all, poor or low-income working families. Their ability to meet the needs of both populations in the long run as mandatory work participation rates increased was doubtful.[94] Child care advocates and state administrators often expressed serious concern that child care needs of TANF recipients would crowd out access to child care for low-income working families. Minnesota, for example, acknowledged that working families that would have been eligible before welfare reform were "losing out" to welfare families. Florida and Washington were among the states that increased child care funding targeted for low-income working families to avoid this development.[95]

Many low-income working families were prevented from receiving federal assistance due to low income cutoffs in their state, high copayment requirements, or low subsidy rates that made out-of-pocket costs "prohibitive." Some politicians and child care advocates speculated that as working poor families lost jobs due to a lack of child care, they would end up on welfare, which would defeat the purpose of the 1996 law. To prevent this from happening, some states enhanced their investment in child care for low-income families.[96] As mentioned earlier, Rhode Island, Delaware, and Wisconsin were among the states that took the lead in expanding income eligibility levels for child care, so that more low-income families would qualify. But these efforts paled in comparison with the enormity of the problem. Meeting the child care needs of low-income working families not on welfare remained one of the most serious challenges of the years after 1996. One child care advocate at the state level summarized this predicament in an interview:

> There is a good amount of public support for child care for welfare moms . . . even though it's not from passion, but from the same perspective as job training and transportation. That is, these things are considered important insofar as they get people off public assistance. But I worry that the same support doesn't exist for other low-income families. If these families don't have child care, they can't work and they'll end up on welfare. In the long run we could end up with more people going on welfare.

Another state advocate explained that although the 1996 welfare law eliminated the guarantee of child care, the fastest way to obtain child care was to be on welfare, while low-income working families struggled to obtain comparable assistance. Thus, dwindling welfare rolls did not eliminate the public policy challenge of ensuring adequate care for children from low-income working families. Furthermore, if welfare recipients took entry-level, low-skilled jobs—as janitors or cashiers, for example—then they often needed care beyond the traditional 9-to-5 shift. Such odd-hour care was typically hard to find and more expensive for providers and parents than traditional care.[97]

Finally, low-income families with a preschooler typically paid a larger proportion of their monthly income on child care than did families with higher incomes. Specifically, in 1997 low-income families spent an average of 16 percent of their earnings on child care compared with an average of 6 percent for higher-income families.[98] The greater economic burden of child care on low-income working families further substantiates calls for increases in assistance from both the public and the private sector directed toward these parents and children.

Lack of data regarding the child care needs of low-income families impeded the ability of policymakers to devise timely solutions. Waiting lists for subsidized child care varied, with some states reporting few, if any, low-income families in need of child care, and others reporting waiting lists of tens of thousands of families.[99] Most states lacked a single agency that tracked families waiting for services. Furthermore, whatever waiting lists were compiled tended to underestimate the need because they counted only those parents willing to apply for assistance. Many others waited or struggled on the sidelines.

Linking Child Care with Other Early Education Initiatives

One of the most striking developments of the 1990s was the increase in state-funded pre-K initiatives. Between 1998 and 1999 forty-two states invested nearly $1.7 billion in pre-K programs, serving approximately 725,000 children. This was two and a half times as much as in 1991/1992. However, state investments in pre-K programs were uneven, with ten states comprising 75 percent of all such funding.[100] Despite the surge of interest in pre-K programs, mostly as a way to enhance school readiness, as of 1996 fewer than half the children aged between three and five were enrolled in pre-K programs. Children in low-income families had the lowest rates of enrollment.[101] Many pre-K programs entailed collaboration among various early education agencies (including Head Start), public schools, and other community child care providers.

As of September 1999, thirty-one states had pre-K programs for three- and four-year-olds; eighteen states targeted four-year-olds; and eight states had broad programs that reached children up to the age of five. Only Georgia spent enough to offer its program to all children in the state. In 1997 New York approved a universal pre-K initiative scheduled to reach all four-year-olds by 2002. Most other states targeted children considered to be at risk for poor academic performance.[102]

States used several different models in designing pre-K programs. *School-based models* relied on public education systems with variations in how much, if at all, they included other schools and agencies. *State-funded Head Start models* used federally funded Head Start agencies as grantees and adhered to the comprehensive quality performance standards of the federal Head Start program. *Community-based models* typically engaged a range of providers, including Head Start and child care, as they tailored programs to meet community needs, often supporting full-day programs.[103]

The politics surrounding state pre-K initiatives sometimes engendered divisiveness. In one camp were those who applauded universal pre-K because of the educational and socialization benefits it offered young children. Many who shared this sentiment viewed public schools as the preferred sponsor because they had existing facilities and infrastructure and could follow the public school precedent of offering services to every child, regardless of income. Some pre-K advocates preferred to rely on child care, Head Start, or other community providers, arguing that local education agencies were too burdened to assume additional responsibilities. Moreover, they claimed, the needs of preschoolers might be best met by early childhood education professionals rather than by elementary school staff. Most policy analysts acknowledged the benefits of a variety of administering agencies for pre-K programs.

At the other end of the spectrum were those who generally opposed universal pre-K. They viewed it as an extension of the government's reach into child care and preferred that families be the mainstay of care for preschoolers. However, with growing interest in reducing illiteracy, enhancing school readiness, and improving academic achievement, pre-K initiatives found a place on most states' agendas. Such initiatives had the potential to offer important resources for children with working parents.

Yet implementation of pre-K programs often presented challenges to working families. Because of limited hours of operation, many pre-K programs were inaccessible to children in low-income families whose parents worked full time. As of 1999, thirty-seven states had pre-K initiatives that operated four hours per day or less. Some of these operated for two and a half hours per day. Seven states ran programs on a school-day schedule of five to seven hours per day. These programs often operated only during the school year.[104]

As of 1999, only three states supported full-day or full-year pre-K. Connecticut's School Readiness Initiative, approved in 1997, funded preschool for three- and four-year-olds and was administered by local School Readiness Councils in thirteen selected towns. The School Readiness Initiative provided the framework for significant increases in Connecticut's early child care infrastructure, in particular, for training family and child care providers. The state provided full reimbursement for children enrolled on a full-time, full-year basis. Eighty-three percent of all children receiving services were enrolled full day and full year.[105] Massachusetts's Community Partnerships also supported full-year, full-day programs for children of working parents. Thirty-five percent of children were enrolled full time. Hawaii's Preschool Open Doors was another state program that funded full-day pre-K, but for only nine months per year.[106]

As states developed pre-K programs, political and economic realities influenced their decisions, making generalizations about the states and their programs difficult. Nonetheless, regardless of the locale, most pre-K programs offered opportunities for collaboration with child care providers and for improving the quality of child care. More than 75 percent of the states with pre-K programs reported collaborating with other early childhood initiatives.[107] Finally, many states (i.e., California, Connecticut, New Jersey, New York, and Rhode Island) expanded preschool and child care programs under Republican governors, thus demonstrating the issue's bipartisan appeal.

Linking Head Start and Child Care

Collaboration between Head Start and child care programs was another emerging aspect of childhood education.[108] Head Start serves three- to five-year-old children from families at or below the federal poverty level. Head Start's comprehensive services and strong parental involvement are exemplars for child care administrators. Its programs fall under the auspices of various entities, usually public schools or community agencies. However, because of limited funding, most Head Start programs serve only four-year-olds and do not reach large numbers of eligible children. Moreover, by the late 1990s approximately half of all Head Start children attended programs for four hours per day or less and 66 percent attended for nine months out of the year or less.[109] By operating less than full time, many Head Start programs are of limited assistance to children of parents working full time.

President Clinton's goal to enroll 1 million children in Head Start by 2002 and strong bipartisan support for the program resulted in steady increases in Head Start funding and enrollment throughout the 1990s. But despite Head Start's popularity, many early childhood experts realized that its original structure could not meet the needs of families living in a society that differed significantly from that of the mid-1960s, when the program had been created. As more low-income parents worked full time and as welfare reform pushed mothers into full-time jobs, new models were needed. As a result, states devised a variety of mechanisms for funding and administering

Head Start and child care partnerships.[110] One model was full-day Head Start. Another was Head Start for part of the day augmented by a child care or other early education program.[111]

Federal Head Start State collaboration grants enabled states to link Head Start with other early childhood and child care programs. By April 1999 all fifty states (and the District of Columbia) received federal Head Start collaboration grants to better meet the needs of low-income families.[112] Some states supplemented Head Start funding to provide full-day care for children enrolled in part-day Head Start programs. Other states found innovative ways of using Head Start as the basis for expanding early childhood programs. For example, through a combination of state and federal resources, Ohio provided a Head Start early childhood experience for 90 percent of its three- and four-year-old children from low-income families.[113]

Structural differences between Head Start and state child care programs presented challenges in designing collaborative programs. For example, Head Start distributes federal funds directly to local agencies, bypassing state governments. In contrast, the CCDBG funds states to administer child care programs and support families and providers. Both Head Start and the CCDBG are under the jurisdiction of the federal Administration for Children and Families but are administered separately by the Child Care and Head Start Bureaus. As a GAO study noted, "according to some child care experts, differences between child care and Head Start program requirements and philosophies can make such collaboration difficult."[114] Nonetheless, because of the advantages that Head Start brings to families and children, such collaboration is likely to increase in the future.

Growing attention to early child development and school readiness create a logical link between early childhood education and child care. But most states find it difficult to merge child care and early childhood education resources within a single program that has elements of both.[115] Turf battles and different funding sources impede such efforts. However, the rising number of preschool programs sponsored by public schools could forge future collaboration between education and child care programs. Given the unmet need for infant and toddler care, the proliferation of private child care centers, and the large number of family child care providers used by working parents, community-based child care incorporating a variety of models will undoubtedly flourish. The challenge to public and private sector leaders is to offer families choices and to ensure that children in a given locale have access to care of the best quality possible.

From Public and Private Partnerships to Tax Credits

Another area that illustrated shifts in the development of child care policymaking was the increase in public and private partnerships. This type of
collaboration has been important for engaging the business community in
child care policymaking. By the late 1990s, public–private partnerships for
child care increased, often as a requirement for state-sponsored programs.
For example, as mentioned earlier, the North Carolina Partnership for Children, which runs Smart Start, was required to match 10 percent of the state
appropriations with private funds.[116]

Roy Romer, former Democratic governor of Colorado, received acclaim
for his 1995 appointment of a twenty-five-member Business Commission on
Child Care Financing, charged with "proposing innovative but realistic
methods to help finance quality child care that is affordable and accessible
for Colorado families."[117] The Colorado Commission made twelve recommendations to enhance the quality of child care and its accessibility and
affordability, several of which the state legislature subsequently approved,
including establishing a dependent care tax credit on the state income tax
for low-income families.[118]

The Indiana Child Care Fund, launched in 1997 with more than
$500,000 in private funds, raised corporate, foundation, and individual con-
tributions to improve child care throughout the state. In subsequent years,
additional funding strengthened the involvement of business and the private
sector. Indiana also sponsored the Cinergy Corporate Mentoring Initiative
and other partnerships among business, government, academia, and the
state's child care resource referral agencies.[119]

Few states can match Florida's activities in promoting business involvement. In 1996 it established the Florida Child Care Executive Partnership,
which led to the enactment of legislation that financed child care for low-
income working families through $10 million in state funds and equal
matching funds from the private sector. The partnerships prompted other
funding and legislative initiatives linking business leaders with child care
policymaking.[120] A handful of other states have launched similar ventures to
promote the involvement of the business community in the child care arena.

The states' child care policies mirror the complexities of American federalism. Governors and other state officials often set the direction of state child
care initiatives, influenced by economics and state politics. As states imple-

ment federal and state child care programs, they have a broad range of options from which to choose. Federal funds provide the basis for most state programs, while state child care policies vary enormously. In the late 1990s many states expanded their investments in child care largely by relying on their TANF block grant funds. In the future, if states fail to achieve TANF surpluses, many child care programs administered by states may be in jeopardy. Using a combination of funds from federal, state, and private sector sources, the states' child care policies featured a kaleidoscope of programs. Implementing them called for innovative ways to collaborate across settings, providers, and policy arenas, such as welfare, education, and health. Those involved with such collaboration often faced administrative and financial hurdles. However, these obstacles failed to thwart the momentum associated with child care as it rose to the top of the agenda of state legislatures across the country. The picture of federal child care policymaking from 1970 to 2000 would not be complete without understanding these trends. The next task is to relate these issues to broader themes emerging from thirty years of legislative deliberations about child care.

9 Looking Back and to the Future

The previous chapters described thirty years of child care policymaking. But to chronicle child care legislation without linking it with larger themes in American public policymaking would be misleading. For the saga of child care policymaking illustrates how issue definition, the structure of American political institutions (Congress and the executive branch), organized interests, and the interactions among these entities influenced public policy outcomes. Because no one theory or framework can sufficiently explain the politics and policies of child care, several are discussed, all of which emphasize structural change.

This final chapter addresses a limited set of puzzling questions concerning developments in child care policymaking. For example, why were the late 1980s characterized by forward motion in child care policymaking when the early 1970s, a period of similar political circumstances (i.e., a conservative Republican president and a Democratic Congress) were a time of stalemate? Given Republicans' long-standing opposition to expanding federal child care programs, why did a conservative Republican president (Bush) and a conservative Republican Congress (1996) approve large expansions in federal child care assistance? How did organized interests influence the outcomes of child care legislation?

Answers to these questions generate some broader questions regarding the linkage between past and future child care politics. For example, what factors enhanced progress in child care policymaking? What do the past thirty years of child care policymaking suggest in regard to what might lie ahead? What directions might policymakers pursue to expand support for child care policies? Answers to these questions show that child care both is similar to other redistributive policies[1] and presents quirks of its own.

It's Not Just Women's Participation in the Labor Force

Child care policymakers repeatedly pointed to the increasing participation of women in the labor force as the critical factor prompting interest in child care legislation. A closer look reveals that demographic changes were important but not sufficient as explanations. Moreover, one needs to distinguish between factors that prompted agenda-setting and those that shaped the politics of enacting child care legislation. The definition of the issue was germane to both. However, in the enactment phase, legislators and organized interests depended more on the structure and procedures of government institutions than during agenda-setting, when other factors helped convert demographic shifts into policy change. In particular, a lag time was needed to create the demand for legislation.

Between 1970 and 2000 the participation rates for females in the labor force, especially for women with young children, actually grew most rapidly from the early 1970s to the mid-1980s (see figure 1.1 and table 1.3). From the mid-1980s to the end of the 1990s, rates continued to increase, but typically at a slower pace than in previous years. The interval between the steep rates of increase starting in the early 1970s and enactment of the CCDBG in 1990 illustrates the delays inherent in building support for policies that respond to broad social changes. Nelson W. Polsby explained that certain policies are "incubated innovations." These take place slowly, over several years, while "political actors" articulate the need for such policies and place them into the "ongoing culture of decision-makers."[2]

Child care policymaking in the 1980s (and to a certain extent in the late 1990s) was an example of an incubated innovation. Lawmakers needed time to become aware of changing demographics and unmet child care needs, decide how their bills would address a perceived problem (whether lack of affordable, high-quality child care, or tax burdens on working families with children), and then engage in negotiations that would bring their bills to enactment. The repeated mention of women's participation in the labor force as the main determinant of child care legislation, without regard for other variables, warrants emphasizing that changing trends do not automatically result in effective policy demand for new laws.

Using John L. Kingdon's framework for agenda-setting, one could argue that growing participation of mothers in the labor force was a changing condition but not a problem that justified action. According to Kingdon, "conditions become defined as problems when we come to believe that we should do something about them." Moreover, problems have an "interpretive element"; people interpret something as a problem based on their values and by classifying conditions into one category or another.[3] It took years for legislators to acknowledge that shifts in the family and work environments of millions of families created gaps in child care that justified federal intervention. Liberals and conservatives had different interpretations of the problems facing low-income working families with children. Each of their definitions of the problem resulted in different legislative solutions (direct child care subsidies versus tax credits) that were part of final outcomes in 1990 and at other times over the past thirty years. Furthermore, it took the work of political entrepreneurs to capitalize on these shifting definitions as they strove to raise child care on the government agenda.

For policy entrepreneurs to succeed at agenda-setting they need to make use of or help create shifts in what Kingdon called the political stream.[4] A classic example of this was when health care became a campaign theme in the 1992 national elections, followed by Clinton's health care reform proposal two years later.[5] Similarly, both parties identified child care as a campaign theme in the 1988 elections, thereby attracting national attention to the issue and promoting subsequent congressional action. In contrast, the difficulties child care advocates faced in making child care a national campaign theme in the 1990s and 2000 depict the hurdles of publicizing child care and getting it on the national and congressional agendas.

Of course, the mere fact that a law is an election issue does not guarantee its enactment. To support federal intervention in the child care arena, lawmakers had to be convinced of market failure and of the benefit of government action in what was traditionally a private family domain. Without that, they at least had to have reasons for going along with a majority of legislators in voting to invest federal dollars in child care programs. These reasons could include not wanting to antagonize party leaders, favoring the enactment of omnibus legislation to which lawmakers attached child care provisions, or fearing electoral losses.

One trend in favor of government involvement in child care was simply the growing importance of child care in American life. Between 1971 and 1990, and continuing into later years, American families of all income levels became increasingly dependent on nonparental care, as did members of Congress and their staffs. The popular image of mothers carrying a briefcase on one arm and a child on the other symbolized the growing numbers of parents (mostly women) who balanced (or more realistically, juggled) family and work. Given these trends, the business community's limited involvement in child care pointed to gaps in child care policies that might warrant federal support.[6]

Once lawmakers had acknowledged the need for federal child care assistance, they had to identify what form a new federal initiative would take. Should they opt for programmatic or tax policy changes? What combination of the two approaches might work? Which populations should they target? The failed 1971 Mondale–Brademas bill included a universal program for all families, paid for on a sliding scale based on income. The 1990 CCDBG targeted low-income families. Some child care policy analysts argued that targeting poor and low-income families reinforced the image of child care as a poverty issue. But by directing public officials' attention to the issue and promoting high-quality child care, the CCDBG offered opportunities for improving child care for all children. The scope of child care policies, including whether they targeted welfare or other low-income working families, depended largely on how the problem was defined.

Issue Definition Presents Challenges and Opportunities

Different versions of social problems generate new ways to evoke interest in an issue. As Frank R. Baumgartner and Bryan D. Jones explained, "Issue definition, then, is the driving force in both stability and instability, primarily because issue definition has the potential for mobilizing the previously disinterested."[7] Issue definition is pivotal to the politics and policies of many social policy concerns, not just child care. For example, one of the reasons for the failure of Clinton's health care proposal was that it simultaneously tried to accomplish many goals about which there was no general consensus, including lowering health care expenditures, expanding health care coverage, and encouraging the use of primary care. Regarding another case illustrating the importance of issue definition, Douglas Imig described how children's advocates shifted their collective focus "to target emerging concerns" in order to remain politically viable.[8]

Between 1970 and 2000 policymakers described child care bills as solutions to several different problems. Sometimes legislators justified voting for child care legislation not because of its value in helping children or working parents per se, but because of the symbolic value that child care assumed in the context of other issues. In so doing, legislators reached a consensus that transcended apparent discord. In reviewing the problems to which child care legislation was a proposed solution over the past thirty years, five major themes emerge: child development, standards, welfare reform, support for low-income working families, and promoting positive behaviors among school-age children. Each of these themes was part of specific legislative proposals (table 9.1).

In the early 1970s, Senator Walter Mondale, Representative John Brademas, and other supporters of child care legislation wanted to establish a federal child care program that would enhance child development. The title of the 1971 Mondale–Brademas bill, the Comprehensive Child Development Act, reflected the importance the bill's sponsors placed on child development. Ironically, among the many reasons for the bill's failure was the widespread publicity over the allegedly damaging effects of child care on child development. Nonetheless, Mondale and Brademas based their legislative proposals on Head Start and the popular notion at the time that a nurturing environment in the first five years of life could enhance subsequent development. By 2000 growing awareness of the importance of high-quality child care for children's development prompted federal and state officials to increase their support for quality enhancement initiatives.[9]

A major theme of child care legislative and regulatory politics in the 1970s and 1980s was that of standards (see chapter 3). Congressional opposition to the FIDCR in 1981 made it difficult for those advocating federal child care standards to make much headway in the years that followed. The controversy over the role of state and federal authorities in setting child care standards continued in the legislative debates in the late 1980s, the ensuing regulatory battles, and, to a lesser extent, the 1996 welfare bill.

For the past thirty years, child care has also been inextricably tied to welfare. Such linkage has both impeded and enhanced the progress of child care legislation at different times. In the early 1970s officials in the Nixon administration were concerned that the Mondale–Brademas child care bill would compete with Nixon's FAP legislation. Carter's proposals for welfare

TABLE 9.1 Major Themes for Child Care Legislation
and Regulation, 1970–2000

Theme	Years	Legislation or regulation
Child development	1969–1973	Mondale–Brademas legislation
	1997–2000	Bills addressing quality enhancement
Standards	1969–1981	FIDCR controversy
	1987–1990	CCDBG and related bills
	1991–1992	Regulations for 1990 child care laws
	1995–1996	PRWORA
Welfare	1969–1971	FAP; Mondale–Brademas legislation
	1977–1979	President Carter's welfare proposal
	1988	FSA
	1996	PRWORA/CCDBG reauthorization
	1997–2000	Implementation of PRWORA
Low-income working families	1987–1990	CCDBG
	1997–2000	Implementation of PRWORA
Reduce harmful behavior (i.e., crime, smoking)	1997–2000	Tobacco settlement revenues School-age child care legislation (21st CCLCs)

reform included child care provisions that sparked controversy among child care advocates. In 1988 the first federal child care guarantee was enacted under welfare legislation. In 1996 changes to the CCDBG and increased funding for child care reflected a consensus that lawmakers could not require welfare recipients to work without providing them with child care assistance. A disadvantage of linking welfare and child care was that it fostered legislators' perception of child care as a poverty issue and detracted from support for federal and state child care policies for low- and middle-income families.

The Act for Better Child Care, introduced in 1987, was an explicit call for federal investment in child care targeting low-income working families.

As enacted in 1990, the CCDBG was also the first legislation that allocated federal funds for quality improvement in child care. Child development was not as salient a feature of the legislation in the 1980s as it had been in the 1970s, largely because of research findings confirming that children were not harmed in child care settings and that the specific effects of child care on a child's development depended on many factors, especially the quality of care.[10] Because of the hurdles that lawmakers faced in enacting a free-standing child care bill, a child care package was included in the 1990 reconciliation bill, mostly because of the redistributive benefits it brought to low-income working families in the context of federal budget negotiations (see chapter 4). The new child care programs enacted in 1990 also demonstrated the ability of lawmakers to reach agreement on highly controversial aspects of child care legislation, such as vouchers, funding of child care sponsored by religious organizations, and standards. In addition, they established parental choice as an essential component of federal and state child care policies. Enactment of two new child care programs in 1990 proved that both parties could reach a middle ground that would endure for more than a decade. The CCDBG also put child care policymaking on a path that endured for years.

When child care next emerged on the congressional agenda in the mid-1990s, as mentioned earlier, it was inextricably connected with welfare reform. In the years immediately after the 1996 PRWORA, child care advocates found it difficult to obtain bipartisan support to expand the CCDBG, especially in the House. In part this was because advocates' legislative strategies lacked a consistent theme. Moreover, state TANF surpluses that could be spent on child care made it difficult to get support for increases in federal child care funding. Lacking a unifying message, child care advocates followed opportunities for CCDBG funding increases as they arose in Congress. In 1997 and 1998 they pushed for increases in funding for child care under legislation for the tobacco settlement, arguing that child care, especially for school-age children, could reduce harmful behaviors, such as smoking. Bipartisan interest in school readiness further fueled support for child care legislation, especially at the state level. The ability of structured child care settings to reduce crime and other harmful behavior offered ways of framing child care as a solution to various social and health problems. By the end of the 1990s, some of these efforts paid off, and care for school-age children under 21st CCLCs and CCDBG quality enhancement received funding boosts, as did overall federal funding for the CCDBG in FY 2001.

In the aftermath of welfare reform, state and federal officials demonstrated growing awareness of the child care needs of low-income working families.

In sum, between 1970 and 2000 child care advocates framed their issue in different ways. Such variations were necessary because their calls for a new federal child care program (1970s and 1980s) and expanding the CCDBG (1990s and 2000) often met with resistance. Some of the advocates' attempts to reframe the issue of child care produced legislative victories. As a result, the federal government's commitment to child care has grown, especially since 1990. But regardless of the spins advocates used, millions of parents still struggled to arrange affordable care and had no choice but to place their children in settings of questionable quality. Hence, child care advocates had yet to craft a message that successfully encompassed the need for child care assistance in its fullest sense. Some of the challenges they faced had to do not so much with problem definition and but more with lack of support for government-sponsored child care and obstacles posed by American political institutions.

What's Institutional Structure Got to Do with It?

In addition to problem definition, the politics of child care legislation showed how the structure of American political institutions influences legislative outcomes. In particular, federalism, separation of powers, polarization between parties, and shifts within the executive branch shaped child care policies between 1970 and 2000.

Federalism

The federalist structure of the American government presented obstacles to consensus building for child care and many other aspects of social policy, such as education, health, and welfare. State and federal authorities frequently bickered over child care standards, financing, and the states' ability to deviate from federal guidelines. The 1971 legislative conflicts over prime sponsorship, regulatory battles implementing the 1990 child care provisions, and the tobacco settlement feuds of the late 1990s were just a few illustrations of how federalism affected the discourse on child care legislation. Efforts to coordinate child care and Head Start were often problematic because each program entailed a different mix of federal, state, and local control. Integrating child care, education, health, and other systems across federal, state, and local levels of government remains an ongoing challenge.

The push for devolution to states, starting in the early 1980s, only partially explains intergovernmental concerns for child care. In addition to the tension between federal and state authorities, federal lawmakers disagreed among themselves over how much flexibility to grant states or local entities. Some legislators approved of federal legislation requiring states to offer child care vouchers but opposed federal mandates regarding health and safety. Moreover, some federal legislators were leery of regulating child care because of its connotation as a family issue but favored government control over other domains, such as transportation. Throughout the political discourse on child care, the federalist structure of American government was an underlying and influencing factor.

Separation of Powers

Another structural feature of American government—the constitutional separation between the executive and legislative branches—creates hurdles in American policymaking.[11] Requiring Congress and the president to work as "tandem-institutions" means that no one branch completely dominates decision making.[12] Enactment of laws, for child care or other issues, requires that both branches agree on some type of action. Lack of presidential interest often hindered enactment of child care laws throughout the 1970s and into the 1980s. Congress often takes actions without presidential support, but without a president pushing child care legislation or at least making it a quid pro quo for other issues, such as welfare, child care bills faced tough going. However, it would be incorrect to claim an eager Congress and a series of reluctant presidents when it came to child care legislation. An increasingly conservative Congress and other structural changes in the legislative branch thwarted child care advocacy efforts.

In reviewing the three major child care legislative episodes between 1970 and 2000 (1971, 1990, and 1996), both the 1990 child care package and the 1996 CCDBG reauthorization were enacted under periods of divided government (different parties controlling the legislative and executive branches). Unified government, such as in the Carter years (1977–1980) and in Clinton's first two years in office (1993–1994), failed to produce the advances in child care that some advocates had anticipated. These patterns indicate that something other than partisanship was at play in the formation of child care policy. Closer examination revealed that these patterns were not unique to child care policies. After all, for most of the postwar period divided government was the norm, and it did not preclude enactment of major laws in areas such as Medicare, Medicaid, disability, and tax policy.

One way of understanding the impact of a divided government on child care policy outcomes is to review scholarship on interbranch relations. David Mayhew, in his path-breaking 1991 book, *Divided We Govern: Party Control, Lawmaking, and Investigations*,[13] showed that divided government did not preclude the enactment of significant laws. This was contrary to conventional thinking until then, which had held that different parties in control of each branch resulted in conflict rather than convergence of views. Based on a review of enacted laws and a retrospective identification of important policy issues between 1946 and 1990, Mayhew showed that many major laws, including the 1990 child care provisions, were enacted under a divided government. But his reasons for why such patterns occurred are open to question.

Mayhew's critics claimed that his measures of significant legislative enactments were either too broad or not inclusive enough. Using different measures, other political scientists have both confirmed and qualified Mayhew's major findings.[14] Mayhew acknowledged that his methods overlooked major legislation embedded in routine bills, such as appropriations or reconciliation. Interestingly, child care was one of the few measures Mayhew counted twice, once under the 1990 reconciliation law and again as a separate landmark measure.[15]

Mayhew's work served as a point of departure for further scholarship on divided government and gridlock.[16] For example, one study of legislation between 1947 and 1992 took a different approach from Mayhew. Instead of analyzing the number of significant laws that were enacted, the researchers looked at the number of bills that were introduced but failed to reach enactment. They found that divided government increased the likelihood of potentially significant legislation failing.[17] Morris Fiorina acknowledged that a divided government affects legislative–executive relations by increasing conflict and tending to have more vetoed bills than would occur under a unified government.[18] His conclusion is applicable to child care politics in that a divided government produced vetoes and prolonged debate, whereas under a unified government (1977–1980, 1993–1994) Congress failed to even pass a child care bill.

While Mayhew and others examined partisan factors in policymaking, a different branch of scholarship emphasized institutional dynamics in determining legislative outcomes. Such models looked at how legislators obtain majorities on certain issues, despite partisan differences. Keith Krehbiel's theory of "pivotal politics" complemented and reinforced Mayhew's finding "that divided versus unified government per se does not affect legislative productivity."[19] Pivotal politics rejected the party-centered approach and instead identified under what circumstances a majority or supermajority could change the status quo. Krehbiel used a game theory model of legislative productivity based on the threat of two supermajority procedures that he considered critical to the enactment of laws: presidential veto and Senate filibuster. A presidential veto requires a two-thirds majority for override. The filibuster requires a three-fifths vote to end debate. For any given political situation, Krehbiel's model enables one to place along an ideological continuum from left to right the positions of the president, the median legislative voter, and the legislators (in both chambers) that would be needed to end gridlock by blocking a veto override or invoking cloture to end the debate.[20] Similar to Mayhew, Krehbiel found that whether the government was divided or unified did not significantly alter legislative productivity. Instead, he argued that changes in the heterogeneity or homogeneity of elected officials' preferences largely determine legislative productivity.[21]

Krehbiel's model implied that gridlock is not inherently bad in that it preserves the status quo and mitigates against frequent and unpredictable change. Politicians and scholars who favor an activist government see things differently. For them, a disadvantage of gridlock resulting from supermajority rules is that it makes it difficult for simple majorities within government to change the status quo.[22]

How does all of this relate to child care legislation? First, it obviates the need to ask why major child care legislation was enacted under periods of divided government. Recent political science research confirms that a unified government doesn't necessarily result in legislative activism, nor does a divided government guarantee gridlock. Instead, a more appropriate question is: Under what circumstances do a majority or supermajority of lawmakers and the president vote for or against a child care measure? Krehbiel's model shifts the analysis away from partisan effects and prompts one to consider how child care legislation can garner support from a simple or supermajority of legislators.

One answer, as discussed earlier, is that Congress and the president enacted child care measures because of the symbolic meaning they brought to other issues. Two examples that readily come to mind were expanding assistance to low-income working families under the 1990 reconciliation bill and promoting the success of welfare-to-work provisions under the PRWORA of 1996. On each occasion, a majority of legislators from both parties reached consensus on significant child care legislation largely because of the meaning child care held in the context of other issues. Divided government may have prolonged the negotiations for these laws and made coalition-building difficult. However, it did not prevent final enactment. Similarly, unified government (as in Clinton's first term and Carter's presidency) may have made it easier for a majority party (typically the Democrats) to negotiate with the president, but it hardly guaranteed the majorities needed to enact major child care bills. The need to attract support from a heterogeneous majority of legislators points to the merits of legislation that combines child care tax credits and direct subsidies. Such was the case with the 1990 reconciliation law and numerous legislative proposals between 1997 and 2000, especially concerning care for school-age children.

Although it is tempting to ponder why child care made important strides under the divided governments of a GOP president in 1990 and a Republican Congress in 1996, partisan explanations of policymaking fall short. Instead, other factors influenced final child care policy outcomes, especially the ability of child care advocates to define the problem and present child care legislation so that it attracted the support of a large and heterogeneous group of lawmakers.

Growing Polarization Between Parties

The discussion so far has minimized the importance of partisan factors. However, they are not to be totally overlooked. One explanation for the difficulty of reaching agreement on child care was the growing polarization between the two major parties. An increased convergence of views within each party, especially in the mid-1990s, further exacerbated difficulties in obtaining bipartisan support. Growing intraparty ideological homogeneity and polarization between parties meant that for most of the 1990s roll-call votes in Congress were divided along party and ideological lines.[23] By the end of 1999 the rate of partisan voting was dipping for the House and only slightly rising for the Senate.[24] Nonetheless, measures of party unity for both parties and both chambers were generally higher in the 1980s and 1990s than in the 1970s.[25] Bipartisan support was especially difficult to achieve for issues such as child care, health care, and education, issues that elicited partisan differences concerning the role of the federal government and definitions of the problem. Consequently, supermajorities that favored the status quo instead of legislative change were often the norm.[26]

Growing intraparty homogeneity and interparty differences were partly due to a decrease in the number of moderates in both parties from the 1970s to the 1990s, especially among northern Republicans.[27] Liberal Republicans in both chambers eased congressional passage of child care legislation in 1971. Senators John Chafee, Olympia Snowe, and Jim Jeffords, and Representative Nancy Johnson were among the moderate Republicans in both chambers who were critical in obtaining bipartisan majorities for child care throughout the 1980s and 1990s. But their dwindling numbers were part of the changing political environment for child care.

Polarization among parties was most visible in floor votes. But many issues failed to reach the floor, either because of partisan differences in the committees or because the leaders in either chamber blocked bills that went against their views. Other partisan battles were fought in conference committee.

The Impact of Committee Structures and Procedures on Child Care Politics

Historically, congressional committees have served numerous functions, ranging from gatekeeping and agenda-setting to enabling legislators to function as information specialists as they move their bills to the full floor.[28] For child care, the House Select Committee on Children, Youth, and Families, started in 1983, was important for agenda-setting during the mid-1980s (see chapter 4). Its elimination in 1991 left a void for child care and other family issues. But because it lacked legislative authority, members of committees in each house with jurisdiction over child care have been most influential in setting the course of child care legislation.

By falling primarily under the jurisdiction of two committees in each chamber (House Committee on Education and the Workforce and Committee on Ways and Means; Senate Committee on Finance and Committee on Health, Education, Labor, and Pensions),[29] child care faced the challenges of other issues, such as health care reform, that required agreement from many disparate individuals and panels. With some lawmakers focusing on tax credits for child care policymaking, others pushing CCDBG funding increases, and many introducing bills that contained both tax credits and programmatic initiatives, coordinating across committees often entangled the policy process. Furthermore, with child care falling under four major committees, politicians' definitions of child care became more complicated, as it was perceived simultaneously as education, welfare, workforce, tax, and social service legislation.

By the late 1990s the education committees in each chamber had jurisdiction over the discretionary stream for the CCDBG, while the tax and revenue committees covered the mandatory funding (entitlements). However, distinctions between these two functions were often blurred, especially regarding the broad contours of child care policy, such as CCDBG reauthorization. Not only was this problematic for child care legislation, but the emergence of new items on the legislative agenda increased the interconnection among many issues. As Frank R. Baumgartner, Bryan D. Jones, and Michael C. MacLeod noted, "Issues and structures co-evolve, in a dynamic dance that, over the long term, changes both the way in which issues are understood and decided, on the one hand, and the manner in which structures are used to channel the consideration of those issues, on the other." The growing number of issues on the congressional agenda, their porous boundaries, and the widening domains of many committees[30] suggest that committee jurisdiction will shape legislative debates. Thus, structural aspects of congressional committees affect the outcomes of many issues, including child care.

In 1990 the decision to establish two federal child care programs largely resulted from committee turf battles in the House, where child care was jointly referred to two committees. This was different from the politics and outcome of the 1971 child care bill when only one committee in each house claimed jurisdiction over legislation under consideration. In the late 1960s and early 1970s, the House Committee on Ways and Means and the Senate Committee on Finance had jurisdiction over child care insofar as it was part of welfare reform or tax credit proposals. However, those committees were not involved in the Mondale–Brademas bills. Other differences between the 1971 and 1990 legislative episodes are discussed in chapter 4.

The impact of the 1995 congressional reforms on child care policymaking were discussed in chapter 6. Basically, the GOP control of Congress fortified the influence of the Republican Party's preferences and reduced the influence of subcommittee and even committee chairs.[31] After the GOP takeover of Congress in 1994, most committees, including traditionally liberal panels such as the House Committee on Education and the Workforce, became increasingly conservative.[32] This created challenges for advocates seeking to increase federal spending on child care.

Yet, despite what some considered their waning influence in the late 1990s, committees remained important as the launching pad for most bills. They also were the forum for amendments that could significantly alter legislative proposals. This was illustrated repeatedly in the course of child care legislation from 1970 through 2000.

Each committee has its own culture and politics. The Senate Committee on Health, Education, Labor, and Pensions (and its predecessors) has been one of the most active committees for child care policymaking. Chairs of its subcommittee on children, most notably Senators Mondale, Alan Cranston, and Christopher Dodd, repeatedly championed child care legislation. The greater amount of child care legislative activity in the Senate compared with the House, especially in the late 1990s, was largely attributable to this Senate panel. But the committee's more liberal inclination,[33] compared with the rest of the chamber, has impeded Senate passage and enactment of its proposals.

The Senate Committee on Finance was more conservative than the Senate labor committee.[34] It also was more centralized than other panels.[35] This meant that the views of the chairperson of the full committee usually dominated committee decisions more than in other committees. In both the Senate Committee on Finance and the House Committee on Ways and Means, child care competed for attention with many high-profile tax and entitlement issues, such as Medicare and Social Security. As a Republican moderate on the Finance Committee, Senator Chafee was important in obtaining bipartisan support for child care on several occasions. Senator Orrin Hatch, a member of the Finance Committee and previously a chair and member of the Senate labor committee, was another source of Republican support for child care bills.

The House Committee on Ways and Means was an important forum for child care deliberations especially in the 1980s when Representative Thomas Downey, as a subcommittee chair, spearheaded many initiatives. Between 1995 and 2000, the conservative positions of the chairman of the full committee, Representative Bill Archer, and his interest in tax reform shaped the committee's activities regarding child care legislation. As a senior member of the committee and then a subcommittee chair, Representative Johnson kept the issue of child care on the committee's agenda.

Organized interests and members of authorizing committees responsible for CCDBG also worked with the appropriations committees in each chamber. The appropriations bill for the Departments of Labor, Health and Human Services, and Education contained hundreds of programs. Getting committee members to approve CCDBG funding increases that a majority of members in both houses would support was no small feat. Krehbiel explained that appropriations bills present particular challenges to pivotal politics because of the hundreds of programs they include and the greater tendency of presidents to veto them.[36] The battles over CCDBG appropriations in the 1990s and 2000 illustrated the contentiousness surrounding child care appropriations.

Moving child care legislation from any committee to full chamber votes was also difficult because of rules and procedures that often required more than simple majorities. Officially, the House Rules Committee determined the timing of moving bills to the floor and the types of amendments allowed, but its members worked closely with the House leadership. Senate rules are more flexible than the House's in terms of what types of amendments members may introduce on the floor. This enhanced the ability of Senate Majority Leader George Mitchell to introduce his child care bill substitute on the Senate floor in 1989 and of Senators Dodd and Jeffords to introduce floor amendments for child care in 1998 and 1999.

Executive Branch

Although Congress was the focus for most of the child care deliberations during the past thirty years, presidents and other executive branch officials also figured prominently. Throughout most of the 1970s and 1980s, presidents had little incentive to sign child care bills. Presidential indifference to child care legislation changed in 1988 when President Bush addressed the concerns of working parents with young children, even if he did so in response to the Democrats' calls for expanded child care policies. President Clinton's interest in child care was a mixed bag. The 1997 White House conferences and his ambitious child care budget proposals for FY 1999, 2000, and 2001 set him apart from previous presidents. But by not designating a realistic funding source for his child care proposals or pushing them through Congress, he signaled his reluctance to make child care a legislative priority. Clinton's willingness to fight publicly for child care funding increased at the end of 2000, most likely because budget surpluses made it easier to justify new appropriations than in the past. Moreover, he had little to lose in pushing for such requests as his second term in office came to a close.

Several factors explain Clinton's wavering on child care. First, like Carter, he was a conservative to moderate Democrat. Especially in the early part of his presidency, when budget deficits ran high, Clinton was not inclined to advocate increases in social spending that would make him look like a tax-and-spend Democrat. Having won the 1992 election with a plurality, but not a majority, he was mindful of the need to broaden his political base. Championing child care could run counter to those electoral goals.

Starting in 1995, Clinton faced a Republican Congress with a strong conservative bent. What benefit did child care legislation hold for him unless it furthered other policy objectives with strong public support and electoral promise, such as welfare reform, school readiness, or crime prevention? Without a show of public opinion in favor of federal child care intervention, Clinton (and Congress) instead went after issues such as education reform and crime prevention that ranked high as national concerns. Child care legislation had some likelihood of success if presidents or other elected officials could frame it in the context of those issues.

Relationships among OMB, DPC, and HHS (or HEW) staff also affected child care legislative and regulatory outcomes. In 1971 White House staff aligned with OMB and DPC defeated Secretary of HEW Elliot Richardson, who saw merit in enacting a federal child care bill. By the late 1980s OMB's rising influence enabled Richard Darman and his staff to take the lead in child care negotiations. OMB continued to influence HHS in the promulgation of regulations pursuant to the 1990 law.

Under Clinton, other parts of the executive branch became influential in child care policymaking. Secretary Donna Shalala provided consistent support for federal involvement in child care during the eight years of her tenure. The creation of the Child Care Bureau under her watch gave a new voice to child care legislation within the executive branch. Observers on both sides of the issue credited (or blamed) Hillary Rodham Clinton for making child care a White House priority. Her interest in the issue gave President Clinton opportunities to showcase child care as a White House initiative, without having to commit himself legislatively.

As Clinton's presidency drew to a close, he could claim credit for an expanded federal commitment to child care. He had vetoed several bills because he thought they lacked adequate child care funding, and Congress usually responded with funding increases. If the Democrats had retained control of Congress in 1995, perhaps Clinton would have more aggressively lobbied for his child care recommendations. But he still would have had to overcome certain structural constraints, such as obtaining consensus between committees, chambers, and parties, and providing feasible ways of funding his proposal. He also had to work with a larger array of organized interests in the child care advocacy coalition than did any of his predecessors.

The Influence of Organized Interests

According to John R. Wright, interest groups help inform legislators. There is always the possibility that they will misinform by manipulating the information they present. But legislators are "generally better informed about politics and policy with interest groups than without them." Organized interests serve as conveyors of information that can block or advance bills. Furthermore, according to Wright, conflict among organized interests is handled within the institutions of national government (i.e., Congress, agencies, and courts). "Thus, the interactions between organized interests and government institutions, not the interactions among interests themselves, are the important connections for understanding and explaining policy outcomes."[37] This certainly applied to child care policymaking where congressional hearings and other deliberations provided the context for debates between organized interests and their allies in Congress.

In analyzing the role of organized interests in child care policymaking, it is important to distinguish between their involvement and their influence. Many organizations were involved. Far fewer were influential. How much organized interests changed legislators' views is difficult to ascertain from this study. At certain key junctures, organized interests provided information and policy alternatives that influenced final outcomes. For example, the initial proposal for the 1987 ABC bill was a combined effort on behalf of staff for certain congressional Democrats and organized interests. CDF and other organizations furnished important data that informed legislative debates. The Heritage Foundation's emphasis on parental choice became a critical component of President Bush's policy and his final child care bill in 1990.

As in many other social policy arenas, the number of organizations and legislators advocating for federal child care programs grew tremendously between 1970 and 2000.[38] Expansion of the number of organized interests working on child care legislation was in some measure a response to changes in the social fabric of American life, especially with regard to women, family, and work. However, growth within a policy domain does not necessarily mean more clout or enacted bills,[39] especially for predominantly liberal groups trying to exert influence on a conservative Congress or White House.

Many organizations advocating for child care legislation (i.e., CDF, NWLC, CWLA, AFSCME, and other labor unions) did not focus exclusively on child care. Rather, child care policymaking gave additional meaning to their organizational missions and major policy concerns. The absence of any one organization solely dedicated to child care legislation strengthened the ability of CDF to take the lead among child care advocacy groups in the political arena. However, for most of its nearly thirty-year history, CDF has focused primarily on improving the well-being of poor and minority children. For some political observers, CDF's focus on poor children has reinforced the negative connotations of child care as a poverty issue. But after all, it is the families with the lowest incomes who most need child care assistance. Furthermore, a closer look reveals that CDF has advocated for issues that affect all families. For child care, this includes its work on DCTC revisions and improving the quality of child care. In recent years CDF has emphasized its concerns with improving the well-being of *all* children. As the lead legislative advocacy group for child care, CDF contributes political expertise, timely data about the states, extensive grassroots networks, and other organizational resources. For the past three decades it has secured for itself a niche at the head of child care legislative advocacy while other groups made their unique contributions to child care policymaking too.[40]

CDF was highly effective in what Jack L. Walker labeled "inside" and "outside" strategies. The former refers to working political contacts within the government, and the latter refers to working the media and the press.[41] CDF's success in negotiating child care was also attributable to Helen Blank, CDF's director of child care policy. Those on both sides of the aisle acknowledged her political sensitivity in advancing an issue as complicated as child care.

Conservative organizations also made important contributions to child care policymaking. In the 1970s conservatives' campaigns against child care lacked organizational strength or cohesiveness. But by the late 1980s, they had garnered considerable influence, largely because of the support of well-endowed foundations and a willingness to lobby aggressively against child care measures they deemed undesirable. By the late 1990s, some groups on the far right and some libertarian groups, such as the Cato Institute, continued to oppose government-sponsored child care programs. But by the late 1990s and into 2000, as discussed in chapter 7, a consensus emerged about the need for federal child care assistance, even though the size and scope of such assistance still generated conflict.

CDF, CCAC, NWLC, FWI, and other organizations involved with child care were among the growing number of citizen-based groups "built around a compelling moral cause or single issue."[42] The Heritage Foundation and other conservative organizations functioned in a similar manner. Unlike professional or trade groups, which relied on dues, citizen-based organizations derived their financial support from individual and corporate contributions. A small group of professionals handled their policy work, compared with the more formal decision-making structures of membership organizations.[43] By the late 1980s, these types of organizations had become the leaders among organized interests in many areas, including child care policymaking. Consequently, they often influenced policy outcomes for a constituency (working families with children) that was not directly engaged in the political arena. The intergovernmental lobby (NGA, NCSL, and APHSA) and others involved with implementing federal child care programs supplemented the information these national advocacy groups offered, especially in commenting on proposed regulations. But the voices of the millions of families who struggled with child care on a daily basis were not strident parts of the battles among organized interests, other than as occasional witnesses at congressional hearings.

Labor unions had a strong interest and presence in child care politics in the late 1960s and early 1970s. Many, especially AFSCME, supported child care legislation in the late 1980s. By the late 1990s, unions had become less visible in all aspects of social policy, in part because of lagging union membership.[44] Nonetheless, by remaining a concern of many female union members, child care held the potential for further legislative activism on the part of the unions.

Business interests were conspicuously absent from child care public policymaking. Most businesses and organizations representing corporate interests typically favored deregulation. Therefore, they were not inclined to support legislation calling for increases in federal child care involvement. The challenge for child care advocates was to convince business leaders of the potential advantages of public child care subsidies in terms of worker productivity.

As explained in more detail in chapter 1, many of the organized interests involved with child care were part of an advocacy coalition whose members shared a set of values and assumptions about the importance of the federal government in child care policymaking.[45] On the other side of the issue was another advocacy coalition whose members pressed for tax credits and spoke on behalf of families with a parent who stayed at home to care for young children. While this advocacy coalition was not as cohesive as the one calling for greater federal involvement in child care, its members adhered to a shared set of values about the importance of parental choice and minimizing government involvement in child care.

Each coalition responded to external cues, in particular the changing demographics of the workforce and research on child development and child care. Between 1970 and 2000, members of both advocacy coalitions experienced policy learning as they recognized the points of compromise that were needed to achieve their goals. CDF and its allies yielded on issues such as vouchers, federal standards, and reshaping their messages to acknowledge parental choice. Those on the other side accepted the CCDBG and other federal child care initiatives, especially in implementing welfare reform. In some ways, those opposed to a federal child care program lost steam as the CCDBG became a solid part of American social policy. But their insistence on tax credits, vouchers, parental choice, and assistance for families with a stay-at-home parent will most likely endure in the years ahead.

The Enigmatic Role of Women in Child Care Policymaking

Given the frequency with which policymakers identified the growing number of women in the workforce as the underlying reason for enacting child care bills, the inconsistent involvement of women's groups is puzzling. Although several national women's organizations were steadfast advocates for an expanded federal role in child care, others were more marginally involved or only gradually increased their interest in the issue over time. As part of this study, when congressional staff or members of Congress were asked about the presence of women's groups, they often answered either that women's groups were conspicuously absent or that they were generally present, but with few exceptions (usually the NWLC) staff and legislators could not identify any particular group. Yet, the lists of organizations lobbying for (and against) child care legislation always included many women's organizations.

The uneven support for child care legislation among women's organizations may be explained by several factors. First, women's groups had to prioritize their legislative agenda. For feminists, other concerns were more pressing than child care. In particular, during the late 1970s and much of the 1980s, equity, nondiscrimination in the workplace, and enactment of the Equal Rights Amendment dominated women's political agendas.[46]

According to many feminists, presenting child care as a woman's issue perpetuated the erroneous assumption that women were responsible for children and child rearing. Vicky Randall referred to this as the "association of childcare with the vexed area of motherhood."[47] Although Randall's comments were based on Great Britain, they were also relevant to the United States. She explained that the women's liberation movement of the 1960s viewed women's childbearing and child-rearing roles as a main cause of female oppression. The "prevailing orthodoxy" was a "guilt by association" for anything that reinforced women's maternal roles.[48] By the late 1970s, the "discovery of motherhood" through baby boomers who fretted about their biological clocks had given voice to a feminist perspective that "celebrated women's distinctive child-rearing capabilities."[49] Yet, this new acceptance of maternity among feminists did not step up feminist activities in advocating for child care legislation, partly because the new mood was not about caring for children, but pertained more to the needs of the mothers involved.[50]

Child care also raised uncomfortable issues about class conflict and equity among women. Both the British and American women's movement drew primarily from middle-class women who typically viewed state-funded child care as a necessity for working-class and low-income women but not for themselves.[51] From another perspective, policymakers, especially conservatives, purported to be supportive of mothers having a range of choices regarding work and family. But conservatives' push for public policies that required welfare mothers with young children to work contradicted their preference that middle-income mothers forfeit work to stay home with their young children.[52] Moreover, policymakers seldom referred to the importance of women having the choice to pursue careers.[53] Such talk was risky when (mostly male) legislators continued to express uneasiness about women leaving young children in the care of others even when forced to work out of economic necessity. Finally, because of varying eligibility criteria for state and federal child care assistance, some low-income women did not receive child care subsidies while others, with the same income and number of children, received welfare and child care benefits.

Another explanation for the uncertainty surrounding women's groups in lobbying for child care legislation was the rise of conservatism. Both conservatism and its perception of the role of women went against feminist political agendas that emphasized the rights of all women to make choices in work, family, political, and economic arenas.[54]

Despite difficulties in enlisting feminist support, many women's groups were active in child care policymaking. Groups such as the NWLC, NCJW, AAUW, YWCA, and AJLI had long histories of child care advocacy. The point here is not to identify which women's groups were involved with child care advocacy. Rather, it is important to appreciate that each organization faced different internal politics in deciding whether to participate in child care advocacy and in determining what form that advocacy should take. The result was a sporadic track record for many women's groups. Finally, women's voices were not monolithic when it came to child care. Not all national women's groups or their members were in concert with feminist ideologies. Moreover, many women's groups advocated traditional roles for women, which also reflected the diversity of women's perspectives on child care. Women's groups on the right were not monolithic either.[55]

In discussing the role of women in child care policymaking, some scholars identified the growing number of women in Congress (13 percent in 2001) and the role of the Congressional Caucus for Women's Issues (table 9.2). But a closer look reveals a more complicated picture of the contribution of women legislators to child care legislation.

First, most of the staunch advocates for child care in Congress, with some exceptions, have been men. Representatives Brademas, Downey, Augustus Hawkins, Dale Kildee, and George Miller, and Senators Cranston, Dodd, Mondale, Chafee, Kennedy, Hatch, and Jeffords, were among the leaders in advocacy for child care legislation. Women, too, have been important champions, in particular, Representatives Rosa DeLauro, Jennifer Dunn, Johnson, Barbara Kennelly, Nita Loewy (D-N.Y.), Carolyn Maloney (D-N.Y.), Patsy Mink, Constance Morella (R-Md.), Patricia Schroeder, Ellen Tauscher, and Lynn Woolsey; and Senators Nancy Kassebaum, Barbara Mikulski, and Snowe. However, it would be inaccurate to characterize child care as a woman's legislative concern when so many of the major players were men, even if this were necessary to garner the requisite level of support. Moreover, women still do not compose a large enough proportion of members to bring

TABLE 9.2 Percentages of Women in Elective Offices

Level of office	1977	1979	1981	1983	1985	1987	1989	1992	1994	1995	1997	1999	2001
U.S. Congress	4%	3%	4%	4%	5%	5%	5%	6%	10%	10%	11%	12%	13%
State legislatures	9%	10%	12%	13%	15%	16%	17%	18%	21%	21%	22%	23%	22%

Sources: Center for Women in Politics, *Fact Sheet, 1/00* (New Brunswick, N.J.: Rutgers University, Eagleton Institute of Politics, CAWP, 2000); Center for Women in Politics, *Election 2000: Summary of Results for Women* (New Brunswick, N.J.: Rutgers University, Eagleton Institute of Politics, CAWP, 2000), available at: www.rci.rutgers.edu~cawp/facts/summary2000.html, accessed 18 December 2000.

child care legislation to enactment. As with women's organizations, not all female legislators viewed child care legislation the same way. While some pushed for increased CCDBG funding, others—typically Republicans— preferred minimal involvement of the federal government and emphasized families with stay-at-home parents. Also, the women's caucus, as all other legislative service organizations, had limited legislative influence, especially after 1994 when the Republican leadership withdrew financial and other organizational resources.

Finally, child care presents challenges when categorized as a women's issue. Noelle Norton's factor analysis of voting behavior among male and female members in Congress from 1989 through 1994 confirmed that ideology is an "adequate explanation of voting patterns when votes of importance to women are not included in the voting models."[56] When she added to her model issues that evoke role changes for women, an additional dimension of voting behavior related to beliefs about gender roles and gender consciousness emerged. However, child care did not follow the same pattern as other issues that suggested role changes for women. Instead, votes on child care loaded highest on the ideological dimension, in contrast to issues such as family planning and abortion that loaded highest on the gender dimension. Norton attributed the aberrant patterns of voting behavior on child care to the growing acceptance of child care in American life by the early 1990s.[57] However, another explanation is that votes on child care, especially between 1989 and 1990, were not always about changing gender roles. Instead, they produced controversies over tax credits versus programmatic expansions, budget priorities, and the delicate balance between federal and state authorities, all of which had more to do with broad ideological concerns than women's changing roles. Thus, when the full context of the politics of child care is taken into consideration, child care does not fall neatly into any single policy domain. Instead it is often a lightning rod for a host of controversial issues, including whether mothers of preschoolers should leave their children in the care of others.

Elsewhere Norton explained that women in Congress have shaped the outcome of legislation pertaining to reproductive rights and welfare reform when they held seats on the subcommittees, full committees, and conference committees with jurisdiction over those issues.[58] As a result of the 2000 elections, women will hold 13 percent of the seats in Congress, an all-time high. While this is a positive development, these women will need to secure seats on committees with jurisdiction over their issues, especially conference committees, if they want to influence the outcomes of legislation on their agenda.

Looking Ahead

The message of this book is that the structures and procedures within and among major political institutions shaped the contours of American child care policies. During the past thirty years, some of these institutional structures, such as federalism and separation of powers, have remained pillars around which key players negotiated various aspects of child care policies. Other structures of Congress, the executive branch, or organized interests have shifted over time. Although it is impossible to discern the effect of any particular factor, together the individuals and entities that comprise the political institutions interacted to create American child care policies.

The definition of child care as a policy issue changed over time. Lawmakers' varying perceptions of the problem to which child care legislation provided a potential solution contributed to different policy outcomes. Since 1970, laws and regulations pertaining to child care have prompted the growth of new structures in the legislative and executive branches and among organized interests. Conversely, new developments among organized interests, especially conservative think tanks, have influenced the course and outcome of federal child care policies since the 1980s. In general, those preferring a federal commitment to child care policymaking made more strides than their counterparts opposed to such measures. It is no longer a question of whether the federal government should have a presence in child care policymaking; the challenge for the foreseeable future is determining what that presence should be. The future holds challenges in determining how to define child care as a women's, children's, workforce, education, or economic concern.

The child care block grant has institutionalized child care within the federal government. However, it is unclear how it will emerge after its reauthorization in 2002. Some combination of tax policies and direct subsidies will inevitably characterize the next round of child care politics and outcomes, especially with a Republican president.

Forecasting social policy is difficult, especially because of unanticipated events.[59] Nonetheless, certain conclusions emerge from the story of child care policymaking since 1970. First, although it is tempting to predict that a Democratic Congress or president or a unified Democratic government might lead to expansions of child care subsidies, recent history and empirical data indicate otherwise. Instead, the ability to obtain majorities to advance child care bills will depend on how legislators define the problem or use child care as a vehicle for other ends. Furthermore, structural changes in Congress and the executive branch will affect the course and outcome of child care legislation, even if only indirectly. Finally, the importance of child care in American work and family life is not about to change and will likely loom larger. Thus, the need for some combination of assistance from both the public and the private sector is more than a passing trend.

As for organized interests, child care cannot survive when defined primarily as a cause that concerns poor or low-income working families. The time is long past to enlarge the child care tent. Although child care legislation has focused on the needs of low-income families, child care remains an important issue for children from middle-class families as well. As Edward Zigler noted at a congressional hearing:

> So there are good homes, and there are bad homes. There is good child care, there is bad child care. What we should do is make it possible for children to have good environments whether they are raised at home or whether they are raised out-of-home, in child care. . . . You are going to find that the problem is much more than just high-risk families. It goes right up through the working class and into the lower middle-class, so you might have to take a little broader look.[60]

Renewed interest in child care from crime prevention and women's groups is encouraging. Business leaders need to come to the table too. As Richard B. Stolley, chairman of the CCAC and president of Time Warner commented, "Fortunately there is high-quality child care in this country, and I often hear from families who have found it. But there is not enough quality, and not enough support from business and government to achieve [that quality]."[61] Thus, in looking to the future, the engagement of business and corporate interest will be critical for shaping American child care policies. This is different from workplace policies that promote family-friendly environments. Both legislative and institutional initiatives that involve business are important.

According to Baumgartner and Jones's framework of punctuated equilibrium, another episode of child care activism will undoubtedly emerge.

Given the unmet need for child care among low-income families, the next episode may move child care beyond welfare. Welfare reform and school readiness catapulted child care to the top of many state agendas, but many children and families, from all walks of life, still struggle with balancing work and family. As long as conservatives and liberals differ in their perception of the problems pertaining to family, society, and budget politics, child care legislation will proceed slowly. But there is reason to believe that future episodes of child care legislation will engage a wider audience than in the past, especially if child care advocates can wisely mesh their message with other policy priorities. The challenge is to make all Americans appreciate that promoting child care policies can bring long-term advantages to all sectors of society, not only to the families who rely on child care for a short period in their lives. Child care has come far since the early 1970s. But there is still a long way to go to make people who are not parents of young children understand that child care policy can affect them by shaping the future generation of workers, parents, and citizens. Future discussions about child care policy are likely to encompass families with stay-at-home parents, a balance between programmatic and tax policies, arguments over how much the federal government should spend on child care, and linkages among child care and other initiatives in education, health, and welfare. Understanding the nature of past debates and the role that political institutions and structures played in shaping policy will help those interested in child care, regardless of their policy preferences, champion the issue in the twenty-first century.

Notes

1. Introduction

1. Gail Richardson and Elisabeth Marx, *A Welcome for Every Child: How France Achieves Quality in Child Care: Practical Ideas for the United States* (New York: French-American Foundation, 1989); Sonya Michel, *Children's Interests/ Mother's Rights: The Shaping of America's Child Care Policy* (New Haven, Conn.: Yale University Press, 1999), 281–97; Ian D. McMahan, "Public Preschool from the Age of Two: The *Ecole Maternelle* in Europe," *Young Children* 47, no. 5 (July 1992): 22–28; Janet C. Gornick, Marcia K. Meyers, and Katherine E. Ross, "Supporting the Employment of Mothers: Policy Variation Across Fourteen Welfare States," *Journal of European Social Policy* 7, no. 1 (1997): 45–70.

2. Ron Haskins, "Similar History, Similar Markets, Similar Policies Yield Similar Fixations," in Michael E. Lamb, Kathleen J. Sternberg, Carl-Philip Hwang, and Anders G. Broberg, eds., *Child Care in Context* (Hillsdale, N.J.: Erlbaum, 1992), 267–80.

3. Poll by Louis Harris and Associates, 14–18 January 1998, available at: Roper POLL, Lexis-Nexis Universe, accession number 0291661, question number 007, accessed 22 January 1999.

4. "Americans Rate Their Society and Chart Its Values: A Roper Center Review of Findings of the General Social Survey and the 1996 Survey of American Political Culture," *Public Perspective* 8, no. 2 (February–March 1997): 1–27. For 1998, to obtain cross tabulations for this item by sex, the author used data from the *General Social Surveys, 1972–1998: Cumulative Codebook* (Chicago: National Opinion Research Center, 1999).

5.   For a discussion of attitudinal changes among Americans that emphasizes grow-
      ing acceptance of working mothers of young children, see Ronald R. Rindfuss,
      Karin L. Brewster, and Andrew L. Kavee, "Women, Work, and Children: Be-
      havioral and Attitudinal Change in the United States," *Population and Devel-
      opment Review* 22, no. 3 (September 1996): 457–82.

6.   U.S. House, Committee on Ways and Means, *1998 Green Book*, 105th Cong.,
      2d sess., 19 May 1998, 664–65, 668.

7.   U.S. Department of Education, National Center for Education Statistics, *Di-
      gest of Education Statistics, 1998* (Washington, D.C.: Government Printing
      Office, 1999), 61.

8.   U.S. Department of Health and Human Services, *Access to Child Care for Low-
      Income Working Families* (Washington, D.C.: DHHS, 1999).

9.   See, for example, Anne Cassidy, "Profiles in Power," *Working Mother*, June
      1999, 20–24.

10.   Andrew J. Cherlin, "By the Numbers," *New York Times Magazine*, 5 April 1998,
      39–41.

11.   U.S. House, Committee on Ways and Means, *1998 Green Book*, 668.

12.   Kristin Smith, *Who's Minding the Kids? Child Care Arrangements: Fall 1995*,
      Current Population Reports, P70-70 (Washington, D.C.: Bureau of the Census,
      2000), 1–5.

13.   Ibid., 16.

14.   James L. Hynes Jr., *Twenty Years in Review: A Look at 1971–1990* (Washington,
      D.C.: National Association for the Education of Young Children, 1991).

15.   U.S. House, Committee on Ways and Means, *1998 Green Book*, 661–63.

16.   Ibid., 1250.

17.   U.S. Department of Commerce, Bureau of the Census, *Money Income in the
      United States, 1997*, Current Population Reports, P60-200 (Washington, D.C.:
      Government Printing Office, September 1998), xi–xiii; Lynn A. Karoly, "The
      Trend in Inequality Among Families, Individuals, and Workers," in Sheldon
      Danziger and Peter Gottschalk, eds., *Uneven Tides* (New York: Russell Sage
      Foundation, 1993), 21; Paul Ryscavage, *Income Inequality in America: An Anal-
      ysis of Trends* (Armonk, N.Y.: Sharpe, 1998); Isaac Shapiro and Robert Green-
      stein, *The Widening Income Gulf* (Washington, D.C.: Center on Budget and
      Policy Priorities, 4 September 1999).

18.   Lawrence Mishel, Jared Bernstein, and John Schmitt, *The State of Working
      America, 1998–99* (Ithaca, N.Y.: Cornell University Press, 1999), 119; Louis
      Uchitelle, "The Middle Class: Winning in Politics, Losing in Life," *New York
      Times*, 19 July 1998, Week in Review, 1, 16.

19.   National Center for Children in Poverty, *Child Poverty in the States: Levels and
      Trends from 1979 to 1998*, Research Brief 2 (New York: National Center for
      Children in Poverty, August 2000).

20. Ibid. In 1974, 15.4 percent of children under the age of eighteen lived in families with incomes below the federal poverty level. U.S. House, Committee on Ways and Means, *1998 Green Book*, 1288; National Center for Children in Poverty, *Young Children in Poverty: A Statistical Update* (New York: National Center for Children in Poverty, June 1999), 2.

21. Greg J. Duncan and Jeanne Brooks-Gunn, eds., *Consequences of Growing Up Poor* (New York: Russell Sage Foundation, 1997).

22. For a discussion of how child care assistance can help diminish childhood poverty, see Barbara Bergmann, "Child Care: The Key to Ending Child Poverty," in Irwin Garfinkel, Jennifer L. Hochschild, and Sara S. McLanahan, eds., *Social Policies for Children* (Washington, D.C.: Brookings Institution, 1996), 112–35.

23. Ellen E. Kisker et al., *A Profile of Child Care Settings: Early Education and Care in 1990*, report prepared by Mathematica Policy Research for the Department of Education (Washington, D.C.: Government Printing Office, 1991), 1:207.

24. Children's Foundation, *The 1999 Child Care Center Licensing Study* (Washington, D.C.: Children's Foundation, 1999), iv. These data differ from 1977 and 1990 supply data because of differences in the organizations sponsoring the surveys and the methodologies they used.

25. Ibid., xiii.

26. Frank R. Baumgartner and Bryan D. Jones, *Agendas and Instability in American Politics* (Chicago: University of Chicago Press, 1993).

27. Ibid., 12, 16.

28. Ibid., 16.

29. Paul A. Sabatier, "An Advocacy Coalition Framework of Policy Change and the Role of Policy-Oriented Learning Therein," *Policy Sciences* 21 (1988): 129–68; Paul A. Sabatier and Hank Jenkins-Smith, eds., *Policy Change and Learning: An Advocacy Coalition Approach* (Boulder, Colo.: Westview Press, 1993).

30. Sabatier, "Advocacy Coalition Framework," 138–39.

31. Paul A. Sabatier, "Policy Change over a Decade or More," in Sabatier and Jenkins-Smith, eds., *Policy Change and Learning*, 19.

32. Sabatier, "An Advocacy Coalition Framework," 149–56.

33. This brief review of the literature is not meant to be comprehensive, but rather summarizes some of the key relevant literature.

34. See, for example, Emily D. Cahan, *Past Caring: A History of U.S. Preschool Care and Education for the Poor, 1820–1965* (New York: National Center for Children in Poverty, 1989); Ann Mitchell, Michelle Seligman, and Fern Marx, *Early Childhood Programs and the Public Schools* (Dover, Mass.: Auburn House, 1989); Barbara Beatty, *Preschool Education in America: The Culture of Young Children from the Colonial Era to the Present* (New Haven, Conn.: Yale

University Press, 1993); and Margaret O'Brien Steinfels, *Who's Minding the Children: A History and Politics of Day Care in America* (New York: Simon and Schuster, 1973), which discusses the politics of child care in the late 1960s and early 1970s.

35. Michel, *Children's Interests/Mother's Rights.*

36. Gilbert Y. Steiner, *The Children's Cause* (Washington, D.C.: Brookings Institution, 1976); Gilbert Y. Steiner, *The Futility of Family Policy* (Washington, D.C.: Brookings Institution, 1981).

37. Marion Frances Berry, *The Politics of Parenthood: Child Care, Women's Rights, and the Myth of the Good Mother* (New York: Viking, 1993).

38. Abbie Gordon Klein, *The Debate over Child Care: 1969–1990* (Albany: State University of New York Press, 1992).

39. Alfred J. Kahn and Sheila B. Kamerman, *Child Care: Facing the Hard Choices* (Dover, Mass.: Auburn House, 1987).

40. Sheila B. Kamerman and Alfred J. Kahn, "Innovations in Toddler Day Care and Family Support Services: An International Overview, *Child Welfare* 74, no. 6 (1995): 1281–1300; Sheila Kamerman and Alfred J. Kahn, "The Possibilities for Child and Family Policy: A Cross-National Perspective," in Frank J. Macchiarola and Alan Gartner, eds., *Caring for Our Children: Proceedings of the Academy of Political Science* 37 (1989): 84–98.

41. Sheila B. Kamerman and Alfred J. Kahn, eds., *Family Change and Family Policies in Great Britain, Canada, New Zealand, and the United States* (New York: Oxford University Press, 1997). A second volume on family policy in Europe is to follow.

42. Ibid., 3–28.

43. See, for example, Edward F. Zigler and Meryl Frank, eds., *The Parental Leave Crisis: Toward a National Policy* (New Haven, Conn.: Yale University Press, 1988); Edward F. Zigler and Edmund W. Gordon, *Day Care: Scientific and Social Policy Issues* (Dover, Mass.: Auburn House, 1982); Edward F. Zigler and Susan Muenchow, *Head Start: The Inside Story of America's Most Successful Educational Experiment* (New York: HarperCollins, 1992); and Edward F. Zigler and Mary E. Lang, *Child Care Choices: Balancing the Needs of Children, Families, and Society* (New York: Free Press, 1991). Other articles by Zigler are cited throughout this book.

44. William T. Gormley Jr., *Everybody's Children: Child Care as a Public Problem* (Washington, D.C.: Brookings Institution, 1995); William Gormley Jr., "Regulating Child Care Quality," *Annals of American Academy of Political and Social Science* 563 (May 1999): 116–29.

45. Among some of the classics relevant to this work are Barbara Nelson, *Making an Issue of Child Abuse* (Chicago: University of Chicago Press, 1984); Eric Redman, *The Dance of Legislation* (New York: Simon and Schuster, 1973);

and Eugene Eidenberg and Roby D. Morey, *An Act of Congress: The Legislative Process and the Making of Education Policy* (New York: Norton, 1969).

46. Theodore R. Marmor, *The Politics of Medicare*, 2d ed. (New York: De Gruyter, 2000).

47. James G. March and Johan P. Olsen, *Rediscovering Institutions: The Organizational Basis of Politics* (New York: Free Press, 1989), 1–2.

48. B. Guy Peters, *Institutional Theory in Political Science: The "New Institutionalism"* (London: Pinter, 1999), 3–11.

49. Ibid., 12.

50. Ibid., 16, citing James G. March and Johan P. Olsen, "The New Institutionalism: Organizational Factors in Political Life," *American Political Science Review* 78 (1984): 738–49.

51. Steven Steinmo and Jon Watts, "It's the Institutions, Stupid! Why Comprehensive National Health Insurance Always Fails in America," *Journal of Health Politics, Policy, and Law* 20, no. 2 (1995): 336; Karen Orren and Stephen Skowronek, "Beyond the Iconography of Order: Notes for a 'New Institutionalism,'" in Lawrence C. Dodd and Calvin Jillson, eds., *The Dynamics of American Politics: Approaches and Interpretations* (Boulder, Colo.: Westview Press, 1994), 311–30, esp. 315–16.

52. Paul Pierson, "Increasing Returns, Path Dependence, and the Study of Politics," *American Political Science Review* 94, no. 2 (2000): 252.

53. Sven H. Steinmo, "American Exeptionalism Reconsidered: Culture or Institutions?" in Dodd and Jillson, eds., *Dynamics of American Politics*, 106–31.

54. Steinmo and Watts, "It's the Institutions," 333.

55. Ibid., 336, quoting Ellen M. Immergut, *Health Politics: Interests and Institutions in Western Europe* (New York: Cambridge University Press, 1992), xiii.

56. Baumgartner and Jones, *Agendas and Instability*, 12.

57. Robert K. Yin, *Case Study Research: Design and Methods*, 2d ed. (Thousand Oaks, Calif.: Sage, 1994), 4–9.

58. The author developed an interview guide for the semistructured interviews and modified it, depending on the interviewees' roles and the need to obtain specific data from certain individuals. Having a core set of questions enhanced reliability (repeatability) and validity (accuracy) of the interview data.

59. Linda T. Kohn, *Methods in Case Study Analysis*, Technical Publications, no. 2 (Washington, D.C.: Center for Studying Health System Change, June 1997), 7.

60. All the interviews conducted between 1996 and 1999 followed a protocol approved by the Yale University School of Nursing Human Subjects Research Review Committee.

61. For further discussions of interviewing politicians and deciding whether or not to tape-record, see Richard E. Fenno Jr., *Watching Politicians: Essays on Participant Observation* (Berkeley, Calif.: Institute of Government Studies, 1990),

81–93, and Robert L. Peabody et al., "Interviewing Political Elites," *PS: Political Science and Politics* 22, no. 3 (1999): 451–55.

2. Politics of Child Care Legislation, 1971

1. Throughout this book, child care advocates include the many legislators, organizations, and individuals who lobbied for federal (and state) funding of child care programs.
2. Margaret O'Brien Steinfels, *Who's Minding the Children: A History and Politics of Day Care in America* (New York: Simon and Schuster, 1973), 34–68; Sonya Michel, *Children's Interests/Mother's Rights: The Shaping of America's Child Care Policy* (New Haven, Conn.: Yale University Press, 1999), 50–117. For an excellent history of child care in Philadelphia between 1890 and 1960 and its linkage to national developments, see Elizabeth Rose, *A Mother's Job: The History of Day Care, 1890–1960* (New York: Oxford University Press, 1998).
3. Geraldine Youcha, *Minding the Children: Child Care in American from Colonial Times to the Present* (New York: Scribner, 1995), 30.
4. Ibid., 34.
5. Robert Melvin Tank, *Young Children, Families, and Society in America Since the 1820s: The Evolution of Health Education and Child Care Programs for Preschool Children* (Ann Arbor: University Microfilms International, 1980), 356–59.
6. Howard Dratch, "The Politics of Child Care in the 1940s," *Science and Society* 38, no. 2 (summer 1974): 169.
7. Ibid., 170–75.
8. For a description of the Lanham Act and early federal involvement in day care, see Sheila Rothman, "Other People's Children: The Day Care Experience in America," *Public Interest* 30 (winter 1973): 21; Steinfels, *Who's Minding the Children*, 66–67.
9. Dratch, "Politics of Child Care," 176; Michel, *Children's Interests/Mother's Rights*, 134–48.
10. Tank, *Young Children, Families, and Society*, 389
11. Susan E. Riley, "Caring for Rosie's Children: Federal Child Care Policies in the World War II Era," *Policy* 26 (1994): 663, citing U.S. House, Committee on Public Buildings and Grounds, *Hearings on H.R. 3178 and H.R. 3278 . . .* , 79th Cong., 1st sess., 16, 22 May 1945, 44.
12. Dratch, "Politics of Child Care," 179; Michel, *Children's Interests/Mother's Rights*, 136–37.
13. Dratch, "Politics of Child Care," 174, 176–77; Michel, *Children's Interests/Mother's Rights*, 134.

14. Youcha, *Minding the Children*, 312.

15. Tank, *Young Children Families, and Society*, 387; Gilbert Y. Steiner, *The Children's Cause* (Washington, D.C.: Brookings Institution, 1976), 387–88.

16. Steiner, *Children's Cause*, 18.

17. U.S. Department of Labor, Women's Bureau, *Working Women and Their Children* (Washington, D.C.: Government Printing Office, 1977), 40.

18. For a thorough discussion of the 1960 White House Conference on Children and Youth and other organizing activities of the public and private sector pertaining to child care in the 1950s and 1960s, see Michel, *Children's Interests/Mother's Rights*, 192–229

19. Steiner, *Children's Cause*, 21; Michel, *Children's Interests/Mother's Rights*, 229–31.

20. Steiner, *Children's Cause*, 21–22.

21. Wilbur J. Cohen and Robert M. Ball, "The Public Welfare Amendments of 1962," *Public Welfare* 20, no. 4 (1962): 191–233.

22. U.S. Department of Labor, Women's Bureau, *A Report of a Consultation on Working Women and Day Care Needs* (Washington, D.C.: Government Printing Office, 1 June 1967), 34, box 148, folder: Child Care Services/Day Care Centers, Albert Quie Papers, Minnesota Historical Society, Minneapolis.

23. U.S. House, Select Subcommittee on Education of the Committee on Education and Labor, *Comprehensive Preschool Education and Child Day Care Act of 1969: Hearings on H.R. 13520*, 91st Cong., 1st and 2d sess., 18, 20 November; 1–4, 9, 10, 16 December 1969; 25, 26 February; 2, 3, 4 March (Washington, D.C.); 21, 23 February 1970 (Chicago), 215.

24. White House Conference on Children, *Report to the President* (Washington, D.C.: Government Printing Office, 1970), 423.

25. For examples of expert testimony presented on child development, see U.S. Senate, Subcommittee on Employment, Manpower, and Poverty of the Committee on Labor and Public Welfare, *Headstart Child Development Act: Hearings on S. 2060*, part 1, 91st Cong., 1st sess., 4–6 August 1969, 71–105, and U.S. House, Select Subcommittee on Education of the Committee on Education and Labor, *Comprehensive Preschool Education and Child Day Care Act of 1969: Hearings on H.R. 13520*, 146–65, 336–44, 538–57, 592–600.

26. Edward Zigler and Karen Anderson, "An Idea Whose Time Had Come: The Intellectual and Political Climate," in Edward Zigler and Jeanette Valentine, eds., *Project Head Start* (New York: Free Press, 1979), 3–19.

27. U.S. House, Committee on Ways and Means, *1998 Green Book*, 105th Cong., 2d sess., 19 May 1998, 661.

28. U.S. Department of Labor, Women's Bureau, *Working Mothers and the Need for Child Care Services* (Washington, D.C.: Department of Labor, 1968), ii, 14–15, 19.

29. Margaret Malone, *Federal Involvement in Day Care* (Washington, D.C.: Library of Congress, Legislative Reference Service, 3 March 1969), 34, box 157, folder: QF, Select Committee on Child Development, Quie Papers.

30. U.S. House, Select Subcommittee on Education of the Committee on Education and Labor, *Comprehensive Preschool Education and Child Day Care Act of 1969: Hearings on H.R. 13520*, 704–11; U.S. Senate, Subcommittee on Employment, Manpower, and Poverty and the Subcommittee on Children of the Committee on Labor and Public Welfare, *Comprehensive Child Development Act of 1971: Hearings on S. 1512*, part 2, 92d Cong., 1st sess., 25, 26 May 1971, 433–520.

31. U.S. Senate, Subcommittee on Employment, Manpower, and Poverty and the Subcommittee on Children of the Committee on Labor and Public Welfare, *Comprehensive Child Development Act of 1971: Hearings on S. 1512*, 440–47.

32. "NOW Statement on Child Care Day Centers, 1967," in "Compilation of NOW Positions on Child Care," 1967–88, courtesy of NOW, Washington, D.C.

33. Mary Keyserling, *Windows on Day Care* (New York: National Council of Jewish Women, 1972).

34. Anne N. Costain, *Inviting Women's Rebellion: A Political Process Interpretation of the Women's Movement* (Baltimore: Johns Hopkins University Press, 1992).

35. M. Margaret Conway, David W. Ahern, and Gertrude A. Steuernagel, *Women and Public Policy: A Revolution in Progress*, 2d ed. (Washington, D.C.: Congressional Quarterly Press, 1999), 152; Sheila B. Kamerman, "Child Care Services: An Issue of Gender Equity and Women's Solidarity," *Child Welfare* 64 (May–June 1985): 260, 268–69.

36. Calvin Tomkins, "Profiles: A Sense of Urgency," *New Yorker*, 27 March 1989, 63.

37. Dona Copper Hamilton and Charles V. Hamilton, *The Dual Agenda* (New York: Columbia University Press, 1997).

38. Tomkins, "Profiles," 63

39. John C. Donovan, *Politics of Poverty*, 2d ed. (Indianapolis: Pegasus, 1973), 83–85.

40. U.S. Senate, Subcommittee on Employment, Manpower, and Poverty and the Subcommittee on Children of the Committee on Labor and Public Welfare, *Comprehensive Child Development Act of 1971*, 524.

41. "Nixon Wins by Narrow Electoral, Popular Vote Margin; GOP Gains Governors; Democrats Hold Senate and House," *Congressional Quarterly Almanac, 1968* (Washington, D.C.: Congressional Quarterly Service, 1968), 943–44.

42. In 1969 the composition of Congress was House: 243 Democrats and 192 Republicans; Senate: 57 Democrats and 43 Republicans. In 1971 the composition was House: 254 Democrats and 180 Republicans; Senate: 54 Democrats and 44 Republicans.

43. John Brademas, *The Politics of Education* (Norman: University of Oklahoma Press, 1987), 35.

44. U.S. House, Select Subcommittee on Education of the Committee on Education and Labor, *Hearings on the Preschool Centers Supplementary Education Act, H.R. 10572*, 90th Cong., 2d sess., 28, 29 February; 15 June 1968, 6–7.

45. Representative Patsy T. Mink, interview by author, Washington, D.C., 2 March 1992.

46. Brademas, *Politics of Education*, 7.

47. U.S. House, Select Subcommittee on Education of the Committee on Education and Labor, *Comprehensive Preschool Education and Child Day Care Act of 1969: Hearings on H.R. 13520*, 1.

48. Ibid., 1–7.

49. Jack Duncan, telephone interview by author, 18 September 1991.

50. Martin LaVor, interviews by author, 1 June 1992 (telephone) and Washington, D.C., 15 June 1992.

51. U.S. House, Select Subcommittee on Education of the Committee on Education and Labor, *Comprehensive Preschool Education and Child Day Care Act of 1969: Hearings on H.R. 13520*, 9–17, 146–74, 815–27.

52. John Iglehart, "Welfare Report/Congress Presses Major Child-Care Program Despite White House Veto Threat," *National Journal* 3 (23 October 1971): 2129.

53. Representative John Dellenback, letter to Secretary Robert Finch, 18 February 1970, tab C of memo from Elliot Richardson to John Ehrlichman, 15 November 1971, box 52, WHCF [EX] WE10, The Nixon Project, National Archives and Records Administration, Alexandria, Va. (hereafter referred to as the Nixon Presidential Materials Staff).

54. John C. Whitaker, "Nixon's Domestic Policy: Both Liberal and Bold in Retrospect," *Presidential Studies Quarterly* 26, no. 1 (winter 1996): 137; Daniel P. Moynihan, *The Politics of a Guaranteed Income: The Nixon Administration and the Family Assistance Plan* (New York: Vintage Books, 1973), 533–34.

55. Dellenback, letter to Finch, 18 February 1970.

56. Martha Phillips, telephone interview by author, 4 December 1991.

57. U.S. House, Select Subcommittee on Education of the Committee on Education and Labor, *Comprehensive Preschool Education and Child Day Care Act of 1969: Hearings on H.R. 13520*, 827.

58. Ibid., 826–28.

59. Phillips, interview.

60. *Congressional Record*, 92d Cong., 1st sess., 30 September 1971, 34285; Martin L. LaVor, "Time and Circumstances," in Fred Weintraub, ed., *Public Policy in the Education of Exceptional Children* (Reston, Va.: Council for Exceptional Children, 1976), 297.

61. *Congressional Record*, 92d Cong., 1st sess., 30 September 1971, 34285.

62. Phillips, interview.

63. Brademas, *Politics of Education*, 41.

64. "Additional Views," drafted by Martin LaVor for Representative Quie, box 157, folder: QF Select Committee on Child Development, Quie Papers.

65. U.S. Senate, Subcommittee on Employment, Manpower, and Poverty of the Committee on Labor and Public Welfare, *Headstart Child Development Act: Hearings on H.R. 2060*, 91st Cong., 1st sess., 15.

66. Walter F. Mondale, letter to Marian Wright Edelman, 15 January 1971, box 32, envelope: 1971, Correspondence; Subcommittee on Children and Youth, Walter F. Mondale Papers, Minnesota Historical Society, Minneapolis.

67. U.S. Senate, Select Committee on Equal Educational Opportunity, *Justice for Children*, 92d Cong., 2d sess., June 1972, Committee Print. This was originally a speech Mondale gave to the Senate on December 9, 1970, addressing the nation's failure to meet the needs of its children.

68. U.S. House, *Conference Report to Accompany S. 2007: Economic Opportunity Amendments of 1971*, 92d Cong., 1st sess., 29 November 1971, 62.

69. Ibid., 61–75.

70. *Congressional Record*, 92d Cong., 1st sess., 2 December 1971, 44446–47, reprint of James J. Kilpatrick, "'Child Development Act' Called Scheme to Sovietize U.S. Youth," *Spokane Daily Chronicle*, 25 October 1971.

71. *Congressional Record*, 92d Cong., 1st sess., 5 November 1971, 39530–33; *Congressional Record*, 92d Cong., 1st sess., 2 December 1971, 44443–48.

72. *Congressional Record*, 92d Cong., 1st sess., 2 December 1971, 44122.

73. *Congressional Record*, 92d Cong., 1st sess., 1 November 1971, 38608.

74. LaVor, interview, 15 June 1992.

75. *Congressional Record*, 92d Cong., 1st sess., 7 December 1971, 45071.

76. Edward Zigler, interview by author, New Haven, Conn., 13 November 1991.

77. Charles A. Byrley, letter to Congressman Albert Quie, 9 June 1971, box 61, folder: Legislation: Education and Labor Committee, Preschool, Quie Papers.

78. Governor Arch A. Moore Jr., telegram to the Honorable Richard M. Nixon, 19 October 1971, [EX] WE, box 25, Children 1/1/71–12/31/72, Nixon Presidential Materials Staff.

79. For example, see Robert Docking, governor of Kansas, telegram to Representative Albert H. Quie, n.d., box 61, folder: Legislation: Education and Labor Committee, Preschool, Quie Papers; Marvin Mandel, letter to all governors, 30 November 1971, box 61, folder: Legislation: Education and Labor Committee, Preschool, Quie Papers.

80. Richard B. Ogilvie, telegram to President Nixon, 1 December 1971, box 25, Children 11/1/71–12/3/72, [EX]WE1, Nixon Presidential Materials Staff.

81. "Special Message to the Congress on the Nation's Antipoverty Programs," 19 February 1969, in *Public Papers of the Presidents of the United States: Richard Nixon, 1969* (Washington, D.C.: Government Printing Office, 1971), 114.
82. Ibid., 270.
83. Ibid., 270–71; John Ehrlichman, memo to the president, 16 August 1969, box 1, [EX] FG 23, WHCF, Nixon Presidential Materials Staff.
84. Checker Finn, memo to Daniel Patrick Moynihan, 19 August 1969, box 1, [EX] FG 23, WHCF, Nixon Presidential Materials Staff.
85. For Zigler's perspective on his appointment, see Edward Zigler and Susan Muenchow, *Head Start: the Inside Story of America's Most Successful Educational Experiment* (New York: HarperCollins, 1992), 74–80.
86. Checker Finn, memo to Daniel Patrick Moynihan, 2 October 1969, box 1, [EX] FG 23, WHCF, Nixon Presidential Materials Staff.
87. Victor G. Cicirelli, *The Impact of Head Start: An Evaluation of the Effects of Head Start on Children's Cognitive and Affective Development* (Athens, Ohio, and New York: Ohio University Press and Westinghouse Learning Corporation, 1969).
88. Zigler and Muenchow, *Head Start*, 65–73.
89. Jack Rosenthal, "Vast Plan for Health, Educational, and Social Service to Children Gains in Congress," *New York Times*, 14 June 1971, 22.
90. Iglehart, "Welfare Report," 2126.
91. Ibid.
92. Ibid., 2127.
93. U.S. Senate, Subcommittee on Employment, Manpower, and Poverty and the Subcommittee on Children and Youth of the Committee on Labor and Public Welfare, *Comprehensive Child Development Act of 1971: Hearings on S. 1512*, 762, 856–60.
94. "Child Development in Danger . . . ," editorial, *New York Times*, 29 November 1971, 38.
95. Child Development-Coordination Section, 14 October 1971, box 157, folder: QF, Select Committee on Child Development, Quie Papers.
96. Edwin L. Harper, "Domestic Policy Making in the Nixon White House: An Evolving Process," *Presidential Studies Quarterly* 26, no. 1 (winter 1996): 41–56, quote on 45; see also 46.
97. Betty Glad and Dwight Ink, "President Nixon's Inner Circle of Advisers," *Presidential Studies Quarterly* 26, no. 1 (winter 1996): 13–40.
98. Paul O'Neill, memo to Kenneth Cole, 6 October 1971, box 52, [EX] WE 10, WHCF, Nixon Presidential Materials Staff.
99. Patrick J. Buchanan, memo to John Ehrlichman and Kenneth Cole, 12 October 1971, box 52 [EX] WE 10, WHCF, Nixon Presidential Materials Staff.
100. Kenneth Cole, memo to John Ehrlichman, 2 November 1971, box 25, [EX] WE 1, WHCF, Nixon Presidential Materials Staff.

101. John Ehrlichman, memo to the president, 15 November 1971; John Ehrlich-
     man, memo to Dwight Chapin, 6 November 1971; John Ehrlichman, schedule
     proposal via Dwight Chapin, 28 September 1971, box 4, [EX] FG 23, WHCF,
     Nixon Presidential Materials Staff.

102. Ehrlichman, memo to the president, 15 November 1971, tab A. The archival
     records do not include the name of the person who wrote the paper, and it is
     unclear if Richardson knew the author.

103. In August 1969 Nixon announced a plan to restructure major domestic pro-
     grams, granting local entities funding for and control over certain functions.
     Richard P. Nathan, "A Retrospective on Richard M. Nixon's Domestic Poli-
     cies," *Presidential Studies Quarterly* 26, no. 1 (winter 1996): 155–64.

104. Ehrlichman, memo to the president, 15 November 1971, Tab B.

105. Ibid.

106. Elliot Richardson, memo to John Ehrlichman, 15 November 1971, box 52,
     [EX] WE 10, WHCF, Nixon Presidential Materials Staff.

107. Ehrlichman, memo to the president, 15 November 1971.

108. John Ehrlichman, memo for the president's file, 3 January 1972, re: Reporting
     on Meeting with Richardson, 15 November 1971, box 4, [EX] FG 23, WHCF,
     Nixon Presidential Materials Staff.

109. Patrick J. Buchanan, memo to H. R. Haldeman, John Ehrlichman, and Ken-
     neth Cole, 17 November 1971, box 86, folder: November 1971, H. R. Halde-
     man, WHSF-SMOF, Nixon Presidential Materials Staff.

110. Patrick J. Buchanan, memo to H. R. Haldeman, 9 December 1971, box 87,
     folder: Buchanan 1971, H. R. Haldeman, WHSF-SMOF, Nixon Presidential
     Materials Staff.

111. Glad and Ink, "President Nixon's Inner Circle," 15, quoted in Stephen Hess,
     Organizing the Presidency, 2d ed. (Washington, D.C.: Brookings Institution,
     1988), 111–12.

112. Buchanan, memo to Haldeman, 9 December 1971.

113. Patrick J. Buchanan, memo to Richard Nixon, 6 January 1971, box 9, folder:
     January 1971, Press Office files, President's Handwriting, WHSF, Nixon Pres-
     idential Materials Staff.

114. P. J. Buchanan, draft message, OEO-Legal Services-Child Development, 8
     December 1971, box 87, folder: Buchanan 1971, H. R. Haldeman, WHSF-
     SMOF, Nixon Presidential Materials Staff; (Andrews) RP veto message,
     OEO-Legal Services-Child Development, 8 December 1971, box 87, folder:
     Buchanan 1971, H. R. Haldeman, WHSF-SMOF, Nixon Presidential Ma-
     terials Staff.

115. "Veto of the Economic Opportunity Amendments of 1971," 10 December
     1971, in *Public Papers of the Presidents of the United States: Richard Nixon,
     1971* (Washington, D.C.: Government Printing Office, 1972), 1174–78.

116. Ibid.

117. Ibid.

118. "White House Press Conference of Frank Carlucci and Stephen Kurzman," 9 December 1971, attachment to memo from Paul O'Neill to Ray Price, 3 December 1971, box 53, folder 12/1/71–12/31/71, [EX] WE 10, WHCF, Nixon Presidential Materials Staff.

119. Steiner, *Children's Cause*, 115; Phillips, interview.

120. See, for example, Walter F. Mondale, *The Accountability of Power* (New York: McKay, 1975), 78–104.

3. From Political Stalemate to Welfare Entitlement, 1972–1988

1. Senate, Subcommittee on Children and Youth and Subcommittee on Employment, Manpower, and Poverty of the Committee on Labor and Public Welfare, *Headstart, Child Development Legislation, 1972*, 92d Cong., 2d sess., 27 March 1972; *Congressional Record*, 92d Cong., 2d sess., 20 January 1972, 629; *Congressional Record*, 92d Cong., 2d sess., 17 February 1972, 4295–96; *Congressional Record*, 92d Cong., 2d sess., 19 June 1972, 21390; *Congressional Record*, 92d Cong., 2d sess., 20 June 1972, 21566–71, 21584–85.

2. U.S. House, Committee on Education and Labor, *Economic Opportunity Act Amendments of 1972: Report to Accompany H.R. 12350*, 92d Cong., 2d sess., 4 February 1972, 82–84.

3. *Congressional Record*, 92d Cong., 2d sess., 17 February 1972, 4296–17.

4. U.S. Senate, Committee on Labor and Public Welfare, *American Families: Trends and Pressures, 1973*, 93rd Cong., 1st sess., 24–26 September 1973.

5. A. Sidney Johnson III, letter to Marian Wright Edelman, 31 May 1973, box 32 folder: CD17 Family Hearings, Walter F. Mondale Papers, Minnesota Historical Society, Minneapolis.

6. Sidney Johnson III, memo to Senator Mondale re: Wedneady's [sic] Breakfast Meeting re. Child Development, 18 December 1973, box 32, folder: ASJ Memos to Senator, June–October, Mondale Papers.

7. U.S. Senate, Subcommittee on Children of the Committee on Labor and Public Welfare, and House, Select Subcommittee on Education of the Committee on Education and Labor, *Joint Hearings on the Child and Family Services Act, 1974*, 93d Cong., 2d sess., 8, 9 August 1974.

8. U.S. House, Subcommittee on Select Education of the Committee on Education and Labor, and U.S. Senate, Subcommittee on Children and Youth and the Subcommittee on Employment, Poverty, and Migratory Labor of the Committee on Labor and Public Welfare, *Child and Family Services Act, 1975: Joint Hearings on S. 626 and H.R. 2966*, parts 1–9, 94th Cong., 1st sess., 20, 21

February; 12, 13 March; 25–26 April (Montpelier, Vt.); 5, 16, 20 June; 15 July 1975.

9.   The leaflet and other pertinent materials can be found in House, Subcommittee on Select Education of the Committee on Education and Labor, *Background Materials Concerning Child and Family Services Act, 1975*, H.R. 2966, 94th Cong., 2d sess., December 1976.

10. *Congressional Record*, 94th Cong., 1st sess., 12 December 1975, 40373.

11. U.S. House, Subcommittee on Select Education of the Committee on Education and Labor, *Background Materials Concerning Child and Family Services Act, 1975*, H.R. 2966, 158–60; copies of letters are on 83–84 as well as in box 94, folder: Child and Family Services Act, Albert H. Quie Papers, Minnesota Historical Society, Minneapolis.

12. Linda Bird Francke, with Diana Camper, "Child Care Scare," *Newsweek*, 5 April 1976, 77; Senators Jacob Javits and Harrison Williams, letter to Honorable Howard Cannon, 4 May 1976, box 1788, folder: Children-General, part 1, Mondale Papers.

13. John Brademas, interview by author, New York, 18 July 1991.

14. U.S. House Committee on Education and Labor, Subcommittee on Select Education, and Senate, Committee on Labor and Public Welfare, Subcommittee on Children and Youth and the Subcommittee on Employment, Poverty, and Migratory Labor, *Child and Family Services Act, 1975: Joint Hearings on S. 626 and H.R. 2966*, part 7, 5, 16 June 1975, 1200.

15. Ibid., 1235.

16. Ibid., 1971.

17. Ibid., 144.

18. Ibid., 191, 1200, 1973. See, for example, testimony presented by the Child Welfare League of America, American Federation of Teachers, and American Federation of State, County, and Municipal Employees in U.S. House and Senate subcommittees.

19. U.S. Senate, Subcommittee on Child and Human Development of the Committee on Labor and Human Resources, *Hearings on Child Care and Child Development Programs, 1977–78*, part 1, 95th Cong., 1st sess., 25 November 1977 (San Francisco); 12 December 1977 (Los Angeles), 1.

20. U.S. Senate, Subcommittee on Child and Human Development of the Committee on Human Resources, *Child Care and Child Development Programs Part 2*, 95th Cong., 2d sess., 8 February 1978 (Washington, D.C.), 696–736, 875.

21. James Kilpatrick, "Launching Another Disaster," *San Francisco Chronicle*, 1 March 1979.

22. Susanne Martinez, interview by author, Washington, D.C., 29 August 1991.

23. "Anatomy of a Failed Legislative Effort: Why and How Cranston Bill Was Withdrawn," *Day Care and Child Development Reports* 8 (26 March 1979): 5–8.

24. Martinez, interview.

25. U.S. Senate, Subcommittee on Child and Human Development of the Committee on Labor and Human Resources, *Hearings on the Child Care Act of 1979*, 96th Cong., 1st sess., 6, 20 February 1979, 221–23.

26. Martinez, interview.

27. "Anatomy of a Failed Legislative Effort," 8.

28. Martinez, interview.

29. Peggy Daly Pizzo, telephone interview by author, 11 November 1992.

30. Suzanne H. Woolsey, "Pied Piper Politics and the Child-Care Debate," *Daedalus* 106 (1977): 143.

31. Lynne M. Casper, Mary Hawkins, and Martin O'Connell, *Who's Minding the Kids? Child Care Arrangements: Fall 1991*, Bureau of the Census, Current Population Reports, P70-35 (Washington, D.C.: Government Printing Office, 1994), 7.

32. Pizzo, interview.

33. Ibid.

34. U.S. Senate, Subcommittee on Child and Human Development of the Committee on Labor and Human Resources, *Hearings on the Child Care Act of 1979*, 238.

35. Pizzo, interview.

36. Charles O. Jones, *The Trusteeship Presidency* (Baton Rouge: Louisiana State University Press, 1988), 124.

37. Stuart E. Eizenstat, quoted in Erwin C. Hargrove, *Jimmy Carter as President: Leadership and the Politics of the Public Good* (Baton Rouge: Louisiana State University Press, 1988), 36.

38. Stuart E. Eizenstat, "President Jimmy Carter, the Democratic Party, and Domestic Policy" (paper presented at Hofstra University, Hempstead, N.Y., 15 November 1990), 19–20.

39. Stuart E. Eizenstat, interview by author, Washington, D.C., 30 October 1992.

40. Most of the information presented here on the FIDCR is based on the detailed history in John R. Nelson, Jr., "The Federal Interagency Day Care Requirements," in Cheryl D. Hayes, ed., *Making Policies for Children* (Washington, D.C.: National Academy Press, 1982), 151–205.

41. Ibid., 169.

42. Ibid., 171.

43. Ibid., 171, 169.

44. U.S. Department of Health, Education, and Welfare, "HEW Day Care Requirements: Proposed Rules; Public Meetings," *Federal Register* 44, no. 14 (15 June 1979): 34754.

45. See, for example, PL. 94-120, P.L. 94-401, and P.L. 95-171; Department of Health, Education, and Welfare, *The Appropriateness of Federal Interagency Day Care Requirements: Report of Findings and Recommendations* (Washington, D.C.: Government Printing Office, 1978), 251.

46. U.S. Department of Health, Education, and Welfare, *Appropriateness of Federal Interagency Day Care Requirements*; Abt Associates, *Children at the Center: Final Report of the National Day Care Study* (Cambridge, Mass.: Abt Associates, 1979).

47. U.S. Department of Health, Education, and Welfare, "HEW Day Care Requirements," 34754–81.

48. Advocates for Children of New York and others, letter to Secretary Harris, 13 September 1979, CY, 1–3, FIDCR, box 12/69, DHHS/OS/IS Official Correspondence 1979, HHS Archives, Suitland, Md.

49. American Academy of Child Psychiatrists and others, letter to Secretary Harris, 8 August 1979, C-Y, 1–3, FIDCR, box 12/69, DHHS/OS/IS Official Correspondence, HHS Archives.

50. Nelson, "Federal Interagency Requirements," 194–96.

51. Patricia Roberts Harris, letter to the Honorable Jim Sasser, September 1979, FIDCR folder, box 12/69, DHHS/OS/IS 1979, Official Correspondence 1979, HEW Archives, Suitland, Md.

52. Peter Libassi, note to Hale Champion, n.d., personal papers of Peter Libassi, FIDCR folder, Yale University, New Haven, Conn.

53. U.S. Department of Health, Education, and Welfare, "Day Care Regulations, Final Rule," *Federal Register* 45, no. 55 (19 March 1980): 17870–85.

54. Pizzo, interview.

55. Eizenstat, interview.

56. *Congressional Record*, 96th Cong., 2d sess., 30 June 1980, 17891.

57. Eleven senators did not vote. *Congressional Record*, 96th Cong., 2d sess., 30 June 1980, 17886–92.

58. Deborah Philips and Edward Zigler, "The Checkered History of Federal Child Care Regulation," in Ernst Z. Rothkopf, ed., *Review of Research in Education* (Washington, D.C.: American Educational Research Association, 1987), 14:21.

59. U.S. House, Committee on Ways and Means, *1990 Green Book*, 101st Cong., 2d sess., 5 June 1990, 742–44.

60. Andrew Rich and R. Kent Weaver, "Advocates and Analysts: Think Tanks and the Politicization of Expertise," in Allan J. Cigler and Burdett A. Loomis, eds., *Interest Group Politics*, 5th ed. (Washington, D.C.: Congressional Quarterly Press, 1998): 235–53.

61. Ibid., 240.
62. Jack L. Walker Jr., *Mobilizing Interest Groups in America: Patrons, Professions, and Social Movements* (Ann Arbor: University of Michigan Press, 1991), 27–40; Kay Lehman Schlozman and John T. Tierney, *Organized Interests and American Democracy* (New York: HarperCollins, 1986), 74–82.
63. Walker, *Mobilizing Interest Groups in America*, 48–51.
64. For an excellent review of the literature on the rise of conservatism in the 1970s and 1980s, see William C. Berman, *America's Right Turn: From Nixon to Bush* (Baltimore: Johns Hopkins University Press, 1994), 171–73.
65. James A. Smith, *The Idea Brokers: Thanks Tanks and the Rise of the New Policy Elite* (New York: Free Press, 1991), 171–72.
66. Niels Bjerre-Poulsen, "The Heritage Foundation: A Second Generation Think Tank," *Journal of Policy History* 3, no. 2 (1991): 158–59.
67. Smith, *Idea Brokers*, 279, 199–201.
68. Bjerre-Poulsen, "Heritage Foundation," 158.
69. Ibid., 159.
70. Smith, *Idea Brokers*, 201.
71. Hilary Stout, "Behind the Scenes: GOP's Welfare Stance Owes a Lot to Prodding from Robert Rector," *Wall Street Journal*, 23 January 1995, 1, 10.
72. U.S. House, Subcommittee on Human Resources of the Committee on Ways and Means, *Hearings on How to Help the Working Poor and Problems of the Working Poor*, 101st Cong., 1st sess., 28 February; 21 March; 27 April 1989, 121–26; U.S. Senate, Subcommittee on Children, Family, Drugs, and Alcoholism of the Committee on Labor and Human Resources, *Hearings on the Act for Better Child Care Services of 1987*, 100th Cong., 2d sess., 15 March; 28 June 1988, 360–80.
73. Sally Covington, *Moving a Policy Agency: The Strategic Philanthropy of Conservative Foundations* (Washington, D.C.: National Committee for Responsive Philanthropy, 1997), 6.
74. Kevin P. Phillips, *Post-Conservative America: People, Politics, and Ideology in a Time of Crisis* (New York: Random House, 1982), 190.
75. Ibid., 184–86.
76. Ibid., 46–50.
77. E. J. Dionne Jr., *Why Americans Hate Politics* (New York: Simon and Schuster, 1991), 111.
78. Ibid., 294.
79. Ibid., 293.
80. "An Interview with Marian Wright Edelman," *Harvard Educational Review* 44 (February 1974): 53–54.
81. Calvin Tomkins, "Profiles: A Sense of Urgency," *New Yorker*, 27 March 1989, 67–68.

82. "Interview with Marian Wright Edelman," 54.

83. Ibid., 54–55.

84. *Children's Defense Fund Annual Report 1989* (Washington, D.C.: CDF, 1990).

85. Rochelle Beck, "The Child Care Policy Stalemate: An Analysis of Federal Policies and an Examination of Options for the 1980s" (Ed.D. diss., Harvard University, 1980), 121.

86. Elinor Guggenheimer, interview by author, New York, 9 March, 1992.

87. Ibid.

88. Ibid.

89. Elinor Guggenheimer, "President's Corner," *Child Care ActioNews* (September–October 1988): 2.

90. *Congressional Record*, 98th Cong., 1st sess., 21 June 1983, S8757–62.

91. Ibid., E32–33.

92. U.S. Senate, *School Facilities Child Care Act*, S. Rept. 98-494, 98th Cong., 2d sess., 25 May 1984, 18–20.

93. "New Programs Added to Head Start Bill," *Congressional Quarterly Almanac, 1984* (Washington, D.C.: Congressional Quarterly, 1985), 485–88.

94. *Congressional Record*, 99th Cong., 1st sess., 28 March 1985, S3670–82.

95. Susan DeConcini, telephone interview by author, 2 October 1991.

96. *Congressional Record*, 98th Cong., 1st sess., 14 November 1983, S16081–82.

97. *Congressional Record*, 99th Cong., 1st sess., 11 December 1985, H11839–43.

98. U.S. House, Committee on Ways and Means, *1998 Green Book*, 105th Cong., 2d sess., 19 May 1998, 678–81, 871–72.

99. In the first year when the DCTC was added to the IRS short form, the number of claimants increased by approximately 1 million, according to Nancy Duff Campbell, telephone interview by author, 13 March 2000.

100. Helen Blank, *Children and Federal Child Care Cuts: A National Survey of the Impact of Federal Title XX Cuts on State Child Care Systems, 1981–1983*, white paper (Washington, D.C.: Children's Defense Fund, 1983), 1–9.

101. U.S. House, Committee on Ways and Means, *1998 Green Book*, 724–25.

102. Joel F. Handler, *The Poverty of Welfare Reform* (New Haven, Conn.: Yale University Press, 1995), 61–62; "After Years of Debate, Welfare Reform Clears," *Congressional Quarterly Almanac, 1988* (Washington, D.C.: Congressional Quarterly, 1989), 349–64.

103. Linda E. Demkovich, "Welfare Reform: Can Carter Succeed Where Nixon Failed?" *National Journal* 9 (27 August 1977): 1331; Linda E. Demkovich, "A Job for Every Welfare Mother, But What About the Kids?" *National Journal* 10 (4 March 1978): 341; U.S. House, Welfare Reform Subcommittee of the Committee on Agriculture, Committee on Education and Labor, Committee on Ways and Means, *Joint Hearings on the Administration's Welfare Reform Proposal, H.R. 9030*, part 1, 95th Cong., 1st sess., 19, 20, 21 September 1977, 18–

22. For a detailed discussion of Carter's welfare program and why it ultimately failed, see David McKay, *Domestic Policy and Ideology: Presidents and the American State, 1964–1987* (Cambridge: Cambridge University Press, 1989), 112–20, and Hargrove, *Jimmy Carter as President*, 54–60.

104. Demkovich, "Job for Every Welfare Mother," 341.

105. Ibid., 341–43.

106. Franna Diamond of CDF, quoted in ibid., 342.

107. "Welfare Reform Stalled," *Congressional Quarterly Almanac, 1978* (Washington, D.C.: Congressional Quarterly, 1979), 600–603; "Welfare Reform," *Congressional Quarterly Almanac, 1979* (Washington, D.C.: Congressional Quarterly, 1980), 509–11.

108. Linda E. Demkovich, "Moynihan on Welfare: From FAP to the Carter Plan," *National Journal* 10, no. 4 (28 January 1978): 146–48.

109. U.S. Senate, Subcommittee on Social Security and Family Policy of the Committee on Finance, *Hearings on Welfare: Reform or Replacement (Child Support Enforcement)*, 100th Cong., 1st sess., 23 January; 2 February 1987, 172.

110. Bureau of the Census, *Statistical Abstracts of the United States, 1992*, 112th ed. (Washington, D.C.: Government Printing Office, 1992), 388.

111. U.S. House, Committee on Ways and Means, *1992 Green Book*, 102nd Cong, 2d sess, 15 May 1992, 1074, 1079; Bureau of Labor Statistics, *Working Women: A Chartbook* (Washington, D.C.: Government Printing Office, 1991), 49.

112. U.S. House, *Welfare Reform Act of 1987*, H. Rept. 100-159, part 2, 100th Cong., 1st sess., 7 August 1987, 100.

113. U.S. House, Committee on Education and Labor, *Hearings on Welfare Reform: H.R. 30, Fair Work Opportunities Act of 1987 and H.R. 1720, Family Welfare Reform Act of 1987*, 100th Cong., 1st sess., 29, 30 April; 5 May 1987, 64, 147.

114. Ibid., 331–32.

115. U.S. House, *Welfare Reform Act of 1987*, part 2, 101.

116. U.S. House, Committee on Education and Labor, *Hearings on Welfare Reform: H.R. 30 and H.R. 1720*, 426.

117. U.S. Senate, Subcommittee on Social Security and Family Policy of the Committee on Finance, *Hearings on Welfare: Reform or Replacement*, 421–22, 426.

118. Government Accounting Office, *Work and Welfare: Current AFDC Work Programs and Implications for Federal Policy*, GAO/HRD-87-34 (Washington, D.C.: GAO, 1987), 4.

119. U.S. House, Subcommittee on Public Assistance and Unemployment Compensation of the Committee on Ways and Means, *Hearings on Welfare Reform*, 100th Cong., 1st sess., 28 January; 19 February; 4, 6, 10, 11, 13 March 1987, 329–30.

120. U.S. House, Subcommittee on Public Assistance and Unemployment Compensation of the Committee on Ways and Means, *Hearings on the Family*

Welfare Reform Act (H.R. 1720), 100th Cong., 1st sess., 30 March; 1 April 1987, 251–54.

121. Ibid., 323–24.

122. Ibid., 327–35, 348.

123. U.S. House, Committee on Education and Labor, *Hearings on H.R. 30 and H.R. 1720*, 321.

124. Ibid., 323.

125. U.S. House, *Family Welfare Reform Act of 1987*, H. Rept. 100-159, part 1, 100th Cong., 1st sess., 17 June 1987, 46–47, 66–69.

126. U.S. House, *Family Welfare Reform Act of 1987*, part 2, 38–41.

127. "After Struggle, House Passes Welfare Reform," *Congressional Quarterly Almanac, 1987* (Washington, D.C.: Congressional Quarterly, 1988), 546–57; U.S. House, *Family Support Act of 1988, Conference Report to Accompany H.R. 1720*, H. Rept. 100-998, 100th Cong., 2d sess., 28 September 1988, 162–65.

128. U.S. House, *Family Support Act of 1988, Conference Report*, 162–65.

129. Ibid., 162.

130. "After Years of Debate, Welfare Reform Clears," 354.

131. Nancy Ebb, *Child Care Tradeoffs: States Make Painful Choices* (Washington, D.C.: Children's Defense Fund, 1994).

132. "After Years of Debate, Welfare Reform Clears," 361–63.

133. Campbell, interview; U.S. House, Committee on Ways and Means, *1998 Greenbook*, 874.

134. Deborah Rankin, "The Tough New Cutbacks in Child Care," *New York Times*, 18 December 1988, section 3, 9.

4. Politics of Child Care Legislation, 1987–1990

1.   Helen Blank, interview by author, Washington, D.C., 12 August 1991.

2.   See for example, U.S. House, Select Committee on Children, Youth, and Families, *Hearing on Child Care: Beginning a National Initiative*, 98th Cong., 2d sess., 4 April 1984; U.S. House, Select Committee on Children, Youth, and Families, *Hearing on Improving Child Care Services: What Can Be Done?*, 98th Cong., 2d sess., 6 September 1984; U.S. House, Select Committee on Children, Youth, and Families, *Hearing on Child Care: Key to Employment in a Changing Economy*, 100th Cong., 1st sess., 10 March 1987; U.S. House, Select Subcommittee on Children, Youth, and Families, *Report on Families and Child Care: Improving the Options*, 98th Cong., 2d sess., September 1984.

3.   Ann Rosewater, e-mail communication to author, 14 November 2000.

4.   Ann Rosewater, telephone interview by author, 7 January 1992.

5.   A review of coverage of child care in the *Readers' Guide to Periodical Literature* revealed an increase from nineteen to sixty-six articles between 1980 and 1986; Sally Solomon Cohen, "Politics of Child Care Legislation: 1970–1990" (Ph.D. diss., Columbia University, 1993, microfiche no. 6194), 467.

6.   Blank, interview.

7.   Act for Better Child Care, S. 1885, *Congressional Record*, 100th Cong., 1st sess., 19 November 1987, S16555.

8.   *Congressional Record*, 100th Cong., 1st sess., 19 November 1987, S16554–71; *Congressional Record*, 100th Cong., 1st sess., 20 November 1987, S16635.

9.   In 1994, Olympia Snowe was elected senator and has continued to fight for child care legislation, as discussed in subsequent chapters.

10.   See, for example, U.S. Senate, Subcommittee on Children, Family, Drugs, and Alcoholism of the Committee on Labor and Human Resources, *Act for Better Child Care Services of 1987*, 100th Cong., 2d sess., 15 March; 28 June 1988; U.S. House, Subcommittee on Human Resources of the Committee on Education and Labor, *H.R. 3660: The Act for Better Child Care Service*, 100th Cong., 2d sess., 25 February 1988; U.S. House, Subcommittee on Human Resources of the Committee on Education and Labor, *Child Care*, 100th Cong., 2d sess., 21 April 1988.

11.   Helen Blank, interview by author, Washington, D.C., 25 September 1992; Jane Seaberry, "Fun Fair Carries Serious Message," *Washington Post*, 25 June 1990; *Children's Defense Fund Annual Report* (Washington, D.C.: CDF, 1991), 19.

12.   Act for Better Child Care (S. 1885), see definition of eligible provider, section 3(6), *Congressional Record*, 100th Cong., 1st sess., 19 November 1987, S16555–62.

13.   Ellen E. Kisker et al., *A Profile of Child Care Settings: Early Education and Care in 1990*, report prepared by Mathematica Policy Research for the Department of Education (Washington, D.C.: Government Printing Office, 1991), 1:36.

14.   Blank, interview, 25 September 1992.

15.   U.S. House, Subcommittee on Human Resources of the Committee on Education and Labor, *Child Care*, 8–9.

16.   U.S. Senate, Committee on Labor and Human Resources, *Act for Better Child Care Services of 1988: Report to Accompany S. 1885*, S. Rept. 100-484, 100th Cong., 2d sess., 1 August 1988, 79–80.

17.   U.S. House, Subcommittee on Human Resources of the Committee on Education and Labor, *H.R. 3660: The Act for Better Child Care Service*, 49.

18.   Lee Boothby, "The Establishment and Free Exercise Clauses and Their Impact on National Child Care Legislation," *Harvard Journal on Legislation* 26 (summer 1989): 549–64; John W. Whitehead, "Accommodation and Equal Treatment of Religion: Federal Funding of Religiously Affiliated Child Care Facili-

ties," *Harvard Journal on Legislation* 26 (summer 1989): 573–90; Kenneth D. Wald, *Religion and Politics in the United States*, 3d ed. (Washington, D.C.: Congressional Quarterly Press, 1997), 73–123.

19. Act for Better Child Care, section 19, *Congressional Record*, 100th Cong., 1st sess., 19 November 1987, S16561.

20. According to the *Random House Dictionary of the English Language* (1966), a secularist is one who holds the "view that public education and other matters of civil policy should be conducted without the introduction of a religious element."

21. Kisker et al., *Profile of Child Care Settings*, 44.

22. Frank Monahan, telephone interview by author, 11 December 1991.

23. Marian Wright Edelman, memo to Members of the Alliance for Better Child Care, 12 February 1988, CDF files, Washington, D.C.

24. Gordon Ambach, executive director of the Council of Chief State School Officers, testimony in U.S. House, Committee on Education and Labor, *Hearings on Child Care*, 101st Cong., 1st sess., 9 February; 6 March; 5 April 1989, 168–215, esp. 207.

25. Helen Blank, memo to Members of the Alliance for Better Child Care, 18 April 1988, CDF files.

26. *Congressional Record*, 100th Cong., 2d sess., 8 June 1988, S744; U.S. Senate, Committee on Labor and Human Resources, *Act for Better Child Care Services of 1988: Report to Accompany S. 1885*, 77.

27. U.S. Senate, Subcommittee on Children, Family, Drugs, and Alcoholism of the Committee on Labor and Human Resources, *Act for Better Child Care Services of 1987*, 79.

28. Allan Carlson, "Taxation and the Family: Philosophical and Historical Considerations," *Insight* (Washington D.C.: Family Research Council, 1994); William R. Mattox Jr., "Tax Fairness for Families: A New Call for Pro-Child Tax Relief," *Family Policy* 4, no. 2 (1991): 1–7; U.S. House, Subcommittee on Public Assistance and Unemployment Compensation of the Committee on Ways and Means, *Hearing on the Child Care Needs of Low-Income Families*, 100th Cong., 2d sess., 9 June 1988, 93.

29. James R. Storey, *EITC: Should It Be Increased to End Poverty for the Working Poor?* (Washington, D.C.: Congressional Research Service, 10 August 1993), 1; U.S. House, Committee on Ways and Means, *1998 Green Book*, 105th Cong., 2d sess., 19 May 1998, 866–69.

30. Mattox, "Tax Fairness for Families," 5.

31. U.S. House, Subcommittee on Human Resources of the Committee on Education and Labor, *Child Care*, 18.

32. Gerald Boyd, "$1,000 Tax Refund Proposed by Bush in Child Care Plan," *New York Times*, 25 July 1988, A1, B6.

33. Republican Platform, *An American Vision: For Our Children and Our Future*, adopted by Republication National Convention, 16 August 1988, 22–23; Michael Oreskes, "Convention a Conservative Gathering," *New York Times*, 14 August 1988, 32; Barbara Kantrowitz, with Pat Wingert, "Who Will Take Care of the Children? Battle at Gender Gap," *Newsweek*, 8 August 1988, 26, 29.

34. Charles Kolb, *White House Daze: The Unmaking of Domestic Policy in the Bush Years* (New York: Free Press, 1994), 95–96.

35. *The 1988 Democratic National Platform* (Washington, D.C.: Democratic National Committee, 1988), 2.

36. Republican Platform, *American Vision*, 22.

37. Bush–Quayle 1988, "George Bush on Child Care Fact Sheet," 24 July 1988, courtesy of George Bush White House staff.

38. The Child Care Act also capped income eligibility for the dependent care tax credit at $50,000. *Congressional Record*, 99th Cong., 2d sess., 8 May 1986, H2488.

39. "The 'ABC' Child Care Bill: An Attempt to Bureaucratize Motherhood," *Issue Bulletin* 145 (Washington, D.C.: Heritage Foundation, 6 October 1988); U.S. House, Subcommittee on Children, Family, Drugs, and Alcoholism of the Committee on Labor and Human Resources, *Act for Better Child Care Services of 1987*, 343–73; Phyllis Schlafly, "What Are the Key Issues in Child Care Legislation?" in Phyllis Schlafly, ed., *Stronger Families or Better Government? The Challenge of Child Care* (Washington, D.C.: Eagle Forum Education and Legal Defense Fund, 1990), 19–25; U.S. House, Subcommittee on Human Resources of the Committee on Education and Labor, *Child Care*, 164–74; Elizabeth Ruppert, *Setting the "Corporate Family" Agenda in the United States* (Washington, D.C.: Family Research Council, 1989), esp. 3–10.

40. U.S. Senate, Committee on Finance, *Child Care Welfare Programs and Tax Credit Proposals, Hearings on S. 5 [and other bills]*, 101st Cong., 1st sess., 18, 19 April 1989, 36–37.

41. U.S. House, Subcommittee on Public Assistance and Unemployment Compensation of the Committee on Ways and Means, *Hearing on the Child Care Needs of Low-Income Families*, 85.

42. Ibid.

43. Ibid., 90.

44. U.S. House, Subcommittee on Human Resources of the Committee on Education and Labor, *Hearing on Child Care*, 100th Cong., 2d sess., 21 April 1988, 164.

45. Karlyn Keene, *The Politics of Child Care Polls* (Washington, D.C.: American Enterprise Institute, 1988), cited in *Congressional Record*, 100th Cong., 2d sess., 21 October 1988, E3662–63.

46. Institute for Research in Social Science, Harris Poll/883013, questions 19 and 23, available at: www.irss.unc.edu/data_archive/, accessed 26 February 2001.

47. National Opinion Research Center polls conducted from February through April in 1989, 1990, and 1991, available at: Public Opinion Online, accession numbers 0093328 (1989), 0142892 (1990), and 0166943 (1991).

48. "Bush: Mixed Results but Veto-Proof," *Congressional Quarterly Almanac, 1990* (Washington, D.C.: Congressional Quarterly, 1991), 30.

49. Donald C. Baumer, "Senate Democratic Leadership in the 101st Congress," in *The Atomistic Congress: An Interpretation of Congressional Change* (Armonk, N.Y.: Sharpe, 1992), 293–332.

50. "Statement on Proposed Child-Care Legislation," 15 March 1989, and accompanying note, in *Public Papers of the Presidents of the United States: George Bush, 1989*, book 1 (Washington, D.C.: Government Printing Office, 1990), 240–41.

51. Robert Rector, "Two Cheers for Bush's Family Tax Cut," *Executive Memorandum*, no. 229 (Washington, D.C.: Heritage Foundation, 22 March 1989), 2.

52. "White House Fact Sheet on the President's Child-Care Principles," in *Public Papers of the Presidents of the United States: George Bush, 1989*, book 1, 527–29.

53. *Congressional Record*, 101st Cong., 1st sess., 16 June 1989, S6798–99.

54. U.S. Senate, Subcommittee on Children, Family, Drugs, and Alcoholism of the Committee on Labor and Human Resources, *Act for Better Child Care Services of 1987*, 225.

55. Ibid., 216.

56. *Congressional Record*, 101st Cong., 1st sess., 25 January 1989, S190; "Child Care Bill Caught in House Spat," *Congressional Quarterly Almanac, 1989* (Washington, D.C.: Congressional Quarterly, 1990), 203–4.

57. In 1987 Senator Orrin Hatch introduced the Child Care Services Improvement Act (S. 1678). Representative Nancy Johnson introduced the companion bill in the House. It provided block grants to states with much lower funding than ABC and featured other provisions, such as child care liability reform.

58. For a lengthy diatribe against Hatch on his child care position, see George Gilder, "An Open Letter to Orrin Hatch," *National Review* 40, no. 9 (13 May 1988): 32–34.

59. *Congressional Record*, 101st Cong., 1st sess., 15 June 1989, S6705.

60. Ibid., S6706.

61. Ibid.

62. *Congressional Record*, 101st Cong., 1st sess., 25 January 1989, S202.

63. *Congressional Record*, 101st Cong., 1st sess., 16 June 1989, S6797–99.

64. U.S. Senate, Committee on Finance, *Federal Role in Child Care*, 100th Cong., 2d sess., 22 September 1988, 8.

65. In addition to the NGA, the other state and local organizations that officially endorsed the final agreement reached with Dodd were the National Association of Counties (NACO), the National Conference of State Legislatures (NCSL), the National League of Cities, the National Association of Regional Councils, and the American Public Welfare Association (APWA). NGA, letter to Senator Christopher Dodd, 12 June 1989.

66. Sections 118 and 119 of ABC as passed by the Senate on 23 June 1989, *Congressional Record*, 101st Cong., 1st sess., 23 June 1989, S7487–89.

67. The groups included were the USCC, NEA, AFT, AJC, United Church of Christ, NCJW, Council of Chief State School Officers, Council of Jewish Federations, Office of the Episcopal Church, Women's Convention-Auxiliary to National Baptist Convention, and General Board of Global Ministries United Methodist Church.

68. Frank Monahan, letter to Senator Christopher Dodd, 20 March 1989.

69. *Congressional Record*, 101st Cong., 1st sess., 16 June 1989, S6790.

70. For Edward Zigler's description of the 21st Century School program, see his testimony in U.S. House, Committee on Education and Labor, *Hearings on Child Care*, 9 February 1989, 7–21. See also Edward Zigler and Elizabeth Gilman, "Day Care and Early Childhood Settings," *Child and Adolescent Psychiatric Clinics of North America* 7, no. 3 (1998): 483–98.

71. U.S. House, Committee on Education and Labor, *Early Childhood Education and Development Act of 1989: Report to Accompany H.R. 3*, H. Rept. 101-190, part 1, 101st Cong., 1st sess., 27 July 1989, 31, 33.

72. Thomas Scully, letter to author, 11 May 1992; Executive Office of the President, Office of Management and Budget, *Statement of Administration Policy: H.R. 3 Early Childhood Education and Development Act*, 28 March 1990.

73. U.S. House, Committee on Education and Labor, *Hearings on Child Care*, 475, 420; "Fact Sheet on Child Care Legislation," National Child Care Association, 1989.

74. Representative Thomas Downey, interview by author, Washington, D.C., 11 September 1991.

75. David Ellwood, *Poor Support* (New York: Basic Books, 1988), 114–21; Christopher Howard, "A Truly Exceptional Social Program: The Politics of the Earned Income Tax Credit" (paper presented at the Annual Meeting of the American Political Science Association, Chicago, 3–6 September 1992), 37–38.

76. Barbara A. Willer, "Federal Comprehensive Child Care Legislation: Much Success in 1989 but More Work Ahead in 1990," *Young Children* 45 (January 1990): 27–49.

77. Paul A. Gigot, "On Child Care, a Liberal Sings Republican Song," *Wall Street Journal*, 9 March 1990, A12; William R. Mattox Jr., telephone interview by author, 3 October 1991. See also Gary Bauer (Family Research Council) and

Marvin H. Kosters (American Enterprise Institute), testimony in U.S. House, Subcommittee on Human Resources of the Committee on Ways and Means, *How to Help the Working Poor and Problems of the Working Poor*, 101st Cong., 1st sess, 28 February; 21 March; 27 April 1989, 121–26, 59–70.

78. *Congressional Record*, 101st Cong., 1st sess., 28 September 1989, H6354.

79. *Congressional Record*, 101st Cong., 1st sess., 3 October 1989, E3264.

80. Jackie Calmes and John R. Cranford, "Bush, Democrats Face Off on Bill to Cut Deficit," *Congressional Quarterly Weekly Report*, 7 October 1989, 2610–13; Ronald D. Elving, "Senate Deficit-Reduction Drive Runs into Capital Gains Bog," *Congressional Quarterly Weekly Report*, 7 October 1989, 2616–19.

81. Frank Swoboda, "Hill Democrats Postpone Action on Child-Care Proposals," *Washington Post*, 16 November 1989, A11; Frank Swoboda, "How the Child-Care Bill Collapsed," *Washington Post*, 20 November 1989, A13.

82. Representatives Tom Downey and George Miller, letter to Marian Wright Edelman, 7 August 1989, CDF files.

83. Marian Wright Edelman, letter to the Honorable Tom Downey and the Honorable George Miller, 31 August 1989, CDF files.

84. Marian Wright Edelman, memo to Tom Downey and George Miller, 14 November 1989, CDF Files.

85. Eleven representatives of Congress, letter to Marian Wright Edelman, 17 November 1989, CDF Files.

86. Scully, letter, 11 May 1992; Executive Office of the President, Office of Management and Budget, *Statement of Administration Policy: H.R. 3 Early Childhood Education and Development Act*, 28 March 1990.

87. Frank Swoboda, "Child-Care Bill Threatened Over Church–State Issue," *Washington Post*, 29 March 1990, A6.

88. Frank Monahan, letter to Representatives of Congress, 29 March 1990.

89. Thomas A. Scully, letter to author, 3 June 1993.

90. John Sununu, letter to Representative William Goodling, inserted by Goodling in *Congressional Record*, 101st Cong., 2d sess., 20 June 1990, H3856.

91. "Childcare Compromise," *Congressional Quarterly Weekly Report*, 8 September 1990, 2837.

92. Stanley Collender, *The Guide to the Federal Budget: Fiscal 1992*, 10th ed. (Washington, D.C.: Urban Institute, 1991), 56.

93. Andrew Rosenthal, "Bush Now Concedes a Need for 'Tax Revenue Increases' to Reduce Deficit in Budget," *New York Times*, 27 June 1990, A1, B6; Richard L. Berke, "Republicans Fear a Kiss of Death as Bush Moves His Lips on Taxes," *New York Times*, 27 June 1990, A1, B6.

94. For detailed accounts of the budget summit, see Susan F. Rasky, "Accord to Reduce Spending and Raise Taxes is Reached: Many in Congress Critical," *New York Times*, 1 October 1990, A1, B8; David E. Rosenbaum, "And the Victor Is Bush?" *New York Times*, 1 October 1990, A1, B8.

95. "Press Conference with the Speaker of the House," 2 October 1990, CDF files.

96. Robert D. Hershey Jr., "Tax Burden Expected to Fall on People of Moderate Means," *New York Times*, 2 October 1990, A1, A24; Robert Pear, "Focus on the Tax Package: Who Will Pay How Much?" *New York Times*, 4 October 1990, D23; Richard I. Berke, "Shouts of Revolt Rise Up in Congressional Ranks," *New York Times*, 1 October 1990, B8.

97. Nathaniel C. Nash, "The Tax Plan: A Big Increase on the Highest Incomes, a Break for the Lowest," *New York Times*, 25 October 1990, B10; Jason DeParle, "Crux of the Tax Debate: Who Pays More?" *New York Times*, 15 October 1990, B9.

98. David E. Rosenbaum, "Bush Rejects Stopgap Bill After Budget Pact Defeat: Federal Shutdown Begins," *New York Times*, 6 October 1990, A1, A8; Michael Oreskes, "Budget Boomerang," *New York Times*, 6 October 1990, 8; Susan Rasky, "A Call for Sacrifice and the Answer Is 'No,'" *New York Times*, 7 October 1990, section 4, 1, 20.

99. Pear, "Focus on the Tax Package," D23.

100. Thomas Scully, interview by author, Washington, D.C., 27 June 1991.

101. Ibid.

102. Nathaniel C. Nash, "Senate and White House Near Pact on Child Care, Lawmakers Say," *New York Times*, 16 October 1990, B9; Julie Rovner, "Negotiators Nearing Accord on Child-Care Package," *Congressional Quarterly Weekly Report*, 20 October 1990, 3511–12.

103. U.S. Senate, Omnibus Budget Reconciliation Act of 1990, report language of Finance Committee recommendations, *Congressional Record*, 101st Cong., 2d sess., 18 October 1990, S15629–15715.

104. *Congressional Record*, 101st Cong., 2d sess., 18 October 1990, S15684–86.

105. Ibid., S15821. For an explanation of this procedural rule, see Collender, *Guide to the Federal Budget 1992*, 53, 56–57.

106. U.S. House, Committee on the Budget, *Omnibus Reconciliation Act of 1990, Report to Accompany H.R. 5835*, H. Rept. 101-881, 101st Cong., 2d sess., 16 October 1990.

107. *Congressional Record*, 101st Cong., 2d sess., 16 October 1990, H10327.

108. Ibid., H10327–28.

109. Rovner, "Negotiators Nearing Accord on Child-Care Package," 3511.

110. David E. Rosenbaum, "Once Near Accord, Budget Talks Lapse into Partisan Squabbling," *New York Times*, 24 October 1990, A20.

111. Nash, "Tax Plan," B10; DeParle, "Crux of the Tax Debate," B9; U.S. House, Committee on Ways and Means, *1991 Green Book*, 102d Cong., 1st sess., 7 May 1991, 1538.

112. Nathaniel C. Nash, "Yet Another Incarnation for a Versatile Tax Credit: Child Care Aid," *New York Times*, 21 October 1990, 28.

113. Bureau of the Census, *Statistical Abstracts of the United States, 1992*, 112th ed. (Washington, D.C.: Government Printing Office, 1992), 387–88; Bureau of Labor Statistics, *Working Women: A Chartbook* (Washington, D.C.: Government Printing Office, 1991), 17.

114. Bureau of the Census, *Who's Minding the Kids? Child Care Arrangements: Fall 1988*, Current Population Reports, P70-30 (Washington, D.C.: Government Printing Office, 1992), 6.

115. Deborah A. Dawson and Virginia S. Cain, "Child Care Arrangements: Health of Our Nation's Children, United States, 1988," *Advance Data from Vital and Health Statistics*, no. 187 (Hyattsville, Md.: National Center for Health Statistics, 1990), 6.

116. Paul Brace and Barbara Hinckley, "George Bush and the Costs of High Popularity: A General Model with a Current Application," *PS: Political Science and Politics* 26, no. 3 (1993): 501–6.

117. Hugh Heclo, "Executive Budget Making," in Gregory B. Mills and John L. Palmer, eds., *Federal Budget Policy in the 1980s* (Washington, D.C.: Urban Institute, 1984), 255–91; Bruce E. Johnson, "From Analyst to Negotiator: The OMB's New Role," *Journal of Policy Analysis and Management* 3 (1984): 501–15; Shelley Lynne Tomkin, *Inside OMB: Politics and Process in the President's Budget Office* (Armonk, N.Y.: Sharpe, 1998), 92–106.

118. Melissa P. Collie and Joseph Cooper, "Multiple Referral and the 'New' Committee System in the House of Representatives," in Lawrence C. Dodd and Bruce I. Oppenheimer, eds., *Congress Reconsidered*, 4th ed. (Washington, D.C.: Congressional Quarterly Press, 1989), 245.

119. Ibid., 249.

120. Roger H. Davidson, "Multiple Referral of Legislation in the U.S. Senate," *Legislative Studies Quarterly* 14 (August 1989): 381, 390.

121. Leroy N. Rieselbach, *Congressional Reform* (Washington, D.C.: Congressional Quarterly Press, 1986), 51–52.

122. Randall Strahan, *New Ways and Means: Reform and Change in a Congressional Committee* (Chapel Hill: University of North Carolina Press, 1990), 39.

123. Gilbert Y. Steiner, *The Children's Cause* (Washington, D.C.: Brookings Institution, 1976), 247.

5. Regulations, Implementation, and High Expectations, 1991–1993

1.   Deborah Phillips and Edward Zigler, "The Checkered History of Federal Child Care Regulation," in Ernst Z. Rothkopf, ed., *Review of Research in Education* (Washington, D.C.: American Educational Research Association, 1987), 3–41.

2.   William T. Gormley Jr., *Everybody's Children: Child Care as a Public Problem* (Washington, D.C.: Brookings Institution, 1995); William Gormley Jr., "Regulating Child Care Quality," *Annals of American Academy of Political and Social Science* 563 (May 1999): 116–29.

3.   Cheryl D. Hayes, John L. Palmer, and Martha J. Zaslow, eds., *Who Cares for America's Children? Child Care Policy for the 1990s* (Washington, D.C.: National Academy Press, 1990), 156; National Association for Education of Young Children, *NAEYC Position Statement on Licensing and Public Regulation of Early Childhood Programs* (Washington, D.C.: NAEYC, 1997), reprinted in NAEYC, *Young Children* 53, no. 1 (January 1998): 43–50.

4.   NAEYC, *NAEYC Position Statement on Licensing.*

5.   Children's Foundation, *The 1999 Child Care Center Licensing Study* (Washington, D.C.: Children's Foundation, 1999), 171.

6.   NAEYC, *NAEYC Position Statement on Licensing*; Deanna S. Gombry et al., "Long-Term Outcomes of Early Childhood Programs: Analysis and Recommendations," *Future of Children* 5, no. 3 (winter 1995): 6–24; W. Steven Barnett, "Long-Term Effects of Early Childhood Programs on Cognitive and School Outcomes," *Future of Children* 5, no. 3 (winter 1995): 25–50; Hirokazu Yoshikawa, "Long-Term Effects of Early Childhood Programs on Social Outcomes and Delinquency," *Future of Children* 5, no. 3 (winter 1995): 51–75; Julee J. Newberger, "New Brain Development Research: A Wonderful Window of Opportunity to Build Public Support for Early Childhood Education," *Young Children* 52, no. 4 (1997): 4–9; Hayes et al., *Who Cares for America's Children?*, 45–144.

7.   NAEYC, *NAEYC Position Statement on Licensing.*

8.   Ibid.

9.   Children's Foundation, *1999 Child Care Center Licensing Study*, iv.

10. Hayes et al., *Who Cares for America's Children?*

11. NAEYC, *NAEYC Position Statement on Licensing*; Ellen Galinsky et al., *The Study of Children in Family Child Care and Relative Care: Highlights of Findings* (New York: Family and Work Institute, 1994); Children's Foundation, *1997 Family Child Care Licensing Study* (Washington, D.C.: Children's Foundation, 1997), vii–x.

12. Children's Foundation, *1997 Family Child Care Licensing Study*, iv, v.

13. Children's Foundation, *1999 Family Child Care Licensing Study*, xiii; Lynne M. Casper, "Who's Minding Our Preschoolers?" *Current Population Reports*, P70-53 (Washington, D.C.: Bureau of the Census, March 1996), 3.

14. NAEYC, *NAEYC Position Statement on Developing and Implementing Effective Public Policies to Promote Early Childhood and School-Age Care Program Accreditation* (Washington, D.C: NAEYC, April 1999).

15. As of October 1, 2000, for example, over 7,500 programs serving more than 680,000 children were accredited by the NAEYC's National Academy of Early

Childhood Programs. A summary of Accredited Programs and Programs Pursuing Accreditation is available at: http://www.naeyc.org/accreditation/center_summary.htm, accessed 20 November 2000. As of April 2000, three hundred licensed child care programs had National Early Childhood Program Accreditation. Suzanne Grace, telephone conversation with author, 12 April 2000.

16. Hayes et al., *Who Cares for America's Children?*, 84–107.

17. Galinsky et al., *Study of Children in Family Child Care and Relative Care*, 46, 81.

18. American Academy of Pediatrics and American Public Health Association, *Caring for Our Children—National Health and Safety Performance: Guidelines for Out-of-Home Child Care Programs* (Washington, D.C.: American Public Health Association, 1992).

19. NAEYC, *NAEYC Position Statement on Licensing*.

20. Charles W. Snow, Jane King Teleki, and Julia T. Reguero-de-Atiles, "Child Care Center Licensing Standards in the United States: 1981 to 1995," *Young Children* (September 1996): 36–41; NAEYC, *NAEYC Position Statement on Licensing*; Kathryn T. Young, Katherine White Marsland, and Edward Zigler, "The Regulatory Status of Center-Based Infant and Toddler Child Care," *American Journal of Orthopsychiatry* 67, no. 1 (1997): 535–44.

21. Government Accounting Office, *Child Care: State Efforts to Enforce Safety and Health Requirements*, GAO/HEHS-00-28 (Washington, D.C.: GAO, 2000), 20.

22. Maryan Wagner Johnson, "The Regulation of Child Care," *Journal of Legislation* 18 (1992): 45–67; Gormley, *Everybody's Children*, 143.

23. Gormley, *Everybody's Children*, 143.

24. Ibid., 144.

25. Anne Stewart, *Implementing Regulations for New Federal Child Care Programs: Selected Issues* (Washington, D.C.: Congressional Research Service, 1991), 4.

26. U.S. House, Subcommittee on Human Resources of the Committee on Ways and Means, *Hearing on the Administration's Proposed Federal Child Care Regulations*, 102d Cong., 1st sess., 26 September 1991, 7.

27. U.S. House, Subcommittee on Human Resources of the Committee on Education and Labor, *Hearing on the Proposed Child Care Regulations for the CCDBG and the At-Risk Child Care Program*, 102d Cong., 1st sess., 31 October 1991, 65.

28. U.S. House, Subcommittee on Human Resources of the Committee on Ways and Means, *Hearing on the Administrations's Proposed Federal Child Care Regulations*, 99.

29. Ibid.

30. "Second-Class Day Care," editorial, *New York Times*, 2 August 1991, A26.

31. "Free the States," editorial, *Washington Post*, 6 August 1991, A20.
32. Jo Anne B. Barnhart, "Choices for the Poor," *Washington Post*, 27 August 1991, A23.
33. Nancy Amidei, "With the Spotlight off Child Care, Administration Panders to Ideologues' Regulations," *Los Angeles Times*, 21 July 1991, 6.
34. Robert Pear, "U.S. Laws Delayed by Complex Rules and Partisanship," *New York Times*, 31 March, 1991, 1, 18.
35. S. K. Wisensale, "White House and Congress on Child Care and Family Leave Policy: From Carter to Clinton," *Policy Studies Journal* 25, no. 1 (1997): 79; Presidential Documents, Executive Order 12606, 2 September 1987, *Federal Register* 52, no. 174 (9 September 1987): 34188; Presidential Documents, Executive Order 12612, 26 October 1987, *Federal Register* 52, no. 210 (30 October 1987): 41685–88; U.S. Department of Health and Human Services, "Final Rule: Aid to Families with Dependent Children At-Risk Child Care Program," *Federal Register* 57, no. 150 (4 August 1992): 34434–36.
36. U.S. Department of Health and Human Services, Administration for Children and Families, "General Reorganization: Statement of Organization, Functions, and Delegations of Authority," *Federal Register* 56, no. 109 (27 August 1991): 42332–50.
37. For a definition of seamless service, see U.S. Department of Health and Human Services, "Interim Final Rule: CCDBG," *Federal Register* (6 June 1991): 26197.
38. Ibid.
39. Ibid., 26196.
40. Robert Rector, letter to Child Care Task Force, 4 August 1991, letter 1439, comments on interim final regulations for CCDBG, Child Care Bureau, Administration for Children and Families, Washington, D.C.
41. Beverly LaHaye, letter to Child Care Task Force, 2 August 1991, letter 1208, comments on interim final regulations for CCDBG, Child Care Bureau files; Phyllis Schlafly, letter to Child Care Task Force, 1 August 1991, letter 1449, comments on interim final regulations for CCDBG, Child Care Bureau files.
42. Gary L. Bauer, letter to the Honorable Louis Sullivan, 5 August 1991, letter 1434, comments on interim final regulations for CCDBG, Child Care Bureau files.
43. See, for example, David S. Liederman, letter to Mark Ragan, 29 July 1991, letter 14427, comments on interim final regulations for CCDBG, Child Care Bureau files; Nancy Duff Campbell and Shirley Sagawa (National Women's Law Center), letter to Mark Ragan, 5 August 1991, letter 1446, comments on interim final regulations for CCDBG, Child Care Bureau files.

44. William T. Pound, letter to Mark Ragan, 5 August 1991, comments on interim final regulations for CCDBG, Child Care Bureau files.

45. U.S. Department of Health and Human Services, "Final Rule: CCDBG," *Federal Register* 57, no. 150 (4 August 1992): 34357.

46. Stewart, *Implementing Regulations for New Federal Child Care Programs*, 10; *Congressional Record*, 101st Cong., 2d sess., 26 October 1990, H12691–12692; U.S. Department of Health and Human Services, "Final Rule: CCDBG," 34376, 34420.

47. Stewart, *Implementing Regulations for New Federal Child Care Programs*, 7.

48. Nancy Ebb, Helen Blank, and Sherrie Lockner, letter to Mark Ragan, 29 July 1991, CDF draft letter, comments on interim final regulations for CCDBG, Child Care Bureau files.

49. U.S. Department of Health and Human Services, "Final Rule: CCDBG," 34377.

50. Raymond G. Scheppach (NGA), letter to Mark Ragan, 2 August, 1991, comments on interim final regulations for CCDBG, Child Care Bureau files.

51. Under the 1990 law, states could spend CCDBG funds on activities to improve child care quality from the 75 percent and 25 percent allocation. However, the law imposed constraints on how states could spend the funds in each allocation. For example, under the 25 percent reserve of funds, not less than 75 percent was to be allocated to early childhood development and before- and after-school care and not less than 20 percent was to be allocated for quality enhancements. The regulations generated controversy over how much flexibility states had in using the 75 percent reserve funds for quality enhancement activities.

52. Sections on child care from the 1990 reconciliation conference report are in the *Congressional Record*, 101st Cong., 2d sess., 26 October 1990, H12691.

53. U.S. Department of Health and Human Services, "Interim Final Rule: CCDBG," *Federal Register* 56, no. 109 (6 June 1991): 26209–11, 26231–32.

54. U.S. House, Subcommittee on Human Resources of the Committee on Ways and Means, *Hearing on the Administration's Proposed Federal Child Care Regulations*, 102d Cong., 1st sess., 26 September 1991, 36–37.

55. Peter M. Weinstein, letter to Mark Ragan, 28 July 1991, letter 995, comments on interim final regulations for CCDBG, Child Care Bureau files.

56. Raymond G. Scheppach, letter to Mark Ragan, 2 August 1991, comments on interim final regulations for CCDBG, Child Care Bureau files.

57. Liederman, letter to Ragan, 29 July 1991.

58. Senators Christopher J. Dodd, Orrin G. Hatch, and Edward M. Kennedy, letter to Jo Anne B. Barnhart, 2 August 1991, comments on interim final regulations for CCDBG, Child Care Bureau files.

59. U.S. Department of Health and Human Services, "Final Rule: CCDBG," 34357.

60. Campbell and Sagawa, letter to Ragan, 5 August 1991.
61. U.S. Department of Health and Human Services, "Final Rule: CCDBG," 34380–81.
62. Stewart, *Implementing Regulations for New Federal Child Care Programs*, 8.
63. Bruce Hershfield, telephone interview by author, 19 December 1996.
64. Stewart, *Implementing Regulations for New Federal Child Care Programs*, 8.
65. Debra DeLee, letter to Mark Ragan, 5 August 1991, letter 14438, comments on interim final regulations for CCDBG, Child Care Bureau files; Arlene Zielke, letter to Mark Ragan, 29 July 1991, comments on interim final regulations for CCDBG, Child Care Bureau files; Campbell and Sagawa, letter to Mark Ragan, 5 August 1991.
66. Dodd, Hatch, and Kennedy, letter to Barnhart, 2 August 1991.
67. U.S. Department of Health and Human Services, "Proposed Rule: Aid to Families with Dependent Children At-Risk Child Care Program," *Federal Register* 56, no. 122 (25 June 1991): 29054–60, quote on 29060. For a full description of standards and treatment of religiously affiliated care, see 29060–61, 29068.
68. Ibid., 29061.
69. U.S. House, Subcommittee on Human Resources of the Committee on Ways and Means, *Hearing on the Administration's Proposed Federal Child Care Regulations*, 23.
70. Ibid., 23–24.
71. Ibid., 26.
72. Ibid., 83.
73. Ibid., 97.
74. Stewart, *Implementing Regulations for New Federal Child Care Programs*, 10.
75. U.S. Department of Health and Human Services, "Proposed Rule: Aid to Families with Dependent Children At-Risk Child Care Program," *Federal Register*, section 257.41 (b).
76. Nancy Ebb, Helen Blank, and Sherrie Lookner, letter to Mary Ann Higgins, re: Proposed Rule for At-Risk Child Care Program, 1 August 1991, CDF files, Washington, D.C.; U.S. House, Subcommittee on Human Resources of the Committee on Education and Labor, *Hearing on the Proposed Child Care Regulations for the CCDBG and the At-Risk Child Care Program*, 26.
77. U.S. Department of Health and Human Services, "Final Rule: Aid to Families with Dependent Children At-Risk Child Care Program," *Federal Register* 57, no. 150 (4 August 1992): section 257.41, 34447, 34461.
78. Ibid., 34448.
79. Ibid., 34449.
80. U.S. Department of Health and Human Services, "Proposed Rule: Aid to Families with Dependent Children At-Risk Child Care Program," 29063.
81. Ebb, Helen, and Lookner, letter to Higgins, 1 August 1991.

82. U.S. House, Subcommittee on Human Resources of the Committee on Ways and Means, *Hearing on the Administration's Proposed Federal Child Care Regulations*, 205.

83. U.S. House, Subcommittee on Human Resources of the Committee on Education and Labor, *Hearing on the Proposed Child Care Regulations for the CCDBG and the At-Risk Child Care Program*, 38.

84. Ebb, Blank, and Lookner, letter to Higgins; U.S. House, Subcommittee on Human Resources of the Committee on Ways and Means, *Hearing on the Administration's Proposed Federal Child Care Regulations*, 138, 148.

85. U.S. Department of Health and Human Services, "Final Rule: Aid to Families with Dependent Children At-Risk Child Care Program," 34437–38.

86. Ibid., 34442.

87. Federal government fiscal years begin on October 1 and are identified by the year in which they end. So, for example, fiscal year 1991 ran from October 1, 1990, to September 30, 1991.

88. Helen Blank, personal communication to the author, 20 January 2000; U.S. House, Conference Committee on Appropriations, *Making Appropriations for the Departments of Labor, Health and Human Services, and Education, and Related Agencies, for the Fiscal Year Ending September 30, 1991, and for Other Purposes*, H. Rept. 101-908, 101st Cong., 2d sess., 20 October 1990, 30, 87.

89. U.S. House, Committee on Ways and Means, *1996 Green Book*, 104th Cong., 2d sess., 4 November 1996, 649.

90. U.S. Department of Health and Human Services, Child Care Bureau, *CCDBG First Annual Report to Congress on State Program Services and Expenditures* (Washington, D.C.: Government Printing Office, 1995), 4.

91. Ibid., 11–22.

92. Danielle Ewen and Anne Goldstein, *Report on the Activities of the States Using CCDBG Quality Improvement Funds* (Washington, D.C.: Child Care Bureau, August 1996), 6.

93. Ibid., 11.

94. Gina Adams, *How Safe? The Status of State Efforts to Protect Children in Child Care* (Washington, D.C.: Children's Defense Fund, October 1995), 3, 14–16.

95. Ibid., 22–23.

96. Ibid., 8.

97. General Accounting Office, *Early Childhood Programs: Multiple Programs and Overlapping Target Groups (Fact Sheet)*, GAO/HEHS-95-4FS (Washington, D.C.: Government Printing Office, 31 October 1994).

98. Gormley, *Everybody's Children*, 123, citing Nancy Ebb, *Child Care Tradeoffs: States Make Painful Choices* (Washington, D.C.: Children's Defense Fund, 1994), 12–13.

99. Gormley, *Everybody's Children*, 124–25.

100. Ebb, *Child Care Tradeoffs*, table 3, appendix B.

101. U.S. House, Committee on Ways and Means, *1996 Green Book*, 662–63.

102. Ebb, *Child Care Tradeoffs*, 13.

103. U.S. House, Committee on Ways and Means, *1996 Green Book*, 664–65.

104. Nancy Duff Campbell, interview by author, Washington, D.C., 1 July 1998.

105. National Women's Law Center, *Child Care Tax Credits Outreach Campaign, April 1991–April 1992: Final Report* (Washington, D.C.: NWLC, 1992).

106. Nancy Duff Campbell, telephone interview by author, 13 March 2000.

107. Bureau of the Census, *Statistical Abstracts of the United States, 1996*, 116th ed. (Washington, D.C.: Government Printing Office, 1996), 271.

108. Elizabeth Drew, *On the Edge: The Clinton Presidency* (New York: Simon and Schuster, 1994), 19.

109. John Brummett, *Highwire: From the Backroads to the Beltway—The Education of Bill Clinton* (New York: Hyperion, 1994), 32.

110. Drew, *On the Edge*, 19.

111. Bill Clinton and Al Gore, *Putting People First: How We Can All Change America* (New York: Time Books, 1992).

112. Ibid., 5, 14, 15, 50.

113. Ibid., 51.

114. Ibid., 165.

115. Ibid., 167; Executive Office of the President, *A Vision of Change for America* (Washington, D.C.: Government Printing Offiice, 17 February 1993), 57.

116. Gerald M. Pomper, "The Presidential Election," in Gerald M. Pomper, ed., *The Election of 1992* (Chatham N.J.: Chatham House, 1993), 140.

117. Ibid.

118. Brummett, *Highwire*, 33.

119. Everett Carll Ladd, "The 1992 Vote for President Clinton: Another Brittle Mandate?" *Political Science Quarterly* 108, no. 1 (1993): 5.

120. M. Stephen Weatherford and Lorraine M. McDonnell, "Clinton and the Economy: The Paradox of Policy Success and Political Mishap," *Political Science Quarterly* 111, no. 3 (1996): 425; Paul J. Quirk and Joseph Hinchliffe, "Domestic Policy: The Trials of a Centrist Democrat," in Colin Campbell and Bert A. Rockman, eds., *The Clinton Presidency: First Appraisals* (Chatham, N.J.: Chatham House, 1996), 266.

121. Drew, *On the Edge*, 32–33, 37–41, quote on 38.

122. Ibid., 53.

123. Lynda Richardson, "Nannygate for the Poor," *New York Times*, 2 May 1990, 52.

124. See, for example, Rochelle Stanfield, "Child Care Quagmire," *National Journal* 25 (27 February 1993): 512–16.

125. "Clinton Signs Family Leave Act," *Congressional Quarterly Almanac, 1993* (Washington, D.C.: Congressional Quarterly, 1994), 389.

126. Executive Office of the President, *Vision of Change for America*, iv.

127. "Clinton Throws Down the Gauntlet," *Congressional Quarterly Almanac, 1993* (Washington, D.C.: Congressional Quarterly, 1994), 85–107; "Remarks to the Children's Defense Fund," 11 March 1993, in *Public Papers of the Presidents of the United States: Papers of William J. Clinton, 1993*, book 1 (Washington D.C.: Government Printing Office, 1994), 272–77; Executive Office of the President, *Vision of Change for America*, 57–58.

128. 1993 Budget Reconciliation Act, *Congressional Quarterly Weekly Report*, 18 September 1993, 2482, 2490, 2494. For an excellent discussion of the politics behind Clinton's efforts to get Congress to enact his economic policies in 1993, see Weatherford and McDonnell, "Clinton and the Economy."

129. "Law Expands, Improves Head Start," *Congressional Quarterly Almanac, 1994* (Washington, D.C.: Congressional Quarterly, 1995), 369–72.

130. President Clinton, "Remarks in a Town Meeting in Cranston, Rhode Island," 9 May 1994, in *Public Papers of the Presidents of the United States: William J. Clinton, 1994*, book 1 (Washington, D.C.: Government Printing Office, 1995), 884.

131. "Excerpts from Television Exchange Held with the President," *New York Times*, 11 February 1993, A26.

132. Cathy Trost, "Patter of Little Feet Begins to Reverberate in the Halls of Power," *Wall Street Journal*, 8 March 1993, A1.

133. "Aid to Families with Dependent Children Child Care Program, Transitional Child Care, and At-Risk Child Care: Child Care and Development Block Grant, Proposed Rule," *Federal Register* 50, no. 90 (11 May 1994): 24510–27.

134. Helen Blank, memo to Mary Jo Bane, re: Proposed Child Care Regulatory Changes, including enclosure, Improving Child Care Licensing, 27 April 1993, CDF files.

135. "Aid to Families with Dependent Children Child Care Program, Transitional Child Care and At-Risk Child Care: Child Care and Development Block Grant, Proposed Rule," 24510–27; Helen Blank and Nancy Ebb, memo to Child Care Advocates, re: Proposed Child Care Regulations Include Positive Changes, 23 May 1994, CDF files.

136. William Tobin, letter to Mary Jo Bane, 30 June 1994, letter 47, comments on 1994 proposed child care regulation, Child Care Bureau files.

137. Gordon White, letter to the Assistant Secretary for Children and Families, 11 July 1994, letter 113, comments on 1994 proposed child care regulation, Child Care Bureau files. White was the director of government relations for the NCCA.

6. Child Care and Welfare Reform, 1994–1996

1. John H. Aldrich and David W. Rohde, "The Transition to Republican Rule in the House: Implications for Theories of Congressional Politics," *Political Science Quarterly* 112, no. 4 (1997–98): 541–67.
2. Ibid., 558.
3. C. Lawrence Evans and Walter J. Oleszek, *Congress Under Fire: Reform Politics and the Republican Majority* (Boston: Houghton Mifflin, 1997), 26–27; Ronald M. Peters Jr., *The American Speakership: The Office in Historical Perspective*, 2d ed. (Baltimore: Johns Hopkins University Press, 1997), 292–393; John Bader, *Taking the Initiative* (Washington, D.C.: Georgetown University Press, 1996), 171–76.
4. Douglas L. Koopman, *Hostile Takeover: The House Republican Party, 1980–1995* (Lanham, Md.: Rowman and Littlefield, 1996), 11, 34.
5. Ibid., 33; Peters, *American Speakership*, 252, 264–83.
6. Evans and Oleszek, *Congress Under Fire*, 26–27.
7. Joseph S. Nye, Philip D. Zelikow, and David C. King, eds., *Why People Don't Trust Government* (Cambridge, Mass.: Harvard University Press, 1997).
8. Roger H. Davidson, "Congressional Committees in the New Reform Era: From Combat to the Contract," in James A. Thurber and Roger H. Davidson, eds., *Remaking Congress: Change and Stability in the 1990s* (Washington, D.C.: Congressional Quarterly, 1995), 30.
9. Gary C. Jacobson, "The 1994 House Elections in Perspective," *Political Science Quarterly* 111, no. 2 (1996): 203–23; Elizabeth Drew, *Showdown: The Struggle Between the Gingrich Congress and the Clinton White House* (New York: Touchstone, 1996), 24.
10. Jacobson, "1994 House Elections," 206–10.
11. Koopman, *Hostile Takeover*," 146; see also Davidson, "Congressional Committees in the New Reform Era."
12. Everett Carll Ladd, "The 1994 Congressional Elections: The Postindustrial Realignment Continues," *Political Science Quarterly* 110, no. 1 (1995): 16.
13. Ibid., 17; Peters, *American Speakership*, 293.
14. Peters, *American Speakership*, 293; see also Jacobson, "1994 House Elections," 204. Several other factors precipitated the Republican takeover and disillusionment with the status quo. Among them was the House bank scandal in 1991, prompted by GAO reports that many representatives had drawn more than 8,000 checks on insufficient funds at the House bank. No checks bounced because there were no rules regarding overdraft. See Koopman, *Hostile Takeover*, 35.
15. Drew, *Showdown*, 24.

16. Koopman, *Hostile Takeover*, 73; Eliza Newlin Carney, "Family Time," *National Journal* 27, no. 30 (29 July 1995): 1947–51; James A. Barnes, "Parent Power," *National Journal* 25, no. 24 (12 June 1993): 1399–1401.

17. Koopman, *Hostile Takeover*, 133–44.

18. Drew, *Showdown*, 32; Koopman, *Hostile Takeover*, 69–72; Ralph Reed, "Casting a Wider Net: Religious Conservatives Move Beyond Abortion and Homosexuality," *Policy Review* (summer 1993): 31–35; James A. Barnes, "Rightward March?" *National Journal* 26, no. 32 (6 August 1994): 1847–51.

19. Koopman, *Hostile Takeover*, 149.

20. Drew, *Showdown*, 32; Ron Haskins, "Does Welfare Encourage Illegitimacy?" *American Enterprise* (July–August 1996): 48–49; George W. Liebmann, "Addressing Illegitimacy: The Roots of Real Welfare Reform," *Backgrounder*, no. 1032 (Washington, D.C.: Heritage Foundation, 6 April 1995).

21. U.S. House, Committee on Ways and Means, *Hearings on Tax Provisions in the Contract with America Designed to Strengthen the American Family*, 100th Cong., 1st sess., 17, 18, 19 January 1995, esp. 120–28, 135–41; Alissa J. Rubin, "Unity Frays Within House GOP over Family Tax Credit," *Congressional Quarterly Weekly Report*, 25 March 1995, 857–59; Drew, *Showdown*, 171–182; "Two Cheers for the American Dream Restoration Act," *In Focus* (Washington, D.C.: Family Research Council, 1994).

22. "Tax Fairness for Families: A New Call for Pro-Child Relief," *Family Policy* 4, no. 2 (Washington, D.C.: Family Research Council, May 1991), 3.

23. Peters, *American Speakership*, 316.

24. Rhodes Cook, "Rare Combination of Forces May Make History of '94," *Congressional Quarterly Weekly Report*, 15 April 1995, 1076–81.

25. Bureau of the Census, *Statistical Abstracts of the United States, 1997*, 117th ed. (Washington, D.C.: Government Printing Office, 1997), 283–85.

26. Evans and Oleszek, *Congress Under Fire*, 12; Davidson, "Congressional Committees in the New Reform Era," 32; Koopman, *Hostile Takeover*, 33.

27. Evans and Oleszek, *Congress Under Fire*, 78.

28. For a discussion of the impact of these rules in diminishing the role of tax committees in budget negotiations, see Jeff Shear, "Vanishing Act," *National Journal* 28, no. 19 (11 May 1996): 1032–36.

29. Peters, *American Speakership*, 295.

30. Davidson, "Congressional Committees in the New Reform Era," 33; Koopman, *Hostile Takeover*, 154; Evans and Oleszek, *Congress Under Fire*, 91, 131, 140; Peters, *American Speakership*, 294.

31. Peters, *American Speakership*, 295.

32. Evans and Oleszek, *Congress Under Fire*, 131, 100.

33. Ibid., 152, 152–56; Richard E. Cohen, "Seismic Shift," *National Journal* 28, no. 20 (18 May 1996): 1084–88.

34. This section focuses on child care as a part of welfare reform. It addresses the broader aspects of welfare reform only insofar as they were relevant to the politics of child care. For summaries of the politics of welfare reform in 1995 and 1996, see "Welfare Bill Clears Under Veto Threat," *Congressional Quarterly Almanac 1995* (Washington, D.C.: Congressional Quarterly, 1996), 7-35–7-52; "Welfare Overhaul: After 60 Years, Most Control Sent to States," *Congressional Quarterly Almanac 1996* (Washington, D.C.: Congressional Quarterly, 1997), 6-3–6-24; Drew, *Showdown*, 87–92, 140–49, 279–83; Daniel P. Moynihan, *Miles to Go* (Cambridge, Mass.: Harvard University Press, 1996); Sheila B. Kamerman and Alfred J. Kahn, *P.L. 104-193: Challenges and Opportunities* (New York: Cross-National Studies Research Program, Columbia University School of Social Work, 1997).

35. Hilary Stout, "GOP's Welfare Stance Owes a Lot to Prodding from Robert Rector," *Wall Street Journal*, 23 January 1995, A1, A10.

36. Ibid., A10.

37. Robert Rector, "The Case for 'Strings-Attached' Welfare Reform," *Heritage Lectures* 524 (1995): 3.

38. Jeffrey L. Katz, "Long-awaited Welfare Proposal Would Make Gradual Changes," *Congressional Quarterly Weekly Report*, 18 June 1994, 1622–1624.

39. Representative Lynn Woolsey introduced H.R. 4318; Representatives Patsy Mink and Matthew Martinez (D-Calif.) introduced H.R. 4498. Representative Robert T. Matsui's (D-Calif.) bill (H.R. 4767) was popular among child care advocates because of its generous child care provisions. For a comparison of the major welfare bills introduced in 1994, see U.S. House, Committee on Education and Labor, *Hearing on H.R. 4605: Work and Responsibility Act of 1994*, 103rd Cong., 2d sess., 2 August 1994, 152–75.

40. See, for example, U.S. House, Committee on Education and Labor, *Hearing on H.R. 4605: Work and Responsibility Act of 1994*; U.S. House, Subcommittee on Human Resources of the Committee on Education and Labor, *Hearing Regarding the Impact of Welfare Reform on Child Care Providers and the Working Poor*, 103rd Cong., 2d sess., 20 September 1994; U.S. House, Subcommittee on Regulation, Business Opportunities, and Technology of the Committee on Small Business, *Who's Minding the Baby? Quality and Availability Programs in Child Care for America's Children*, 103rd Cong., 2d sess., 9 December 1994.

41. U.S. House, Committee on Ways and Means, Subcommittee on Human Resources, *Hearings on Welfare Reform Proposals, Including H.R. 4605: The Work and Responsibility Act of 1994*, 103rd Cong., 2d sess., 14, 26–29 July; 9, 16 August 1994.

42. U.S. House, Subcommittee on Human Resources of the Committee on Education and Labor, *Hearing Regarding the Impact of Welfare Reform on Child Care Providers and the Working Poor*, 5–6.

43. Ibid., 15.

44. Ibid., 70–74. See, for example, testimony of Bruce Hershfield.

45. General Accounting Office, *Child Care: Working Poor and Welfare Recipients Face Service Gaps*, GAO/HEHS-94-87 (Washington, D.C.: Government Printing Office, 13 May 1994).

46. Nancy Ebb, statement in U.S. House, Subcommittee on Human Resources of the Committee on Education and Labor, *Hearing Regarding the Impact of Welfare Reform on Child Care Providers and the Working Poor*, 44.

47. George Gallup Jr., *The Gallup Poll: Public Opinion, 1994* (Wilmington, Del.: Scholarly Resources, 1995), 87.

48. Alissa J. Rubin, "Archer: A Quiet Conservative with an Explosive Agenda," *Congressional Quarterly Weekly Report*, 12 August 1995, 2426–32.

49. Aldrich and Rohde, "The Transition to Republican Rule in the House," 550–51.

50. Senator Christopher Dodd, prepared statement in U.S. Senate, Committee on Labor and Human Resources, *Hearings on the Impact of Welfare Reform on Children and Their Families*, 104th Cong., 1st sess., 28 February; 1 March 1995, 4–5.

51. General Accounting Office, *Child Care Subsidies Increase Likelihood that Low Income Mothers Will Work*, GAO/HEHS-95-20 (Washington, D.C.: Government Printing Office, 31 December 1994).

52. U.S. House, Subcommittee on Early Childhood, Youth, and Families of the Committee on Economic and Educational Opportunities, *Hearing on the Contract with America: Child Welfare and Childcare*, 104th Cong., 1st sess., 31 January 1995, 110.

53. Ibid., 111.

54. U.S. House, Subcommittee on Human Resources of the Committee on Ways and Means and the Subcommittee on Early Childhood, Youth, and Families of the Committee on Economic and Educational Opportunities, *Hearing on Child Care and Child Welfare*, 104th Cong., 1st sess., 3 February 1995.

55. Ibid., 84.

56. Patty Siegal, statement in U.S. House, Subcommittee on Early Childhood, Youth, and Families of the Committee on Economic and Educational Opportunities, *Hearing on the Contract with America: Child Welfare and Childcare*, 115.

57. Coats was elected to replace Dan Quayle as a representative in 1980 and then was appointed to Quayle's Senate seat in 1988. Coats won the Senate election in 1992, but in 1996 he announced that he would not run for reelection in 1998. Michael Barone and Grant Ujifusa, "The Almanac of American Politics 1998," in *National Journal* (Washington, D.C.: National Journal, 1997), 525–26.

58. U.S. Senate, Subcommittee on Children and Families of the Committee on Labor and Human Resources, *Hearing on the CCDBG: How Is It Working?* 104th Cong., 1st sess., 16 February 1995.

59. Ibid., 52–59, quote on 56.

60. Ibid., 7.

61. Ibid., 25–52, 65–74.

62. Ibid., 3.

63. Ibid., 11–25.

64. Sandra Hofferth, statement in U.S. Senate, Committee on Labor and Human Resources, *Hearings on the Impact of Welfare Reform on Children and Their Families*, 5.

65. Helen Blank, telephone interview by author, 26 November 1996.

66. U.S. House, Committee on Economic and Educational Opportunities, *Welfare Reform Consolidation Act of 1995*, H. Rept. 104-75, part 1, 104th Cong., 1st sess., 10 March 1995, 7, 65, 69.

67. Ibid., 397; Chery Wetzstein, "Welfare Reform's Limited Day Care Worries Goodling," *Washington Times*, 5 March 1995, reprinted in ibid., 418–19.

68. U.S. House, Committee on Economic and Educational Opportunities, *Welfare Reform Consolidation Act of 1995*, 32–38, quote on 34.

69. Helen Blank, testimony in U.S. House, Subcommittee on Human Resources of the Committee on Ways and Means and Subcommittee on Early Childhood, Youth, and Families of the Committee on Economic and Educational Opportunities, *Hearing on Child Care and Child Welfare*, 62–63.

70. Jeffrey L. Katz, "GOP Moderates Central to Welfare Overhaul," *Congressional Quarterly Weekly Report*, 18 March 1995, 813.

71. "Q and A on Child Care Developments in Congress," 27 July 1995, CDF files, Washington, D.C.; "Provisions of the House Welfare Bill," *Congressional Quarterly Weekly Report*, 18 March 1995, 816.

72. *Congressional Record*, 104th Cong., 1st sess., 23 March 1995, H3582–86.

73. Drew, *Showdown*, 145–47; *Congressional Record*, 104th Cong., 1st sess., 23 March 1995, H3582–86.

74. Quoted in Jeffrey L. Katz, "House Passes Welfare Bill: Senate Likely to Alter It," *Congressional Quarterly Weekly Report*, 25 March 1995, 872.

75. Drew, *Showdown*, 144–45.

76. "Remarks to the National Governors' Association Summit on Young Children in Baltimore, MD," 6 June 1995, in *Public Papers of the Presidents of the United States: William J. Clinton, 1995*, book 1, (Washington, D.C.: Government Printing Office, 1996), 821.

77. Katz, "House Passes Welfare Bill," 873.

78. *Congressional Record*, 100th Cong., 2d sess., 7 October 1988, S15055.

79. Child Care Legislative Update, 5 June 1995, CDF files; see also CDF Alert, telephone tree message for Senate Finance Committee Action on Child Care, 17 May 1995, CDF files; Jeffrey L. Katz, "Senate Plan Falls in Line, Shifts Welfare to States," *Congressional Quarterly Weekly Report*, 27 May 1995, 1503–6; U.S. Senate, Committee on Finance, *Report on the Family Sufficiency Act of 1995*, S. Rept. 104-96, 104th Cong., 1st sess., 9 June 1995.

80. Phil Duncan, ed., *Politics in America 1994, 103rd Congress* (Washington, D.C.: Congressional Quarterly, 1993), 308.

81. Quoted in Allan Freedman, "With Child Care Bill, Panel Aims to Influence Welfare Debate," *Congressional Quarterly Weekly Report*, 27 May 1995, 1507.

82. Ibid.

83. U.S. Senate, Committee on Labor and Human Resources, *Report on CCDBG Amendments Act of 1995*, S. 850, S. Rept. 104-94, 104th Cong., 1st sess., 8 June 1995, 1–11.

84. Ibid., section 658 T.

85. *Congressional Record*, 104th Cong., 1st sess., 11 August 1995, S12513.

86. "Teleconference Remarks with the U.S. Conference of Mayors," 20 June 1995, in *Public Papers of the Presidents: William J. Clinton, 1995*, book 1, 909.

87. "Q and A on Child Care Developments in Congress," 27 July 1995; quoted in Jeffrey L. Katz, "Senate GOP Puts Overhaul on Hold to Muster Votes," *Congressional Quarterly Weekly Report*, 12 August 1995, 2445.

88. *Congressional Record*, 104th Cong., 1st sess., 11 August 1995, S12428–511.

89. "Dole Bill Summary," 9 August 1995, CDF files.

90. Executive Office of the President, Office of Management and Budget, "Statement of Administration Policy on S. 1120: Work Opportunity Act of 1995," 5 August 1995, CDF files.

91. Katz, "Senate GOP Puts Overhaul on Hold," 2443.

92. Jeff Shear, "The Right Turn," *National Journal* 27, no. 45 (11 November 1995): 2799–2802.

93. Jeffrey L. Katz, "GOP Moderates Flex Muscles," *Congressional Quarterly Weekly Report*, 16 September 1995, 2805.

94. *Congressional Record*, 104th Cong., 1st sess., 8 September 1995, S12979; Raymond C. Scheppach (NGA), William Pound (NCSL), and A. Sidney Johnson (APWA), letter to senators, 14 June 1995, CDF files.

95. *Congressional Record*, 104th Cong., 1st sess., 11 September 1995, S13179.

96. Jeffrey L. Katz, "GOP Focuses on Resolving Overhaul Disputes," *Congressional Quarterly Weekly Report*, 9 September 1995, 2722; Jeffrey L. Katz, "Uneasy Compromise Reached on Welfare Overhaul," *Congressional Quarterly Weekly Report*, 16 September 1995, 2804–8.

97. *Congressional Record*, 104th Cong., 1st sess., 11 September 1995, S13173.

98. Ibid., S13179.

99. Jeffrey L. Katz, "Governors Group Sidelined in Welfare Debate," *Congressional Quarterly Weekly Report*, 20 May 1995, 1423–25.

100. Robin Toner, "Defeat for Child-Care Aid in Welfare Bill," *New York Times*, 12 September 1995, A20.

101. Katz, "Uneasy Compromise Reached," 2808.

102. Marian Wright Edelman, "Say No to This Welfare Reform," *Washington Post*, 3 November 1995, A23; Dana Milbank, "Children's Defense Fund and Its Lauded Leader Lose Clout as Social Policy Shifts to the States," *Wall Street Journal*, 28 May 1996, A28.

103. "Remarks on Vetoing the Budget Reconciliation Legislation," 6 December 1995, in *Public Papers of the Presidents: William J. Clinton, 1995*, book 2 (Washington, D.C.: Government Printing Office, 1996), 1851–53; "Message to the House of Representatives, Returning Without Approval Budget Reconciliation Legislation," in ibid., 6 December 1995, 1853–55.

104. Peters, *American Speakership*, 306; Jeff Shear, "Going for the Silver," *National Journal* 28, no. 42 (19 October 1996): 2219–22.

105. Helen Blank, memo to Child Care Advocates, re: Welfare Reform Bill Is Vetoed, 16 January 1996, CDF files.

106. "Message to the House of Representatives Returning Without Approval Legislation on the Welfare System," 9 January 1996, in *Public Papers of the Presidents: William J. Clinton, 1996*, book 1 (Washington, D.C.: Government Printing Office, 1997), 22–23.

107. Alissa J. Rubin, "Governors Hope Welfare, Medicaid Plan Will Lead to Overall Budget Deal," *Congressional Quarterly Weekly Report*, 10 February 1996, 352–53.

108. Helen Blank, memo to Child Care Advocates, re: NGA Proposals on Welfare and Medicaid, 13 February 1996, CDF files.

109. Lori Nitschke, "Committees Stoke the Fire for Another Veto Battle," *Congressional Quarterly Weekly Report*, 15 June 1996, 1684–86.

110. Lisa Clagett Weintraub, "Key Changes Approved," *Congressional Quarterly Weekly Report*, 15 June 1996, 1685.

111. U.S. House, Committee on the Budget, *Report to Accompany the Welfare and Medicaid Reform Act of 1996: H.R. 3734*, H. Rept. 104-651, 104th Cong, 2d sess., 27 June 1996, 869–70.

112. U.S. House, *Personal Responsibility and Work Opportunity Reconciliation Act of 1996: Conference Report to Accompany H.R. 3734*, H. Rept. 104-725, 104th Cong., 2d sess., 30 July 1996, 406–17; Jeffrey Katz, "Conferees May Determine Fate of Overhaul Bill," *Congressional Quarterly Weekly Report*, 20 July 1996, 2048–51.

113. CDF, "Key Questions About Federal Child Care Issues," July 1996, CDF files.

114. Sheila Zedlewski et al., *Potential Effects of Congressional Welfare Reform Legislation on Family Incomes* (Washington, D.C.: Urban Institute, 26 July 1996).

115. U.S. House, *Personal Responsibility and Work Opportunity Reconciliation Act of 1996*, 406–17; Raymond C. Scheppach, letter to Senate Finance Committee, 26 June 1996, CDF files.

116. Jeffrey L. Katz, "After 60 Years, Most Control Is Passing to States," *Congressional Quarterly Weekly Report*, 3 August 1996, 2190–96.

117. Presidential News Conference, "Clinton Says Welfare Bill Is 'Real Step Forward,'" *Congressional Quarterly Weekly Report*, 3 August 1996, 2217.

118. U.S. House, *Personal Responsibility and Work Opportunity Reconciliation Act of 1996*, 406–17.

119. U.S. House, Committee on the Budget, *Report to Accompany the Welfare and Medicaid Reform Act of 1996: H.R. 3734*, 869–70.

120. Yankelovich Partners, Time/CNN Poll, 10 May 1996.

121. Bruce Hershfield, telephone interview by author, 9 July 1998.

122. Joan Lombardi, telephone interview by author, 18 February 2000.

123. Carole Ashkinaze, "Child Care and the Media: Will Interest Last?" *ChildCare ActioNews* 13, no. 2 (March–April 1996): 1, 4–5.

124. April 19th Collaborative Working Committee, memo to Ratifying Organizations, 31 August 1994, re: Ratification of Guiding Principles for Child Care/ Early Education System.

125. April 19th Group, "Building and Maintaining an Effective Child Care/Early Education System in Your State," September 1996.

126. Milbank, "Children's Defense Fund and Its Lauded Leader Lose Clout," A28.

127. Helen Blank, telephone conversation with author, 4 August 1998.

128. Moynihan, *Miles to Go*, 38, 61.

129. Hillary Rodham Clinton, *It Takes a Village and Other Lessons Children Teach Us* (New York: Simon and Schuster, 1996), esp. 221–38.

130. Helen Blank, letter to State Child Care Advocates, 29 February 1996, CDF files.

131. Dorothy Gilliam, "For Kids, It's the Day After that Counts," *Washington Post*, 25 May 1996, B1.

132. Cindy Loose, "Memorial Bridge to Resound with the Patter of Little Feet," *Washington Post*, 29 May, 1996, B1.

133. Ibid.

134. "The State of the Union: Clinton Aims for the Center, Praises GOP Themes," *Congressional Quarterly Almanac, 1996* (Washington, D.C.: Congressional Quarterly, 1997), D5–6.

7. High Hopes, 1997–2000

1.   Frank R. Baumgartner and Bryan D. Jones, *Agendas and Instability in American Politics* (Chicago: University of Chicago Press, 1993).

2.   William Schneider, "Small Change," *National Journal* 28, no. 45 (9 November 1996): 2406–7.

3.   Ibid., 2406.

4.   Deborah Kalb, "Women of Freshmen Class Not Easily Labeled," *Congressional Quarterly Weekly Report*, 14 December 1996, 3399.

5.   Richard E. Cohen, "Soft Center," *National Journal* 28, no. 50 (14 December 1996): 2682.

6.   Richard E. Cohen, "A Lott of Change," *National Journal* 28, no. 45 (9 November 1996): 2438–42, esp. 2441; John K. Iglehart, "Politics and Compromise: Senator Jim Jeffords," *Health Affairs* 16, no. 4 (July–August 1997): 82–90.

7.   Graeme Browning, "Class Acts," *National Journal* 28, no. 51 (21 December 1996): 2742.

8.   Ibid., 2743.

9.   For a detailed chronology of the 1997 budget law, including the child tax credits, see Daniel J. Palazzolo, *Done Deal? The Politics of the 1997 Budget Agreement* (New York: Chatham House, 1999).

10.   George Hager, "Clinton, GOP Congress Strike Historic Budget Agreement," *Congressional Quarterly Weekly Report*, 3 May 1997, 993.

11.   Ronald D. Elving and Andrew Taylor, "A Balanced-Budget Deal Won, a Defining Issue Lost," *Congressional Quarterly Weekly Report*, 2 August 1997, 1835; David E. Rosenbaum, "In Balanced-Budget Deal, Bush Is Off the Seesaw," *New York Times*, 8 August 1997, A23; Nicholas F. Brady, "George Bush Was Right," *Wall Street Journal*, 9 March 1998, A18.

12.   Clinton originally wanted the child tax credit for couples with incomes of up to $60,000 and children through age thirteen. But in exchange for making more low-income families eligible, he went along with the GOP position of phasing out the credit for couples with incomes above $110,000 and extending the eligibility age to seventeen. Richard W. Stevenson, "Accord Reached on Tax Measure, G.O.P. Leaders Say," *New York Times*, 23 July 1997, A19; "Highlights of the Agreement," *Congressional Quarterly Weekly Report*, 2 August 1997, 1834; Adam Clymer, "White House and the G.O.P. Announce Deal to Balance Budget and to Trim Taxes," *New York Times*, 29 July 1997, A1, 16.

13.   Robert Pear, "G.O.P. Leadership Agrees on a Plan to Cover Children," *New York Times*, 24 July 1997, A1, B8; Alison Mitchell, "Clinton Makes a Broad Case for Budget Cuts," *New York Times*, 29 July 1997, A1, A16.

14.   John T. Bruer, "The Brain and Child Development: Time for Some Critical Thinking," *Public Health Reports* 113 (September–October 1998): 388–97.

15.   Carnegie Corporation, *Starting Points: Meeting the Needs of Our Youngest Children* (New York: Carnegie Corporation of New York, 1994); Rima Shore, *Rethinking the Brain: New Insights into Early Development* (New York: Families and Work Institute, 1997), xvii.

16. Carnegie Corporation, *Starting Points*, 3; Shore, *Rethinking the Brain*.

17. Julee J. Newberger, "New Brain Development Research: A Wonderful Opportunity to Build Public Support for Early Childhood Education," *Young Children* 52 no. 4 (May 1997): 4–9; Shore, *Rethinking the Brain*.

18. Mary B. W. Tabor, "Actor-Director Focusing on Children," *New York Times*, 6 August 1997, B8.

19. Available at: www.iamyourchild.org, accessed 4 December 2000.

20. Tabor, "Actor-Director Focusing on Children," B8.

21. Lynn A. Karoly et al., *Investing in Our Children: What We Know and Don't Know About the Costs and Benefits of Early Childhood Interventions* (Santa Monica, Calif.: RAND, 1998), xii.

22. See, for example, "Your Child" [special edition], *Newsweek*, spring–summer 1997; J. Madeline Nash, "Special Report: Fertile Minds," *Time*, 3 February 1997, 48–56; and "Nurturing Development of the Brain," *New York Times*, editorial, 28 April 1997, A14.

23. Bruer, "Brain and Child Development," 389.

24. John T. Bruer, *The Myth of the First Three Years: A New Understanding of Early Brain Development and Lifelong Learning* (New York: Free Press, 1999).

25. Ibid., 60.

26. John T. Bruer, "Education and the Brain: A Bridge Too Far," *Educational Researcher* 26, no. 8 (1997): 4–16.

27. Zero to Three, Response to *The Myth of the First Three Years*, by John T. Bruer, available at: www.zerotothree.org/no-myth.html, accessed 4 December 2000.

28. Barbara Vobejda, "Experts Describe New Research on Early Learning: White House Panel Stresses Importance of First 3 Years," *Washington Post*, 18 April 1997, A03.

29. National Institute of Child Health and Human Development, *The NICHD Study of Early Child Care*, NICHD Publication No. 98-4319 (Washington, D.C.: NICHD, April 1998), 15, 17. See also NICHD Early Child Care Research Network, "The Effects of Infant Child Care on Infant–Mother Attachment Security: Results of the NICHD Study of Early Child Care," *Child Development* 68, no. 5 (1997): 860–79.

30. See, for example, Ellen Galinsky et al., *The Study of Children in Family Child Care and Relative Care: Highlights of Findings* (New York: Families and Work Institute, 1994); Cost, Quality, and Child Outcomes Study Team, *Cost, Quality and Child Outcomes in Child Care Centers*, Executive Summary, 2d ed. (Denver: Economics Department, University of Colorado at Denver, 1995). For an excellent summary report on child care quality, see Deborah Lowe Vandell and Barbara Wolfe, "Child Care Quality: Does It Matter and Does It Need to be Improved?" available at: www.aspe.hhs.gov/hsp/ccquality00/ccqual.htm, accessed 12 September 2000.

31. "Clintoncare for Kids," *Wall Street Journal*, 8 January 1998, A8. The $2.1 billion referred to in this editorial was proposed by Clinton in 1998.
32. Laura Shapiro, "The Myth of Quality Time," *Newsweek*, 12 May 1997, 62–69; Arlie Hochschild, *The Time Bind: When Work Becomes Home and Home Becomes Work* (New York: Holt/Metropolitan Books, 1997); Penelope Leach, *Children First: What Our Society Must Do—and Is Not Doing—For Our Children Today* (New York: Knopf, 1994).
33. Christopher Dodd's bill was cosponsored by Minority Leader Tom Daschle in the Senate; Representative Lynn Woolsey introduced its counterpart (H.R. 899) in the House.
34. U.S. Senate, Subcommittee on Children and Families of the Committee on Labor and Human Resources, *Hearing on Pre to 3: Policy Implications of Child Brain Development*, 105th Cong., 1st sess., 5 June 1997, 1.
35. Ibid., 16.
36. Ibid., 33.
37. Ibid., 41.
38. U.S. Senate Committee on Labor and Human Resources, *Hearing on Improving the Quality of Child Care*, 105th Cong, 2d sess., 17 July 1997.
39. Among the tax-related features of CIDCARE were provisions making the DCTC refundable, increasing tax breaks for families that used accredited child care, and supplementing the dependent care assistance plans that some employers offered to employees.
40. Senator Herb Kohl's amendment was based on his bill, the Child Care Infrastructure Act of 1997 (S. 82), which was introduced in the House by Representative Carolyn Maloney (D-N.Y.) as H.R. 1706.
41. Jonathan Alter, "Making Child Care Macho," *Newsweek*, 3 November 1997, 70.
42. "About the Conference: The White House Conference on Child Care," 23 October 1997, available at: http://www.whitehouse.gov/WH/work/102397.html, accessed 4 December 2000; Barbara Vobejda, "President Announces Child-Care Initiatives," *Washington Post*, 24 October 1997, A16.
43. "Remarks Announcing Proposed Legislation on Child Care," 7 January 1998, in *Public Papers of the Presidents of the United States: William J. Clinton, 1998*, book 1 (Washington, D.C.: Government Printing Office, 1999), 6.
44. Robert Pear, "Child Care Talks Return First Lady to Spotlight," *New York Times*, 23 October 1997, A24.
45. Ibid.; Katharine Q. Seelye, "Hillary Clinton Begins Drive to Improve Care for Children," *New York Times*, 1 October 1997, A20;
46. Robert Pear, "Clinton to Offer a Child Care Plan, White House Says," *New York Times*, 14 December 1997, A1, 38.
47. Joan Lombardi, telephone interview by author, 18 February 2000.
48. Association for Supervision and Curriculum Development and thirty-two other

organizations, letter to the Honorable William Jefferson Clinton, 20 October 1997, CDF files, Washington, D.C.

49. Stanley I. Greenspan, "The Reason Why We Need to Rely Less on Day Care," *Washington Post*, 19 October 1997, C01

50. Gina C. Adams and Nicole Oxendine Poersch, *Key Facts About Child Care and Early Education: A Briefing Book* (Washington, D.C.: Children's Defense Fund, 1997); Gina Adams, Karen Schulman, and Nancy Ebb, *Locked Doors: States Struggling to Meet the Child Care Needs of Low-Income Working Families* (Washington, D.C.: Children's Defense Fund, March 1998). CDF also issued state reports on child care grouped by region; see, for example, Gina Adams and Karen Schulman, *The Northeast: Child Care Challenges* (Washington, D.C.: Children's Defense Fund, May 1998).

51. National Women's Law Center, *There Is No Conflict Between Helping Working Families Meet Their Child Care Needs and Supporting "Stay-at Home" Parents* (Washington, D.C.: NWLC, March 1998).

52. National Women's Law Center, *How the Clinton Administration's Child Care Initiative Would Expand the DCTC* (Washington, D.C.: NWLC, January 1998); National Women's Law Center, *Tax Relief for Employed Families: Improving the DCTC* (Washington, D.C.: NWLC, April 1998).

53. Lawrence O. Gostin, Peter S. Arno, and Allan Brandt, "FDA Regulation of Tobacco Advertising and Youth Smoking: Historical, Social and Constitutional Perspectives," *Journal of the American Medical Association* 277, no. 5 (5 February 1997): 410–18.

54. "Response to Increases in Cigarette Prices by Race/Ethnicity, Income, and Age Group: United States, 1976–1993," *Morbidity and Mortality Weekly Report* 47, no. 29 (31 July 1998): 605–9; General Accounting Office, *Tobacco: Issues Surrounding a National Tobacco Settlement*, GAO/RCED-98-110 (Washington, D.C.: GAO, April 1998), 2–3.

55. Sue Kirchhoff, "Clinton's Child Care Proposal Draws Supporters and Critics," *Congressional Quarterly Weekly Report*, 10 January 1998, 78–79.

56. "Remarks Announcing Proposed Legislation on Child Care," 7 January 1998, 8; Katharine Q. Seelye, "Clinton Proposes $21 Billion over 5 Years for Child Care," *New York Times*, 8 January 1998, A1, 18.

57. Seelye, "Clinton Proposes $21 Billion"; John F. Harris, "Clinton Rolls Out Child Care Plan," *Washington Post*, 8 January 1998, A01.

58. "Address Before a Joint Session of the Congress on the State of the Union," 27 January 1998, in *Public Papers of the Presidents of the United States: William J. Clinton, 1998*, book 1, 112–23.

59. "Remarks to the National Council of Jewish Women," 24 February 1998, in *Public Papers of the Presidents of the United States: William J. Clinton, 1998*, book 1, 276–82; "Remarks at Housatonic Community-Technical College in

Bridgeport, Connecticut," 10 March 1998, in *Public Papers of the Presidents of the United States: William J. Clinton, 1998*, book 1, 343–47; "Remarks on the Child Care Initiative and an Exchange with Reporters," 23 April 1998, in *Public Papers of the Presidents of the United States: William J. Clinton, 1998*, book 1, 604–6.

60. "Address Before a Joint Session of the Congress on the State of the Union," 27 January 1998, 112–23; Executive Office of the President, Office of Management and Budget, *Budget of the United States Government, Fiscal Year 1999* (Washington, D.C.: Government Printing Office, 1999), 61–67.

61. U.S. Department of the Treasury, *Investing in Child Care: Challenges Facing Working Parents and the Private Sector Response* (Washington, D.C.: Department of the Treasury, 1998); U.S. Department of Labor, *Meeting the Needs of Today's Workforce: Child Care Best Practices* (Washington, D.C.: Department of Labor, 1998).

62. Harris, "Clinton Rolls Out Child Care Plan," A01; Seelye, "Clinton Proposes $21 Billion," 18.

63. One of the marriage penalties in the federal income tax code is the increase in taxes that some married couples incur because they pay taxes as couples rather than as individuals. The income from the second worker pushes the couple's total earnings into a higher tax bracket than if the second worker were taxed separately. The marriage penalty does not apply to single-earner couples, the constituency that conservatives were most concerned about in the context of child care policy. National Center for Policy Analysis, "The Marriage Penalty," Policy Backgrounder No. 145, 2 February 1998, available at: www.ncpa.org/bg/bg145.html, accessed 4 December 2000; Lori Nitschke, "Marital Status and Taxes? Irreconcilable Differences?" *Congressional Quarterly Weekly*, 30 October 1999, 2581–85.

64. Robert Rector and Patrick Fagan, "The Clinton Day Care Proposal: An Attack on Parents and Children," *Executive Memorandum*, no. 506 (Washington, D.C.: Heritage Foundation, 14 December 1998).

65. "Clintoncare for Kids," A8.

66. "Flawed Day-Care Plans," *New York Times*, 27 December 1997, A10.

67. National Women's Law Center, *How the Chafee–Johnson Child Care Bill Would Change the DCTC* (Washington, D.C.: NWLC, March 1998), 2; "105th Congress Continues Debate on Child Care Initiatives in Second Session," *Young Children* 53, no. 2 (March 1998): 82.

68. ACCESS legislation allowed families with one parent staying at home to care for a child under the age of one to claim up to $90 per month of child care expenses as a tax credit.

69. For a detailed discussion, see "Child-Care Options," *Congressional Quarterly Researcher* 8, no. 18 (8 May 1998): 409–32.

70. U.S. Senate, Committee on Finance, *Hearing on Child Care*, 105th Cong., 2d sess., 22 April 1998.

71. Mott Foundation, "Special Report: 21st Century Community Learning Centers, 1998 Poll Findings," available at: www.mott.org/21stcentury/announcements/polls/html, accessed 4 December 2000. This Web site also has results of 1999 and 2000 polls indicating ongoing strong public support for after-school programs.

72. U.S. House, Committee on Ways and Means, *1998 Green Book*, 105th Cong., 2d sess., 19 May 1998, 663.

73. Kristin Smith, *Who's Minding the Kids? Child Care Arrangements: Fall 1995*, Current Population Reports, P70-70 (Washington, D.C.: Bureau of the Census, 2000), 17.

74. Fight Crime: Invest in Kids, *Quality Child Care and After-School Programs: Powerful Weapons Against Crime* (Washington, D.C.: Fight Crime: Invest in Kids, February 1998), 29, citing B. M. Miller et al., *I Wish the Kids Didn't Watch So Much TV: Out-of-School Time in Three Low Income Communities* (Wellesley, Mass.: Wellesley College, National Institute on Out-of-School Time, 1996).

75. Jodi Wilgoren, "The Bell Rings but the Students Stay, and Stay," *New York Times*, 24 January 2000, A1, A18. For an excellent review of research findings related to after-school care, see Deborah Lowe Vandell and Hsiu-chih Su, "Child Care and School-Age Children," *Young Children* 54, no. 6 (November 1999): 62–71.

76. Adams and Poersch, *Key Facts About Child Care and Early Education*, H-1; National Institute on Out-of-School Time (NIOST), Center for Research on Women, *Fact Sheet on School-Age Children* (Wellesley, Mass.: NIOST, January 2000), available at: www.wellesley.edu/WCW/CRW/SAC/factsht.html, accessed 4 December 2000.

77. Howard N. Snyder, "Juvenile Justice Arrests, 1997," *Juvenile Justice Bulletin* (Washington, D.C.: Department of Justice, Office of Juvenile Justice and Delinquency Prevention, December 1998), available at: www.ncjrs.org/pdffiles1/97arrest.pdf, accessed 4 December 2000.

78. Fight Crime: Invest in Kids, *Quality Child Care and After-School Programs*, 12–25.

79. U.S. Department of Education and U.S. Department of Justice, *Safe and Smart: Making the After-School Hours Work for Kids* (Washington, D.C.: Government Printing Office, 1998).

80. Elliot Richardson was an interesting choice, as he was the only U.S. attorney general (1973) who also served as a state attorney general (Massachusetts) and as a federal prosecutor. Sanford Newman, telephone interview by author, 26 October 1998.

81. Fight Crime: Invest in Kids, *A Public Awareness Project to Help Americans See Their Self-Interest in Investing in All of America's Children and Youth* (Washington, D.C.: Fight Crime: Invest in Kids, August 1998).

82. Newman, interview.

83. Fight Crime: Invest in Kids, *Quality Child Care and After-School Programs*; Fight Crime: Invest in Kids, "415 Police Chiefs, Prosecutors, and Victims Unveil School and Youth Violence Prevention Plan," press release, 13 October 1998.

84. Sanford Newman, letter to author, 9 November 1998.

85. *Congressional Record*, 105th Cong., 2d sess., 2 March 1998, S1202–5; *Congressional Record*, 105th Cong., 2d sess., 4 February 1998, S388–93; Executive Office of the President, Office of Management and Budget, *Budget of the United States Government, Fiscal Year 1999*, 64.

86. Staff, Senate Committee on Labor and Human Resources, "21st Century Community Learning Centers: Comparison Between Statute and Department of Education Rules/Application," February 1998, 8–9; Katina R. Stapleton, *21st Century Community Learning Centers: A Summary of the Program* (Washington, D.C.: Congressional Research Service, 7 August 1998).

87. Stapleton, *21st Century Community Learning Centers*.

88. Senate, Committee on Labor and Human Resources, *Hearing on Non-School Hours: Mobilizing School and Community Resources*, 105th Cong., 2d sess., 25 February 1998.

89. Stapleton, *21st Century Community Learning Centers*.

90. According to a Gallup Poll taken in January 1998, respondents ranked education and crime as the two top issues they would like the president and Congress to address. Child care was not even mentioned although tax credits for families with children ranked as a secondary priority. George Gallup Jr., *The Gallup Poll: Public Opinion, 1997* (Wilmington, Del.: Scholarly Resources, 1998), 24–26.

91. *Congressional Record*, 105th Cong., 2d sess., 31 March 1998, S2805.

92. Ibid., S2809.

93. Executive Office of the President, Office of Management and Budget, *Historic Tables: Budget of the United States Government, Fiscal Year 2001* (Washington, D.C.: Government Printing Office, 2000), 19–20.

94. "Background, Support the Dodd, Kennedy, Murray Child Care Amendment" (Washington, D.C.: Children's Defense Fund, March 1998).

95. *Congressional Record*, 105th Cong., 2d sess., 31 March 1998, S2811; Senator Barbara Mikulski was absent that day, but probably would have voted for Dodd's amendment had she been there.

96. Allan Freedman, "Action on Tobacco Agreement Not Expected Before Fall," *Congressional Quarterly Weekly Report*, 21 June 1997, 1442; Jonathan Weis-

man, "Congress Casting a Wary Eye at Tobacco Deal's Details," *Congressional Quarterly Weekly Report*, 28 June 1997, 1508–9.

97. "Tobacco Use Among High School Students: United States, 1997," *Morbidity and Mortality Weekly Report* 47, no. 12 (3 April 1998): 229–33.

98. A 10 percent increase in the price of cigarettes caused a 4 to 9 percent decrease in the percentage of youths who smoked. General Accounting Office, *Tobacco*, 10; "Response to Increases in Cigarette Prices by Race/Ethnicity, Income, and Age Groups: United States, 1976–1993."

99. U.S. Senate, *National Tobacco Policy and Youth Smoking Reduction Act*, S. Rept. 105-180, 105th Cong., 2d sess., May 1988, "Title II: Reductions in Underage Tobacco Use."

100. "Youth Smoking Rises 73% in 9 Years," *New York Times*, 9 October 1998, A14; Gostin, Arno, and Brandt, "FDA Regulation of Tobacco Advertising and Youth Smoking."

101. For example, Senator Edward Kennedy's bill (S. 1492) used tobacco revenues to fund early childhood programs. Senator Orrin Hatch, chair of the Judiciary Committee, introduced legislation (S. 1530) that, among other things, increased penalties imposed on cigarette companies for not meeting targets for reducing youth smoking.

102. "Issue: Tobacco Settlement," *Congressional Quarterly Weekly Report*, 6 December 1997, 2997–98; Alan K. Ota, "Tobacco Industry Courts the Hill with Compromise, Conciliation," *Congressional Quarterly Weekly Report*, 8 November 1997, 2727–33.

103. U.S. Senate, *National Tobacco Policy and Youth Smoking Reduction Act*.

104. The discussion of child care and tobacco legislation is based largely on a telephone interview with David Kass, 14 April 2000.

105. Nancy Duff Campbell, Judith C. Appelbaum, and Cristina Firvida of NWLC, letter on behalf of American Association of University Women and other women's organizations to senators, 5 June 1998, NWLC files, Washington, D.C.

106. Rebecca Carr, "Federal–State Tobacco Dispute May Land in Congress," *Congressional Quarterly Weekly Report*, 22 November 1997, 2907.

107. Governor George V. Voinovich and other governors, letter to Senators Lott and Daschle, inserted into *Congressional Record*, 105th Cong., 2d sess., 17 June 1998, S6448.

108. Governor George V. Voinovich and Governor Thomas R. Carper, letter to Senator Lott, 20 May 1998, NGA files, Washington, D.C.

109. The Kerry–Bond amendment had cosponsorship of Senators John Chafee, Kennedy, Dodd, Paul Wellstone, Kohl, Tim Johnson (D-S.D.), Barbara Boxer, Arlen Specter, Mary Landrieu (D-La.), Richard Durbin (D-Ill.), Max Baucus (D-Mont.), and even Bob Graham, who had previously expressed opposition to the settlement because of the federal government's usurping of state funds.

110. *Congressional Record*, 105th Cong., 2d sess., 11 June, 1998, S6155–56, quote on S6155.
111. Ibid., S6139–56.
112. David E. Rosenbaum, "Senate Drops Tobacco Bill with '98 Revival Unlikely: Clinton Lashes Out at G.O.P.," *New York Times*, 18 June 1998, A1, A24.
113. Jeffrey Goldberg, "Big Tobacco's Endgame," *New York Times Magazine*, 21 June 1998, 41; Alan Greenblatt, "Tobacco Debate Rages on, Keeping Bill Alive, if Unwieldy," *Congressional Quarterly Weekly*, 13 June 1998, 1605–7.
114. National Governors Association, "The Tobacco Settlement Agreement: Implications for States," 9 December 1998, available at: www.nga.org/pubs/issue briefs/1998/981209tobacco.asp, accessed 4 December 2000; Stephanie Stapleton, "States Jockey for Use of Tobacco Funds," *American Medical News*, 24 May 1999, 1, 30, 31.
115. Sue Kirchhoff, with Mary Agnes Carey, "Medical Research and Education Are Big Winners in Spending Bill," *Congressional Quarterly Weekly*, 24 October 1998, 2985–97.
116. Children's Defense Fund, "Child Care Advocacy Newsletter," 26 October 1998, available at: cdfchildcare@childrensdefense.org and www.childrensdefense.org/ ccadvoc_newsletter_archives.htm.
117. Kirchhoff, with Carey, "Medical Research and Education Are Big Winners in Spending Bill."
118. Children's Defense Fund, "Child Care Advocacy Newsletter," 16 October 1998.
119. This view was expressed by Robert D. Reischauer, former CBO director and now a senior fellow at the Brookings Institution, cited in Carroll J. Doherty, "Clinton Case Overshadows 105th's Legislative Legacy," *Congressional Quarterly Weekly*, 3 October 1998, 2635.
120. David Hosansky, "Hastert Wins High Marks from the Business Community," *Congressional Quarterly Weekly*, 2 January 1999, 22–24.
121. Jeffrey L. Katz, "Shakeup in the House," *Congressional Quarterly Weekly*, 7 November 1998, 2989.
122. Michael Barone and Grant Ujifusa, *The Almanac of American Politics, 2000* (Washington, D.C.: National Journal, 1999), 373–78.
123. Executive Office of the President, Office of Management and Budget, *Historic Tables: Budget of the United States Government, Fiscal Year 2000* (Washington, D.C.: Government Printing Office, 1999), 20; Executive Office of the President, Office of Management and Budget, *Historic Tables: Budget of the United States Government, Fiscal Year 2001*, 19–20.
124. Andrew Taylor, "Clinton, GOP Hope to Make History out of Their Differences," *Congressional Quarterly Weekly*, 17 July 1999, 1702–3.
125. David Wessel and Greg Hitt, "Burden of Choice: Lawmakers Discover that Surpluses Can Be as Vexing as Deficits," *Wall Street Journal*, 29 July 1999, A1, A12.

126. Adam S. Marlin, "A Will of Their Own," *Congressional Quarterly Weekly*, 30 January 1999, 250.

127. "State of the Union Address," 19 January 1999, in *Weekly Compilation of Presidential Documents, William J. Clinton*, for week ending Friday January 22, 1999 (Washington, D.C.: Government Printing Office, 1999), 35: 78–88.

128. Executive Office of the President, Office of Management and Budget, *Budget of the United States Government, Fiscal Year 2000* (Washington, D.C.: Government Printing Office, 1999).

129. *Congressional Record*, 106th Cong., 1st sess., 19 January 1999, S375–86.

130. *Congressional Record*, 106th Cong., 1st sess., 11 March 1999, S2592–98.

131. For a summary of child care legislative proposals and actions in 1999 to 2000, see Melinda Gish and Karen Spar, *Child Care Issues in the 106th Congress* (Washington, D.C.: Congressional Research Service, 18 February 2000).

132. U.S. House, Subcommittee on Human Resources of the Committee on Ways and Means, *Hearing on Child Care Financing*, 106th Cong., 1st sess., 16 March 1999; Sue Kirchhoff, "As Lawmakers Push to Expand Federal Funding for Child Care, GOP Accuses States of Hoarding," *Congressional Quarterly Weekly*, 20 March 1999, 706.

133. Representative Nancy L. Johnson, letter to each governor, 16 March 1999, courtesy of Representative Johnson's office.

134. Kirchhoff, "As Lawmakers Push to Expand Federal Funding for Child Care, GOP Accuses States of Hoarding."

135. Jason DeParle, "Leftover Money for Welfare Baffles, or Inspires, States," *New York Times*, 29 August 1999, A1, A30.

136. U.S. Department of Health and Human Services, Administration for Children and Families, "Access to Child Care for Low-income Working Families," 1999, available at: www.acf.dhhs.gov/programs/ccb/research/ccreport/ccreport.htm, accessed 4 December 2000.

137. Andrew Taylor, "Adoption of GOP Budget Resolution Is Small Victory with Big Asterisk," *Congressional Quarterly Weekly*, 17 April 1999, 881–82.

138. Gish and Spar, *Child Care Issues in the 106th Congress*, 13.

139. U.S. House, *Conference Report to Accompany H.R. 2488*, H. Rept. 106-289, 106th Cong., 1st sess, 4 August 1999, 219–23, 229, 545.

140. William J. Clinton, "Veto Message," 23 September 1999, reprinted in *Congressional Quarterly Weekly*, 25 September 1999, 2248.

141. *Congressional Record*, 106th Cong., 1st sess., 30 September 1999, S11716–17.

142. *Congressional Record*, 106th Cong., 1st sess., 3 November 1999, H11441–43.

143. Children's Defense Fund, "Child Care Advocacy Newsletter," 16 November 1999.

144. Executive Office of the President, Office of Management and Budget, *Budget of the United States Government, Fiscal Year 2001* (Washington, D.C.: Government Printing Office, 2000), 57–61.

145. David Nather, "House Braces for More Slow Going on Labor–HHS Spending Bill as GOP Leaders Scramble for Support," *Congressional Quarterly Weekly*, 10 June 2000, 1398–99; Children's Defense Fund, "Child Care Advocacy Newsletter," 9 June 2000; Children's Defense Fund, "Child Care Advocacy Newsletter," 15 June 2000.

146. White House, Office of the Press Secretary, "Statement by the President," 6 December 2000, available at: http://www.pub.whitehouse.gov/uri.oma.eop.gov/us/2000/12/6/5.text.1, accessed 7 December 2000; U.S. Department of Health and Human Services, "New Statistics Show Only Small Percentage of Eligible Families Receive Child Care Help," press release, 6 December 2000.

147. Children's Defense Fund, "Child Care Advocacy Newsletter," 18 December 2000.

148. Bob Herbert, "Children's Champions?" *New York Times*, 31 August 2000, A25; Marian Wright Edelman, "There's No Trademark on Concern for Kids," *New York Times*, 29 July 2000, A13.

149. Irvin Molotsky, "Study Shows Importance of Preschool and Child-Care Quality in Education," *New York Times*, 9 June 1999, B11; Cost, Quality, and Outcomes Study Team, *The Children of the Cost, Quality, and Outcomes Study Go to School, Executive Summary* (Chapel Hill: University of North Carolina, Frank Porter Graham Child Development Center, June 1999), available at: www.fpg.unc.edu/~ncedl/PAGES/cq.htm, accessed 22 June 2001.

150. Committee on Integrating the Science of Early Childhood Development, *From Neurons to Neighborhoods: The Science of Early Childhood Development*, ed. Jack P. Shonkoff and Deborah A. Phillips (Washington, D.C.: National Academy Press, 2000), 10.

151. U.S. Department of Health and Human Services, Child Care Bureau and Maternal and Child Health Bureau, *Healthy Child Care America: Blueprint for Action* (Washington, D.C.: Government Printing Office, 1996).

152. Congressional Caucus for Women's Issues, 106th Cong., Legislative Agenda, available at: www.house.gov/maloney/issues/womenscaucus/106thagenda.html, accessed 4 December 2000.

153. National Council of Jewish Women, *Opening a New Window on Child Care: A Report on the Status of Child Care in the Nation Today* (New York: National Council of Jewish Women, 1999).

154. Leslie Calman, personal correspondence, 17 September 1999.

155. *Lifetime Television, the Congressional Caucus for Women's Issues, and Advocacy Groups Advance New Effort to Make Women's Voices Heard in the National Conversation on Child Care* (New York: Lifetime, n.d.).

156. Family Research Council, *Building the Family, Building the Republic: Policy Proposals for the 106th Congress* (Washington, D.C.: FRC, 1998), 27–30; Daniel J. Mitchell, "Time to Sunset the Tax Code," *Heritage Foundation Executive Memorandum* (Washington, D.C.: Heritage Foundation, 28 January 2000). Republicans' efforts to enact legislation alleviating the marriage penalty were stymied in September 2000 when the House failed to override President Clinton's veto of legislation that included such provisions. Tax reform legislation enacted in May 2001 included a phaseout of the marriage penalty, starting in 2005. Glenn Kessler and Juliet Eilperin, "Congress Passes $1.35 Trillion Tax Cut: Lawmakers Hand Bush a Big Legislative Victory," *Washington Post*, 27 May 2001, A1.

157. Gwen J. Broude, "The Realities of Day Care," *Public Interest* 125 (fall 1996): 95–105; Darcy Olsen, *The Advancing Nanny State: Why the Government Should Stay out of Child Care* (Washington, D.C.: Cato Institute, 23 October 1997).

8. *A View from the States, 1996–2000*

1.   James Hosek and Robert Levine, "An Introduction to the Issues," in James Hosek and Robert Levine, eds., *The New Fiscal Federalism and the Social Safety Net: A View from California*, 1–8 (Santa Monica, Calif.: RAND, 1996), available at: www.rand.org/publications/CF/CF123/hosek.levine/index.html, accessed 11 December 2000.

2.   Ann O. M. Bowman and Richard C. Kearney, *The Resurgence of the States* (Englewood Cliffs, N.J.: Prentice-Hall, 1986), 6.

3.   John D. Donahue, *Disunited States* (New York: Basic Books, 1997), 30.

4.   Bowman and Kearney, *Resurgence of the States*, 6.

5.   Thomas J. Anton, "New Federalism and Intergovernmental Fiscal Relationships: The Implications for Health Policy," *Journal of Health, Politics, Policy, and Law* 22, no. 3 (1997): 704.

6.   Donahue, *Disunited States*, 10.

7.   Richard P. Nathan, *The Newest New Federalism for Welfare: Where Are We Now and Where Are We Headed?* (Albany, N.Y.: Nelson A. Rockefeller Institute of Government, 30 October 1997), 7.

8.   Garry Wills, "The War Between the States and Washington," *New York Times Magazine*, 5 July 1998, 29.

9.   Bowman and Kearney, *Resurgence of the States*, 10–31; Anton, "New Federalism and Intergovernmental Fiscal Relationships," 694–95.

10. These results of these polls were not consistent. For some area—such as health care, the environment, civil rights, and the economy—respondents favored federal over state authorities. Donahue, *Disunited States*, 13, 186.

11. Richard L. Cole and John Kincaid, "Public Opinion and American Federalism: Perspectives on Taxes, Spending, and Trust—An ACIR Update," *Publius: The Journal of Federalism* 30, nos. 1–2 (2000): 189–201, data reported on 191–192.

12. Anton, "New Federalism and Intergovernmental Fiscal Relationships," 694.

13. Ibid., 708–11.

14. Ibid., 706.

15. Alan Greenblatt, "States vs. Congress, Governors: Leave It to Us," *Congressional Quarterly Weekly*, 20 February 1999, 425.

16. Nathan, *Newest New Federalism for Welfare*, 5.

17. U.S. National Commission on Excellence in Education, *A Nation at Risk: The Imperative for Educational Reform: A Report to the Nation and the Secretary of Education, U.S. Department of Education* (Washington, D.C.: National Commission on Excellence in Education, 1983).

18. For a thorough discussion of Goal 1 and its implementation, see Lorrie A. Shepard, Sharon L. Kagan, and Emily Wurtz, eds., *Principles and Recommendations for Early Childhood Assessments* (Washington, D.C.: National Education Goals Panel, February 1998).

19. U.S. Department of Education, "Goals 2000: Reforming Education to Improve Student Achievement—April 30, 1998; Part I: Goals 2000: History," available at: www.ed.gov/pubs/G2KReforming/g2ch1.html, accessed 11 December 2000. Many excellent documents describing Goals 2000 are available on-line through the Department of Education's Web site: www.ed.gov/G2K.

20. U.S. Department of Education, "Goals 2000: Educate America Act, October 1996 Update," available at: www.ed.gov/G2K/g2k-fact.html, accessed 11 December 2000.

21. As part of this focus on the first three years, the National Governors Association published *The First Three Years: A Governor's Guide to Early Childhood* (Washington, D.C.: NGA, 1996), which covered state initiatives, financing strategies, public engagement, and other topics pertaining to early childhood and health.

22. National Governors Association, Center for Best Practices, *Promising Practices to Improve Results for Young Children* (Washington, D.C.: NGA, n.d.); Mary L. Culkin, Scott Groginsky, and Steve Christian, *Building Blocks: A Legislator's Guide to Child Care* (Denver: National Conference of State Legislatures, December 1997), 65–67; Office of the Governor George V. Voinovich, *The Ohio Family and Children First Initiative: A Record of Results Toward School Readiness, Update* (Columbus: Office of the Governor, October 1996), 1, 4.

23. The NGA Center for Best Practices, started in 1996, works in a number of policy fields, many of which focus on children's issues. Its activities in early childhood care include showcasing the states' efforts and promoting the governors' roles in implementing them. National Governors Association, Center

for Best Practices, *Investing in America's Future: Achieving Results for Young Children, What Works?* [conference brochure] (Washington, D.C.: NGA, 1997); National Governors Association, Center for Best Practices, *Investing in America's Future: Early Childhood Activities in the States, 1996–98* (Washington, D.C.: NGA, 1998).

24. George Voinovich was elected senator from Ohio in 1998, and Thomas Carper was elected senator from Delaware in 2000.

25. National Governors Association, *Policy Statement on Child Care and Early Education, EC-11* (Washington, D.C.: NGA, 1998).

26. Ibid.

27. National Governors Association, *Head Start in the States: Strengthening Collaborative Relationships* (Washington, D.C.: NGA, 1996).

28. Scott Groginsky, Steve Christian, and Laurie McConnell, *Early Childhood Initiatives in the States: Translating Research into Policy*, State Legislative Report 23, no. 14 (Denver: National Conference of State Legislatures, June 1998); National Governors Association, *Policy Statement on Child Care and Early Education*; Culkin, Groginsky, and Christian, *Building Blocks*, 15.

29. Groginsky, Christian, and McConnell, *Early Childhood Initiatives in the States*, 8.

30. Kevin Sack, "Georgia's Chief Reveling in His Sky-High Ratings," *New York Times*, 16 February 1998, A9; Anthony Raden, *Universal Prekindergarten in Georgia: A Case Study of Georgia's Lottery-Funded Pre-K Program* (New York: Foundation for Child Development, 1999).

31. This view is eloquently documented in an analysis of states' child care policies in the late 1980s: Monica Lynn Herk, "Helping the Hand that Rocks the Cradle: The Politics of Child Care Policy at the State Level" (Ph.D. diss., Princeton University, 1993).

32. Jennifer Preston, "Investing in Future, States Spend More on Preschool Classes," *New York Times*, 22 March 1998, 40.

33. U.S. Department of Health and Human Services, Administration for Children and Families, "Child Care and Development Fund: Notice of Proposed Rulemaking," *Federal Register* 62, no. 141 (23 July 1997): 39609–57. The proposed and final rule changed the name of the child care block grant to Child Care and Development Fund. However, because it continued to be referred to as the Child Care and Development Block Grant (CCDBG), that term is used for this and subsequent discussions.

34. U.S. Department of Health and Human Services, Administration for Children and Families, "Child Care and Development Fund: Final Rule," *Federal Register* 63, no. 142 (24 July 1998): 39936.

35. U.S. Department of Health and Human Services, Administration for Children and Families, "Child Care and Development Fund: Notice of Proposed Rulemaking," 39610.

36. Ibid.
37. Sharon K. Long et al., *Child Care Assistance Under Welfare Reform: Early Responses by the States* (Washington, D.C.: Urban Institute, 22 August 1998).
38. See, for example, Carl Tubbesing, deputy executive director, NCSL, letter to the Assistant Secretary for Children and Families, n.d., courtesy of NCSL.
39. U.S. Department of Health and Human Services, Administration for Children and Families, "Child Care and Development Fund: Final Rule," 39958.
40. U.S. Department of Health and Human Services, Administration for Children and Families, "Child Care and Development Fund: Notice of Proposed Rulemaking," 39625–26.
41. U.S. Department of Health and Human Services, Administration for Children and Families, "Child Care and Development Fund: Final Rule," 39959.
42. See, for example, Yasmina Vinci, National Association of Child Care Resource and Referral Agencies, comment, 22 September 1997, re: Proposed Amendments to the Child Care and Development Block Grant Regulation, obtained from ACF, on-line; Barbara Willer, National Association for the Education of Young Children, comment, 22 September 1997, re: Proposed Amendments to the Child Care and Development Block Grant Regulation, obtained from ACF, on-line; Karabelle Pizzigati and Bruce Hershfield, Child Welfare League of America, letter to the Assistant Secretary of HHS for Children and Families, 22 September 1997, Child Care Bureau, Administration for Children and Families, Washington, D.C.; Helen Blank and Nancy Ebb, memo to Child Care Advocates, 10 August 1997, re: Proposed Child Care Regulations Include Many Positive Features, CDF files, Washington. D.C.; and Lynn White, National Child Care Association, comments, 22 September 1997, re: Proposed Amendments to the Child Care and Development Block Grant Regulation, obtained from ACF, on-line.
43. See, for example, Carmen Schulze, Missouri Department of Social Services, Division of Family Services, comment, 29 September 1997, re: Proposed Amendments to the Child Care and Development Block Grant Regulation, obtained from ACF, on-line; Suzanne Zafonte Sennett, New York Bureau of Early Childhood Services, comment, 26 September 1997, re: Proposed Amendments to the Child Care and Development Block Grant Regulation, obtained from ACF, on-line; Patti Campbell, Idaho Department of Health and Welfare, comment, 22 September 1997, re: Proposed Amendments to the Child Care and Development Block Grant Regulation, obtained from ACF, on-line; and Verna S. Weber, memo to Joan Lombardi, 22 September 1997, re: Comments for Child Care Regs., Child Care Bureau files.
44. U.S. Department of Health and Human Services, Administration for Children and Families, "Child Care and Development Fund: Final Rule," 39959.
45. U.S. Department of Health and Human Services, Administration for Children and Families, "Child Care and Development Fund: Notice of Proposed Rulemaking," 39626.

46. Robert E. Hannemann, president, American Academy of Pediatrics, letter to the Assistant Secretary for Children and Families, 22 September 1997, re: Child Care and Development Fund, Notice of Proposed Rulemaking, courtesy of AAP.

47. U.S. Department of Health and Human Services, Administration for Children and Families, "Child Care and Development Fund: Final Rule," 39953–57, 39987–88.

48. See, for example, Blank and Ebb, memo to Child Care Advocates, 10 August 1997, 3, and Alvin Collins, Maryland Department of Human Resources, comment, 26 September 1997, re: Proposed Amendments to the Child Care and Development Block Grant Regulation, obtained from ACF, on-line.

49. U.S. Department of Health and Human Services, Administration for Children and Families, "Child Care and Development Fund: Final Rule," 39946.

50. See, for example, White, comments, 22 September 1997.

51. U.S. Department of Health and Human Services, Administration for Children and Families, "Child Care and Development Fund: Final Rule," 39942–943.

52. Ibid., 39965, 39990.

53. Tubbesing, letter to the Assistant Secretary for Children and Families, n.d.

54. See, for example, William T. Gormley Jr., *Everybody's Children: Child Care as a Public Problem* (Washington, D.C.: Brookings Institution, 1995); Alfred J. Kahn and Sheila B. Kamerman, *Child Care: Facing the Hard Choices* (Dover, Mass.: Auburn House, 1987); and Helen Blank and Nicole Oxendine Poersch, *State Child Care and Early Education Developments: Highlights and Updates for 1998* (Washington, D.C.: Children's Defense Fund, 1999).

55. See, for example, Government Accounting Office, *Welfare Reform: States' Efforts to Expand Child Care Programs*, GAO/HEHS-98-27 (Washington, D.C.: GAO, January 1998); Government Accounting Office, *Welfare Reform: Implications of Increased Work Participation for Child Care*, GAO/HEHS-97-75 (Washington, D.C.: GAO, May 1997); Sharon K. Long and Sandra J. Clark, *The New Child Care Block Grant: State Funding Choices and Their Implications* (Washington, D.C.: Urban Institute, October 1997); Helen Blank and Gina Adams, *State Developments in Child Care and Early Education 1997* (Washington, D.C.: Children's Defense Fund, 1997); Blank and Poersch, *State Child Care and Early Education Developments*; American Public Welfare Association, *Meeting the Child Care Challenge: State Child Care Status Survey* (Washington, D.C.: American Public Welfare Association, 1998); Culkin, Groginsky, and Christian, *Building Blocks*; National Governors Association, Center for Best Practices, Employment and Social Services Policy Studies Division, and U.S. Department of Health and Human Services, Administration for Children and Families (hereafter referred to as NGA and DHHS), *Improving Services for Children in Working Families* (Washington, D.C.: NGA, 1998); U.S.

Department of Health and Human Services, Child Care Bureau, "Child Care and Development Fund, FFY 1998 Tables and Charts, 15 March 2000," available at: www.acf.dhhs.gov/programs/ccb/data/charts/cover.htm, accessed 25 April 2000.

56. Government Accounting Office, *Welfare Reform: States' Efforts to Expand Child Care Programs*, 5.

57. U.S. House, Committee on Ways and Means, *1998 Green Book*, 105th Cong., 2d sess., 19 May 1998, 685.

58. Blank and Poersch, *State Child Care and Early Education Developments*, 9.

59. Some of these transfers included carryovers of unobligated TANF funds from previous years. U.S. Department of Health and Human Services, Administration for Children and Families, "TANF Program Expenditures for 1999 through the 4th Quarter, 1 June 2000," available at: www.acf.dhhs.gov/programs/ofs/data/q499, accessed 7 July 2001.

60. American Public Welfare Association, *Meeting the Child Care Challenge*, 2; Blank and Adams, *State Developments in Child Care and Early Education 1997*, 14.

61. Blank and Poersch, *State Child Care and Early Education Developments*, 10.

62. Ibid., 10–13.

63. Ibid., 9.

64. Ibid., 9–11.

65. Children's Defense Fund, "Child Care Advocacy Newsletter," 13 March 2000, available at: cdfchildcare@childrensdefense.org.

66. Government Accounting Office, *Welfare Reform: States' Efforts to Expand Child Care Programs*; "Child Care in California: A Short Report on Subsidies, Affordability, and Supply," available at: http://aspe.hhs.gov/hsp/Child-Care99/ca-rpt.htm, accessed 11 December 2000.

67. Blank and Poersch, *State Child Care and Early Education Developments*, 16.

68. Ibid., 29–35.

69. Ibid., 26–27.

70. Raymond Hernandez, "Albany Funds for Child Care Going Unspent," *New York Times*, 25 October 1999, B1, B7.

71. Government Accounting Office, *Welfare Reform: States' Efforts to Expand Child Care Programs*, 3.

72. U.S. Department of Health and Human Services, Administration for Children and Families, "Child Care and Development Block Grant/Child Care and Development Fund Children Served in Fiscal Year 1999 (average monthly)," available at: www.acf.dhhs.gov/news/cctable.htm, accessed 11 December 2000.

73. Individual state and aggregate data described in this section were obtained from U.S. Department of Health and Human Services, Child Care Bureau, "Child Care and Development Fund: FFY 1998 Tables and Charts, 15 March 2000."

See also State Policy Documentation Project, "Low-Income Child Care Programs March 2000," available at: www.spdp.org/tanf/childcare.htm, accessed 11 December 2000.

74. NGA and DHHS, *Improving Services for Children in Working Families*, 8–11; Scott Groginsky, Susan Robison, and Shelley Smith, *Making Child Care Better: State Initiatives* (Denver: National Conference of State Legislatures, 1999).

75. Blank and Poersch, *State Child Care and Early Education Developments*, 23–30.

76. Groginsky, Robison, and Smith, *Making Child Care Better*, 10–11, 38–39.

77. Culkin, Groginsky, and Christian, *Building Blocks*, 63–64; "Smart Start Facts," available at: www.smartstart-nc.org/resources&evaluation/childfacts.htm, accessed 11 December 2000.

78. Culkin, Groginsky, and Christian, *Building Blocks*, 63; "Frequently Asked Questions," available at: www.smartstart-nc.org/information/faq.htm, accessed 11 December 2000.

79. "Frequently Asked Questions"; Blank and Poersch, *State Child Care and Early Education Developments*, 12; Karen Schulman, Helen Blank, and Danielle Ewen, *Seeds of Success: State Prekindergarten Initiatives, 1998–99* (Washington, D.C.: Children's Defense Fund, 1999), 163.

80. Culkin, Groginsky, and Christian, *Building Blocks*, 22; Blank and Poersch, *State Child Care and Early Education Developments*, 54–55, 58–59.

81. North Carolina Department of Health and Human Services, "North Carolina Cares, Committed to Attracting and Retaining Educated Staff," available at: www.state.nc.us/DHR/docs/nccare.htm, accessed 11 December 2000; Blank and Poersch, *State Child Care and Early Education Developments*, 23; Groginsky, Robison, and Smith, *Making Child Care Better*, 17.

82. Blank and Poersch, *State Child Care and Early Education Developments*, 5.

83. U.S. Department of Health and Human Services, Administration for Children and Families, "Change in TANF Caseloads," as of June 2000, available at: www.acf.dhhs.gov/news/stats/caseload.htm, accessed 11 December 2000.

84. Jason DeParle, "A Sharp Decline in Welfare Cases Is Gathering Speed," *New York Times*, 2 February 1997, A1, 18; Wendell Primus et al., *The Initial Impacts of Welfare Reform on the Incomes of Single-Mother Families* (Washington, D.C.: Center on Budget and Policy Priorities, 1999), 27–29.

85. For an excellent review of state responses to the 1996 welfare law in areas such as child care, see Jack Tweedie, "From D.C. to Little Rock: Welfare Reform at Midterm," *Publius: The Journal of Federalism* 30, nos. 1–2 (2000): 69–97.

86. Jason DeParle, "U.S. Welfare System Dies as State Programs Emerge," *New York Times*, 30 June 1997, A1.

87. Sue Shellenbarger, "Back-to-Work Effort Has Strained Supply of Good Child Care," *Wall Street Journal*, 22 October 1997, B1.

88. Pamela Loprest, *Families Who Left Welfare: Who Are They and How Are They Doing?* (Washington, D.C.: Urban Institute, 1999).

89. Growing Up in Poverty Project, *Executive Summary: Remember the Children: Mothers Balancing Work and Child Care under Welfare Reform. Wave 1 Findings, California, Connecticut, and Florida* (New Haven, Conn.: Bush Center, 2000), 2.

90. S. Jody Heymann and Alison Earle, "The Impact of Welfare Reform on Parents' Ability to Care for Their Children's Health," *American Journal of Public Health* 89, no. 4 (1999): 502–5.

91. Growing Up in Poverty Project, *Executive Summary: Remember the Children*, 4.

92. Ron Haskins, "Welfare Reform Works," *News and Issues* (New York: National Center for Children in Poverty, winter 1999): 4–6; Wendell Primus, "Success of Welfare Reform Unclear," *News and Issues* (New York: National Center for Children in Poverty, winter 1999): 5–6.

93. Robert Pear, "States Declining to Draw Billions in Welfare Money," *New York Times*, 8 February 1999, A1, A19.

94. General Accounting Office, *Welfare Reform: States' Efforts to Expand Child Care Programs.*

95. Long et al., *Child Care Assistance Under Welfare Reform*, 9.

96. Helen Blank et al., *Child Care Falling Short for Low Income Working Families* (Washington, D.C.: Children's Defense Fund, 23 March 1998); Gina Adams, Karen Schulman, and Nancy Ebb, *Locked Doors: States Struggling to Meet the Child Care Needs of Low-Income Working Families* (Washington, D.C.: Children's Defense Fund, March 1998); Blank and Poersch, *State Child Care and Early Education Developments.*

97. General Accounting Office, *Welfare Reform: Implications of Increased Work Participation for Child Care*, 3.

98. Linda Giannerilli and James Barsimantov, *Child Care Expenses of America's Families*, Occasional Paper No. 40 (Washington, D.C.: Urban Institute, 2000), 7.

99. Childrens' Defense Fund, "Child Care Advocacy Newsletter," 22 November 1999.

100. Schulman, Blank, and Ewen, *Seeds of Success*, xiii.

101. Ibid., 5.

102. Ibid., xx, 199.

103. Ibid., 13–20.

104. Ibid., 128–29.

105. Connecticut Commission on Children, "School Readiness and Early Reading Success: Connecticut Leads the Way," *School Readiness Update* 2, no. 1 (March 1999): 1; Schulman, Blank, and Ewen, *Seeds of Success*, 131–32.

106. Schulman, Blank, and Ewen, *Seeds of Success*, 130.

107. Ibid., 169.

108. Nicole Oxendine Poersch and Helen Blank, *Working Together for Children: Head Start and Child Care Partnerships* (Washington, D.C.: Children's Defense Fund, 1996); Groginsky, Christian, and McConnell, *Early Childhood Initiatives in the States*, 14.

109. Government Accounting Office, *Head Start Programs: Participant Characteristics, Services, and Funding*, GAO/HEHS-98-65 (Washington, D.C.: GAO, 1998).

110. Poersch and Blank, *Working Together for Children*, 7–23.

111. Government Accounting Office, *Head Start: Challenges Faced in Demonstrating Program Results and Responding to Societal Changes*, GAO/T-HEHS-98-3 (Washington, D.C.: GAO, 9 June 1998), 2–3.

112. U.S. Department of Health and Human Services, Head Start Collaboration Office, "Fact Sheet on Head Start–State Collaboration Offices," September 1998; Karen Mitchell, U.S. Head Start Office, personal communication, 12 April 1999.

113. Schulman, Blank, and Ewen, *Seeds of Success*, 200.

114. Government Accounting Office, *Welfare Reform: States' Efforts to Expand Child Care Programs*, 22.

115. Long et al., *Child Care Assistance Under Welfare Reform*, 12.

116. NGA and DHHS, *Improving Services for Children*, 6.

117. Colorado Department of Human Services, Division of Child Care, *Report of the Colorado Business Commission on Child Care Financing* (Denver: Colorado Department of Human Services, 1995).

118. Ibid., 8–13; Culkin, Groginsky, and Christian, *Building Blocks*, 50–51.

119. Helen Blank and Nicole Oxendine Poersch, *State Developments in Child Care and Early Education 1999* (Washington, D.C.: Children's Defense Fund, 2000), 107.

120. Ibid., 106.

9. *Looking Back and to the Future*

1. Redistributive policies entail the reallocation of resources or rights among groups or social classes. Theodore J. Lowi, "American Business, Public Policy, Case Studies, and Political Theory," *World Politics* 16: 677–715.

2. Nelson Polsby, *Political Innovation in America: The Politics and Policy of Initiation* (New Haven, Conn.: Yale University Press, 1984), 153.

3. John L. Kingdon, *Agendas, Alternatives, and Public Policies*, 2d ed. (New York: HarperCollins, 1995), 115–17.

4. Ibid., 145–164. Kingdon's framework for agenda-setting relies on the merging of three streams: politics, problem, and policy. The political stream encompasses broad changes in national moods often reflected in national elections and public opinion.

5. Jacob S. Hacker, *The Road to Nowhere: The Genesis of President Clinton's Plan for Social Security* (Princeton, N.J.: Princeton University Press, 1997), 10–11.

6. According to a 1997 FWI study, 13 percent of respondents had an employer who offered direct financial assistance for child care; 20 percent had employers offering assistance in finding child care; and 29 percent had employers putting pretax dollars into an account to pay for child or other dependent care. A very small percentage (less than 3 percent) of employers offered on-site child care. James T. Bond, Ellen Galinsky, and Jennifer E. Swanberg, *The 1997 National Study of the Changing Workforce* (New York: Families and Work Institute, 1998), 96.

7. Frank R. Baumgartner and Bryan D. Jones, *Agendas and Instability in American Politics* (Chicago: University of Chicago Press, 1993), 16.

8. Douglas Imig, "Advocacy by Proxy: The Children's Lobby in American Politics," *Journal of Children and Poverty* (1996): 31–53.

9. Committee on Integrating the Science of Early Childhood Development, *From Neurons to Neighborhoods: The Science of Early Childhood Development*, ed. Jack P. Shonkoff and Deborah A. Phillips (Washington, D.C.: National Academy Press, 2000), 297–327.

10. Thomas J. Gamble and Edward Zigler, "Effects of Infant Day Care: Another Look at the Evidence," *American Journal of Orthopsychiatry* (January 1986): 26–42; Edward Zigler and Edmund W. Gordon, *Day Care: Scientific and Social Policy Issues* (Dover, Mass.: Auburn House, 1982); Cheryl D. Hayes, John L. Palmer, and Martha J. Zaslow, *Who Cares for America's Children? Child Care Policy for the 1990s* (Washington, D.C.: National Academy Press, 1990), esp. 71–73.

11. The literature on legislative–executive branch relations is extensive. See, for example, Charles O. Jones, *The Presidency in a Separated System* (Washington, D.C.: Brookings Institution, 1994); Mark A. Peterson, *Legislating Together* (Cambridge, Mass.: Harvard University Press, 1990); and James L. Sundquist, *Constitutional Reform and Effective Government*, rev. ed. (Washington, D.C.: Brookings Institution, 1992).

12. Peterson, *Legislating Together*, 7–9. For an analysis of interbranch bargaining and the role of presidential vetoes, with the 1996 welfare law as a case in point, see Charles M. Cameron, *Veto Bargaining: Presidents and the Politics of Negative Power* (New York: Cambridge University Press, 2000).

13. David R. Mayhew, *Divided We Govern: Party Control, Lawmaking, and Investigations, 1946–1990* (New Haven, Conn.: Yale University Press, 1991).

14. Sean Q. Kelly, "Divided We Govern? A Reassessment," *Polity* 25, no. 3 (1993): 475–84; Morris Fiorina, *Divided Government*, 2d ed. (Boston: Allyn and Bacon, 1996), 163; Cameron, *Veto Bargaining*, 38–40.

15. Mayhew, *Divided We Govern*, 39n, 40n.

16. For a discussion of Mayhew's work, how it differed from conventional thinking and generated subsequent scholarship, see Sarah A. Binder, "The Dynamics of Legislative Gridlock, 1947–96," *American Political Science Review* 93, no. 3 (September 1999): 519–33. Other scholars have extended Mayhew's analysis and concluded that divided government diminishes the enactment of landmark legislation but has no major impact on bills considered important, albeit not landmark. William Howell, Scott Adler, Charles Cameron, and Charles Reimann, "Divided Government and the Legislative Productivity of Congress, 1945–94," *Legislative Studies Quarterly* 25, no. 2 (May 2000): 285–312.

17. George C. Edwards III, Andrew Barrett, and Jeffrey Peake, "The Legislative Impact of Divided Government," *American Journal of Political Science* 41, no. 2 (April 1997): 545–63.

18. Fiorina, *Divided Government*, 166.

19. Keith Krehbiel, *Pivotal Politics: A Theory of U.S. Lawmaking* (Chicago: University of Chicago Press, 1998), 74–75.

20. Ibid., 23.

21. Ibid., 75.

22. Ibid., 230–31.

23. Keith T. Poole and Howard Rosenthal, *Congress: A Political Economic History of Roll-Call Voting* (New York: Oxford University Press, 1997); Alan K. Ota, "Partisan Voting on the Rise," *Congressional Quarterly Weekly*, 9 February 1999, 79–80.

24. The rate of partisan voting in the House dropped from 55.5 percent in 1998 to 47.1 percent in 1999. It increased in the Senate from 55.7 percent in 1998 to 62.8 percent in 1999—slightly lower than earlier years of the decade. Daniel J. Parks, "Partisan Voting Holds Steady," *Congressional Quarterly Weekly*, 11 December 1999, 2975–76.

25. Norman J. Ornstein, Thomas E. Mann, and Michael J. Malbin, *Vital Statistics on Congress* (Washington, D.C.: American Enterprise Institute for Public Policy Research, 1999), 201–3.

26. For a discussion of this issue as it related to Medicare, see Theodore R. Marmor, *The Politics of Medicare*, 2d ed. (New York: De Gruyter, 2000), 174.

27. Norman J. Ornstein, Robert L. Peabody, and David W. Rohde, "The U.S. Senate Toward the Twenty-First Century," in Lawrence C. Dodd and Bruce I. Oppenheimer, eds., *Congress Reconsidered*, 6th ed. (Washington, D.C.: Congressional Quarterly Press, 1997), 1–28.

28. Steven S. Smith and Christopher J. Deering, *Committees in Congress*, 2d ed.

(Washington, D.C.: Congressional Quarterly Press, 1990); Keith Krehbiel, *Information and Legislative Organization* (Ann Arbor: University of Michigan Press, 1992), 254–56.

29. These four major committees do not include appropriations committees in each house and other panels, such as government operations, which also dealt with child care.
30. Frank R. Baumgartner, Bryan D. Jones, and Michael C. MacLeod, "The Evolution of Legislative Jurisdictions," *Journal of Politics* 62, no. 2 (2000): 321–49.
31. Dan Carney, "Transforming the Nation by Fits and Starts," *Congressional Quarterly Weekly*, 29 January 2000, 162–67.
32. Ornstein, Mann, and Malbin, *Vital Statistics on Congress*, 207–13.
33. Richard F. Fenno Jr., *Congressmen in Committees* (Boston: Little, Brown, 1973), 169; Ornstein, Mann, and Malbin, *Vital Statistics on Congress*, 214–19.
34. Its Conservative Coalition support scores rose considerably from 58 percent in 1993 to 78 percent in 1997. In contrast, the Conservative Coalition support scores for the Senate Committee on Health, Education, Labor, and Pensions rose from 43 to 53 percent over the same period. Ornstein, Mann, and Malbin, *Vital Statistics on Congress*, 214–15.
35. Fenno, *Congressmen in Committees*, 182; Smith and Deering, *Committees in Congress*, 141.
36. Krehbiel, *Pivotal Politics*, 208.
37. John R. Wright, *Interest Groups and Congress: Lobbying, Contributions, and Influence* (Boston: Allyn and Bacon, 1996), 200, 4–5, 173.
38. Frank R. Baumgartner and Jeffrey C. Talbert,"Interest Groups and Political Change," in Bryan D. Jones, ed., *The New American Politics: Reflections on Political Change and the Clinton Administration* (Boulder, Colo.: Westview Press, 1995), 101.
39. Robert H. Salisbury, "The Paradox of Interest Groups in Washington: More Groups, Less Clout," in Anthony King, ed., *The New American Political System: Second Version* (Washington, D.C.: American Enterprise Institute Press, 1990), 203–29.
40. For a discussion of these issues as they apply to children's advocacy groups, see Imig, "Advocacy by Proxy."
41. Jack L. Walker Jr., *Mobilizing Interest Groups in America: Patrons, Professions, and Social Movements* (Ann Arbor: University of Michigan Press, 1992), 9–11.
42. Ibid., 34; Theda Skocpol, "Associations Without Members," *American Prospect* (July-August 1999): 66–73.
43. Walker, *Mobilizing Interest Groups in America*, 53.
44. Wright, *Interest Groups and Congress*, 25–26.
45. Paul A. Sabatier and Hank Jenkins-Smith, eds., *Policy Change and Learning: An Advocacy Coalition Approach* (Boulder, Colo.: Westview Press, 1993).

46. Katherine Teghtsoonian, "The Work of Caring for Children: Contradicting Themes in American Child Care Policy Debates," *Women & Politics* 17, no. 2 (1997): 79–80; Marion Frances Berry, *The Politics of Parenthood: Child Care, Women's Rights, and the Myth of the Good Mother* (New York: Viking, 1993); Sonya Michel, *Children's Interests/Mother's Rights: The Shaping of America's Child Care Policy* (New Haven, Conn.: Yale University Press, 1999).

47. Vicky Randall, "Feminism and Child Daycare," *Journal of Social Policy* 25, no. 4 (1996): 497.

48. Ibid., 498.

49. Ibid.

50. Ibid., 500–501.

51. Ibid., 502.

52. Katherine Teghtsoonian, "Promises, Promises: 'Choices for Women' in Canadian and American Child Care Policy Debates," *Feminist Studies* 22, no. 1 (1996): 119–46.

53. Teghtsoonian, "Work of Caring for Children," 88.

54. Randall, "Feminism and Child Daycare," 493; Katherine Teghtsoonian, "Institutions & Ideology: Sources of Opposition to Federal Regulation of Child Care Services in Canada and the United States," *Governance: An International Journal of Policy and Administration* 5, no. 2 (April 1992): 197–223; Teghtsoonian, "Promises, Promises," 119–22.

55. Rebecca E. Klatch, *Women of the New Right* (Philadelphia: Temple University Press, 1987), 152–53.

56. Noelle H. Norton, "Uncovering the Dimensionality of Gender Voting in Congress," *Legislative Studies Quarterly* 24, no. 1 (1999): 65–86, quote on 77.

57. Ibid., 80.

58. Noelle Norton, "Transforming Congress from the Inside: Women in Congress" (paper presented at the Annual Meeting of the American Political Science Association, Washington, D.C., 31 August–3 September 2000).

59. See, for example, Theodore R. Marmor, "Forecasting American Health Care: How We Got Here and Where We Might Be Going," *Journal of Health, Politics, Policy, and Law* 23, no. 3 (June 1998): 551–71.

60. U.S. Senate, Subcommittee on Children and Families of the Committee on Labor and Human Resources, *Hearing on Pre to 3: Policy Implications of Child Brain Development*, 105th Cong., 1st sess., 5 June 1997.

61. Richard B. Stolley, "Chairman's Corner," *ChildCare ActioNews* (March–April 1999), 2–3.

Index

POWER, CONFLICT, AND DEMOCRACY:
AMERICAN POLITICS INTO THE TWENTY-FIRST CENTURY

John G. Geer, *From Tea Leaves to Opinion Polls: A Theory of Democratic Leadership*

Kim Fridkin Kahn, *The Political Consequences of Being a Woman: How Stereotypes Influence the Conduct and Consequences of Political Campaigns*

Kelly D. Patterson, *Political Parties and the Maintenance of Liberal Democracy*

Dona Cooper Hamilton and Charles V. Hamilton, *The Dual Agenda: Race and Social Welfare Policies of Civil Rights Organizations*

Hanes Walton Jr., *African-American Power and Politics: The Political Context Variable*

Amy Fried, *Muffled Echoes: Oliver North and the Politics of Public Opinion*

Russell D. Riley, *The Presidency and the Politics of Racial Inequality: Nation-Keeping from 1831 to 1965*

Robert W. Bailey, *Gay Politics, Urban Politics: Identity and Economics in the Urban Setting*

Ronald T. Libby, *ECO-WARS: Political Campaigns and Social Movements*

Donald Grier Stephenson Jr., *Campaigns and the Court: The U.S. Supreme Court in Presidential Elections*

Kenneth Dautrich and Thomas H. Hartley, *How the News Media Fail American Voters: Causes, Consequences, and Remedies*

Douglas C. Foyle, *Counting the Public In: Presidents, Public Opinion, and Foreign Policy*

Ronald G. Shaiko, *Voices and Echoes for the Environment: Public Interest Representation in the 1990s and Beyond*

Hanes Walton Jr., *Reelection: William Jefferson Clinton as a Native-Son Presidential Candidate*

Demetrios James Caraley, editor, *The New American Interventionism: Lessons from Successes and Failures—Essays from* Political Science Quarterly

Ellen D. B. Riggle and Barry L. Tadlock, editors, *Gays and Lesbians in the Democratic Process: Public Policy, Public Opinion, and Political Representation*

Robert Y. Shapiro, Martha Joynt Kumar, Lawrence R. Jacobs, Editors, *Presidential Power: Forging the Presidency for the Twenty-First Century*

Kerry L. Haynie, *African American Legislators in the American States*

Marissa Martino Golden, *What Motivates Bureaucrats? Politics and Administration During the Reagan Years*

Geoffrey Layman, *The Great Divide: Religious and Cultural Conflict in American Party Politics*